D0771052

The Visual Miscellaneum

THE BESTSELLING CLASSIC, Revised & Reimagined

The Visual Miscellaneum

A Colorful Guide to the World's Most Consequential Trivia

David McCandless

HARPER DESIGN
An Imprint of HarperCollins Publishers

ERNEST J. ALLEN LIBRARY
Palomar College/Escondido

The Visual Miscellaneum: Revised and Reimagined

Copyright © 2012 by David McCandless

All rights reserved. No part of this book may be used or reproduced in any manner whatsoever without written permission, except in the case of brief quotations embodied in critical articles and reviews. For information, address Harper Design, 10 East 53rd Street, New York, NY 10022.

HarperCollins books may be purchased for educational, business, or sales promotional use. For information, please write: Special Markets Department, HarperCollins*Publishers*, 10 East 53rd Street, New York, NY 10022.

Published in 2012 by:
Harper Design
An Imprint of HarperCollins*Publishers*
10 East 53rd Street
New York, NY 10022
Tel (212) 207-7000
harperdesign@harpercollins.com
www.harpercollins.com

First published in 2009 by:
HarperCollins*Publishers*

Library of Congress Control Number: 2012943296
ISBN: 978-0-06-223652-4

Printed in Hong Kong, 2012

FSC
www.fsc.org
MIX
Paper from responsible sources
FSC C007454

FSC™ is a non-profit international organisation established to promote the responsible management of the world's forests. Products carrying the FSC label are independently certified to assure consumers that they come from forests that are managed to meet the social, economic and ecological needs of present and future generations, and other controlled sources.

Find out more about HarperCollins and the environment at
www.harpercollins.co.uk/green

ESC CTR
AG
250
.M353
2012

to the beautiful internet

Introduction

This book started out as an exploration. Swamped by information, I was searching for a better way to see it all and understand it. Why not visually?

In a way, we're all visual now. Every day, every hour, maybe even every minute, we're seeing and absorbing information via the web. We're steeped in it. Maybe even lost in it. So perhaps what we need are well-designed, colourful and – hopefully – useful charts to help us navigate. A modern-day map book.

But can a book with the minimum of text, crammed with diagrams, maps and charts, still be exciting and readable? Can it still be fun? Can you make jokes in graphs? Are you even allowed to?

So I started experimenting with visualizing information and ideas in both new and old ways. I went for subjects that sprang from my own curiosity and ignorance — the questions I wanted answering. I avoided straightforward facts and dry statistics. Instead, I focused on the relationship between facts, the context, the connections that make information meaningful.

So, that's what this book is. Miscellaneous facts and ideas, interconnected visually. A visual miscellaneum. A series of experiments in making information approachable and beautiful. See what you think.

David McCandless

POP

Billion-Dollar-O-Gram 010
International Number Ones 020
Books Everyone Should Read 028
The "In" Colours 032
The "Interesting" Colours 034
Simple Part I 060
Better than Bacon 146
Who Clever Are You? 164
Types of Facial Hair 172
Good News 180
Immortality 182
Red vs Blue 188
Simple Part II 198
Most Popular US Girls' Names 212
Most Popular US Boys' Names 214

WEB

The One Machine 086
What Does China Censor Online? 092
Google Insights 136
Looking for Love Online 178
Articles of War 160
Fast Internet 192
Selling Your Soul 238

THOUGHT

Left vs Right 014
Three's a Magic Number 036
What is Consciousness? 066
Colours and Culture 076
Stages of You 077
World Religions 098
Moral Matrix 100
Postmodernism 132
2012: The End of the World? 184
Being Defensive 208
Enneagram 236

NATURE

Small Carbon 026
Which Fish are Okay to Eat? 030
Stock Check 042
Amazon 044
Carbon Conscious 068
Rising Sea Levels 074
Water Towers 094
The Carbon Dioxide Cycle 102
Kyoto Targets 139
30 Years Makes a Difference 142
Big Carbon 158
Amphibian Extinction Rates 176

SCIENCE

Creation Myths 046
The Book of You 050
The Book of Me 052
Personal Computer Evolution 084
Low Resolution 104
Climate Sceptics vs The Consensus 122
Nature vs Nurture 130
Scale of Devastation 174
Radiation Dosage 206
The Future of Energy 219
The Future of the Future 240

HEALTH

Snake Oil? 018
Drugs World 096
The Sunscreen Smokescreen 112
The Remedy 117
What are the Chances? 147
Some Things You Can't Avoid 148
Body By 151
Microbes Most Dangerous 152
Cosmetic Ingredients 153
Things That'll Give You Cancer 154
Alternative Medicine 204

FOOD

'aste Buds 106
'he Poison 116
'he Remedy 117
alad Dressings 118
Not Nice 119
'ass the... 129
'ypes of Coffee 156
'he Buzz vs The Bulge 166
Daily Diets 168
Calories In, Calories Out 170

POWER

Who Runs the World? 038
Who *Really* Runs the World? 040
Behind Every Great Man... 126
War Chests 183
Peters Projection 202
The Middle East 216
The Middle East: Some Context 218

LIFE

Reduce Your Chances... 072
20th-Century Death 120
Death Spiral 134
The Varieties of Romantic Relationship 140
Motive, Timing and Delivery 178
Man's Humanity to Man 190

FILM

'ime Lines 016
22 Stories 222
Most Profitable Stories 2007 224
Most Profitable Stories 2008 226
Most Profitable Stories 2009 228
Most Profitable Stories 2010 230
Most Profitable Stories 2011 232
Most Profitable Stories of All Time 234

MEDIA

Mountains out of Molehills 022
X "is the new" Black 024
Horoscoped 144
Types of Information Visualization 128

MUSIC

Dance Genre-ology 048
Rock Genre-ology 058
Most Successful Rock Bands 220

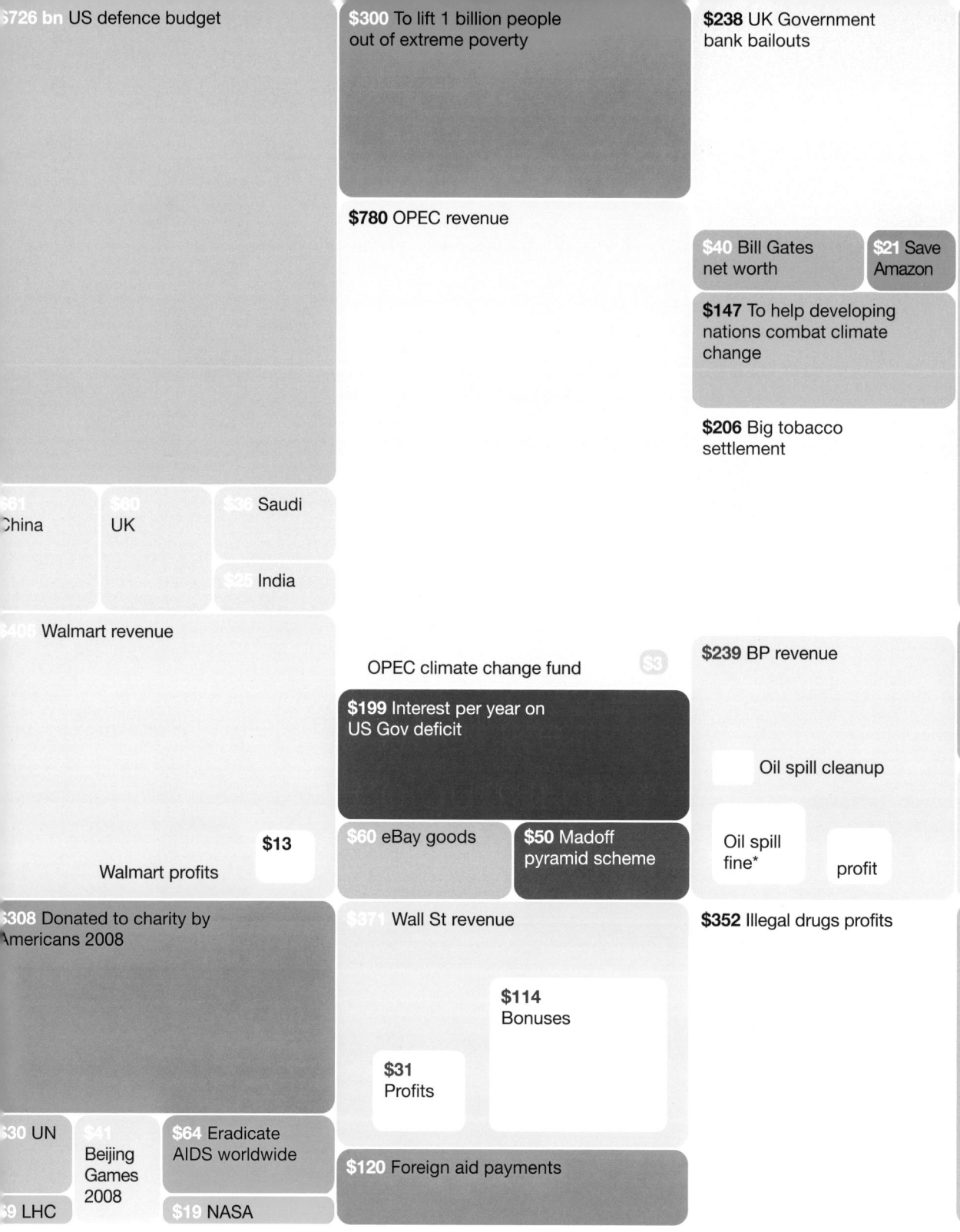

Billion-Dollar-O-Gram

Billions spent on this. Billions spent on that. It's all relative, right?

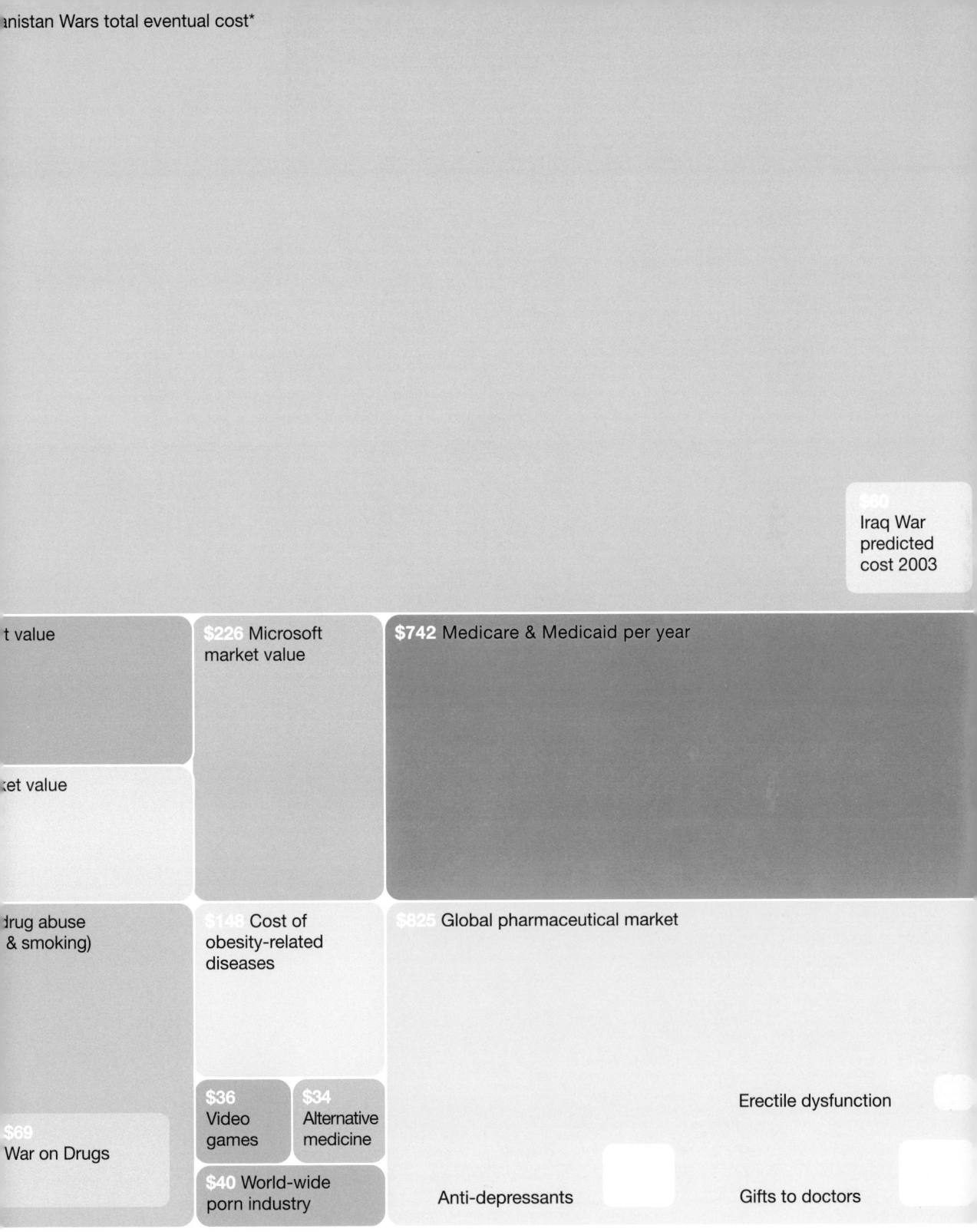

* estimated

source: MSNBC, Guardian, Washington Post, Forbes, UNODC, BBC News. All figures 2009 unless otherwise stated.

$12,700bn Worldwide cost of the financial crisis

source: Wikipedia, Guardian, Business Week, Ritzholtz.com

Left

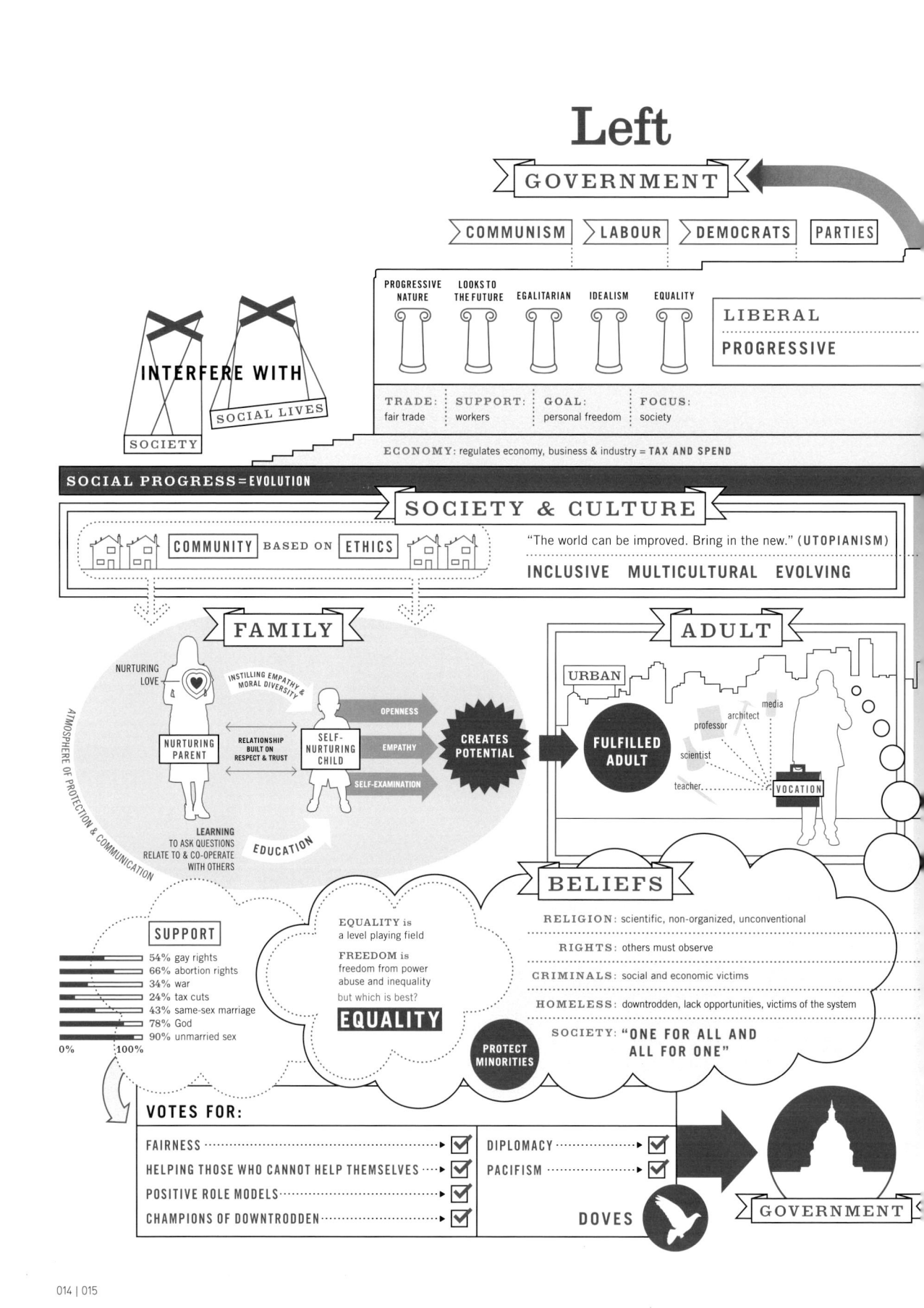
GOVERNMENT
COMMUNISM
LABOUR
DEMOCRATS
PARTIES
PROGRESSIVE NATURE
LOOKS TO THE FUTURE
EGALITARIAN
IDEALISM
EQUALITY
LIBERAL
PROGRESSIVE
INTERFERE WITH
SOCIETY
SOCIAL LIVES
TRADE: fair trade
SUPPORT: workers
GOAL: personal freedom
FOCUS: society
ECONOMY: regulates economy, business & industry = TAX AND SPEND
SOCIAL PROGRESS=EVOLUTION
SOCIETY & CULTURE
COMMUNITY BASED ON ETHICS
"The world can be improved. Bring in the new." (UTOPIANISM)
INCLUSIVE MULTICULTURAL EVOLVING
FAMILY
NURTURING LOVE
INSTILLING EMPATHY & MORAL DIVERSITY
NURTURING PARENT
RELATIONSHIP BUILT ON RESPECT & TRUST
SELF-NURTURING CHILD
OPENNESS
EMPATHY
SELF-EXAMINATION
CREATES POTENTIAL
ATMOSPHERE OF PROTECTION & COMMUNICATION
LEARNING TO ASK QUESTIONS RELATE TO & CO-OPERATE WITH OTHERS
EDUCATION
ADULT
URBAN
FULFILLED ADULT
media
architect
professor
scientist
teacher
VOCATION
SUPPORT
54% gay rights
66% abortion rights
34% war
24% tax cuts
43% same-sex marriage
78% God
90% unmarried sex
0%
100%
EQUALITY is a level playing field
FREEDOM is freedom from power abuse and inequality
but which is best?
EQUALITY
PROTECT MINORITIES
BELIEFS
RELIGION: scientific, non-organized, unconventional
RIGHTS: others must observe
CRIMINALS: social and economic victims
HOMELESS: downtrodden, lack opportunities, victims of the system
SOCIETY: "ONE FOR ALL AND ALL FOR ONE"
VOTES FOR:
FAIRNESS
HELPING THOSE WHO CANNOT HELP THEMSELVES
POSITIVE ROLE MODELS
CHAMPIONS OF DOWNTRODDEN
DIPLOMACY
PACIFISM
DOVES
GOVERNMENT

Right

GOVERNMENT

PARTIES | REPUBLICAN | CONSERVATIVE | NATIONALIST

CONSERVATIVE
TRADITIONAL

EQUITY | PRAGMATISM | MERITOCRACY | LOOKS TO THE PAST | CONSERVATIVE NATURE

FOCUS: individual | GOAL: economic freedom | SUPPORT: employers | TRADE: free trade

ECONOMY: de-regulated economy, business & industry = DON'T TAX AND SPEND

DON'T INTERFERE WITH

SOCIETY | SOCIAL LIVES

SOCIAL PROGRESS=STATUS QUO

SOCIETY & CULTURE

"Protect the good things about the world." (PRESERVATION)

TRADITIONAL NATIONALISTIC EXCLUSIVE

COMMUNITY BASED ON MORALS

ADULT

RURAL

police
military
stockbroker
business
judge

VOCATION

SELF-RELIANT ADULT

BUILDS CHARACTER

FAMILY

SELF-DEFENCE
MORAL STRENGTH
SELF-DISCIPLINE

SELF-RELIANT CHILD

RELATIONSHIP BUILT ON RESPECT & FEAR

STRICT PARENT

INSTILLING MORAL STRENGTH & ABSOLUTES

TOUGH LOVE

EDUCATION

SKILLS
TO SUCCEED
TO COMPETE
INDIVIDUALISM

ATMOSPHERE OF REWARD & PUNISHMENT

BELIEFS

RELIGION: theistic, organized, conventional

RIGHTS: others must not interfere

CRIMINALS: choose to be criminals

HOMELESS: no work ethic, no values, no sense of shame

SOCIETY: "SURVIVAL OF THE FITTEST"

IMMIGRATION CONTROL

EQUALITY is opportunity

FREEDOM is the chance to achieve or fail

but which is best?

FREEDOM

SUPPORT

gay rights	44%
abortion rights	43%
war	91%
tax cuts	84%
same-sex marriage	12%
God	87%
unmarried sex	80%

0% — 100%

VOTES FOR:

- AGGRESSION ☑
- MILITANCY ☑
- UPHOLDING ORDER ☑
- HELPING THOSE WHO HELP THEMSELVES ☑
- STRONG ROLE MODELS ☑
- CHAMPIONS OF OPPORTUNITY ☑

HAWKS

GOVERNMENT

source: Wikipedia, Britannica.com, New Scientist, Conservative-resources.com

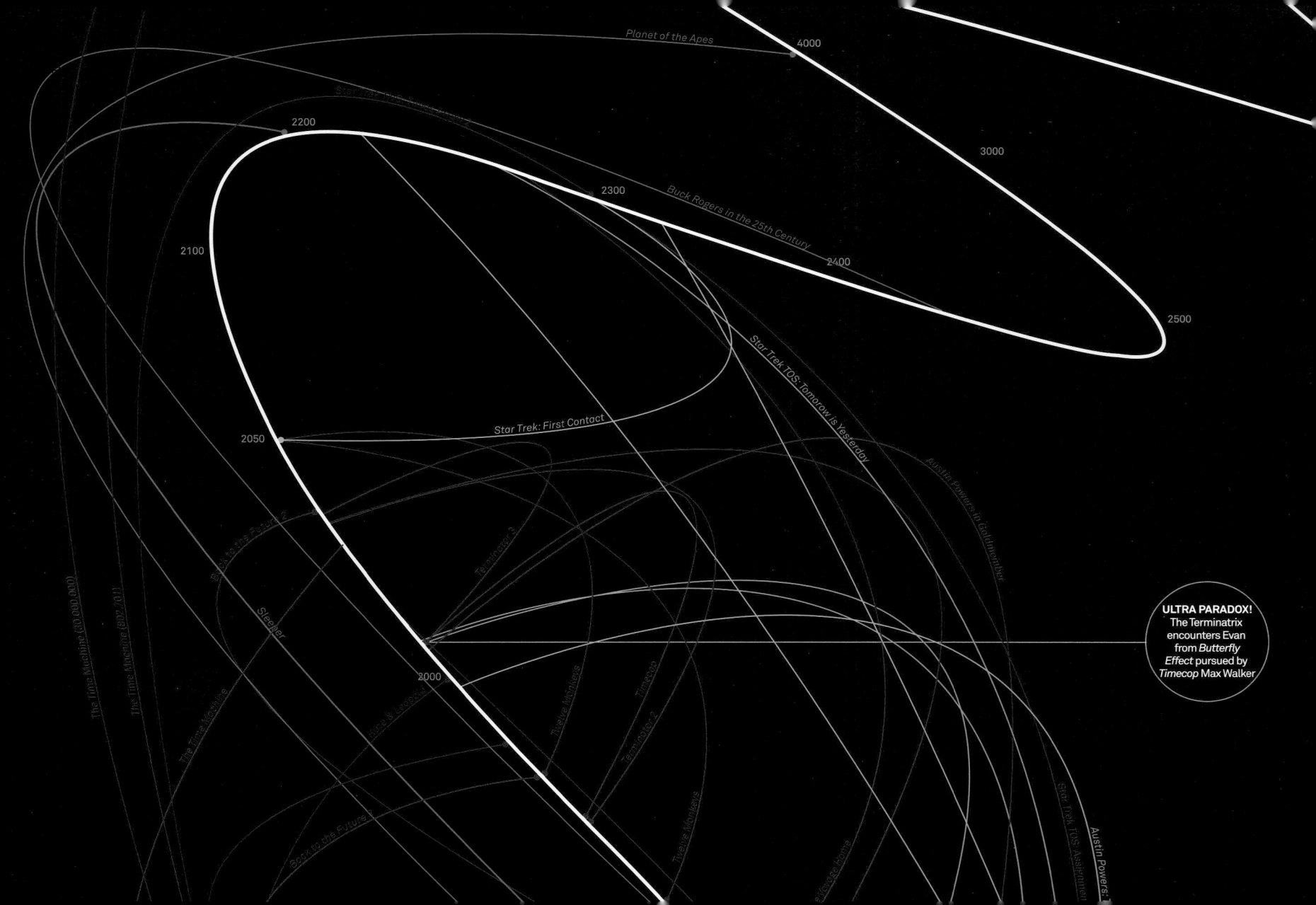

ULTRA PARADOX! The Terminatrix encounters Evan from *Butterfly Effect* pursued by *Timecop* Max Walker

Time Lines

Time travel plots in TV and film

Snake Oil?

Scientific evidence for popular dietary supplements showing tangible health benefits when taken orally by an adult with a healthy diet.

EVIDENCE

STRONG

GOOD

PROMISING

folic acid
certain birth defects

fish oil/ omega 3
heart disease

garlic
blood pressure

melatonin
insomnia

niacin (vitamin B3)
heart disease

vitamin D
general health, all cause mortality

zinc
colds

dark chocolate
blood pressure

green tea
cholesterol

calcium+ vitamin D
breast cancer

omega 6
heart health

bone health

tyrosine
alertness, wakefulness, memory

anti-oxidants
infertility in men

CoQ10
blood pressure

colorectal cancer

olive leaf extract
blood pressure, cholesterol

vitamin K2
bone health

devil's claw
arthritis

cancer symptoms

NAC
mental health

peppermint oil
IBS

rhodiola rosea L.
fatigue

hawthorn
blood pressure

creatine
cognition

WORTH IT LINE

WORTH IT LINE

red yeast rice
cholesterol, heart disease

calcium
osteoporosis

depression, mental illness

honey
coughs in children

nettle
urinary

vitamin B8
OCD

echinacea
colds

ginger

krill oil
PMS

magnesium
blood pressure

magnesium +vitamin B6

probiotics
IBS*

valerian
insomnia

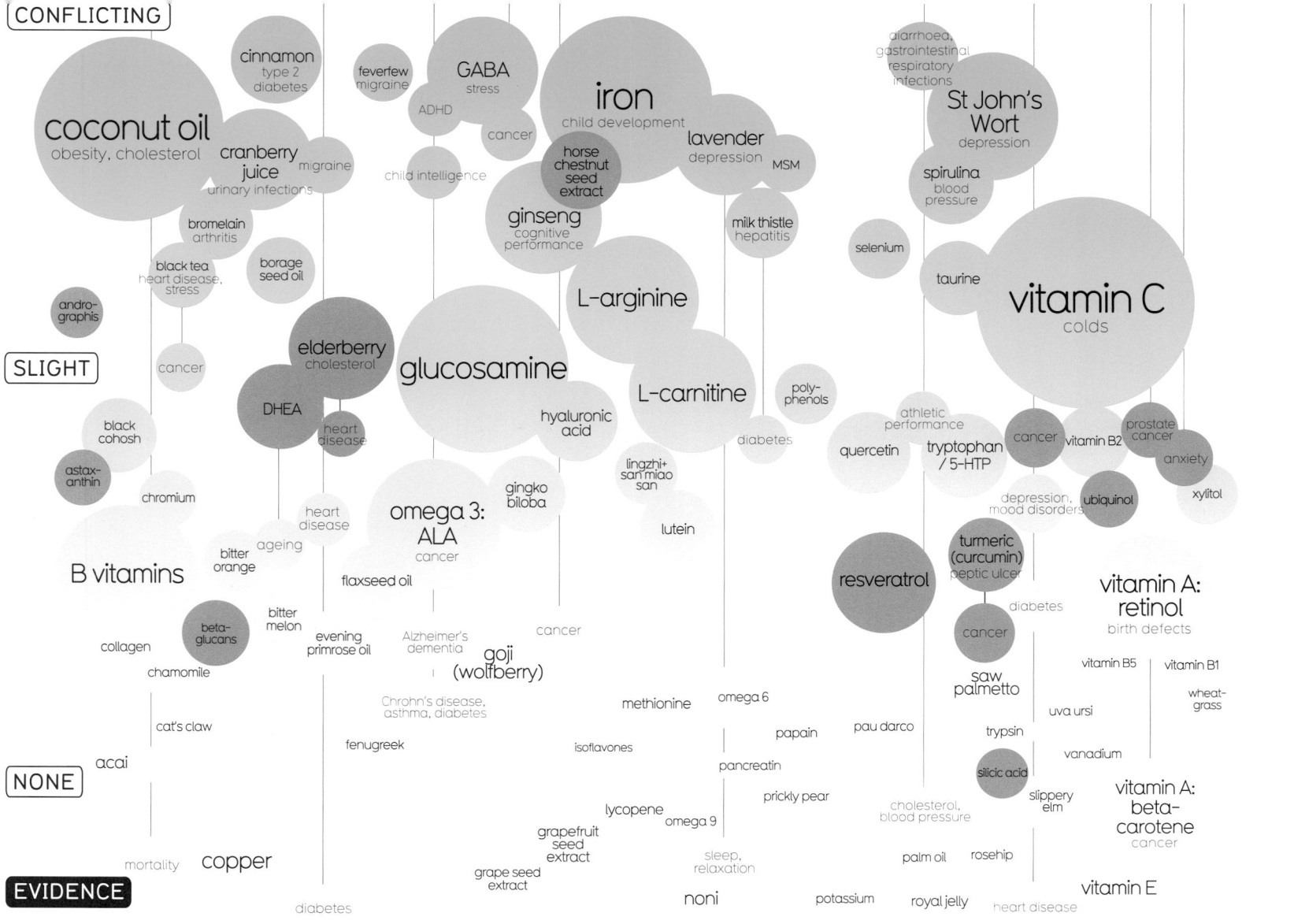

source: English language placebo-controlled double-blind human trials on PubMed.org and Cochrane.org, The US Office of Dietary Supplements, Herbmed.org, European Medicines Agency

International Number Ones

Because every country is the best at something

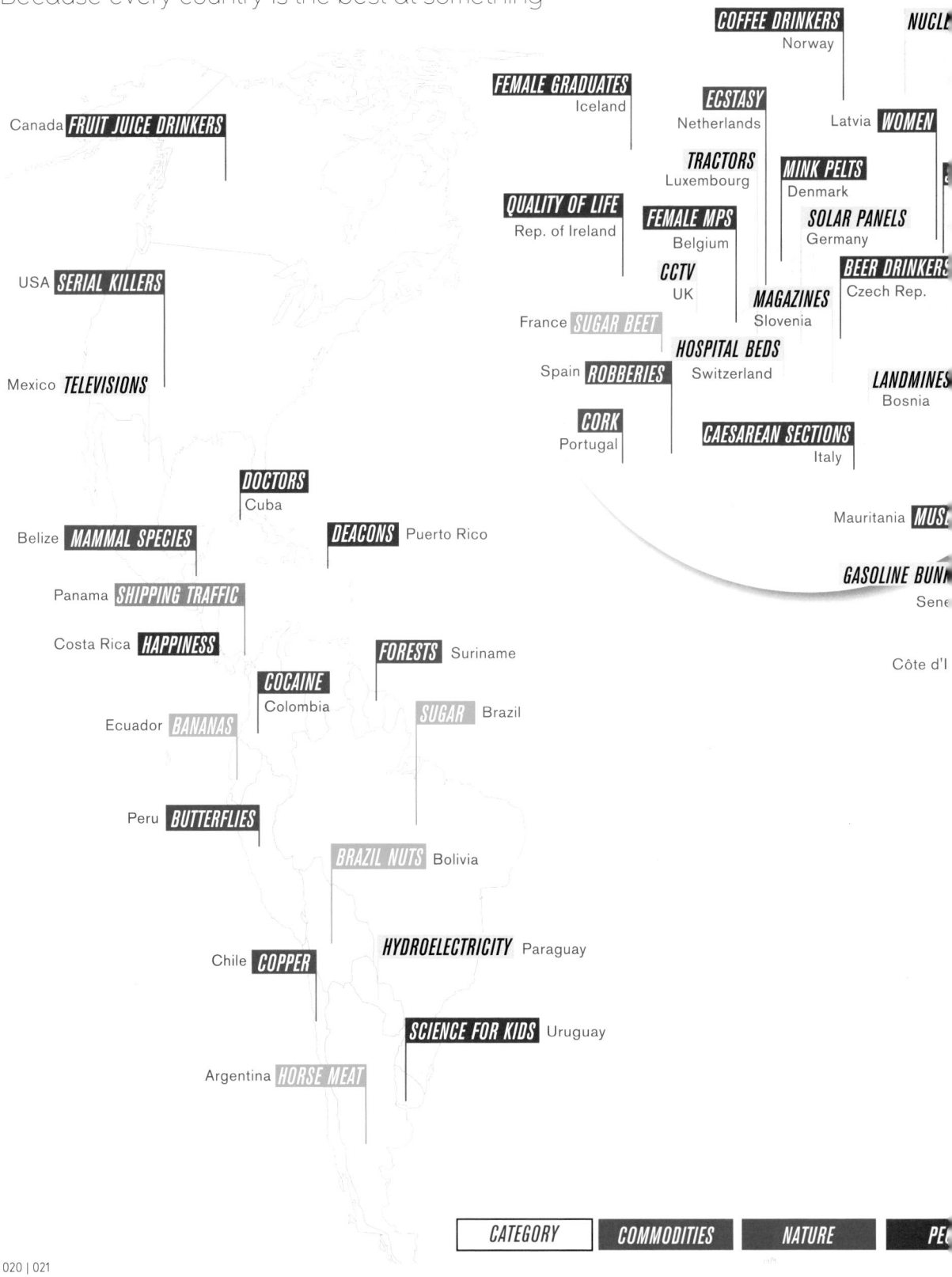

source: per capita data from Newscientist.com, Unstats.un.org, NationMaster.com

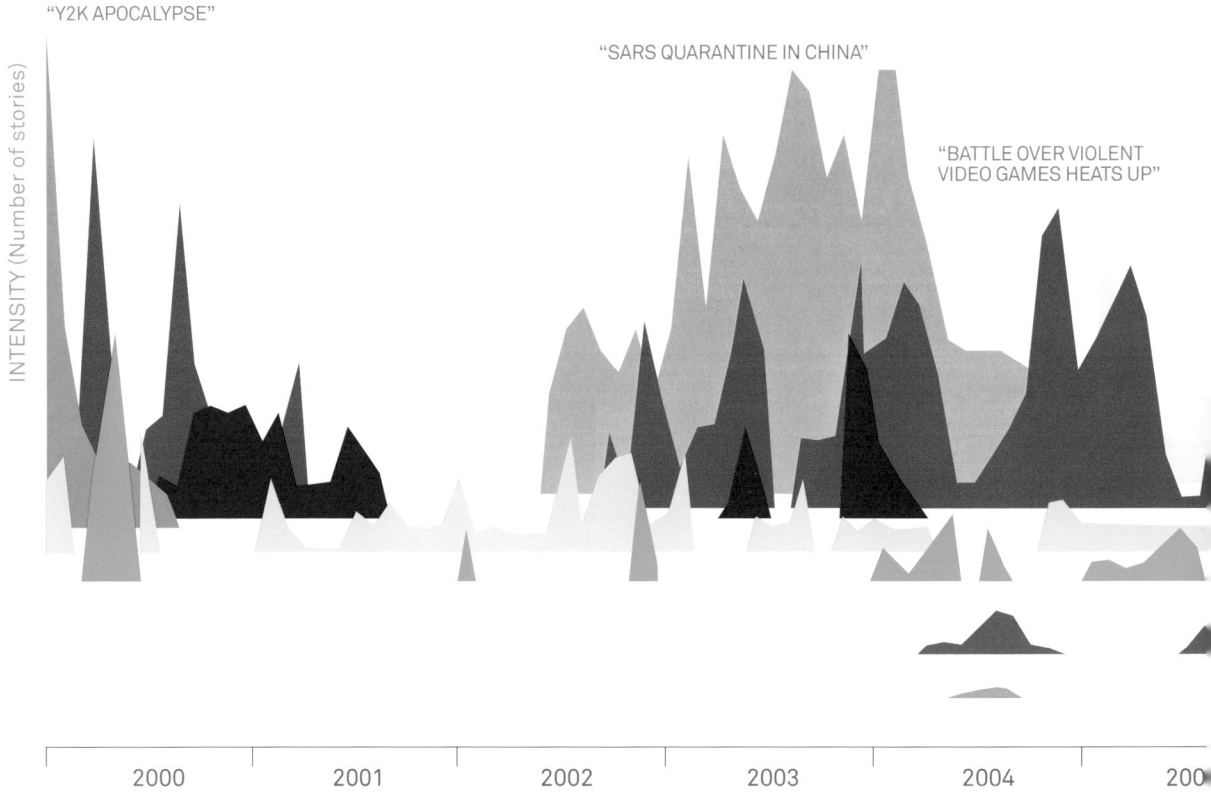

Story *(approximate worldwide deaths)*

- Killer Wasps *(1000)*
- Killer Wifi *(0)*
- Mobile Phones & Tumours *(0)*
- Autism Vaccinations *(0)*
- Asteroid Collision *(0)*
- Millennium Bug *(0)*
- Mad Cow Disease *(204)*
- Violent Video Games *(Unknown)*
- SARS *(774)*
- Bird Flu *(262)*
- Swine Flu *(702)*

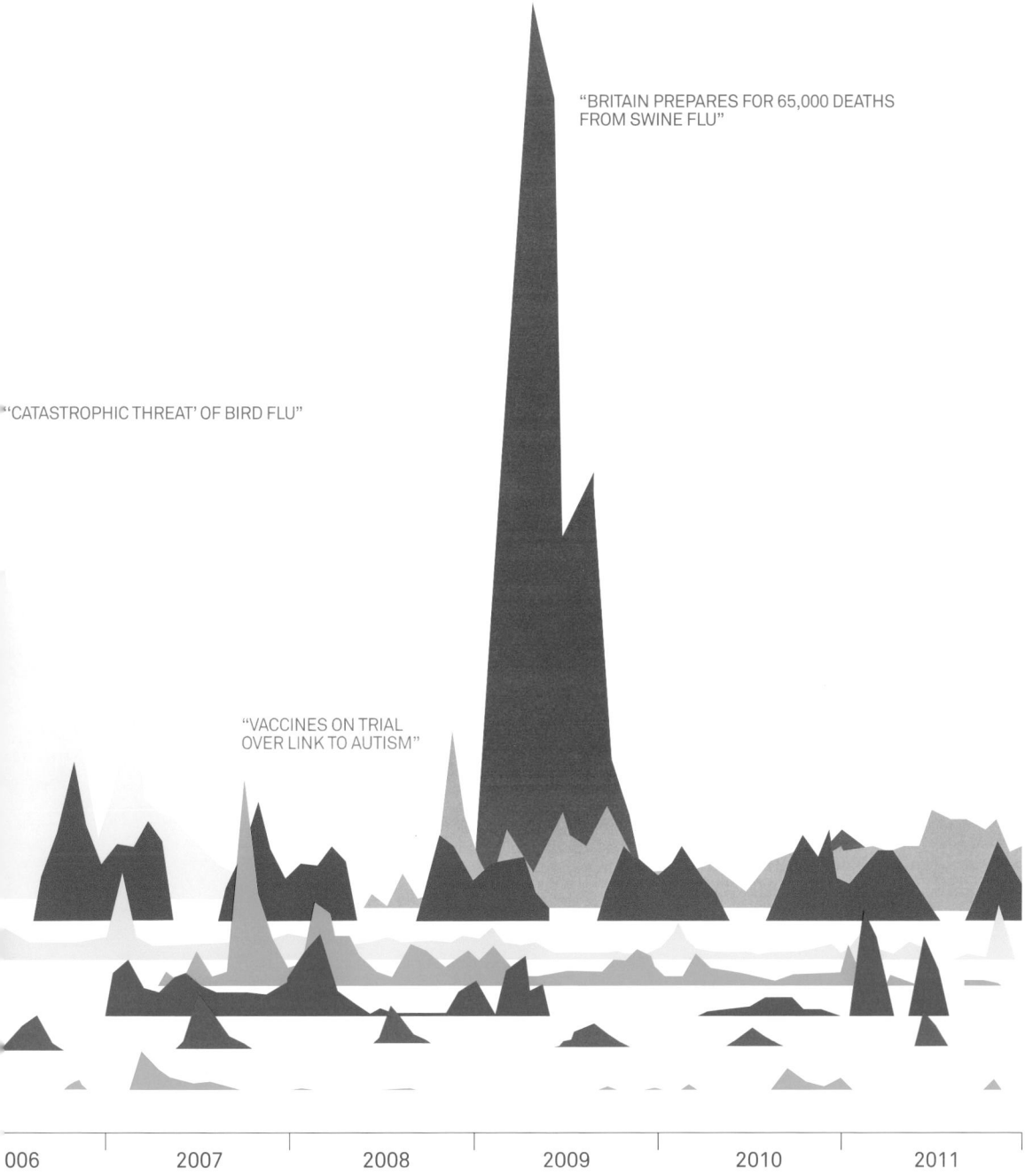

Mountains out of Molehills

A timeline of global media scare stories

source: Google News and Insights for Search (worldwide deaths at time of print)

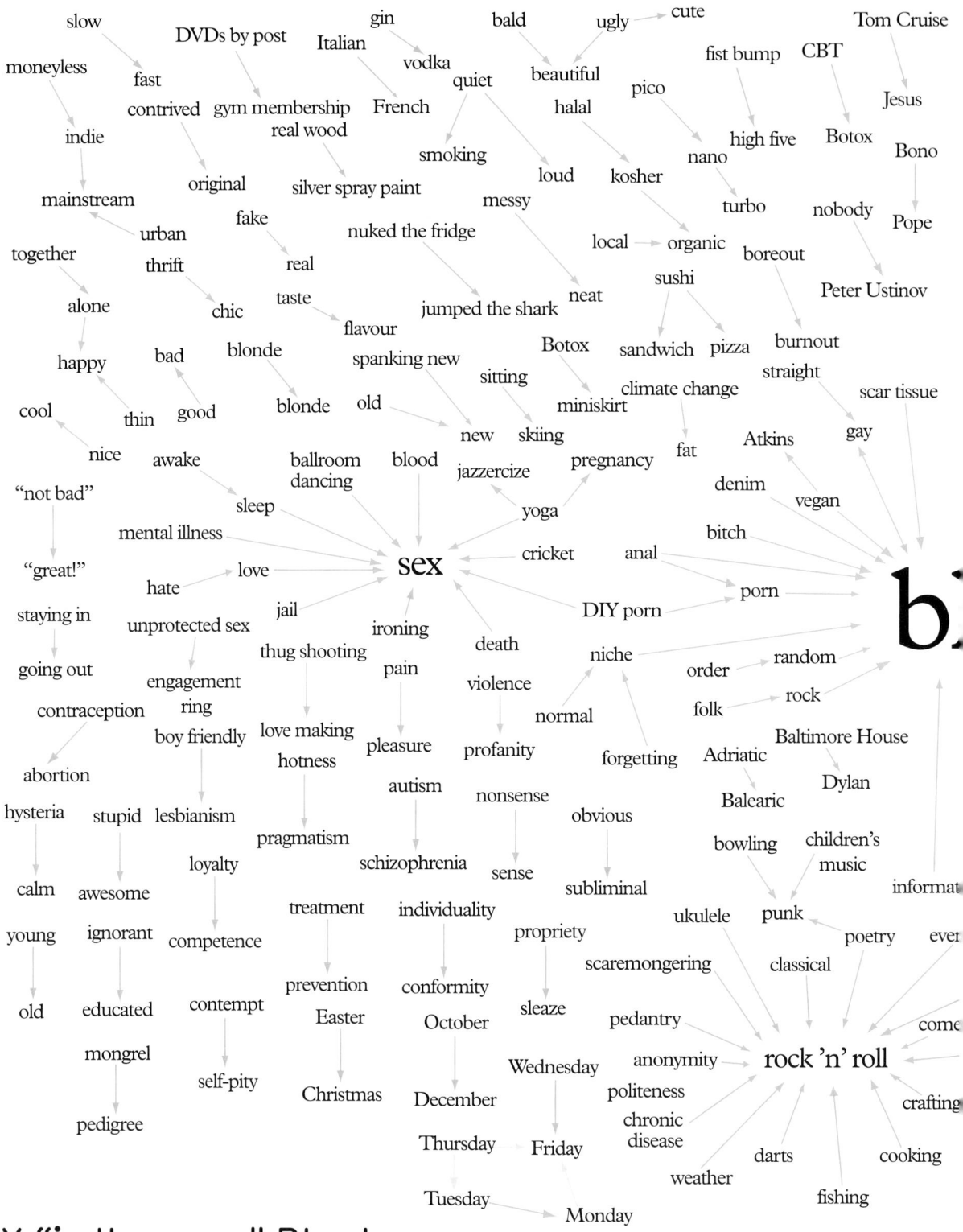

X "is the new" Black

A map of clichés

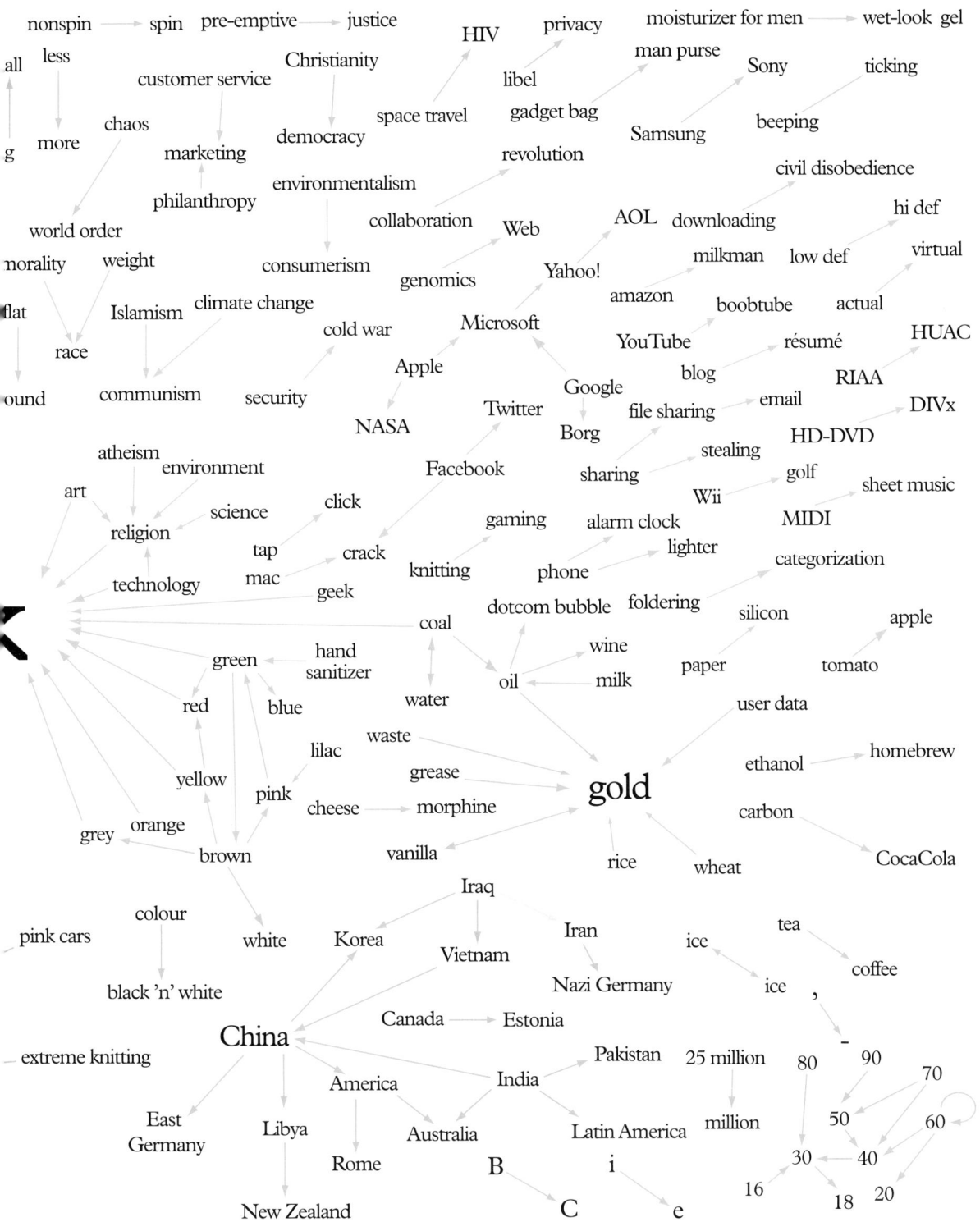

Searches for the phrase "is the new" on various media websites.

idea: Randall Szott // source: Google, Guardian.co.uk, NewScientist.com, Wired.com, Nytimes.com

Kilograms of Carbon

Emissions per year

your facebook page

to heat the average

average meat-based diet

vegetarian diet

vegan diet

breathing

electric kettle

cappucino
(one a day)

low energy bulb

toilet roll

drying washing
on line

lapto

21" iMac computer

incandescent bulb

electric shower
(once a day)

tumbledryer
(3 times a week)

emails
(20 a day)

cremation

burial

amount absorbed by a
tree in its lifetime

wine

28" LCD TV

mobile phone calls
(2 mins per day)

mobile phone calls
(1 hour per day)

source: New York Times, Environmental Protection Agency, IPCC, Energy Information Administration, UNESCO

Books Everyone Should Read

A consensus cloud

n Front
Dorian Gray Atonement
e Bovary A Clockwork Orange
thering Heights Of Human Bondage
East of Eden Fahrenheit 451
hings Past The Road The Little Prince
Disgrace The Curious Incident of the Dog in the Night-Time
lies On the Road The Kite Runner The Bell Jar
dred Years of Solitude Dracula
One Flew Over the Cuckoo's Nest Little Women
y Finn Beloved 1984 Stranger in a Strange Land
Moby-Dick
Mockingbird The Old Man and the Sea
The Master and Margarita Frankenstein
o the Galaxy War and Peace
The Glass Bead Game Twilight Do Androids Dream of Electric Sheep?
New World A Confederacy of Dunces Foundation
A Tale of Two Cities
ishment Catch-22 Possession
Cold Comfort Farm Memoirs of a Geisha
ables Anna Karenina The Wind in the Willows
Atlas Shrugged
erfield Slaughterhouse-Five Ender's Game
Ulysses
The Amazing Adventures of Kavalier and Clay
Animal Farm Rebecca
Wrath For Whom the Bell Tolls
Oscar and Lucinda
he Good Earth

source: Desert Island Discs, Pulitzer Prize, AskMetafilter.com, World Day Book Poll, Booker Prize, BBC Big Reads, Oprah's Book Club List & the author's own top five

ERNEST J. ALLEN LIBRARY
Palomar College/Escondido

YES

Farmed

Coho Salmon

Arctic Char

Barramundi (US)

Cobia

Striped Bass

Rainbow Trout

Catfish

Tilapia

Atlantic

Sardine (CORNWALL)

Dab

Flounder

Herring (NORWAY)

Mackerel

Gurnard

Seabass (LINE & GILLNET)

Spider Crab (POT)

Red Mullet

MAYBE

Crayfish (CHINA)

Basa

Sturgeon

Haddock (LINE)

Lemon Sole (SEINE)

Coley/Saithe (TRAWL)

Pollock (ALASKA)

Cod (HOOK & LINE, GULF OF MAINE)

Cod (NON TRAWL, ICELAND)

NO

Gilthead Bream

Tilapia (CHINA)

Salmon

Salmon

Monkfish

Cod

H

Eel

Tiger Prawns

Herring (W. ATLANTIC)

Sea Trout

Spiny Dogfish (LINE)

Yellowtail Tuna

Cobia (ASIA)

Chilean Seabass

Plaice

Anchov (MEDITERRA

Seabass

Yellowfin Tuna

Ha

Which Fish are Okay to Eat?

Crashing fish stocks. Pollution. Near-extinction.

Atlantic/Pacific

ack Bream

Albacore Tuna
(POLE)

gfin Squid
(SEINE)

Big Eye Tuna
(POLE)

Squid
(JIG)

Spiny Lobster

Skipjack Tuna
(POLE & LINE)

Dover Sole

Shark

Red Snapper

Swordfish

Orange Roughy

Any Tuna
(LONGLINE)

Skate

Pacific

Anchovy
(PERU & CHILE)

Blackcod/Sablefish

Halibut

Crimson Snapper
(AUSTRALIA, TRAP)

Salmon
(ALASKA)

Cod
(LONGLINE, JIG, TRAP)

Dungeness Crab
(TRAP)

Pink Shrimp
(OREGON)

Sardine

Striped Bass

White Seabass

Lingcod

Flounder

Californian Halibut
(HOOK & LINE)

American Lobster
(TRAP)

Pomfret

Sole

Mahi Mahi
(LONGLINE)

Squid

Turbot

Yellowfin Tuna

Blue Marlin

Spiny Lobster

Grenadier

Hoki

King Crab

Californian Halibut

Mahi Mahi

Cod
(IMPORTED)

Rockfish
(TRAWL)

Toothfish

Salmon

source: Marine Conservation Society, Greenpeace, Seafood Watch // data:bit.ly/whichfish

SUMMER | WINTER

The "In" Colours

Women's fashion colours

source: pantone.com

The "Interesting" Colours

Selected women's fashion colours

SUMMER

2002

pinkle	lily green	poppy red	03
tigerlily	cadmium	plaza taupe	04
coral reef	kelp	begonia pink	05
french vanilla	melon	clove	06
silver peony	tarragon	golden apricot	07
golden olive	croissant	snorkel blue	08
lucite green	dark citron	rose dust	09
roccoco red	deep ultramarine	cameo pink	10
blue curaçao	peapod	russet	11

2002

gypsy lavender | turkish coffee | peacock

03

hollyhock | cognac | dull gold

04

tango red | norse blue | elderberry

05

moroccan blue | rattan | moss

06

simple taupe | apple cinnamon | red mahogany

07

carafe | chilli pepper | lemon curry

08

royal lilac | shiitake | withered rose

09

split pea | dark plum | raspberry

10

rose dust | purple orchid | woodbine

11

honeysuckle | deep teal | quarry

WINTER

source: pantone.com

Three's a Magic Number

BIZARRE LOVE TRIANGLES

hmmmmm

70s

cough

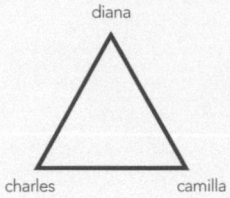

80s

wha–?

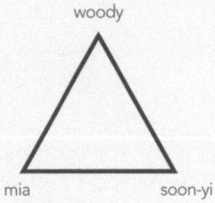

90s

THREE THINKING

dialectics

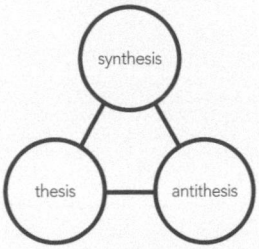

HEGEL

types of thinking

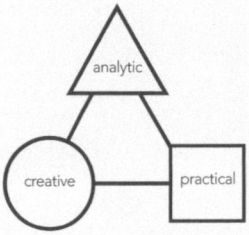

APPARENTLY

journalistic

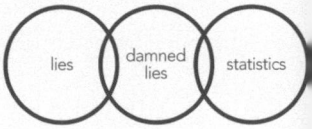

MARK TWAIN

THE THREE DOMAINS OF LIFE

the domains

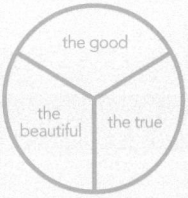

PLATO

their disciplines

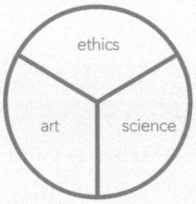

their types of truth

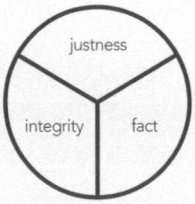

CHRISTIAN TRINITIES

God is a happy family

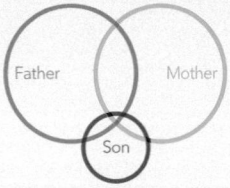

GNOSTIC (100 AD)

1 god, 3 persons

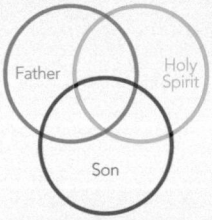

EARLY (200 AD)

all separate

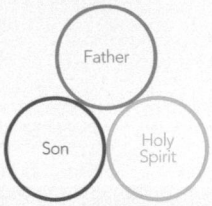

NICENE (325 AD)

HEALTHREE

life essentials

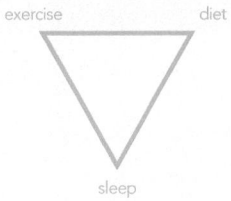

COMMON SENSE

types of fitness

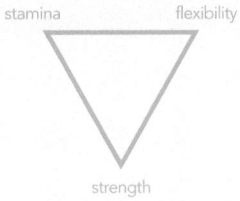

SHAWN PHILLIPS

relationship essentials

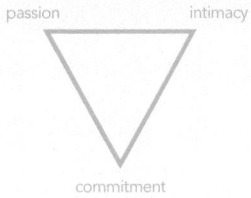

GOOD LUCK!

3-part mind

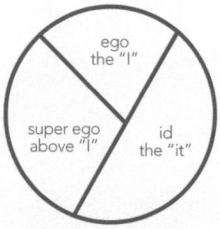

FREUD

3-part brain

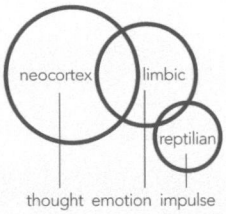

PAUL D MACLEAN

3 voices in the mind

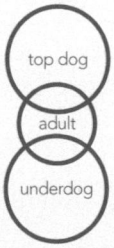

FRITZ PERLS

THREEDOM

pre-modern values

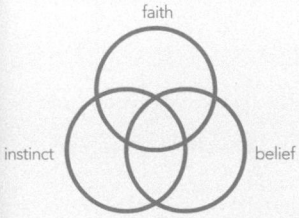

PRE 1700

modern values

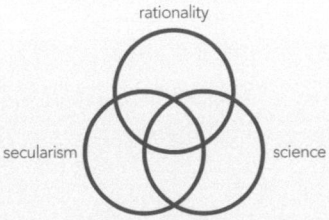

1700–1945

post-modern values

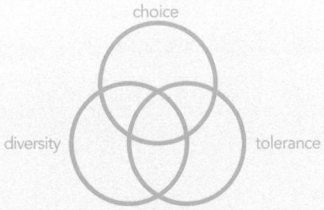

1945+

o, son both human & divine

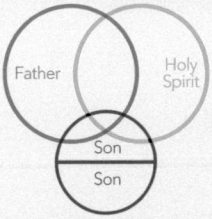

CALCEDON (451 AD)

er, son created by union

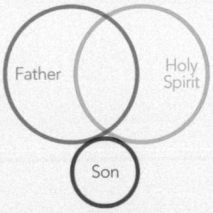

ORIENTAL ORTHODOXY (451 AD)

I know! Father creates *both*

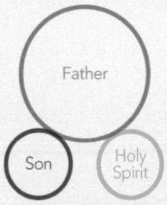

EASTERN ORTHODOXY (1054 AD)

source: Wikipedia, The Gale Encyclopedia of Religion

Who Runs the World?

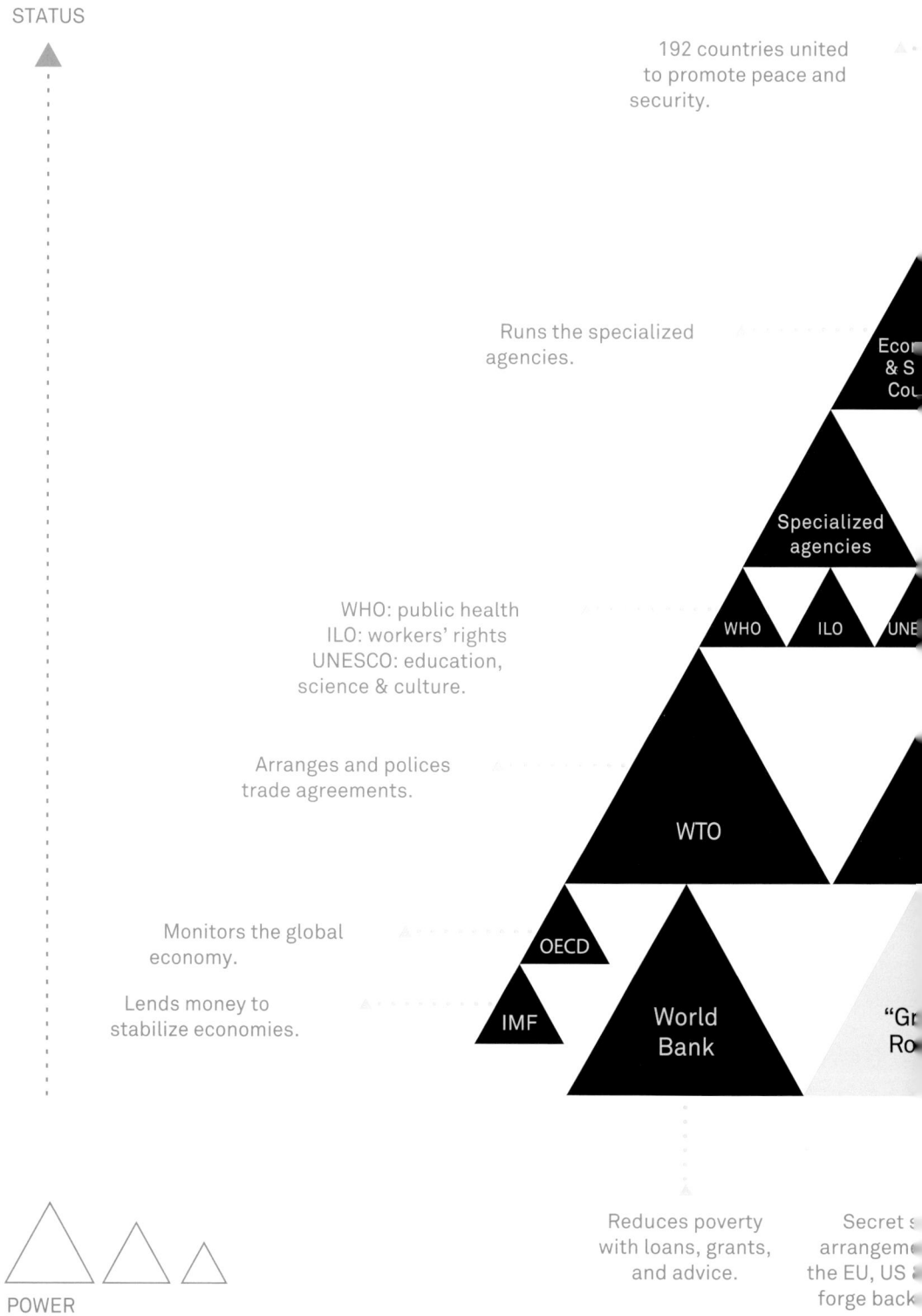

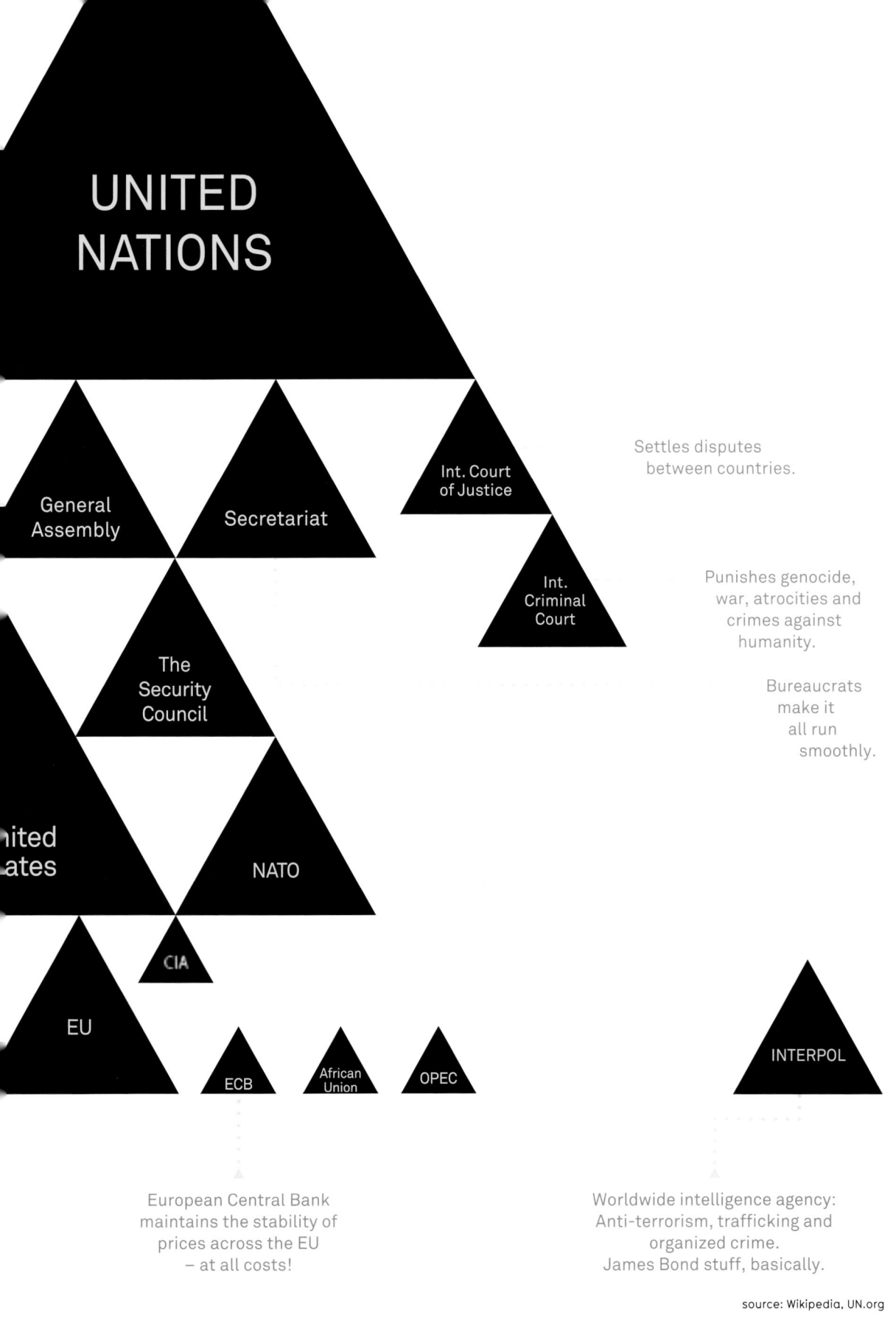

source: Wikipedia, UN.org

Who *Really* Runs the World?

Conspiracy theory

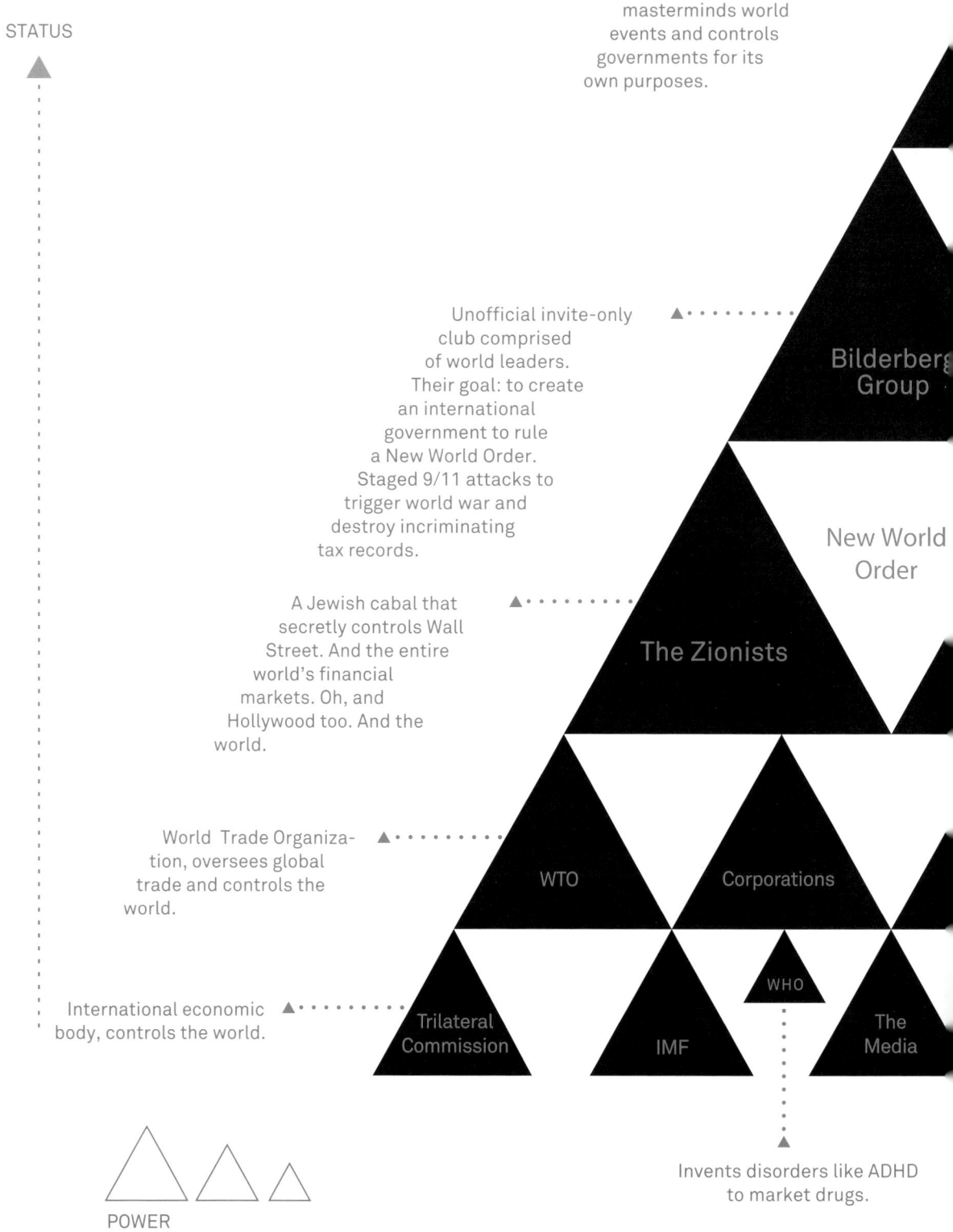

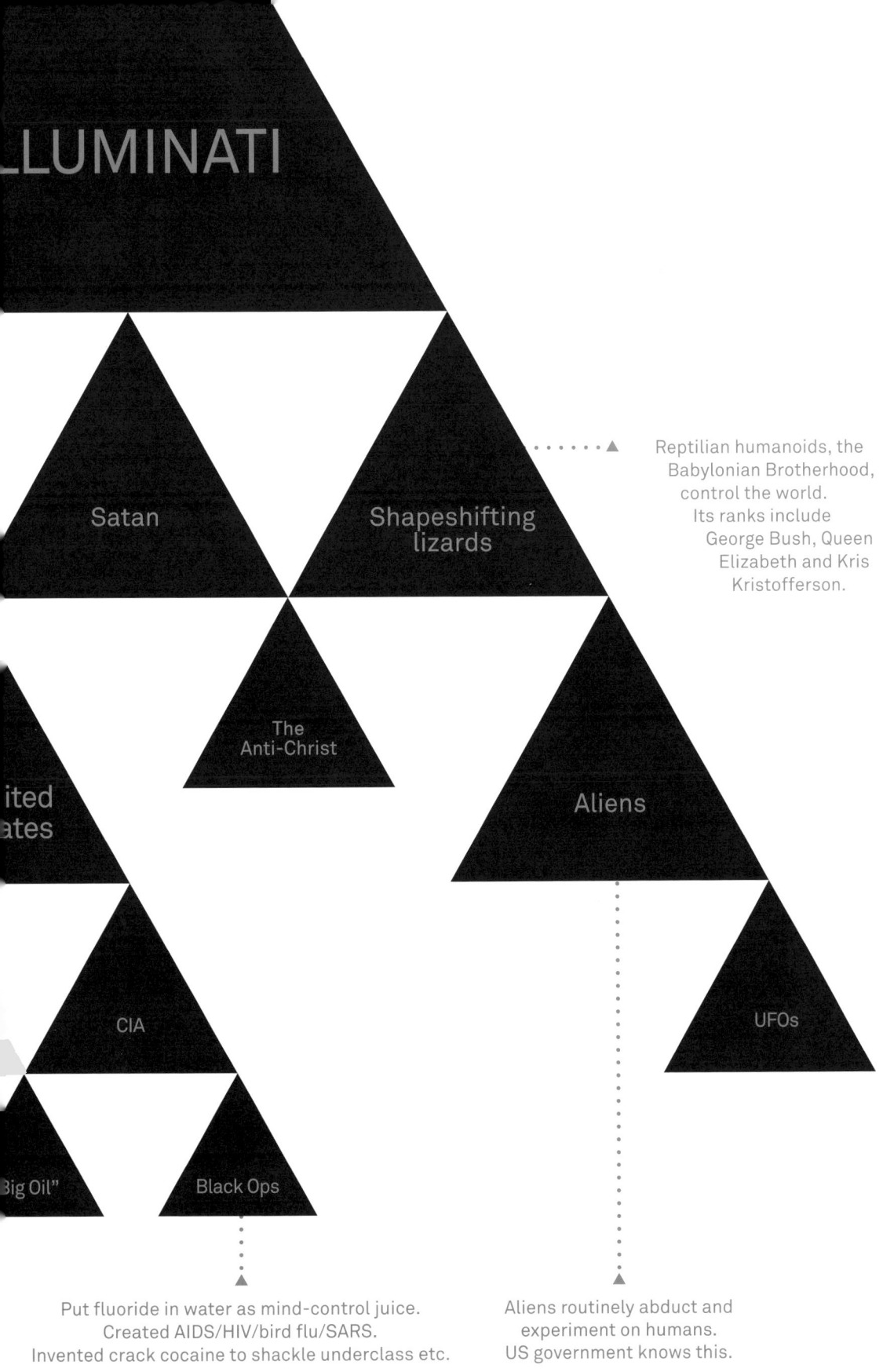
LLUMINATI
Satan
Shapeshifting lizards
Reptilian humanoids, the Babylonian Brotherhood, control the world. Its ranks include George Bush, Queen Elizabeth and Kris Kristofferson.
The Anti-Christ
ited ates
Aliens
CIA
UFOs
Big Oil"
Black Ops
Put fluoride in water as mind-control juice. Created AIDS/HIV/bird flu/SARS. Invented crack cocaine to shackle underclass etc.
Aliens routinely abduct and experiment on humans. US government knows this.

Stock Check

Estimated remaining world supplies of non-renewable resources

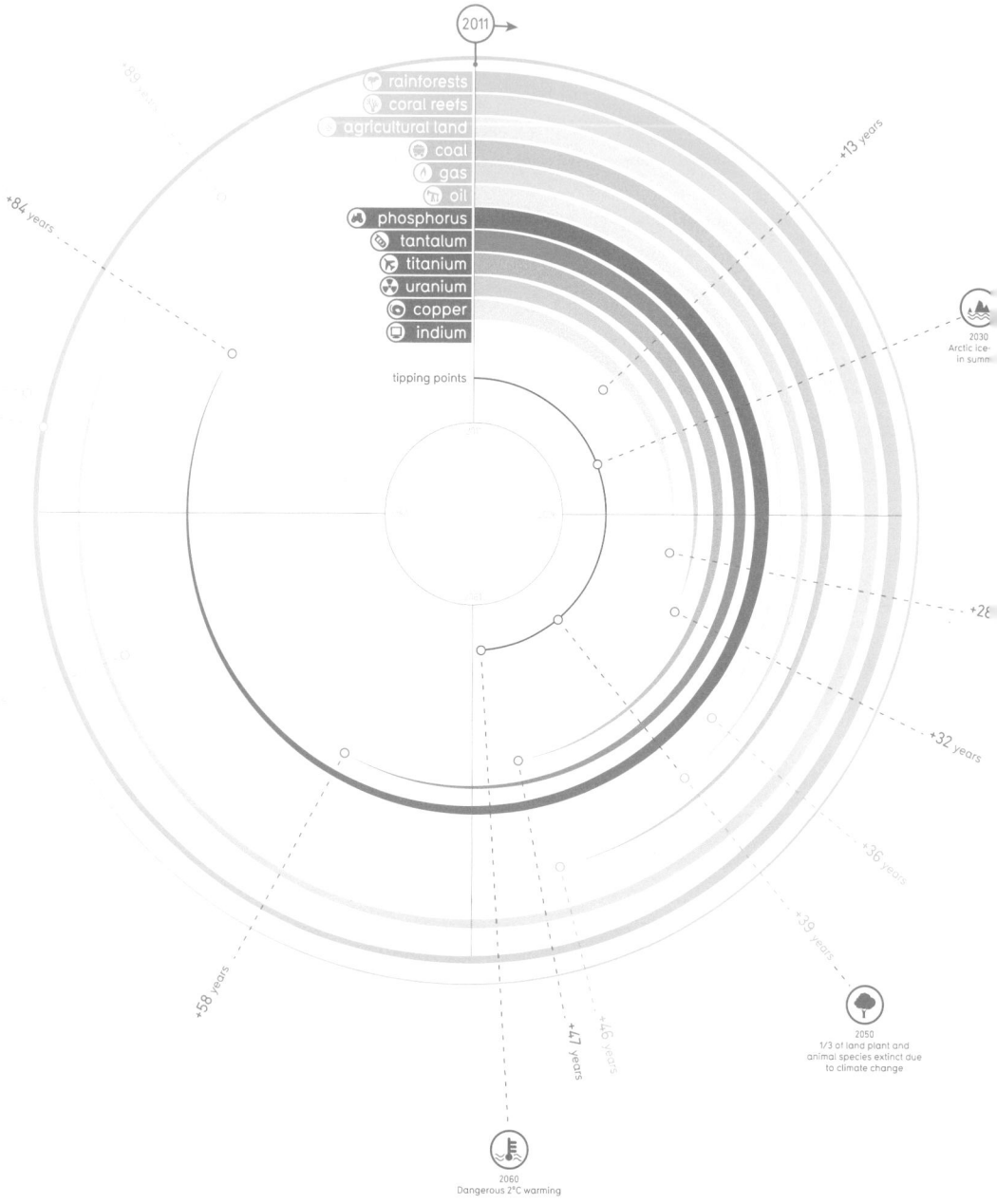

note: worst-case based on published estimates, assuming fixed % yearly consumption rate

source: UN TEEB, US Geological Survey, BP, Worm et al (2006), London Metal Exchang

source: Costanza et al, World Bank (2010)

Amazon

1979

2009

source: Global Forest Watch

Creation Myths

How did it all start?

Ex Nihilo (Out of Nothing)

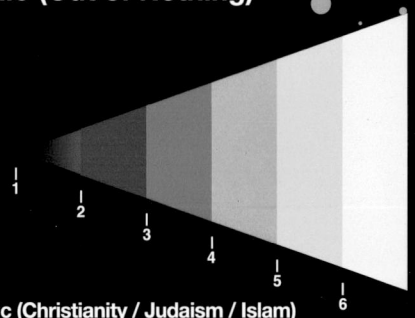

Abrahamic (Christianity / Judaism / Islam)
Day 1. God created light and darkness.
Day 2. He created water and sky.
Day 3. Separated dry ground from oceans, created all vegetation.
Day 4. Created sun, moon and stars.
Day 5. Created all water-dwelling creatures and birds.
Day 6. Created all creatures of the world.
Day 7. Had a nice rest.

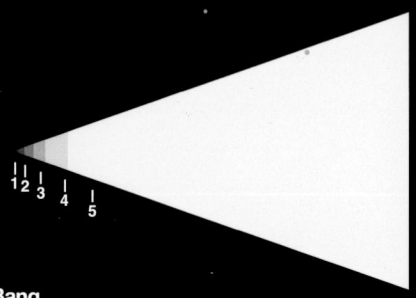

The Big Bang
1. 15,000 million years ago all the matter in the Universe bursts out from single point. **2.** Inflates from the size of an atom to the size of a grapefruit in a microsecond. **3.** Three minutes in, the universe is a superhot fog, too hot for even light to shine. **4.** 300,000 years later, everything is cool enough to form the first atoms. Light shines! **5.** After a billion years, clouds of gas collapse. Gravity pulls them in to form the first galaxies and stars.

Primordial "Soup"

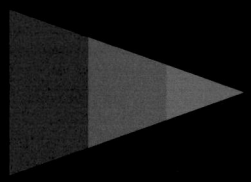

Hinduism
In a dark vast ocean, Lord Vishnu sleeps. A humming noise trembles. With a vast "OM!" Vishnu awakes. From his stomach blossoms a lotus flower containing Brahma, who splits the lotus flower into heaven, earth and sky.

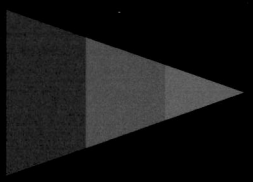

Chinese (Taoist)
There was a mist of chaos. The mist separated and the light rose to heaven and the heavy sank and formed the earth. From heaven and earth came yin and yang, masculine and feminine. Together they keep the world in harmony.

Infinite Universe / Continuous Creation

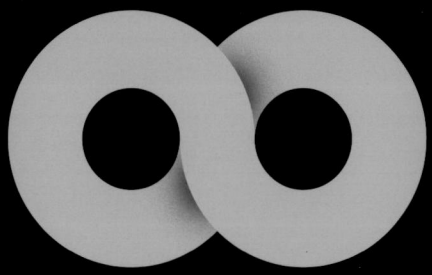

Steady State Theory
Matter is generated constantly as the universe expands.
No beginning, no end.

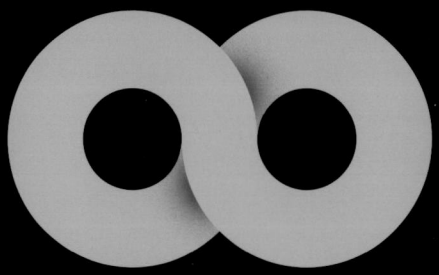

Buddhism
The universe is not fixed in a state of "being", but of "becoming". At any moment some stars and galaxies are born while others die

nfinite Universe / Cyclical

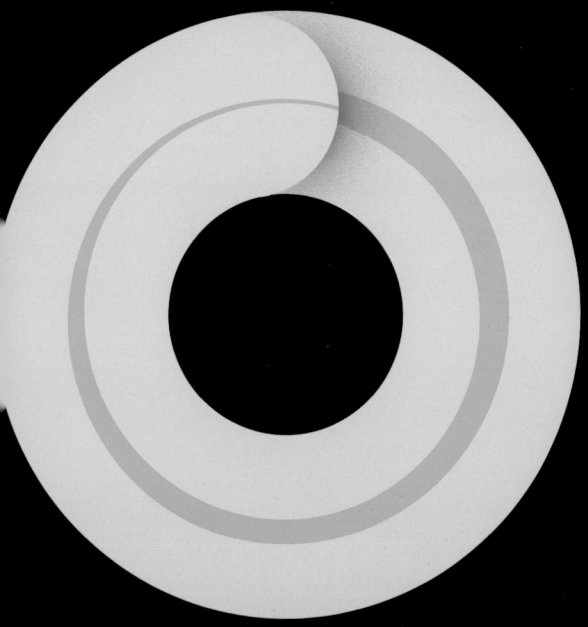

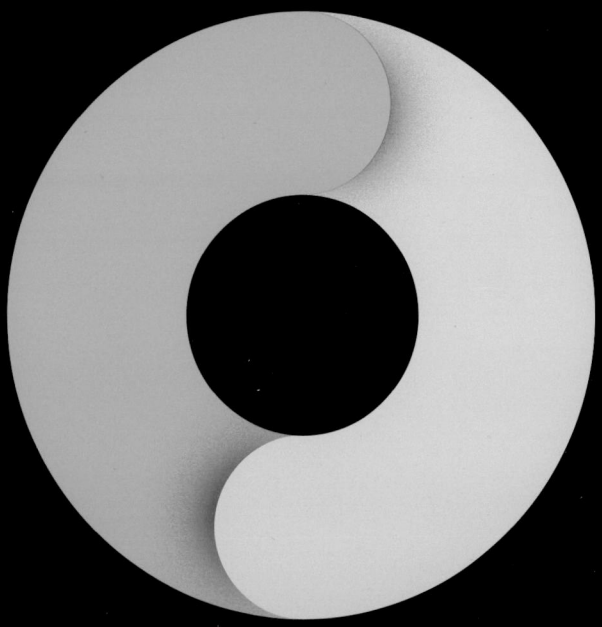

ig Bangs, Big Crunches
ndless cycles of big bangs and big crunches, with each cycle sting about a trillion years. All matter and radiation is reset, but e cosmological constant is not. It gradually diminishes over many ycles to the small value observed in today's universe.

Involution / Evolution (Hinduism, Theosophy)
Infinite number of universes in an infinite cycle of births, deaths and rebirths. Each cycle lasts 8.4 billion years. The universe involves (in breath), gathers all the material, then 'evolves' (out breath) and expands. This cycle repeats infinitely.

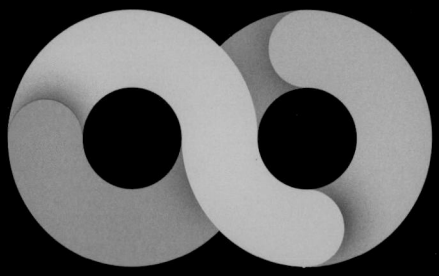

uasi Steady State (QSS) Theory
he cosmos has always existed. Explosions, of all different sizes, ccur continuously, giving the impression of a big bang in our locality.

Bubble Universe
Our universe is a bubble spawned off a larger "foam" of other universes. Each bubble is different. Ours is finely tuned to support life.

source: Wikipedia, NewScientist.com

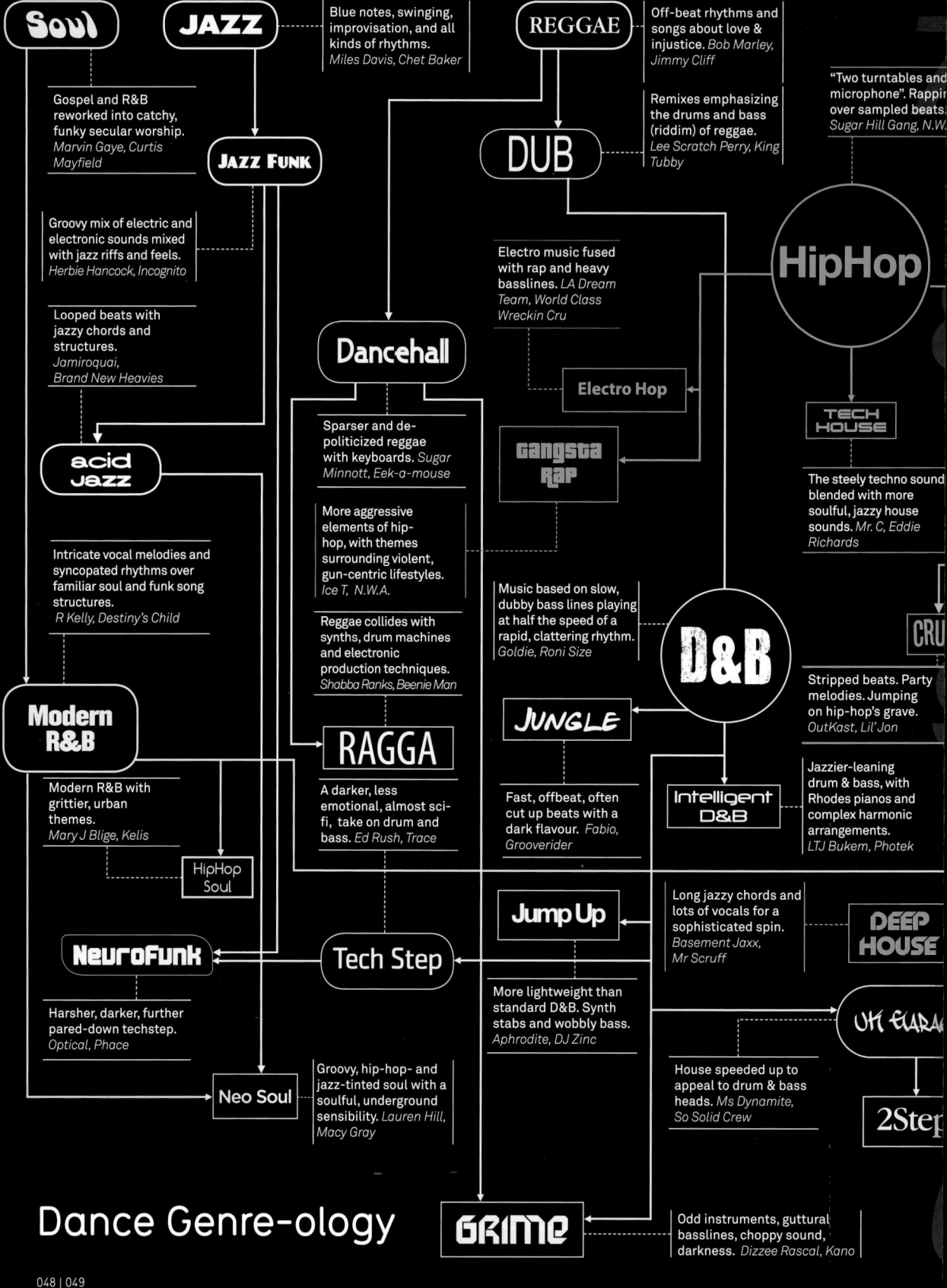

Dance Genre-ology

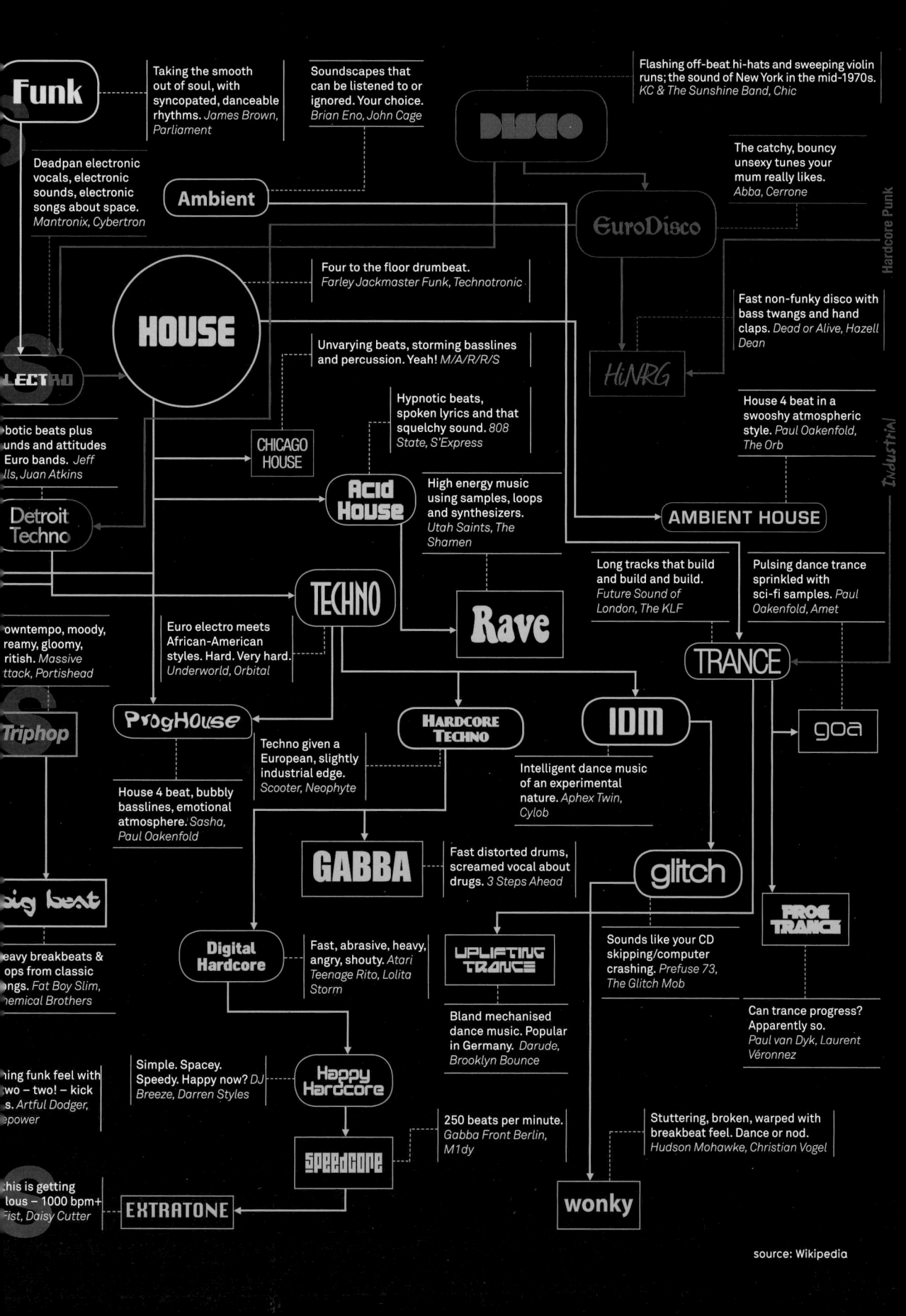

source: Wikipedia

The Book of You

A copy in every one of your 10,000,000,000 cells

The Book

Your complete DNA (or "genome") – 3.2 billion words

Your Page

The only part that varies from person to person ("genotype")
0.06%

The Chapters

Organized sections inside the book ("chromosomes"). Made of genes
23 pairs

The Paragraphs

Genes are clumps of DNA made up of base pairs
20 – 25,000

The Words

Individual two letter "words" of DNA
2 million

The Letters

Letters made of just four individual molecules

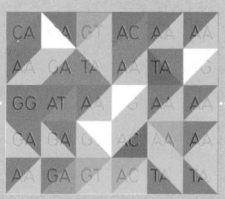

Responsible for all your physical characteristics, susceptibility to certain diseases, and even earwax
We have identified the effects of around 5000 out of 2,000,000 (0.25%)

source: Decodeme.com, Wikipedia

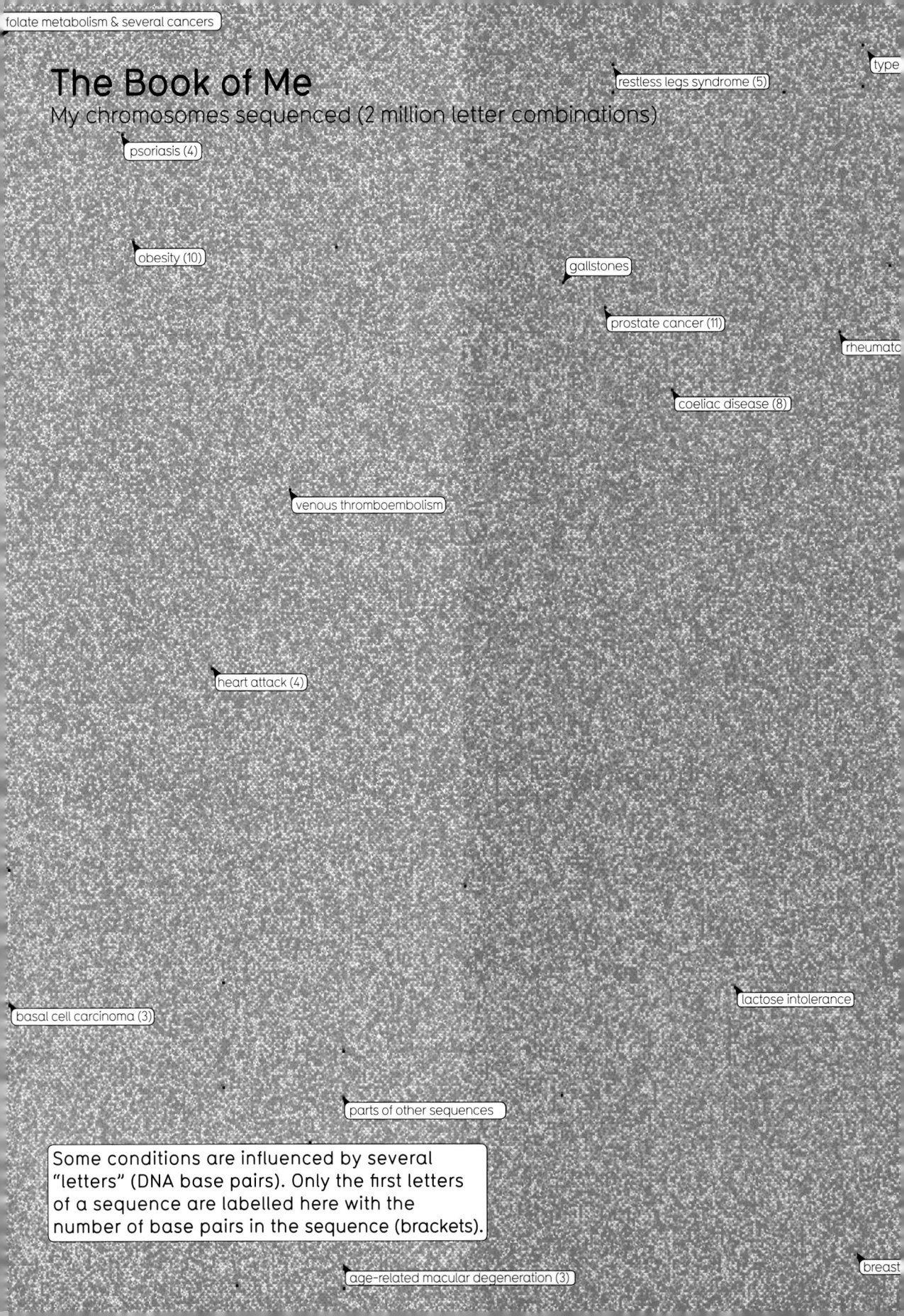
The Book of Me
My chromosomes sequenced (2 million letter combinations)
folate metabolism & several cancers
restless legs syndrome (5)
type
psoriasis (4)
obesity (10)
gallstones
prostate cancer (11)
rheumato
coeliac disease (8)
venous thromboembolism
heart attack (4)
lactose intolerance
basal cell carcinoma (3)
parts of other sequences
Some conditions are influenced by several "letters" (DNA base pairs). Only the first letters of a sequence are labelled here with the number of base pairs in the sequence (brackets).
breast
age-related macular degeneration (3)

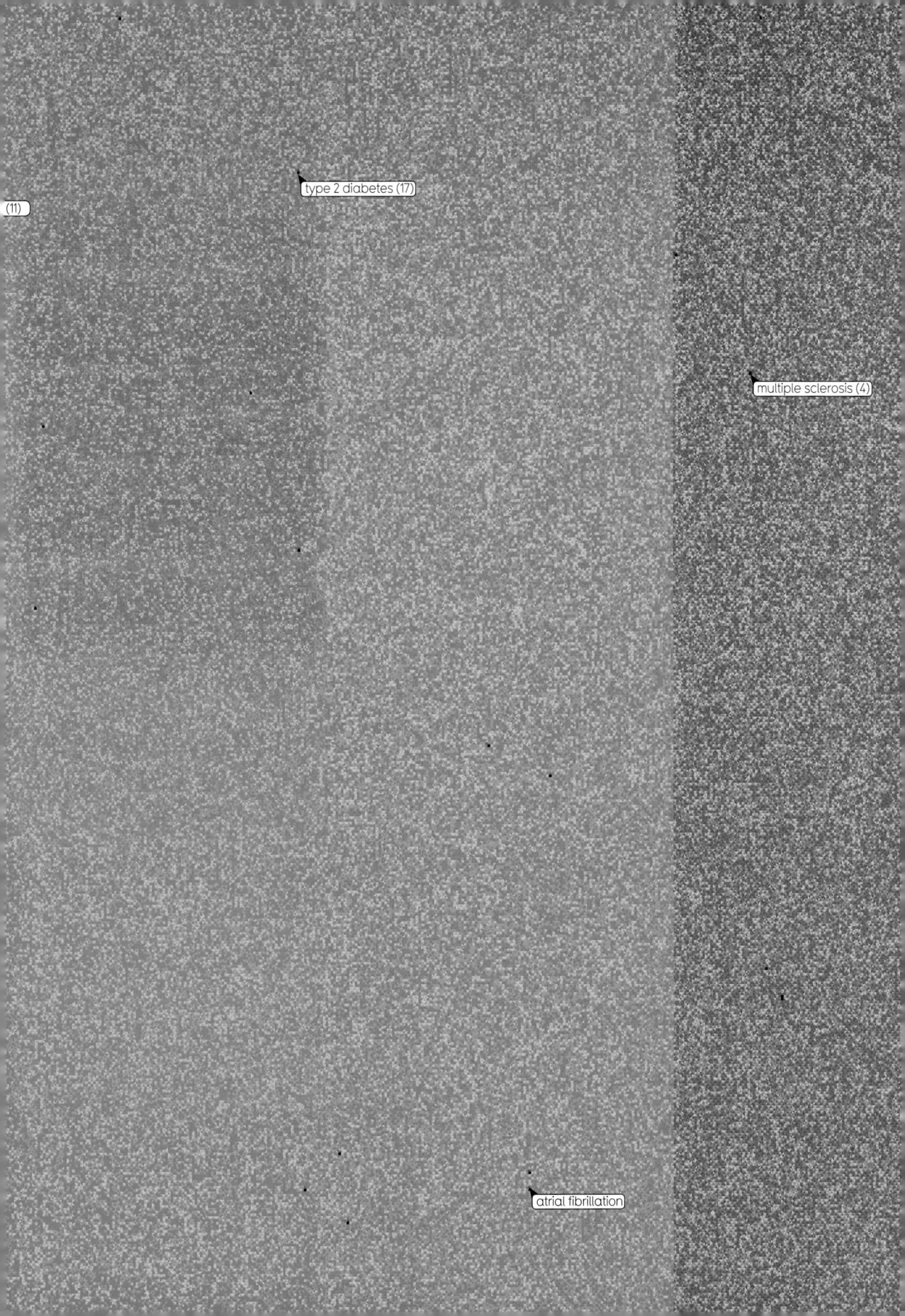
type 2 diabetes (17)
(11)
multiple sclerosis (4)
atrial fibrillation

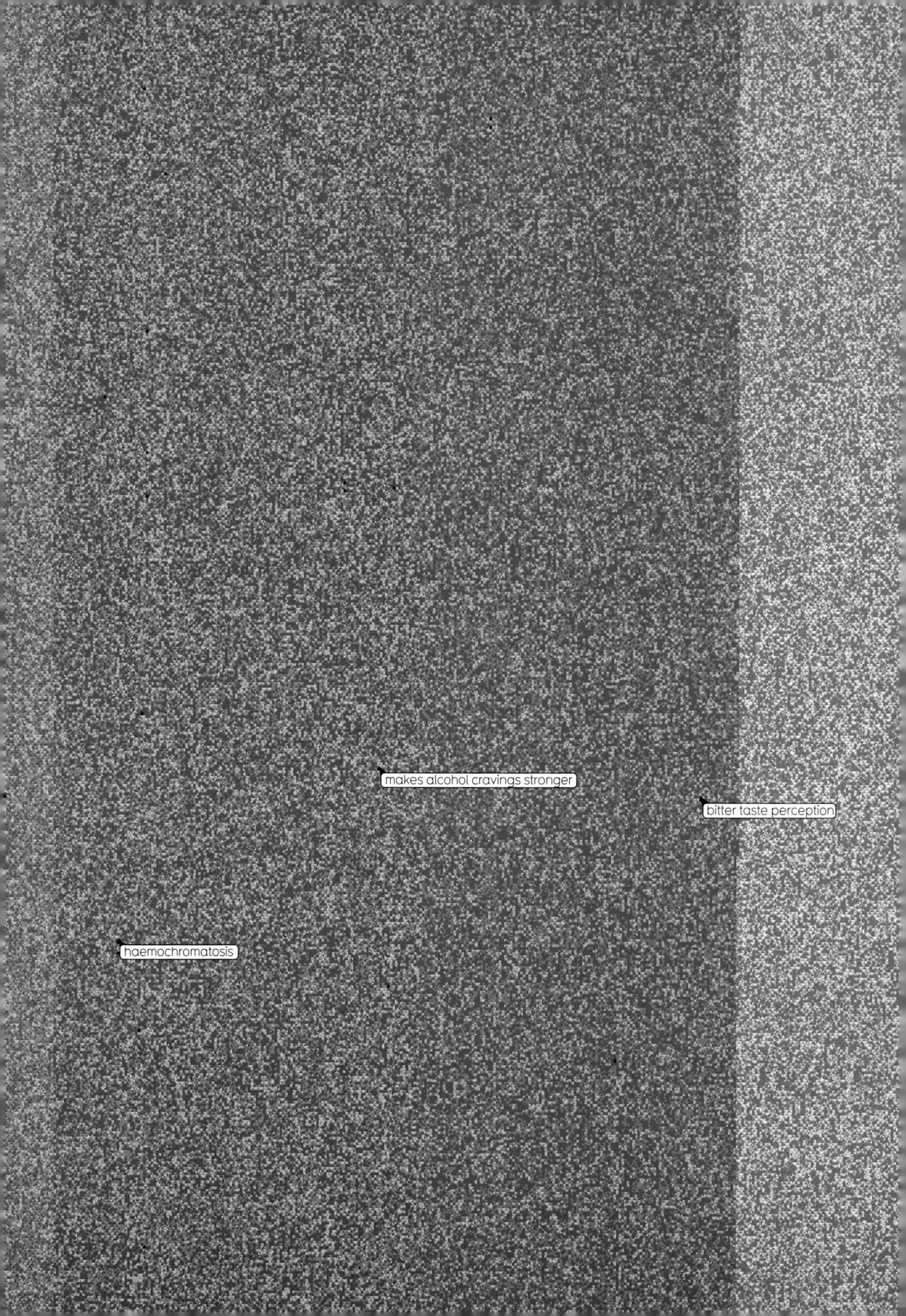
makes alcohol cravings stronger
bitter taste perception
haemochromatosis

intercranial aneurysm

sensitivity to pleasure

endurance athletics

warfarin metabolism (3)

adder cancer

colorectal cancer (6)

nicotine dependence

determin

alcoholic flush reaction

exfoliation glaucoma

green eye colour

blue eye colour

asthma
increased Alzheimer's risk (3)
baldness
source: Decodeme.com / programming : Mattias Gunneras
varied cognitive effects

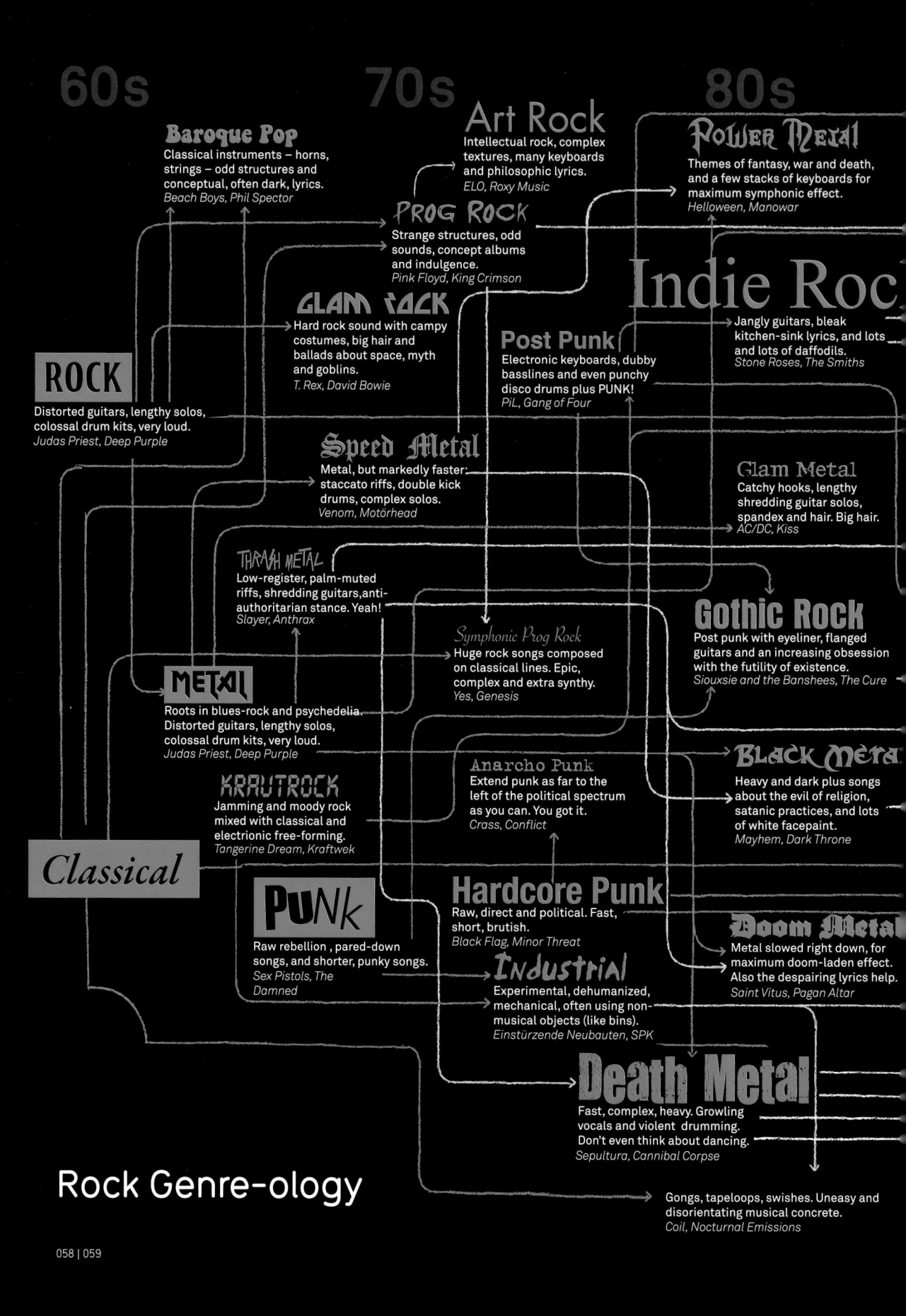

Rock Genre-ology

80s 90s 00s

POST ROCK
Often purely instrumental. Uses rock instruments to create textures, tones and atmospheres.
Tortoise, Mogwai

Mathrock
Complex, difficult, lopsided time signatures and bizarre arrangements to not quite tap your foot to.
Battles, Dirty Projectors

Symphonic Post Rock
Ambient soundscapes. Orchestras. Walls of sound.
Godspeed You! Black Emperor, Sigur Rós

GRUNGE
The distortion and ferocity of hardcore punk and metal with angsty lyrics and more accessible tune-ship.
Mudhoney, Nirvana

Mathcore
Offshoot of doom metal.
The Dillinger Escape Plan

post grunge
Distorted guitar, angsty lyrics but easier on the ear.
Silverchair, Puddle of Mudd

INDIE POP
Indie rock fused with 60s influences for a more pop-oriented sound.
The Wedding Present, Orange Juice

britpop
Fusing the rock and pop elements of indie music and sold back to the major labels in the 1990s.
Oasis, Blur

DEATH DOOM
Growling, incomprehensible vocals, double kick drum and sheets of guitars.
Paradise Lost, Anathema

RAP ROCK
White-style shouted rap, hardcore guitars over live hip-hop style beats.
Rage Against the Machine, Red Hot Chili Peppers

MELODIC BLACK METAL
Reining in the distortion, a few more tunes, but no let-up on the obsession with death and destruction.
Satyricon, Dark Fortress

DEATHCORE
Heavy muted riffing, dissonance, growling and screaming. Melodic riffs in there somewhere.
Abscess, Unseen Terrrors

College Rock
Poppy but edgy guitar rock with artsy, poignant and jangly qualities.
REM, They Might Be Giants

Symphonic Black Metal
The addition of orchestral instruments and classical influences to the black metal.
Dimmu Borgir, Antestor

GOTH METAL
Aggressive guitar mushed with melancholic vibes, dark atmospheres & epic lyrics.
Evanescence, Paradise Lost

Melodic Death Metal
Reining in the distortion, a few more tunes, but no let-up on the obsession with death and destruction.
In Flames, Dark Tranquillity

METAL CORE
All the ferocity of metal, with all the political posturing of hardcore punk.
Biohazard, Suicidal Tendencies

Gothic Black Metal
Operatic female vocals, ambient keyboards and dark guitaring.
Cradle of Filth, Moonspell

Drone Doom
Heavy, heavy, repetitive, slow. "Not unlike listening to an Indian raga in the middle of an earthquake".
Sunn O))), Earth

TECHNICAL DEATH METAL
Noise, plus prog-style tempo changes and bizarre time signatures.
Meshuggah, Suffocation

THRASH CORE
Incredibly fast punk songs with blasting beats and rebellious shouty lyrics.
Septic Death, Nuclear Assault

INDUSTRIAL METAL
Lots of drum machines. Lots of guitars. Lots of bleak lyrics. All with a tight computerized edge.
Ministry, Nine Inch Nails

GRINDCORE
Very heavy guitars, very fast rhythms, very short songs (sometimes only seconds).
Napalm Death, Carcass

MARTIAL INDUSTRIAL
Orchestral elements of classical music fused with rock music, parading and military uniforms.
Laibach, Death in June

BRUTAL DEATH METAL
Absurdly fast drumming, plus growling, shrieking and shredding guitars.
Spawn of Posession, Devourment

source: Wikipedia

Simple Part I

Think of the Children

% of children living in poverty

source UNICEF 2007. Numbers rounded up.

Farty Animals

Annual methane emissions in equivalent CO_2

source: UN Environmental Programme, theregister.co.uk

Who Reads the Most?

Amazon book stock as % of population size

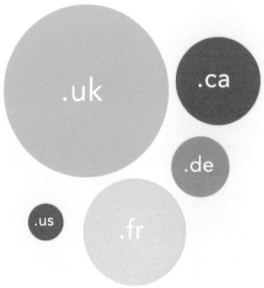

source: Data scraped from Amazon websites.

Wave of Generosity

% of promised tsunami aid money actually paid

Greece 100%
New Zealand
Iceland UK Norway
Japan 90%
Australia Canada 75%
Portugal Netherlands
Italy France 50%
USA 35%
Germany 26%

source: OECD

Celebrities with Issues

umber of celebs behind each cause

ostly male celebs

qual men & women

ostly female celebs

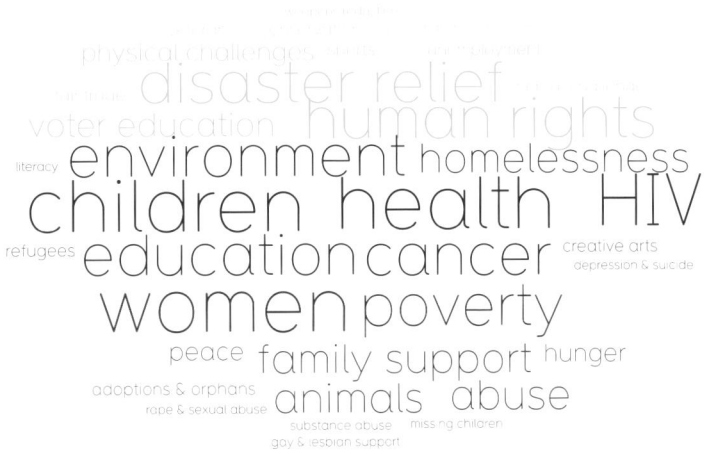

ea: Richard Rogers @ govcom.org // source: looktothestars.org

How Rich?

early earnings of world's wealthiest nations as combined earnings of US states

007

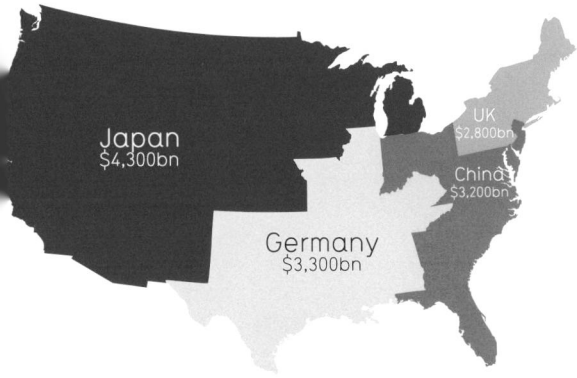

2010

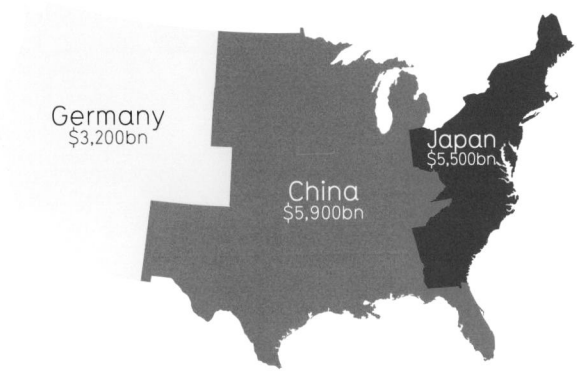

urce: WorldBank, ASecondHandConjecture.com

Sex Education

% virgin students by university subject

source: MIT/Wellesley College magazine, Counterpoint (2001)

Godless Swedes

% of atheists, agnostics & non-believers

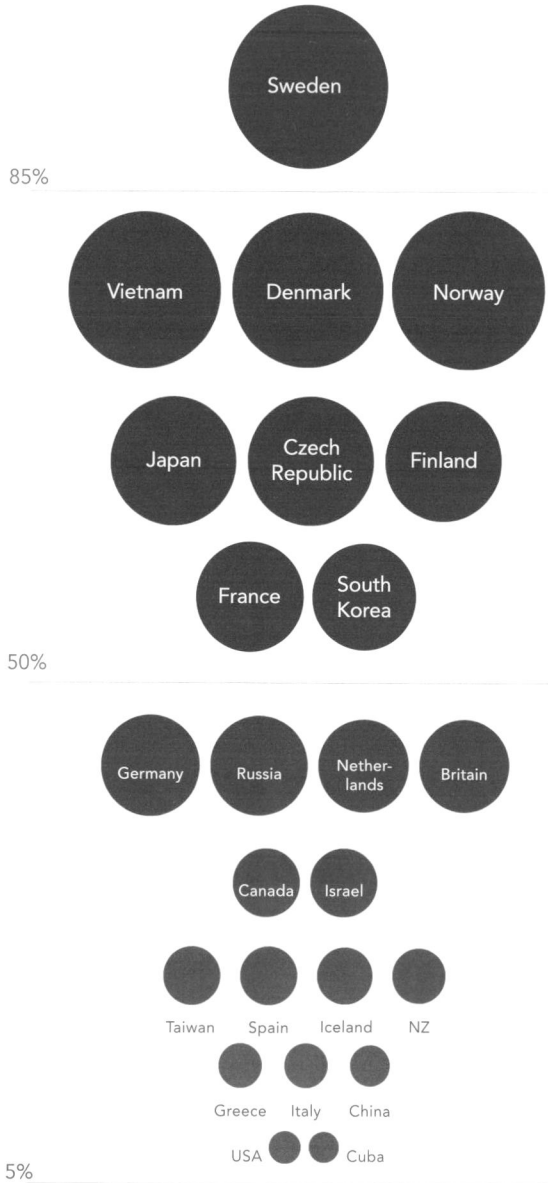

source: Adherents.com

Net Increase

nternet traffic growth

ntire internet per year
993

Internet per second
2008

nternet per year, 2000

YouTube per month, 2008

urce: Cisco

Left-Hand Path

Increased wealth of left-handed men

Does not apply to left-handed women.

source: Lafayette College and Johns Hopkins University study

Goggle Box

he cognitive surplus...

100 million hours
to create
Wikipedia

urce: Cognitive Surplus. Clay Shirky (Allen Lane, 2010)

Clear Cut

Drop in HIV transmission in circumcised males

source: University of Melbourne, BBC News

Excuse Us

Reasons for divorce

source: Insidedivorce.com

National Hypochondriacs Service

op health searches

UK

Sciatica Shingles
Thyroid
Pregnancy
Ringworm
Chickenpox
Anaemia
Glandular Fever

source: NHS Direct

USA

Stroke Asthma
ADHD
Pregnancy
Arthritis
Cancer
HIV

source: About.com

Germany

Arthritis
Anorexia Flu Spots
Hemorrhoids
Diabetes
MS

source: Google Insights

For Cod's Sake

tocks of cod in the North Atlantic (100,000 tons)

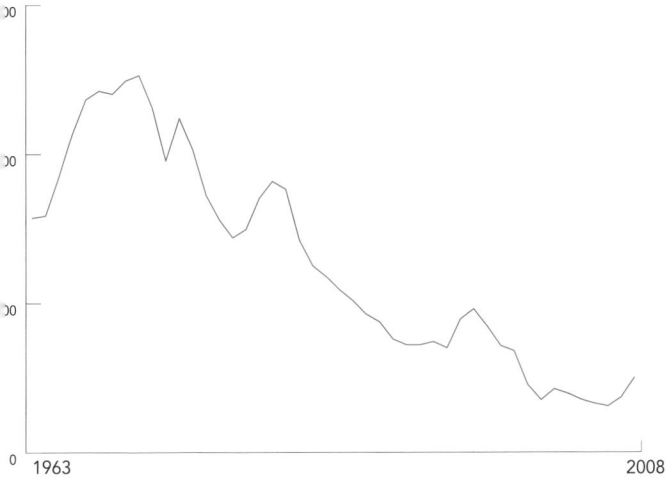

ource: Fisheries Research Service

Ups and Downs

Cover vs coverage

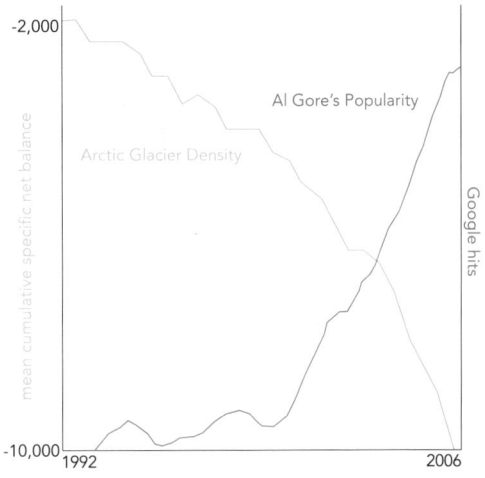

source: Google Insights

What is Consciousness?

Make up your own mind

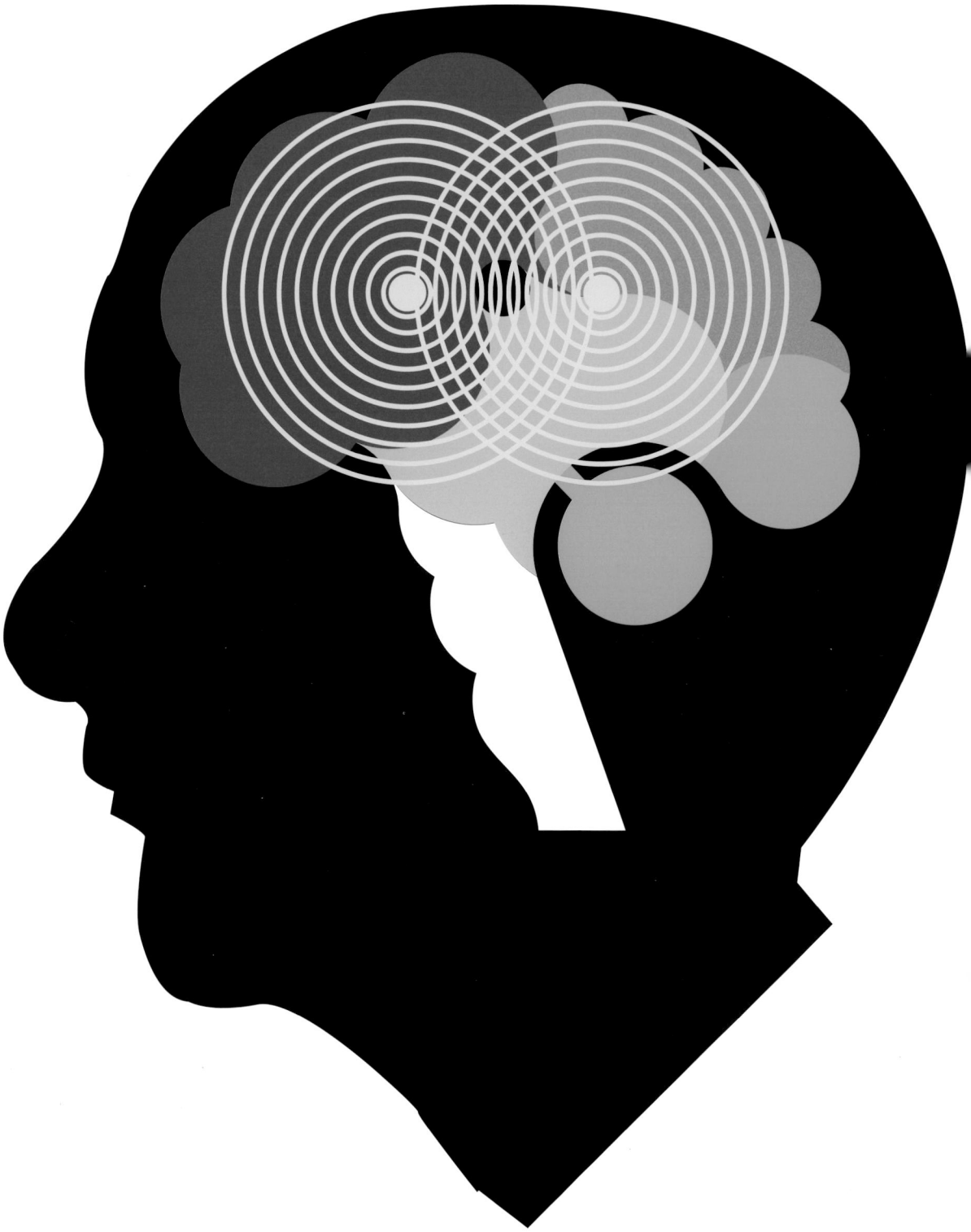

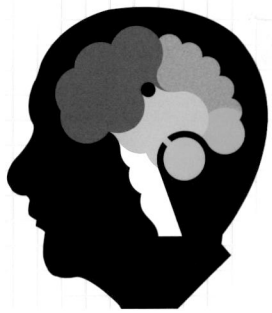

A field that exists in its own parallel "realm" of existence outside reality, so can't be seen.
(Substance Dualism)

A sensation that "grows" inevitably out of complicated brain states.
(Emergent Dualism)

A physical property of all matter, like electromagnetism, just not one scientists know about.
(Property Dualism)

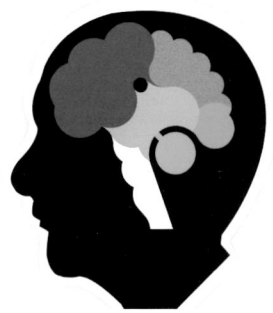

All matter has a psychic part. Consciousness is just the psychic part of our brain.
(Panpsychism)

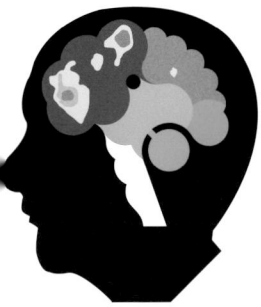

Mental states are simply physical events that we can see in brain scans.
(Identity Theory)

Consciousness and its states (belief, desire, pain) are simply functions the brain performs.
(Functionalism)

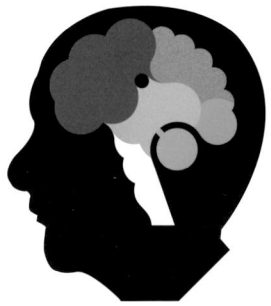

Literally just behaviour. When we behave in a certain way, we appear conscious.
(Behaviourism)

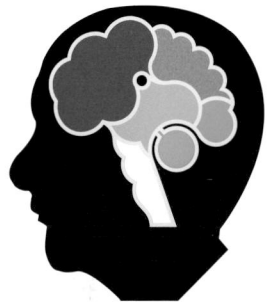

An accidental side-effect of complex physical processes in the brain.
(Epiphenomenalism)

Not sure. But quantum physics, over classical physics, can better explain it.
(Quantum Consciousness)

The sensation of your most significant thoughts being highlighted.
(Cognitivism)

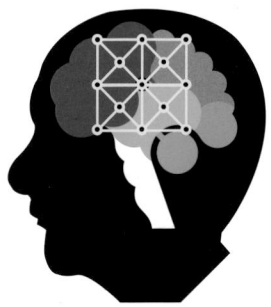

Consciousness is just higher-order thoughts (thoughts about other thoughts).
(Higher-Order Theory)

A continuous stream of ever-recurring phenomena, pinched like eddies into isolated minds.
(Buddhism)

source: Wikipedia

Carbon Conscious

Tweak your day

source: UNESCO, Environmental Protection Agency, Energy Information Administration including everyone in the UK & USA

4,187,280,000 tons

including everyone in the UK & USA

1,752,000,000 tons

(Equivalent to Japan's annual CO_2 emissions)

including everyone in the UK

907,244,000 tons

used per year

527,644,000

tons saved

including everyone in the UK

379,600,000 tons

used per year

2,435,280,000 tons
saved
(equivalent to Russia & India's total combined CO_2 emissions per year)

Reduce Your Chances of Dying in a Plane Crash

A pre-flight check

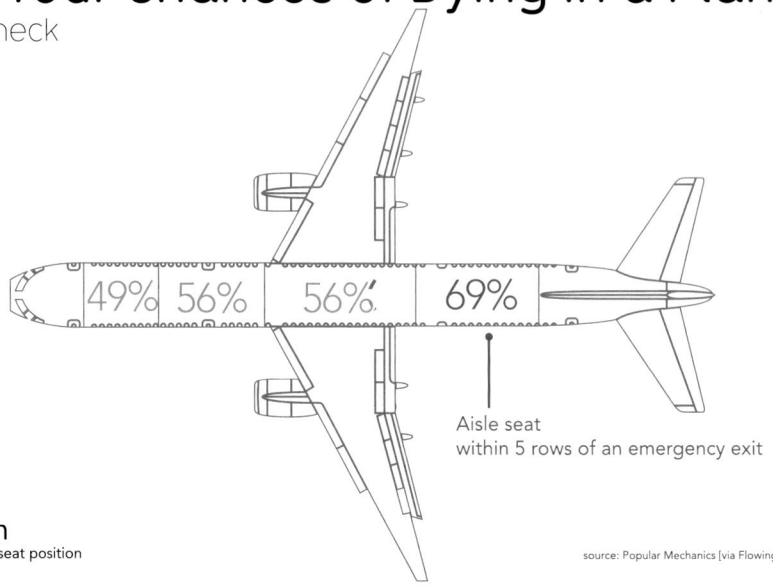

Seating Plan

Survival rate relative to seat position

source: Popular Mechanics [via FlowingData.com], University of Greenwich study

Squadron Leaders

Fatal accidents by aircraft type

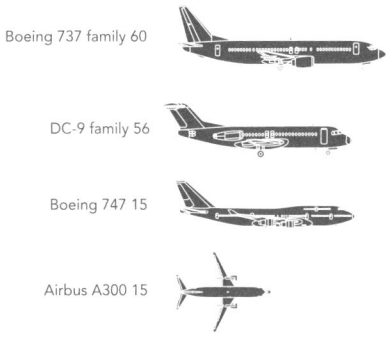

2nd Squadron Leaders

Ratio of number of planes in services to fatal accidents (the higher, the better)

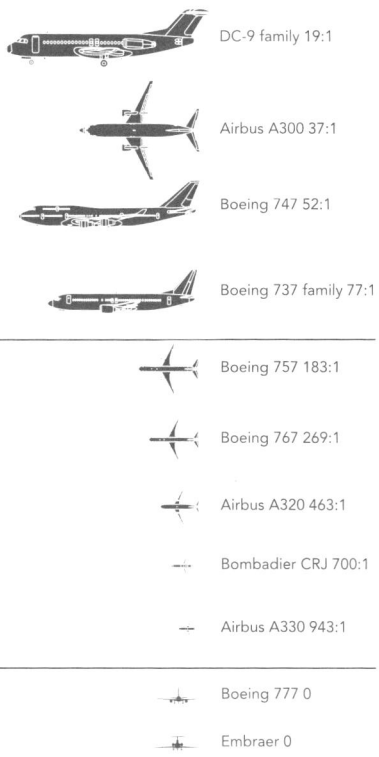

source: www.ascendworldwide.com [via Guardian Datablog]

Bad Month

Months with the most fatal airline accidents 1942–2009

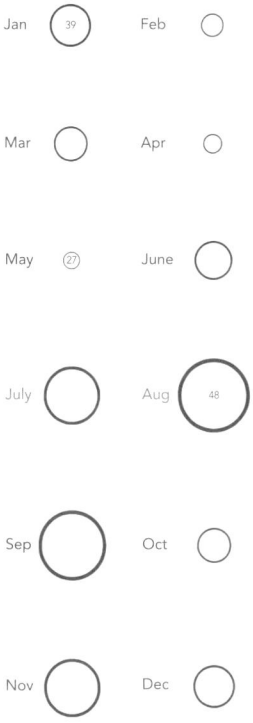

source: Wikipedia/List_of_air_disasters

Safety Record

Fatal accidents by airline (7 or more) 1950–2008

AIR FRANCE
KOREAN AIR
PIA Pakistan International
AIR INDIA
CUBANA
AmericanAirlines®
TURKISH AIRLINES
AEROFLOT
UNITED
Garuda Indonesia
Air Philippines
CHINA AIRLINES
U·S AIRWAYS

source: airdisaster.com

Final Destination

Density of fatal accidents 1942–2009

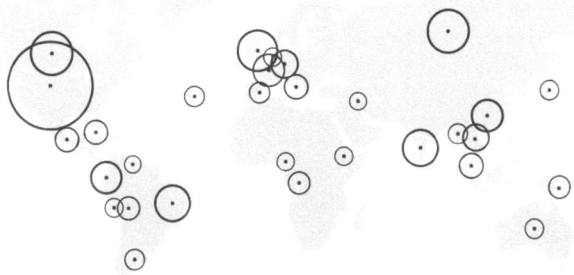

USA (2613 accidents), Russia (626), UK, India, Canada, Brazil, France, China, Colombia, Germany, Vietnam, Indonesia, Mexico, Italy, Cuba, Bolivia, Philippines, Congo (former Zaire), Spain, Argentina, Atlantic Ocean (and associated seas like Mediterranean, Caribbean), Myanmar, Australia, Japan, Venezuela, Netherlands, Sudan, Nigeria, Iran, Peru, Angola, Papua New Guinea, Afghanistan, Poland, Egypt, Pakistan, Thailand, Turkey, Ecuador (75)

source: www.aviation-safety.net/database/country

The Odds

Chances of actually dying in a plane crash

Falling down	Heat stroke	Lightning	Nuclear accident	Plane crash	Bee sting	Mountain lion attack	Blogging
20,666:1	950,000:1	2,320,000:1	10,000,000:1	11,000,000:1	15,000,000:1	32,000,000:1	35,000,000:1

source: Google

Rising Sea Levels

How long have we got?

years sea level

8000 80m

1000 20m

8m

7m

400 6m

5m

300 4m

200 3m

2m

100 1m

HOLLYWOOD

Venice

Los Angeles

Amsterdam

Hamburg

St Petersburg

San Francisco

Lower Manhattan

source: IPCC, UN Sea Levels Report, Realclimate.org, Telegraph.co.uk

Colours and Culture

The meanings of colours around the world

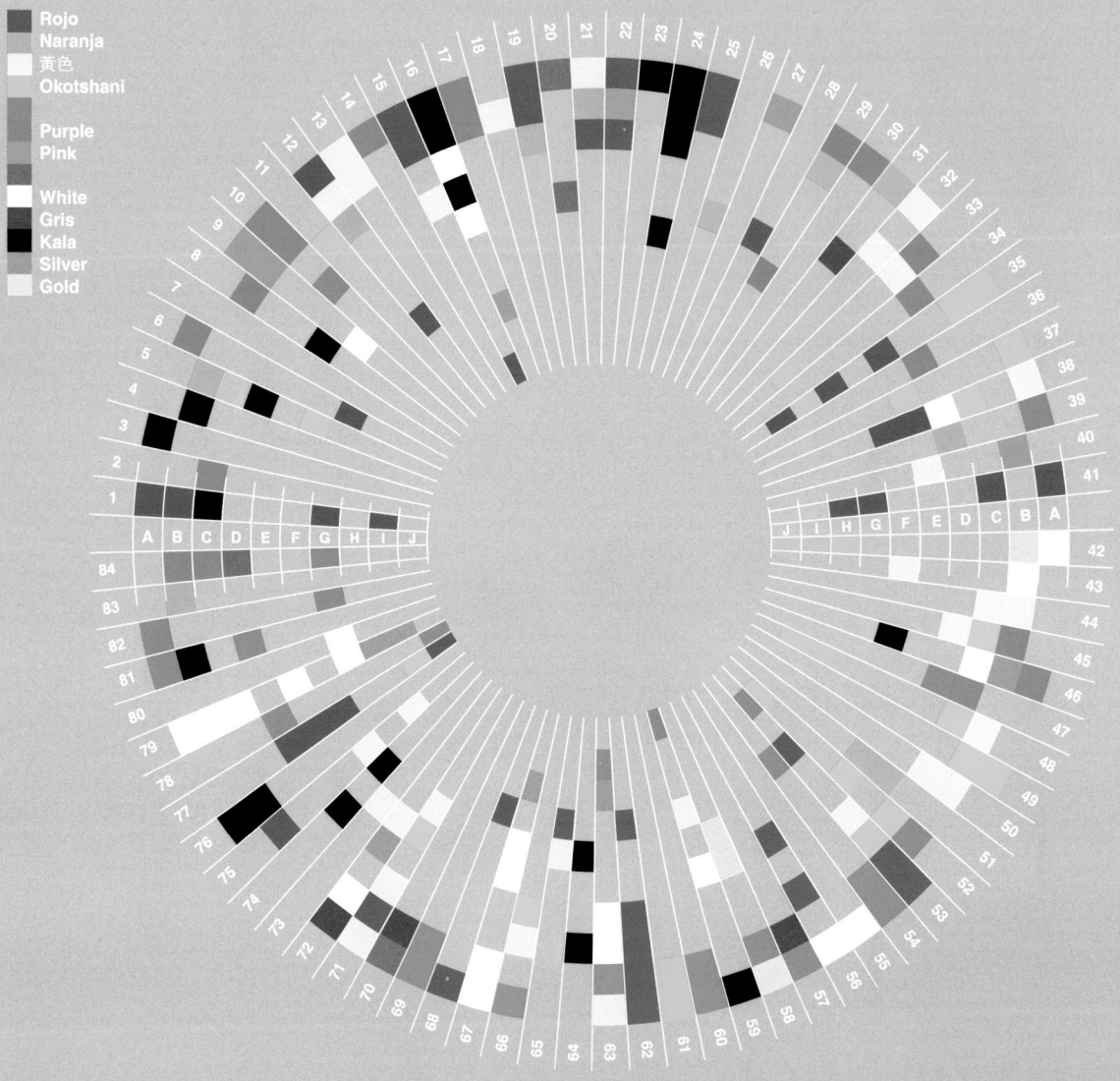

A American
B Japanese
C Hindu
D Native American
E Chinese
F Asian
G Eastern European
H Muslim
I African
J South American

1 Anger
2 Art / Creativity
3 Authority
4 Bad Luck
5 Balance
6 Beauty
7 Calm
8 Celebration
9 Children
10 Cold
11 Compassion
12 Courage
13 Cowardice
14 Cruelty
15 Danger
16 Death
17 Decadence
18 Deceit
19 Desire
20 Earth
21 Energy
22 Eroticism
23 Eternity
24 Evil
25 Excitement
26 Family
27 Femininity
28 Fertility
29 Flamboyance
30 Freedom
31 Friendliness
32 Fun
33 God
34 Gods
35 Good Luck
36 Gratitude
37 Growth
38 Happiness
39 Healing
40 Healthiness
41 Heat
42 Heaven
43 Holiness
44 Illness
45 Insight
46 Intelligence
47 Intuition
48 Religion
49 Jealousy
50 Joy
51 Learning
52 Life
53 Love
54 Loyalty
55 Luxury
56 Marriage
57 Modesty
58 Money
59 Mourning
60 Mystery
61 Nature
62 Passion
63 Peace
64 Penance
65 Political Power
66 Personal Power
67 Purity
68 Radicalism
69 Rationality
70 Reliability
71 Repelling Ev
72 Respect
73 Royalty
74 Self-cultivati
75 Strength
76 Style
77 Success
78 Trouble
79 Truce
80 Trust
81 Unhappiness
82 Virtue
83 Warmth
84 Wisdom

source: Wikipedia, general we

Stages of You

Children grow in phases. Do adults too? If so, what are the stages? Some theories..

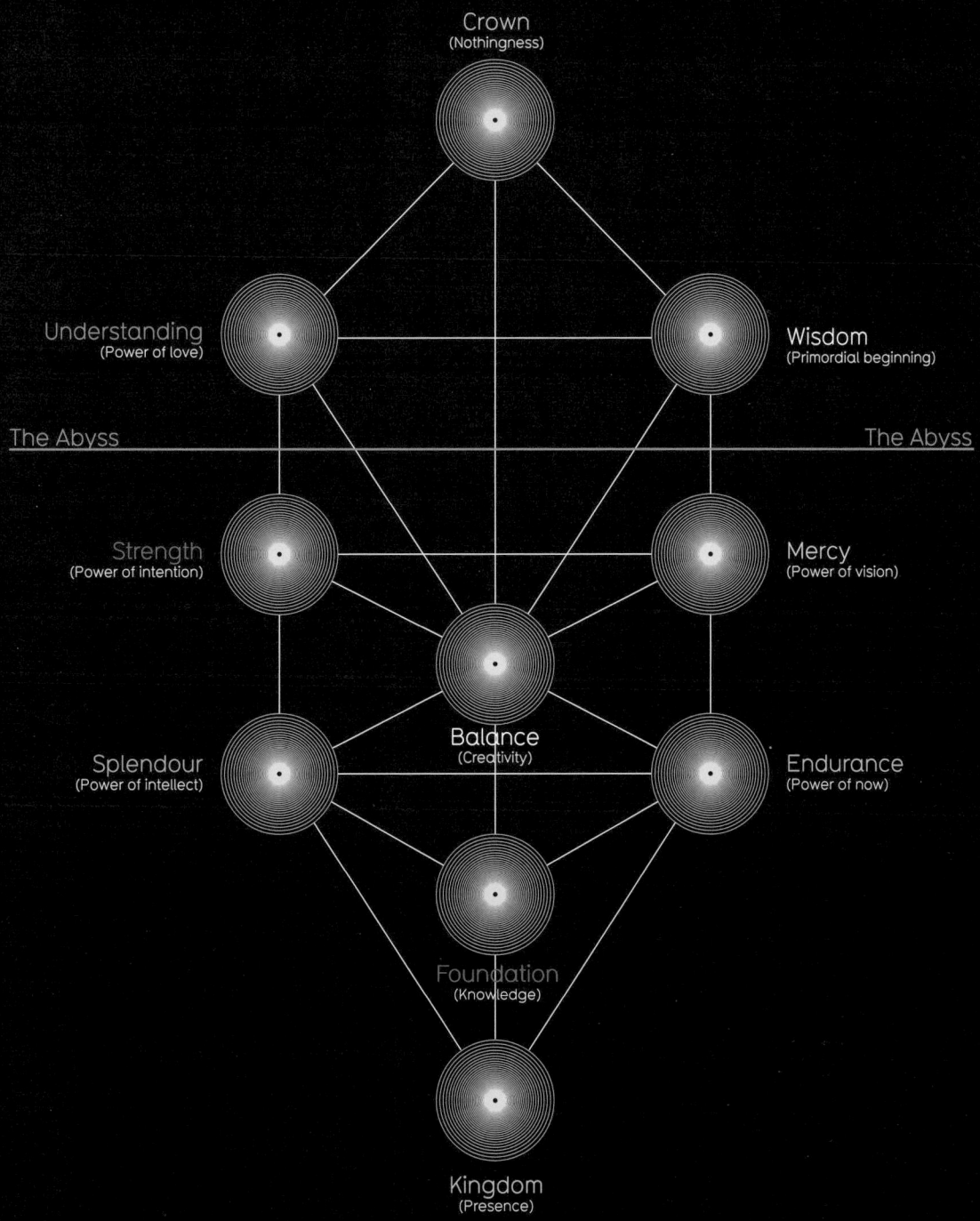

The Tree of Life

In the Jewish Kabbalah, these are the ten stages through which the universe was created. They're also the ten qualities of God. As an adult grows, they ascend the tree and acquire these qualities for themselves.

CRITICS SAY: "Where's the evidence?"

Sufism

In the mystical form of Islam, the soul or self (nafs) has seven degrees of development, each with increasing purity.

world <

The Pure Self

Self is entirely transcended. No ego or separate self left. Only the Divine exists. Any sense of individuality or separateness is an illusion.

The Self Pleasing to God

Inner marriage of self and soul. All power to act comes from God. You can do nothing by yourself. You no longer fear anything nor ask for anything. Genuine inner unity and wholeness.

The Pleased Self

You are content with your lot, and pleased with even the difficulties and trials of life, realizing that these difficulties come from God. Very different from the usual way of experiencing the world (i.e. focused on seeking pleasure and avoiding pain).

The Contented Self

The struggles of the earlier stages are basically over. The self is at peace. Old desires and attachments still exist but are no longer binding. Grateful, trusting, and adoring. One accepts difficulties in the same way one accepts benefits. The ego-self begins to let go, allowing the individual to come more closely in contact with the Divine.

The Inspired Self

Beginning to taste the joys of spiritual experience. Genuine pleasure from prayer, meditation and other spiritual activities, motivated by compassion, service and morals. Though not free from desires and selfishness, their power is significantly reduced. Emotional maturity is dawning.

The Regretful Self

Insight dawns. The negative effects of a habitually self-centred approach to the world become apparent. Wants and desires still dominate. But now you can see your faults. Regret and a desire for change grow. Attempts to follow higher impulses follow – not always successfully.

The Commanding Self

A false personality created by parents, school and culture. Selfish, controlling and lacking compassion. Must be recognized and bypassed (not destroyed) to grow.

> self

The Arc of Ascent

CRITICS SAY
"Says who?"

Source: Sufi (Laleh Bakhtair), Sufi.org, Wikipedia, Idries Sha

The Seven Chakras

In this Eastern system, you develop by mastering life-force energy expressed through certain energy centres or "chakras" (roughly centred on various glands and organs). Imbalances in these energy wheels create feelings of blockage and dissatisfaction.

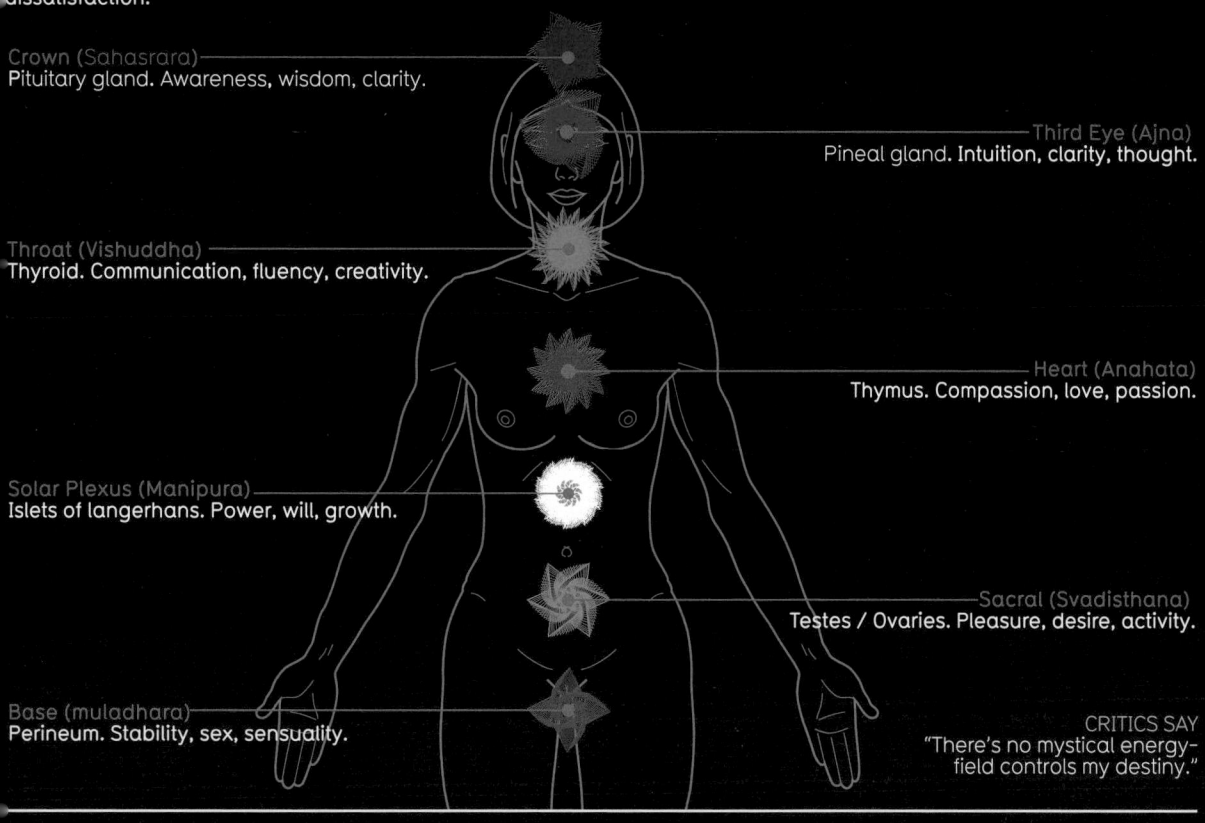

CRITICS SAY
"There's no mystical energy-field controls my destiny."

Maslow's "Hierarchy of Needs"

Psychologist Abraham Maslow believed that adult growth occurs in seven stages. But only after certain needs are fulfilled in your life.

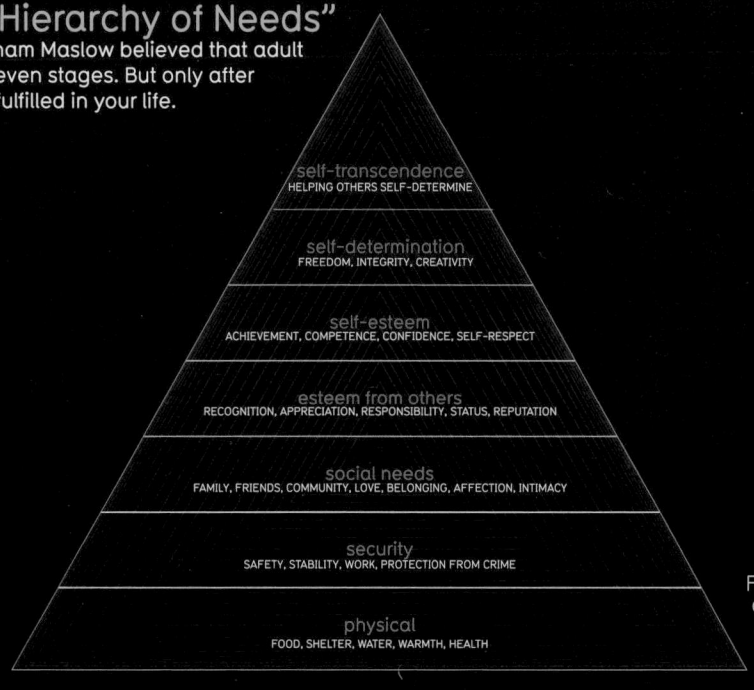

CRITICS SAY
"Little evidence. Fundamental human needs don't change over time and certainly can't be ranked in a hierarchy."

source: Wikipedia, Sufi.org, IdriesShah.com

Loevinger's Stages of Self-Development

Psychologist Jane Loevinger's system emphasizes the maturing of conscience. Social rules govern most people's personal decisions. But if differences appear between social rules and your behaviour, you must adapt to resolve the conflict, i.e. you have to grow.

	Opportunist	Diplomat	Expert
DEFINED BY	mistrust & manipulation	the group (tribe, family, nation)	knowledge
POSITIVES	energetic	dependable	ideas & solutions
SELF-DEFINITION	self-centred	self-in-group	self-autonomy
ACTION	whatever	obeying	doing
INTERESTS	domination, control	neatness, status, reputation	efficiency, improv perfection
THINKING	black & white	concrete	watertight
BEHAVIOUR	opportunistic	controlled	superior
WORLD VIEW	hostile, dangerous place	conformist, fundamentalist	rational, scientific
LOOKING FOR	rewards	acceptance	perfection
MORALITY	for self-interest only	given by the group	self-righteous
LANGUAGE HABITS	polarities: good/bad, fun/boring	superlatives, platitudes, clichés	"yes but..."
COMMON FLAWS	selfish	hostility to "outsiders"	selfish
FEAR OF	being overpowered	disapproval, rejection	loss of uniquenes
DEFENCES	blaming, distortion	suppression, projection, idealization	intellectualizing, h humour, blaming
SOCIALLY	two-faced, hostile	facilitator, socialite	seek to stand out crowd
RELATIONSHIPS	exploitative, volatile	useful for status	useful or not?
WHEN OPPOSED	tantrums, harsh retaliation	meekly accept	argumentative, b opinionated

Achiever	Individualist	Strategist	Alchemist
independence	unconventionality	strength & autonomy	complexity, authenticity
conviction, fairness, enthusiasm	inspiring & spontaneous	insightful, principled, balanced	charismatic, authentic leaders
self-in-society	self as individual	self-determination	transparent self
perfecting	being & feeling	integrating	playing, reinventing
ons, causes, goals, effectiveness	unique personal achievements	patterns, trends, processes, complexity	problems of language and meaning
rational, sceptical	holistic	visionary	intuitive
lenging, supportive	creative	highly collaborative, spontaneous	free
stmodern, scientific	paradoxical, no need to explain everything	multi-faceted, ambiguous	chaotic
root causes	uniqueness	authenticity	truths
self-chosen	non-judgemental, almost amoral	deeply principled, will sacrifice self for values	very high moral standards
ask lots of "why" questions	contrasting ideas, vivid language	complex, lyrical	fluid orators
exhaustion, over-nsion, self-criticism	can appear aloof & unapproachable	impatient with theirs & others' development	feeling better than others
lure, loss of control	self-deception	not fulfilling their potential	fearless
rationalization, self-criticism	sublimation, spiritualization	suppression, humour, altruism	sublimation, humour
genuinely friendly	fun!	great communicators	can talk to anyone
diverse, intense & meaningful	intense & mutually rewarding	vital for intimacy & growth	deeply empathic
"we agree to differ"	respectful, differences are celebrated	tolerant, insightful, responsive	empathetic

CRITICS SAY: The "self" is a complex of developing parts, not governed by a single factor.

source: Susanne Cook-Greuter, Ego Development: Nine Levels of Increasing Embrace, Wikipedia

Spiral Dynamics

Measures how people think. The intensity with which you embrace or reject each coloured value system reveals how high you are up the development spiral. Can also be applied to societies and cultures.

Developed by Professor Clare Graves, Dr Don Beck and Chris Cowan

Yellow Autonomous

Behaviour Ecological thinking. **Embraces** Change and chaos. Self-directed. **Attitude** See the big picture. Life is learning. **Decision-making** Highly principled. Knowledge based. **Admires** The competent. **Seeks** integrity. **Loves** Natural systems, knowledge, multiplicity. **Wants** Self-knowledge. **Hides** Attachment. **Good side:** Free. Wise. Aware. **Bad side:** Overly intellectual, excessively sceptical, angst ridden.

Orange Achiever

Behaviour Strategic. Scientific thinking. Competes for success. Driven. Competitive. **Attitude** Goal orientated. Play to win. Survival of the fittest. **Decisions** Bottom line. Test options for best results. Consult experts. **Admires** The successful. **Seeks** Affluence. Prosperity. Rational truth. **Loves** Success, status. **Wants** Self-expression. **Hides** Lies **Good side:** Great communication and creativity. Risk taking. Optimistic. **Bad side:** Workaholic. Babbling. Fearful.

Red Egocentric

Behaviour Self-centred. **Attitude** Do what you want, regardless. Live for the moment. The world is a jungle. Might makes right. **Decisions based on** what gets respect, what feels good now. **Admires** The powerful. **Seeks** Power, glory and revenge. **Loves** Glitz, conquest, action. **Wants** Self-definition. **Hides** Shame. **Good side**: Spontaneous, purposeful. **Under pressure**: Dominating, blaming, aggressive. **Bad side**: Passive, sluggish, fearful.

Beige Instinctive

Behaviour Instinctive. Materialistic. Greedy. Fearful. **Attitude** Do what you can to stay alive. **Seeks** Food, water, warmth, security.

Turquoise Whole View

Behaviour Holistic intuitive thinking. **Attitude** Global. Harmonious. An ecology of perspectives. **Decision-making** Flow. Blending. Looking up and downstream. Long range. **Admires** Life! **Seeks** Interconnectedness. Peace in an incomprehensible world. **Loves** Information. Belonging. Doing.

Green Communitarian

Behaviour Consensus-seeking. Harmony within the group. Accepting. Dialogue. **Attitude** Everybody is equal. **Decision-making** Consensus. Collaborative. Accept everyone's input. **Admires** The charismatic. **Seeks** Inner peace with caring community. **Loves** Affection, good relationships, beneficial resolution. **Wants** Self-reflection. **Hides** Doubts. **Good side:** Listens well. Receptive. Perceptive, imaginative. **Bad side:** "Politically correct", inauthentic.

Blue Absolutist

Behaviour Authoritarian. Cautious. Careful. Fit in. Discipline. Faith. **Attitude** Only one right way. **Decision-making** based on obeying rules, following orders, doing "right". **Admires** The righteous. **Seeks** Peace of mind. **Loves** Everything in its right place. **Wants** Self-acceptance. **Hides** Grief. **Good side:** Balanced, compassionate. **Bad side:** Needy, possessive, jealous, bitter, critical.

Purple Tribal

Behaviour Impulsive. Honour the "old ways". **Attitude** Self-gratifying. **Decision-making** Based on custom and tradition. **Seeks** Safety, security. **Admires** The clan. **Hides** Guilt. **Good side:** Fluid with a healthy sexuality. **Bad side:** Overly emotional, obsessive, frigid, impotent, numb.

CRITICS SAY: "Says who? Exact characteristics for advance stages are unclear and speculative."

source: spiraldynamics.net, wikipedia

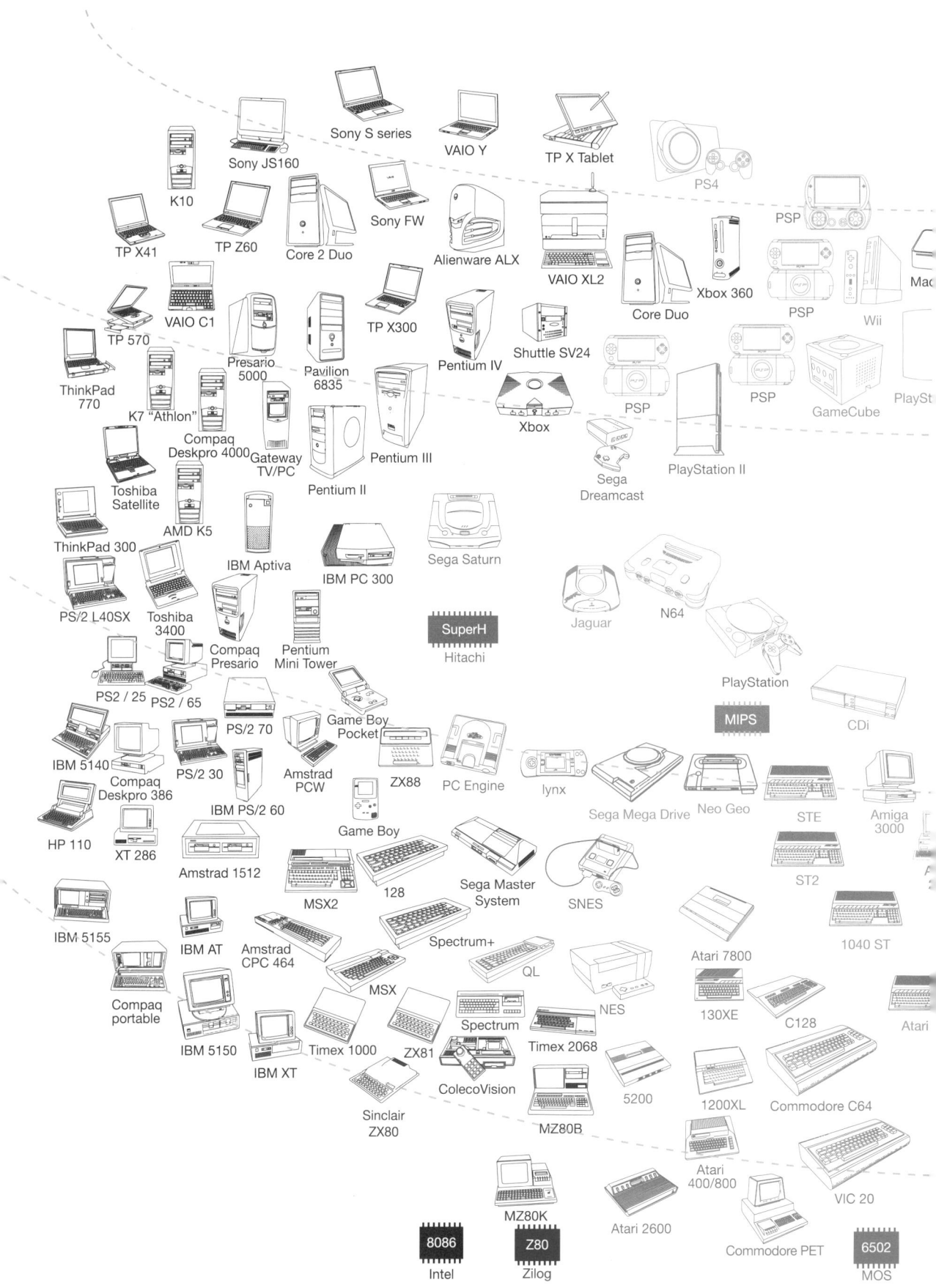
Sony S series
VAIO Y
TP X Tablet
PS4
Sony JS160
K10
TP X41
TP Z60
Core 2 Duo
Sony FW
Alienware ALX
VAIO XL2
Core Duo
Xbox 360
PSP
PSP
Wii
VAIO C1
TP 570
TP X300
Presario 5000
Pavilion 6835
Pentium IV
Shuttle SV24
ThinkPad 770
K7 "Athlon"
Compaq Deskpro 4000
Gateway TV/PC
Pentium III
Pentium II
Xbox
PSP
PSP
GameCube
Sega Dreamcast
PlayStation II
Toshiba Satellite
AMD K5
ThinkPad 300
IBM Aptiva
IBM PC 300
Sega Saturn
PS/2 L40SX
Toshiba 3400
Compaq Presario
Pentium Mini Tower
SuperH
Hitachi
Jaguar
N64
PlayStation
PS2 / 25
PS2 / 65
PS/2 70
Game Boy Pocket
MIPS
CDi
IBM 5140
Compaq Deskpro 386
PS/2 30
Amstrad PCW
ZX88
PC Engine
lynx
Sega Mega Drive
Neo Geo
STE
Amiga 3000
IBM PS/2 60
Game Boy
HP 110
XT 286
Amstrad 1512
MSX2
128
Sega Master System
SNES
ST2
IBM 5155
IBM AT
Amstrad CPC 464
Spectrum+
Atari 7800
1040 ST
Compaq portable
MSX
QL
NES
130XE
C128
Atari
IBM 5150
IBM XT
Timex 1000
ZX81
Spectrum
Timex 2068
ColecoVision
5200
1200XL
Commodore C64
Sinclair ZX80
MZ80B
Atari 400/800
VIC 20
MZ80K
Atari 2600
Commodore PET
8086
Intel
Z80
Zilog
6502
MOS

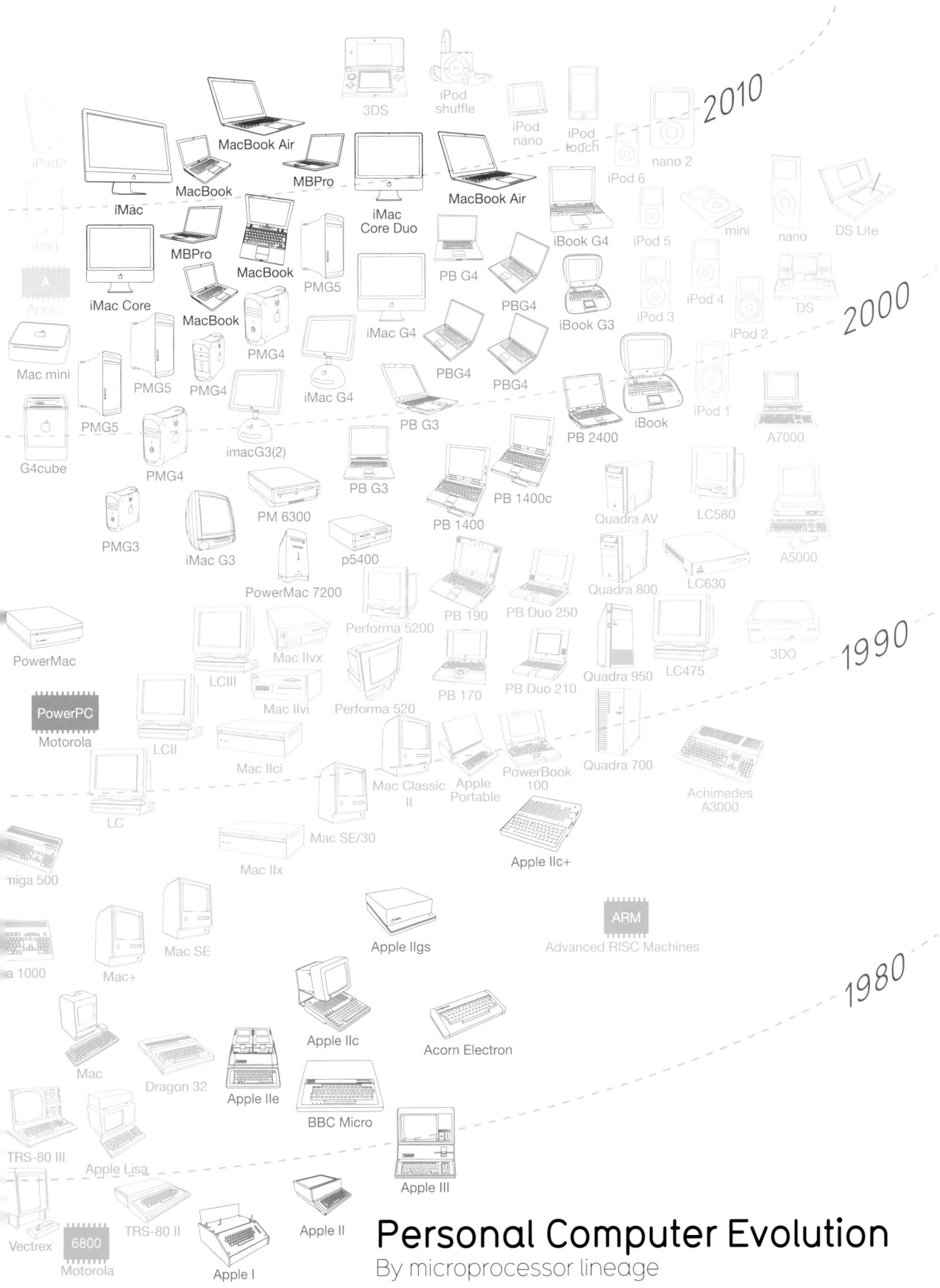

Personal Computer Evolution

By microprocessor lineage

source: Wikipedia

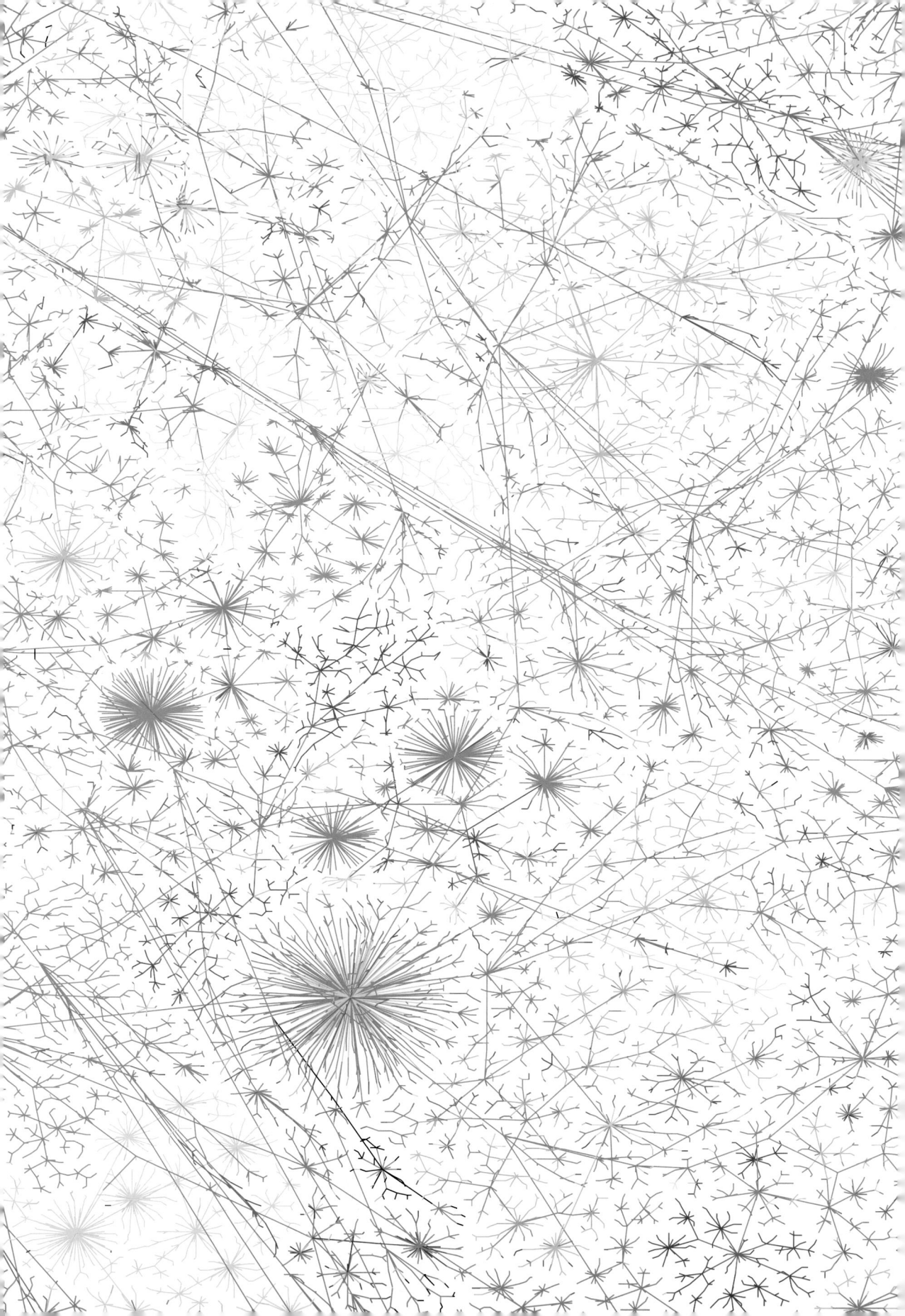

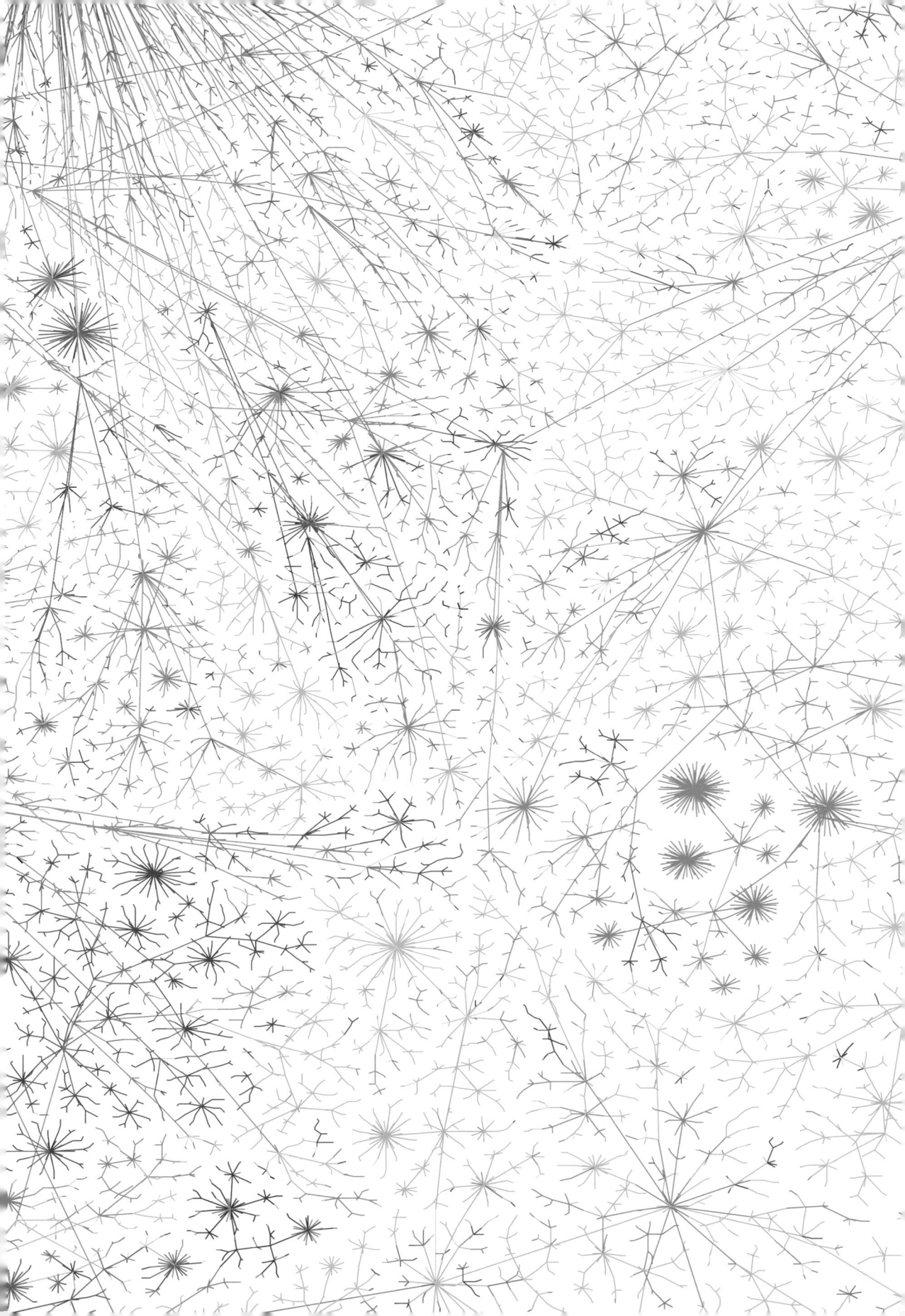

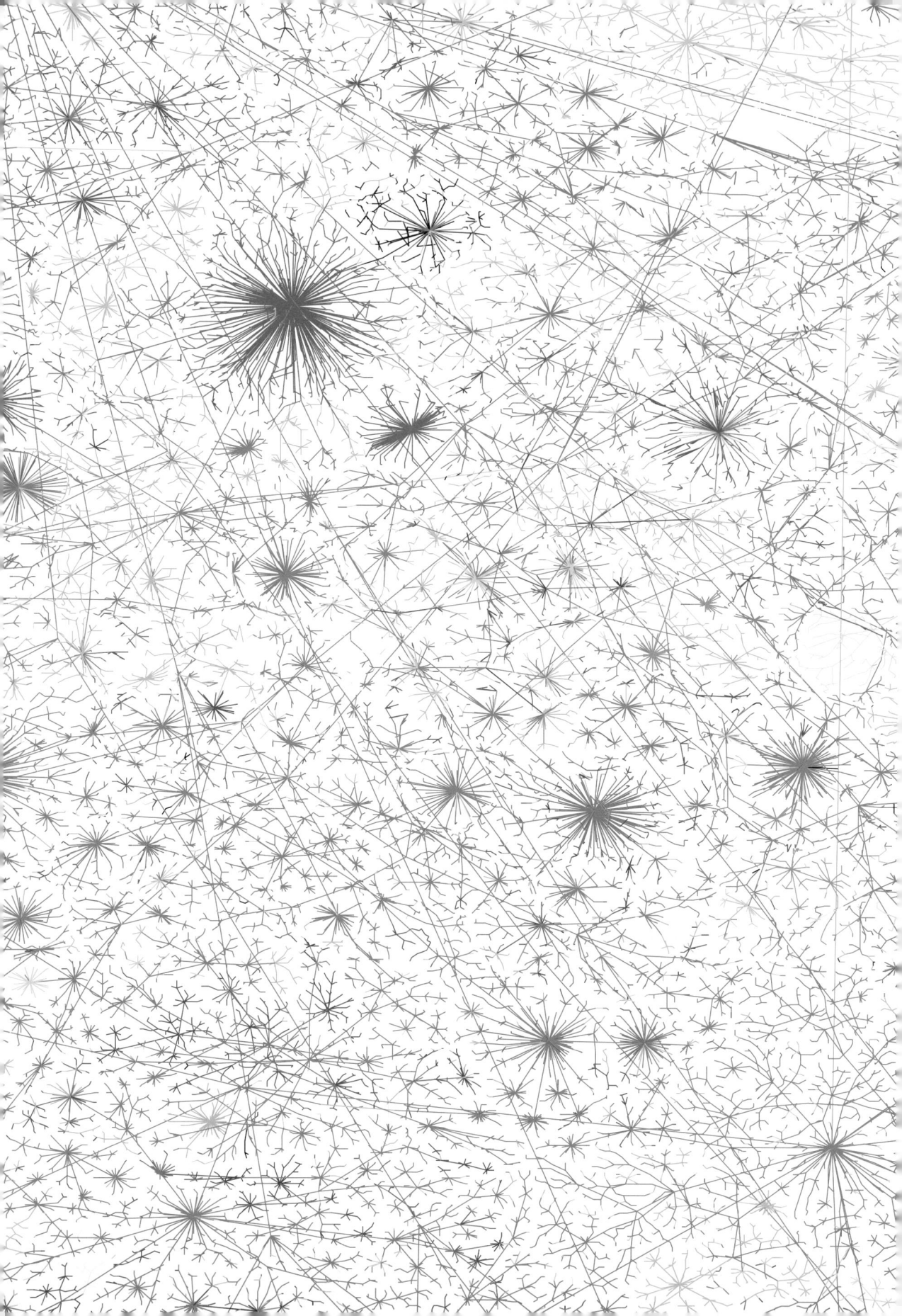

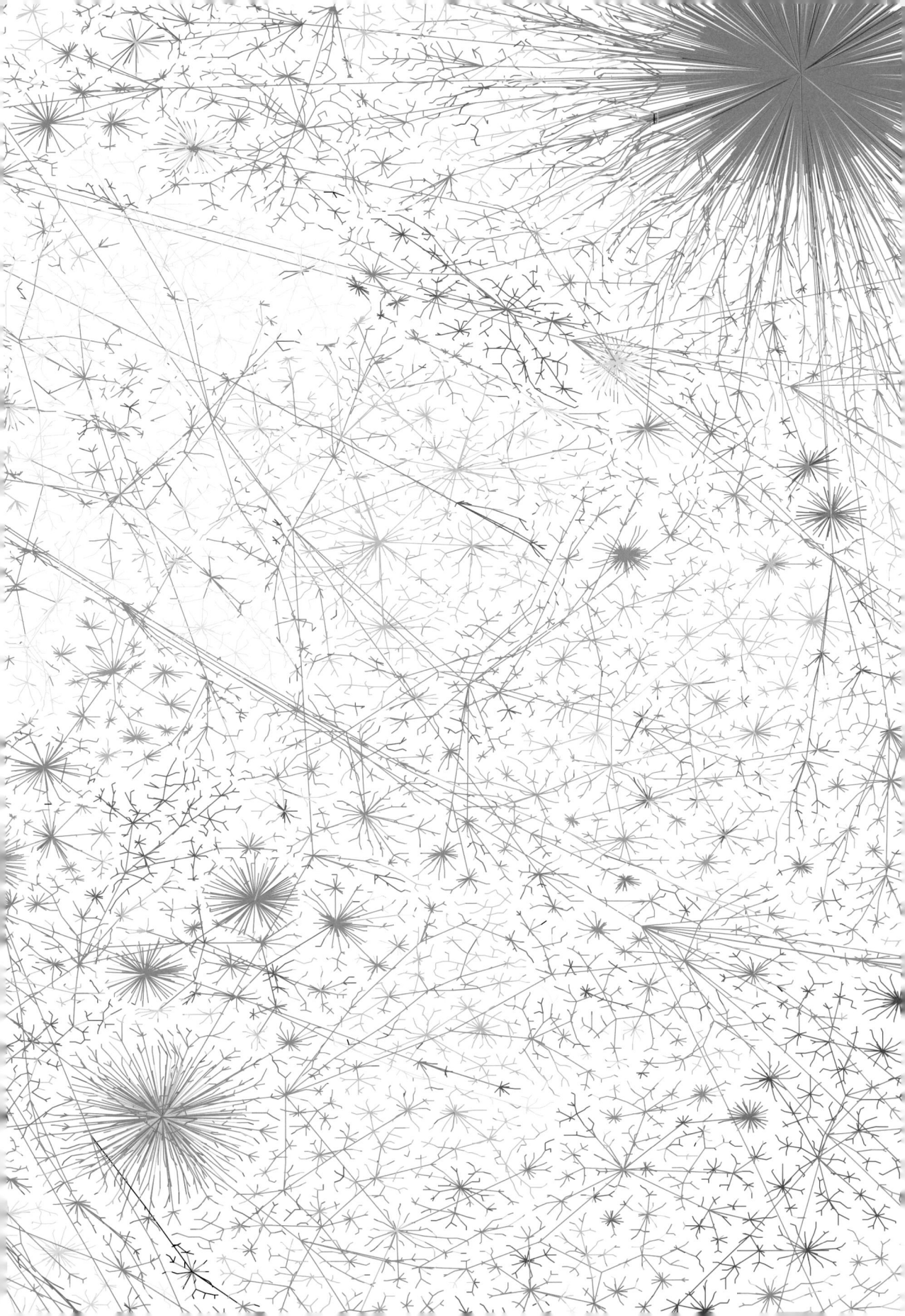

The One Machine

Map of the internet

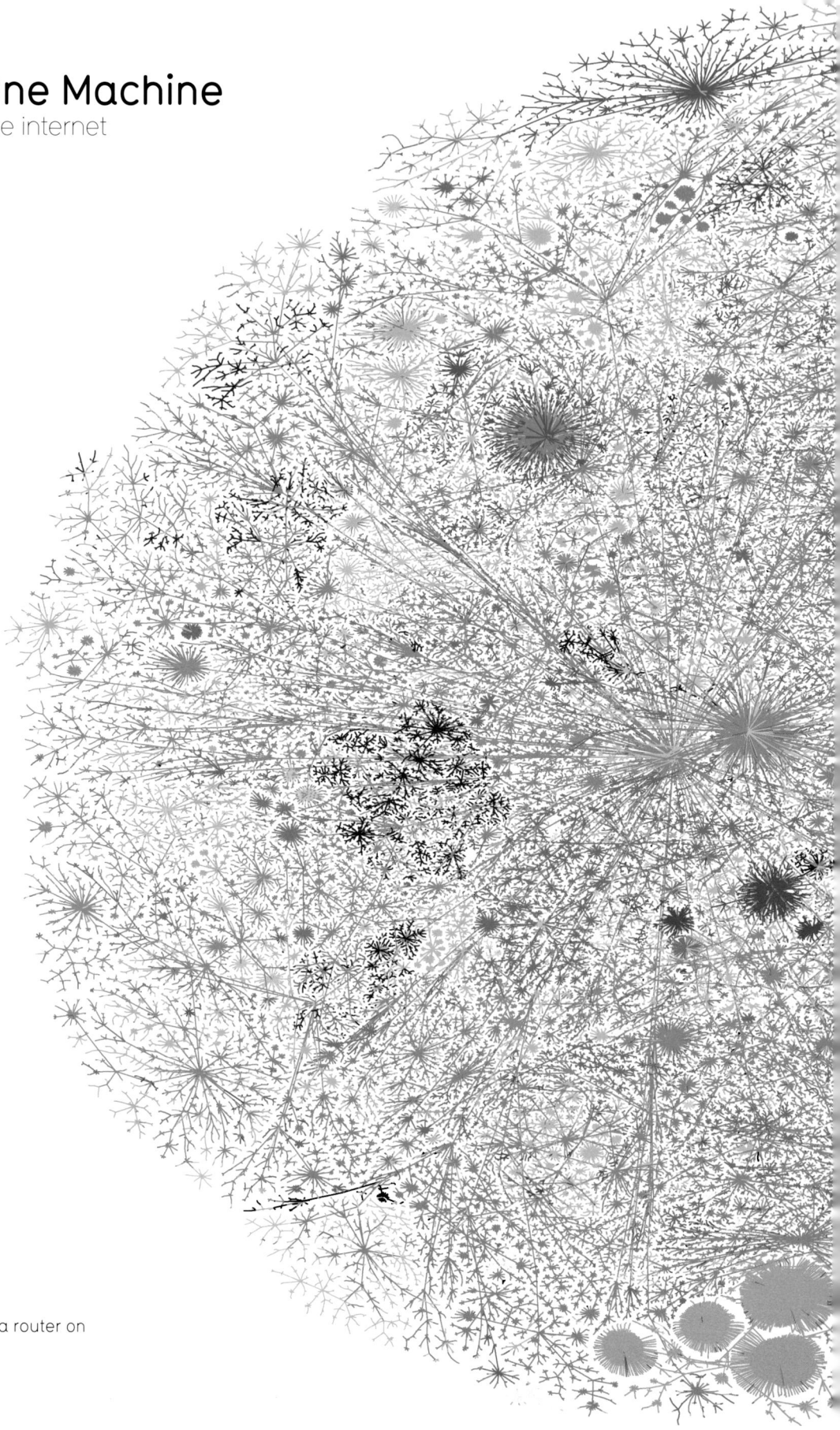

Each node is a router on the internet.

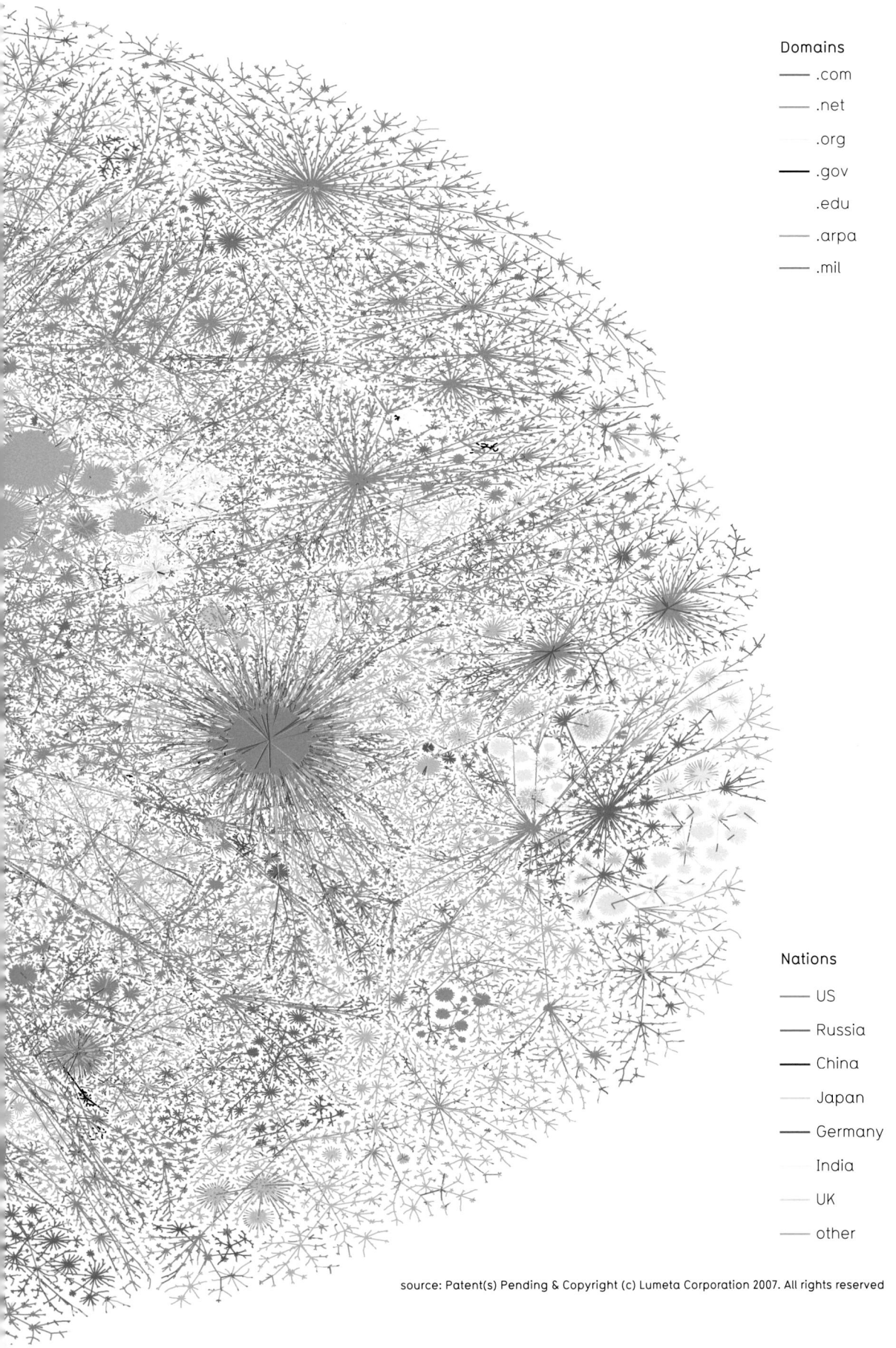

source: Patent(s) Pending & Copyright (c) Lumeta Corporation 2007. All rights reserved

What Does China Censor Online?

Blocked keywords and websites

01net.com 2ch.net 4chan.org 6park.com ad
amnestyinternational.org antro.cl aol.com
bbc.com bbspot.com bebo.com bild.de blo
bundestag.de cbc.ca china.ch china.cn china
cnn.com collegehumor.com crailtap.com cy
de.wikipedia.org delfi.lt democracy.co
drudgereport.com e-gold.com ebaumsv
ehrenselmundo.es el "brain wash"elpais.cc
facebook.com fark"censorship jail"flickr.com
friendster.com ga movement" gamefaqs.c
globo.com goo "dalai" "democracy" ogle.c
googl "democratic progressive party" "despc
great "dissident" "eighty-nine" "buddha stre
home Times" "eroticism" "evil" "exile" "falu
indym Nyima" "genocide" "gerontocracy" "
level.ro liberta"lun gong" "Ma Sanjia" "Mein
marca.es mc browser" "oppression" "perse
msn.com m Department" "political dissident"
nhl.com through labor" "Shanghai clique"
arcade.com "student federation" "student m
purepwnage.co Chinese Students and Schol
sapo.pt seznam.cz Mothers" "Tiananmen Sc
stern.de studivz.de suchar.ne tagesscha ir
tibet.com traffic4u.nl tw.yahoo.com tumblr.
usa.gov userfriendly.org vatican.va v
whatreallyhappened.com whitehouse.com w
wikipedia.org wordpress.com worldofwarc
xanga.com yahoo.cn yahoo.co.jp yahoo.co
yandex.ru yle.fi youtube.com ytmnd.com
6park.com addictinggames.com afton
amnestyinternational.org antro.cl aol.com

Falun Gong
A qigong-like spiritual practice violently supressed after followers protested against the government.

Gedhun Choekyi Nyima
2nd highest-ranking Tibetan spiritual leader after Dalai Lama. Arrested by the authorities in 1995. Not seen since.

Xinjiang
Northwest province, home to the Uyghur people and much ethnic tension.

June 4th
The usual name for the Tiananmen Square protests of 1989. (The word "Tiananmen" does not have the same association. It usually refers to the geographical place.)

com amazon.com amnesty.com amnesty.org
.com asahi.com barrapunto.com bbc.co.uk
ogspot) boingboing.net bundesregierung.de
china.org china "anti-communist" rin.com
dagbladet.no "Beijing Spring" motion.com
rt.com digg.com "anti-society" isney.com
bay.com ebay.de "blocking" com com
en.wikipedia.org "brutal torture" n espn.com
s.com free.fr "Chinese democracy tibet.org
t.com gay "communist bandits" geenstijl.nl
uk goog "democracy movement" google.de
ol "dictatorship" cn greatfirewallofchina.org
and hands" "Epoch rg heise.de hi5.com
g" "Gedhun Choekyi.com imdb.com index.hu
i people riot" "human rights" org lemonde.fr
vs blackout" "no-limit m mail.ru marca.com
ese Central Propaganda lip.com mitbbs.com
ed Terror" "reeducation com news.bbc.co.uk
y burial" "Sino-Russian border" no.be penny-
dependent Federation of prisonplanet.com
en incident" "Tiananmen a.it runescape.com
e" "Tibet Talk" "Tibetan sony.com spiegel.de
"Voice of the People" n.com thoonsen.com
und church" "Xinjiang g uol.com.br usa.com
ence" "yilishen" "yellow peril" wenxuecity.com
g "Freedom Forum of pedia.com wikipedia.de
iversity" "June 4th".pl wretch.cc wwe.com
m.cn yahoo.com.hk yahoo.com.tw yahoo.fr
org01net.com 163.com 2ch.net 4chan.org
mazon.com amnesty.com amnesty.org
.com asahi.com barrapunto.com bbc.co.uk

Beijing Spring
Brief period of political liberalization in 1977. The public were allowed to criticise the regime. Lasted a year.

Communist Bandits
Derogatory term for communists used by the Taiwan National Party.

buddha stretches a thousand hands
A Falun Gong pose.

Ma Sanjia
Forced labour camp where Falun Gong followers were detained.

Shanwei
Refers to Dongzhou, a village where a series of protests against government plans ended in a number of villagers being shot.

Yilishen
A company which scammed more than one million Chinese investors by promising ants could be bought, bred and sold back at a profit. Revealed as a Ponzi scheme in 2007.

Websites are either completely blocked or have offending pages removed.

source: ConceptDoppler.com, Wikipedia, GreatFirewallofChina.org (2008)

Water Towers

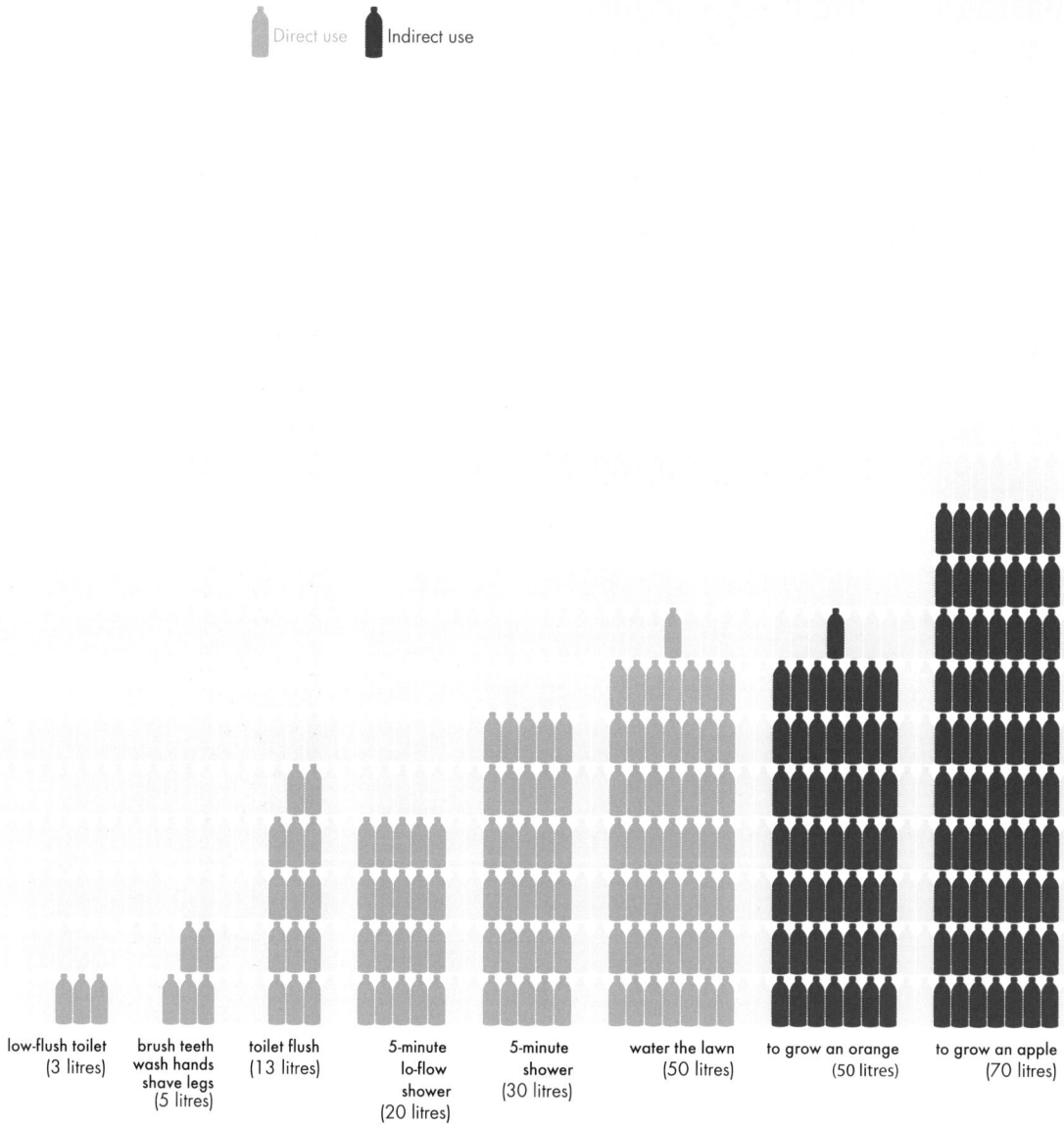

source: Wikipedia, Good Magazine

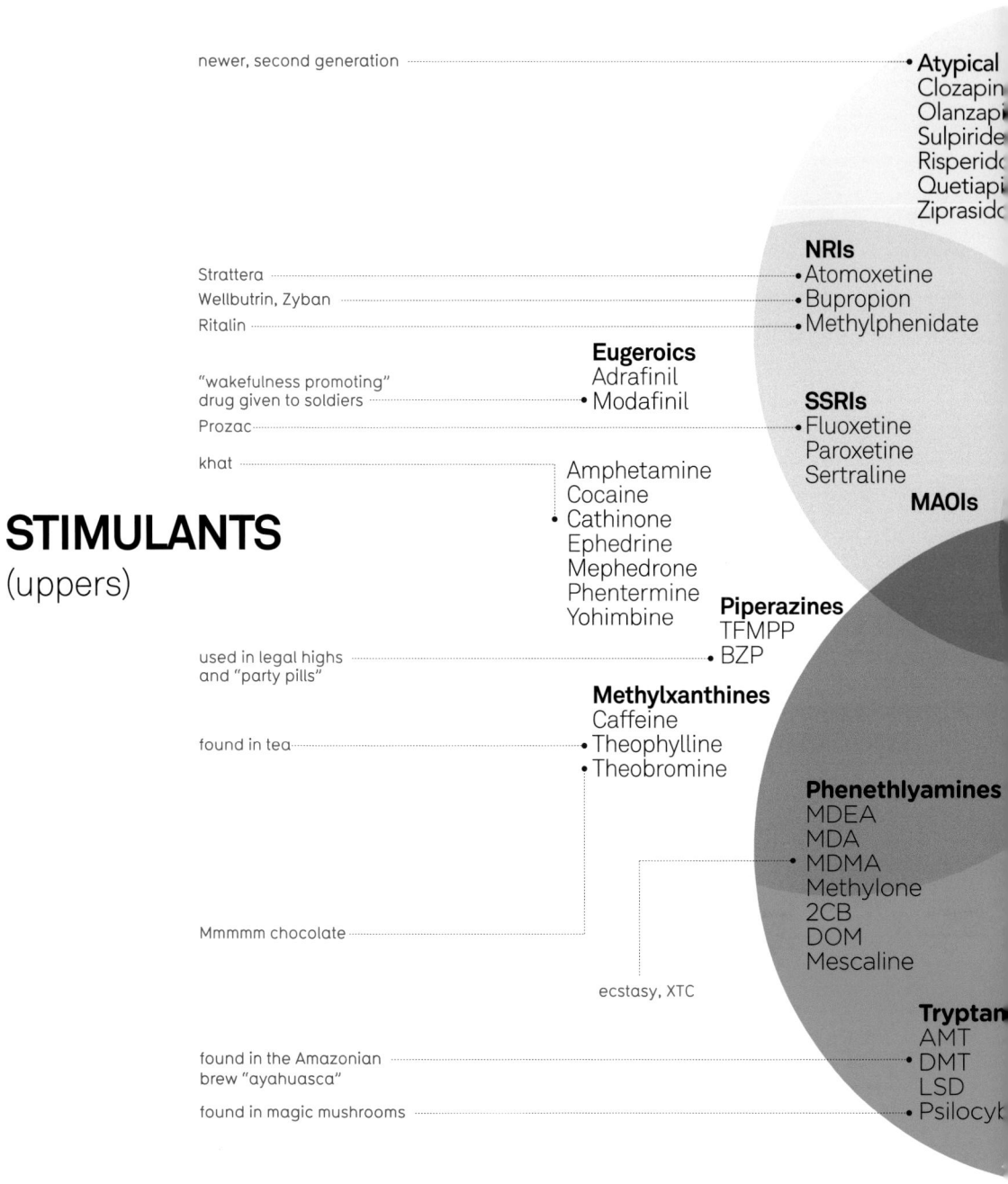
Anti
(tr
newer, second generation
Atypical
Clozapin
Olanzapi
Sulpiride
Risperido
Quetiapi
Ziprasido
NRIs
Strattera
Atomoxetine
Wellbutrin, Zyban
Bupropion
Ritalin
Methylphenidate
Eugeroics
Adrafinil
"wakefulness promoting" drug given to soldiers
Modafinil
SSRIs
Prozac
Fluoxetine
Paroxetine
Sertraline
khat
Amphetamine
Cocaine
Cathinone
Ephedrine
Mephedrone
Phentermine
Yohimbine
MAOIs
STIMULANTS
(uppers)
Piperazines
TFMPP
used in legal highs and "party pills"
BZP
Methylxanthines
Caffeine
found in tea
Theophylline
Theobromine
Phenethlyamines
MDEA
MDA
MDMA
Methylone
2CB
DOM
Mescaline
Mmmmm chocolate
ecstasy, XTC
Tryptam
AMT
found in the Amazonian brew "ayahuasca"
DMT
LSD
found in magic mushrooms
Psilocyb
Hall

tics
s)

al •
peridol
idazine
zide
henazine
rpromazine
hanazine

older, first generation

another active ingredient in cannabis

Benzodiazepines
Alprazolam
Diazepam •
Flunitrazepam
Temazepam
Lorazepam

Valium

acyclics
rotiline
odone

Sedative Hypnotics
Alcohol
Ether
Barbiturates
Chloroform
Methaqualone •

quaaludes

Depressants
(downers)

GHB
GBL

valactones •

Narcotic Analgesics

Codeine	Methadone
Fentanyl	Morphine
Heroin	Opium
Hydrocodone	Oxycodone

found in kava-kava

active ingredient in cannabis

found in the African ceremonial root Iboga

Dissociatives
A
DXM
Ketamine
PCP
Nitrous Oxide

enic Acid
cimol •

found in fly agaric mushrooms (the red and white ones)

iants •
olamine
pine
camine

found in Datura ("Jimson weed")

ns

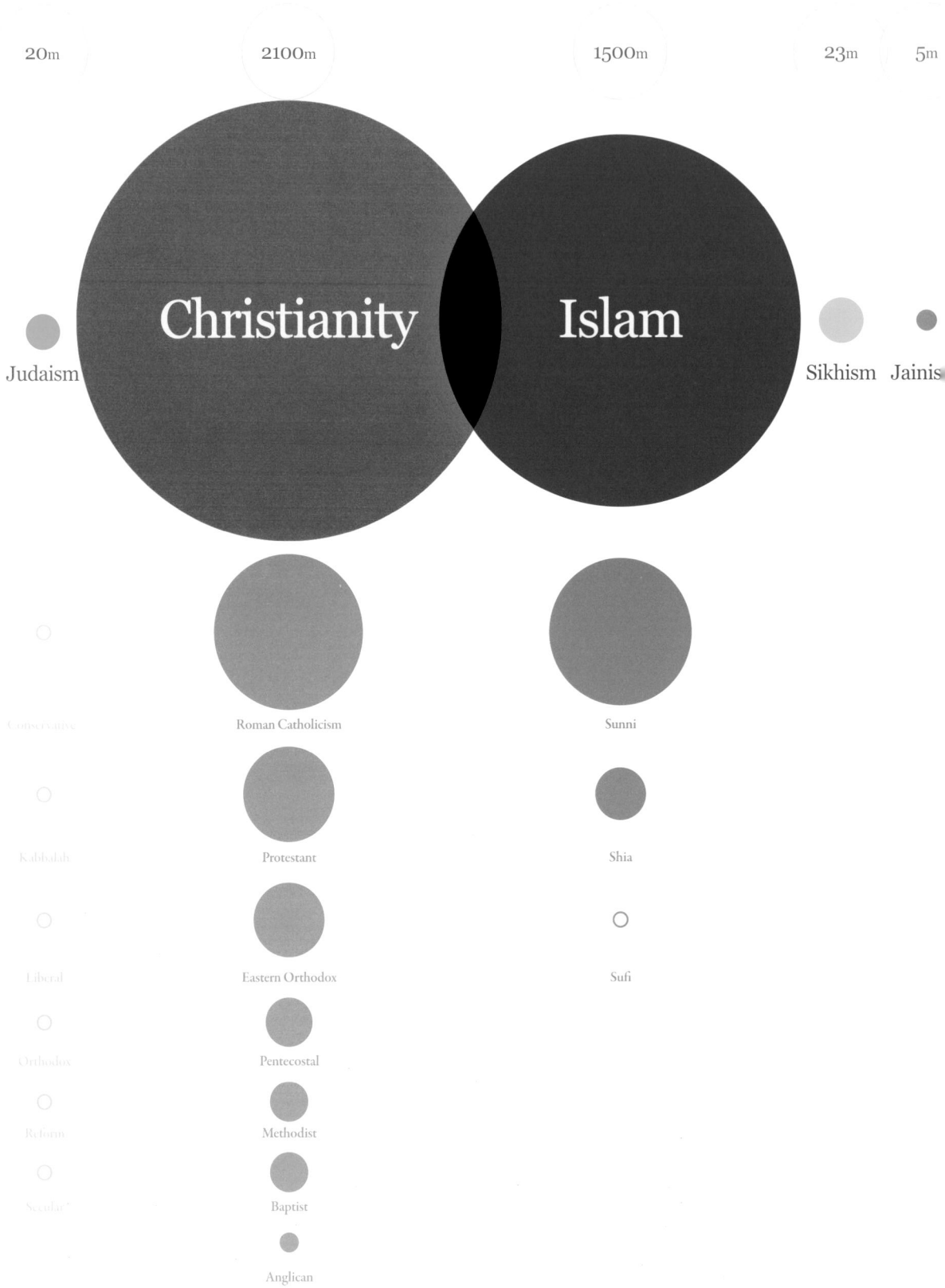
20m
2100m
1500m
23m
5m
Christianity
Islam
Judaism
Sikhism
Jainis
Roman Catholicism
Sunni
Protestant
Shia
Eastern Orthodox
Sufi
Pentecostal
Methodist
Baptist
Anglican

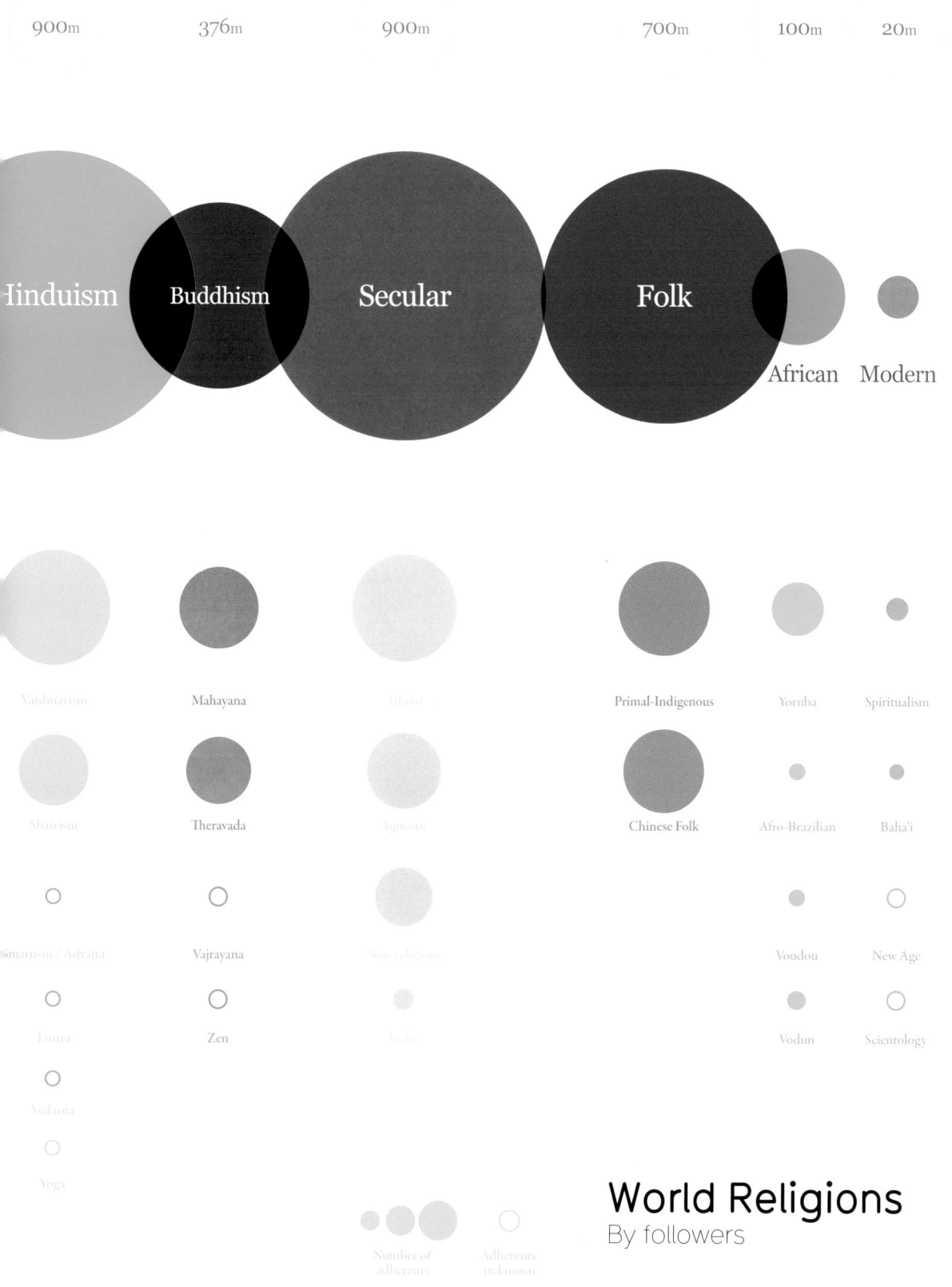

World Religions

By followers

source: Adherents.com

Moral Matrix

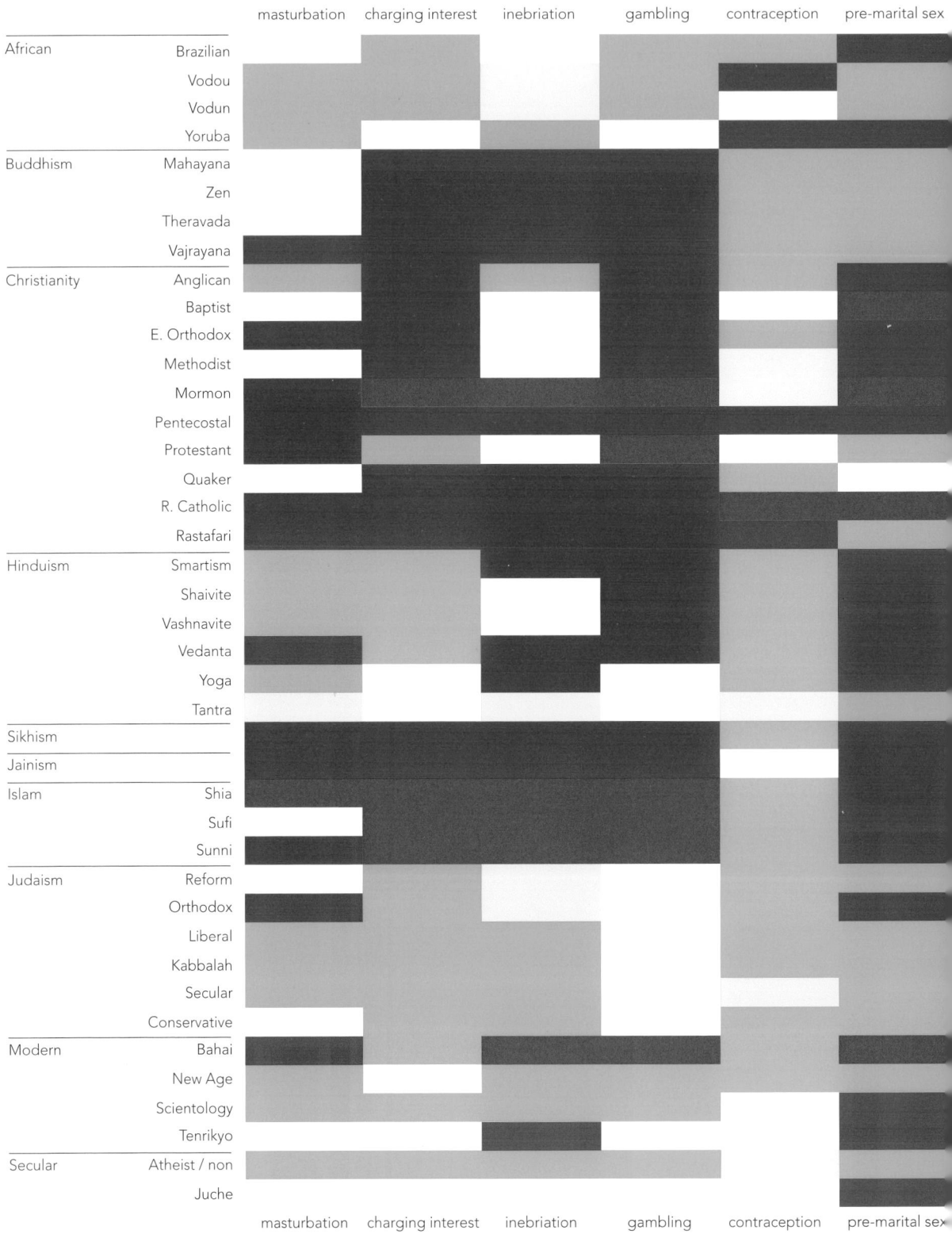

source: Wikipedia, Adherents.com

The Carbon Dioxide Cycle

Yearly man-made vs natural carbon emissions in gigatons (g)

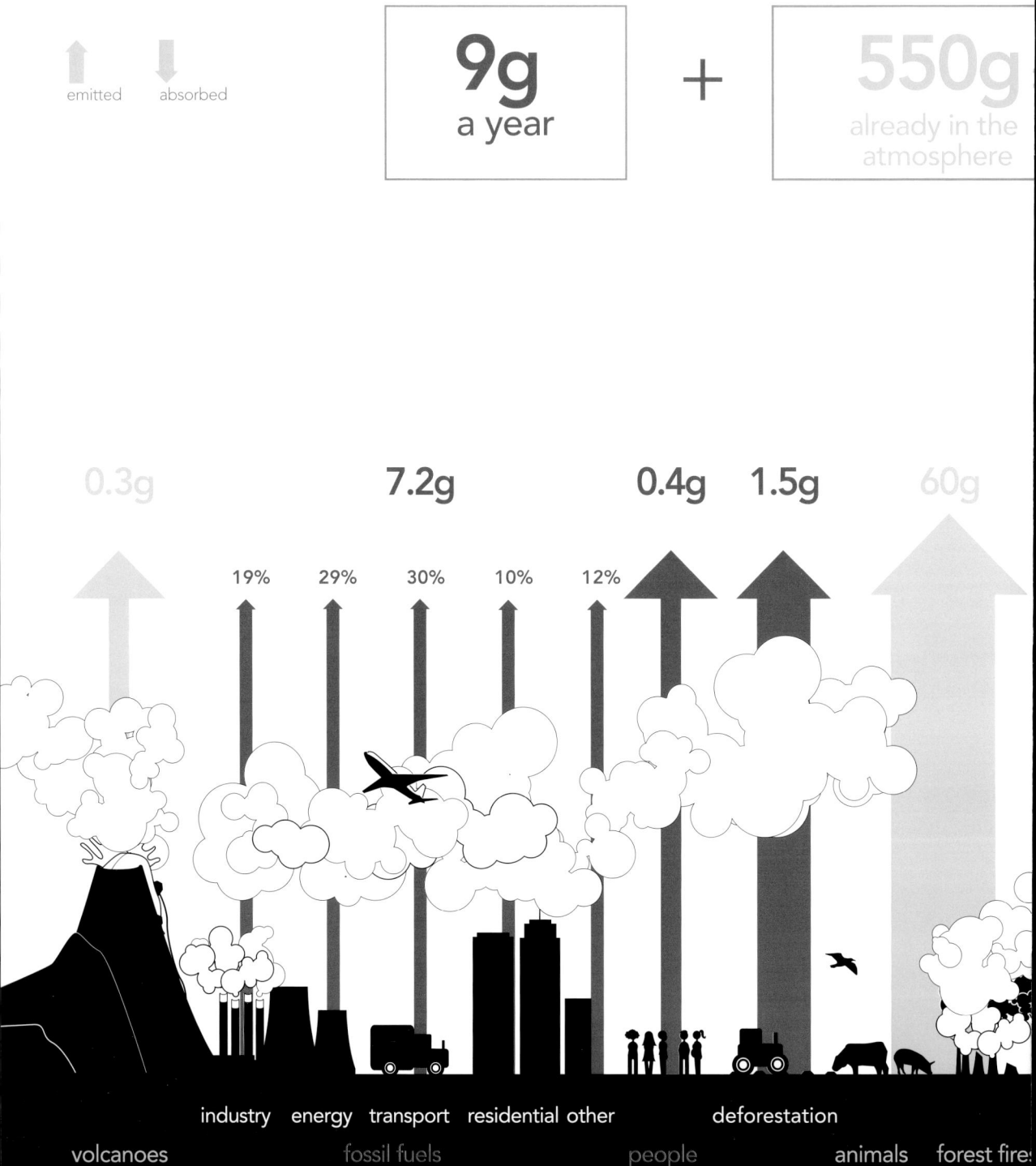

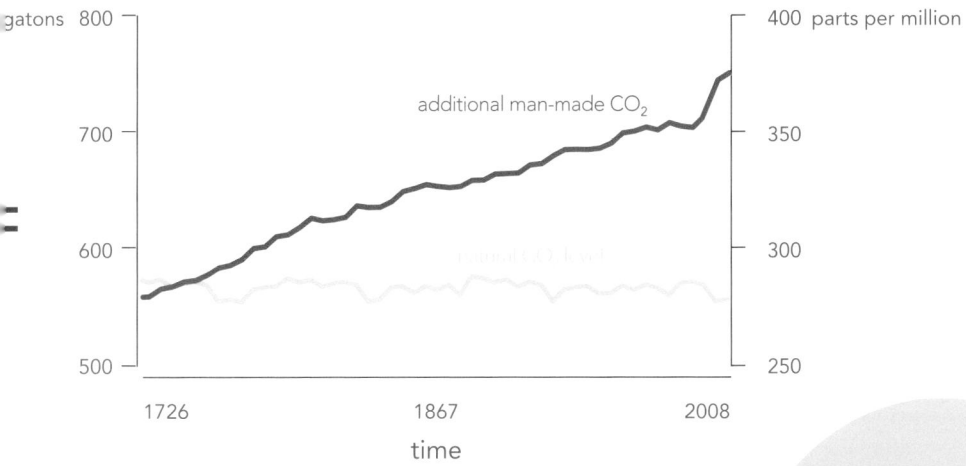

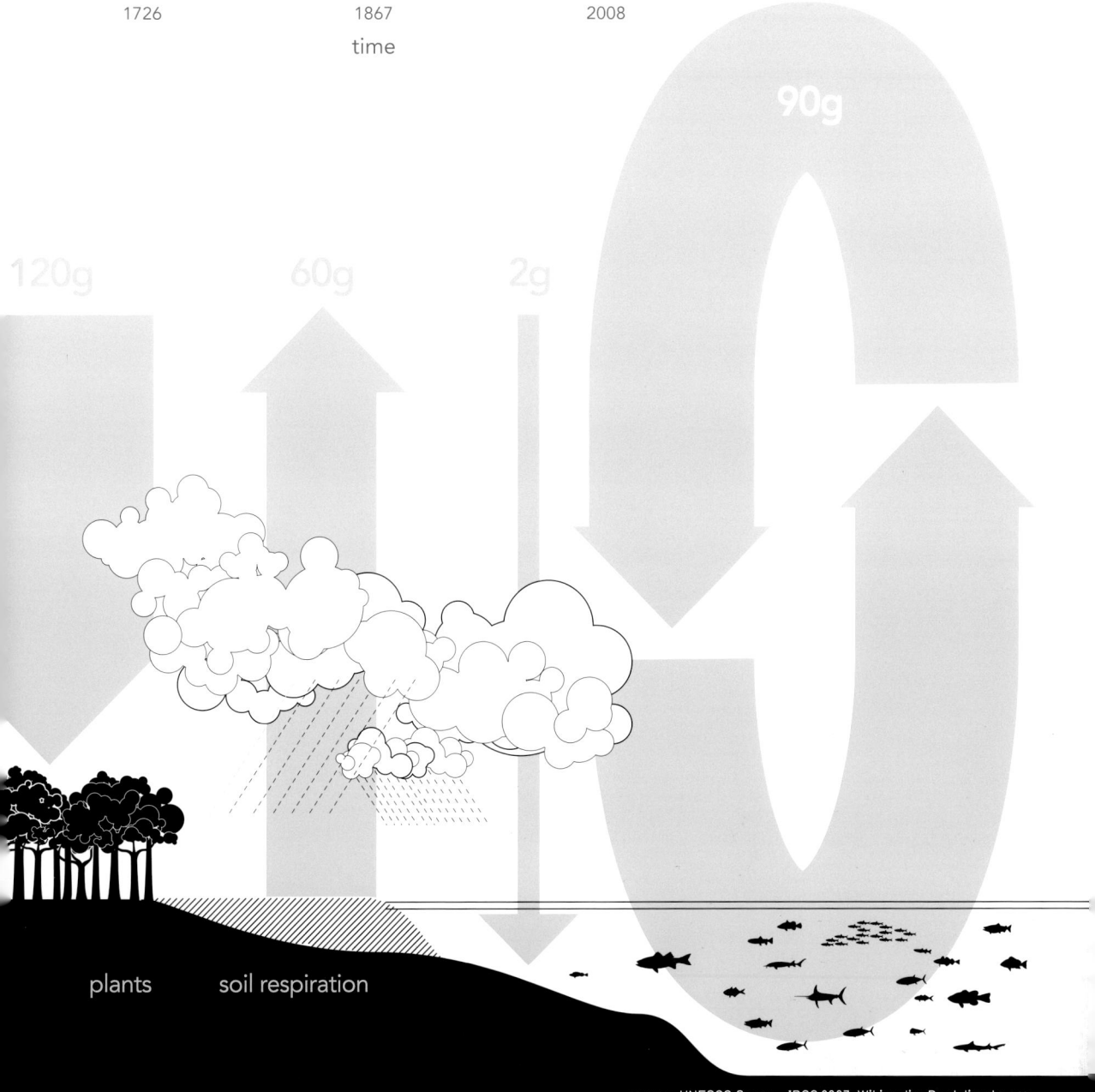

source: UNESCO Scope, IPCC 2007, Wikipedia, Realclimate.org

1250 MB/s

same bandwidth as a computer network

125 M

USB ke

Low Resolution

Amount of sensory information reaching the brain per second

Amount consciously perceived (0.045%)

source: Tor Nørretranders, The User Illusion: Cutting Consciousness Down to Size

Taste Buds

Complementary tastes

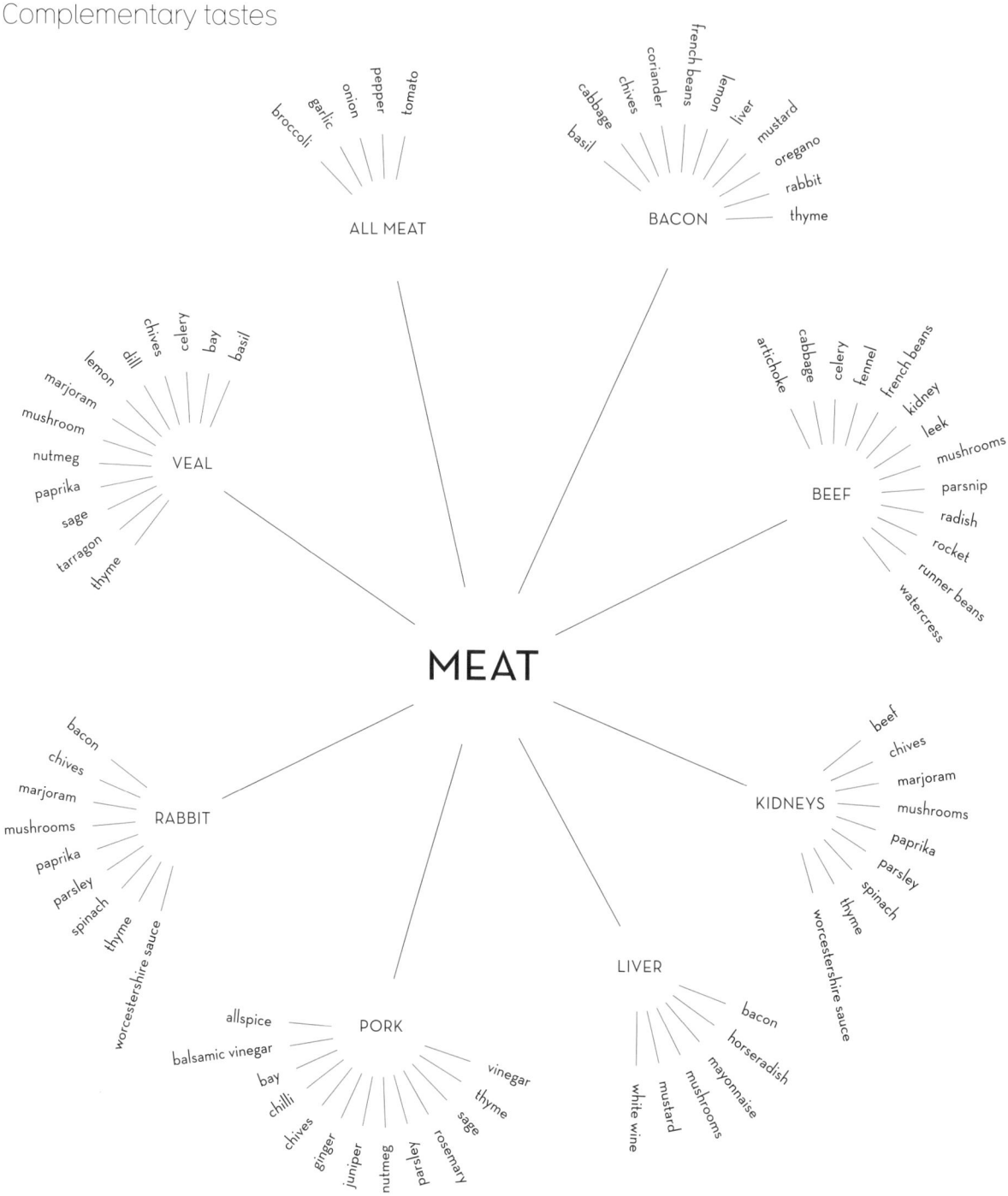

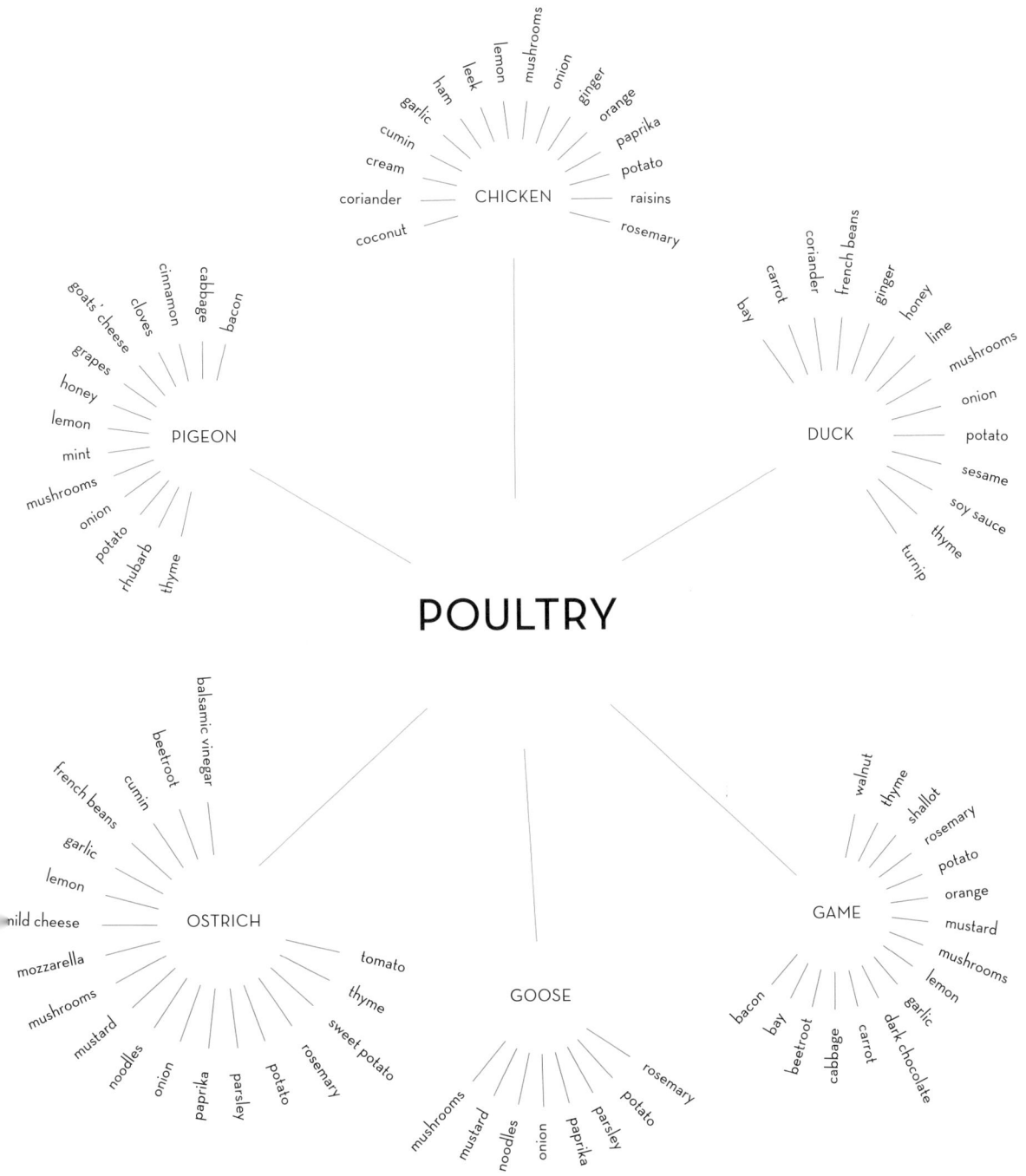
CHICKEN
coconut
coriander
cream
cumin
garlic
ham
leek
lemon
mushrooms
onion
ginger
orange
paprika
potato
raisins
rosemary
PIGEON
bacon
cabbage
cinnamon
cloves
goat's cheese
grapes
honey
lemon
mint
mushrooms
onion
potato
rhubarb
thyme
DUCK
bay
carrot
coriander
french beans
ginger
honey
lime
mushrooms
onion
potato
sesame
soy sauce
thyme
turnip
POULTRY
OSTRICH
balsamic vinegar
beetroot
cumin
french beans
garlic
lemon
nild cheese
mozzarella
mushrooms
mustard
noodles
onion
paprika
parsley
potato
rosemary
sweet potato
thyme
tomato
GOOSE
mushrooms
mustard
noodles
onion
paprika
parsley
potato
rosemary
GAME
walnut
thyme
shallot
rosemary
potato
orange
mustard
mushrooms
lemon
garlic
dark chocolate
carrot
cabbage
beetroot
bay
bacon

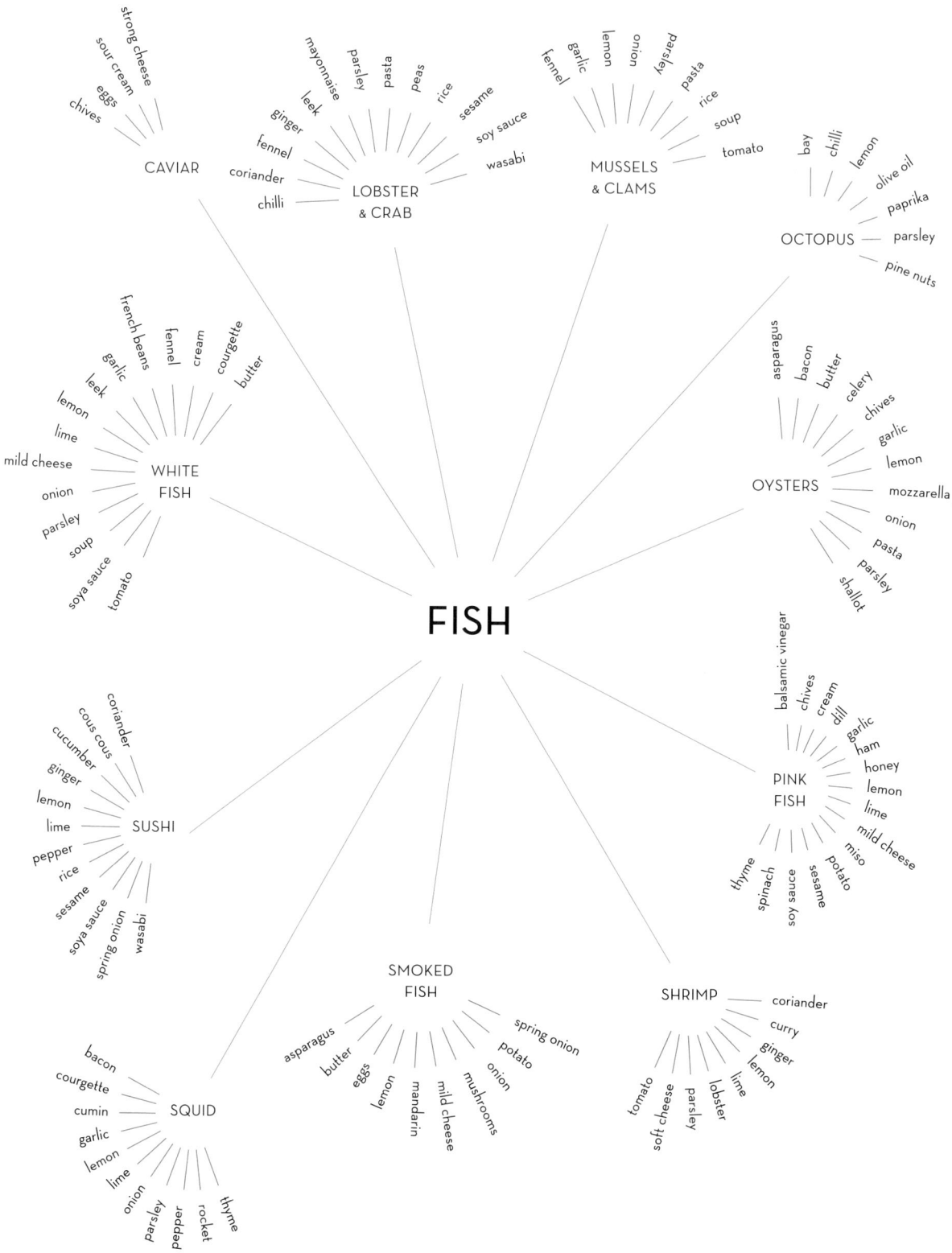
FISH
CAVIAR
strong cheese
sour cream
eggs
chives
LOBSTER & CRAB
mayonnaise
parsley
pasta
peas
rice
sesame
soy sauce
wasabi
leek
ginger
fennel
coriander
chilli
MUSSELS & CLAMS
fennel
garlic
lemon
onion
parsley
pasta
rice
soup
tomato
OCTOPUS
bay
chilli
lemon
olive oil
paprika
parsley
pine nuts
WHITE FISH
french beans
fennel
cream
courgette
butter
garlic
leek
lemon
lime
mild cheese
onion
parsley
soup
soya sauce
tomato
OYSTERS
asparagus
bacon
butter
celery
chives
garlic
lemon
mozzarella
onion
pasta
parsley
shallot
SUSHI
coriander
cous cous
cucumber
ginger
lemon
lime
pepper
rice
sesame
soya sauce
spring onion
wasabi
PINK FISH
balsamic vinegar
chives
cream
dill
garlic
ham
honey
lemon
lime
mild cheese
miso
potato
sesame
soy sauce
spinach
thyme
SMOKED FISH
asparagus
butter
eggs
lemon
mandarin
mild cheese
mushrooms
onion
potato
spring onion
SHRIMP
coriander
curry
ginger
lemon
lime
lobster
parsley
soft cheese
tomato
SQUID
bacon
courgette
cumin
garlic
lemon
lime
onion
parsley
pepper
rocket
thyme

GREENS & SALAD
ALFALFA
almond
avocado
bread
butter beans
cream cheese
mung beans
mushrooms
sesame
soya bean
soy sauce
vinegar
BEETROOT
asparagus
balsamic vinegar
beef
bread
dark chocolate
eggs
ham
honey
cream cheese
orange
pink fish
radish
strong cheese
thyme
BROCCOLI
basil
carrot
cashew nut
ham
mild cheese
olive oil
soy sauce
tomato
vinegar
BABY SPINACH
bacon
eggs
french beans
mild cheese
mushrooms
pasta (creamy)
smoked fish
strong cheese
tomato
vinegar
WATERCRESS
apple
avocado
balsamic vinegar
beef
bread
eggs
lemon
mild cheese
mint
miso
parsley
pink fish
rice
tofu
white fish
yoghurt
BRUSSELS SPROUTS
bacon
butter
chestnut
chicken
eggs
leek
mild cheese
mushrooms
onion
shallots
SPINACH
pasta (creamy)
pine nuts
pink fish
strong cheese
walnut
eggs
chickpeas
chicken
bacon
avocado
CABBAGE
bacon
balsamic vinegar
bay
butter
carrot
cloves
game
mushrooms
shallots
thyme
SEAWEED
bacon
blackberry
cucumber
ginger
lemon
miso
noodles
sesame
small fish
soy sauce
CRESS
chicken
eggs
mayonnaise
pink fish
potato
ROCKET
beef
beetroot
bread
garlic
ham
pepper
mild cheese
olive oil
onion
lemon
pink fish
pizza
rice
small fish
tomato
PEPPER
asparagus
balsamic vinegar
eggs
garlic
mild cheese
pine nuts
pineapple
potato
rocket
small fish
strong cheese
tomato
tortilla
LETTUCE
beef
beetroot
chicken
lemon
lime
mild cheese
olive oil
onion
orange
peas
rice

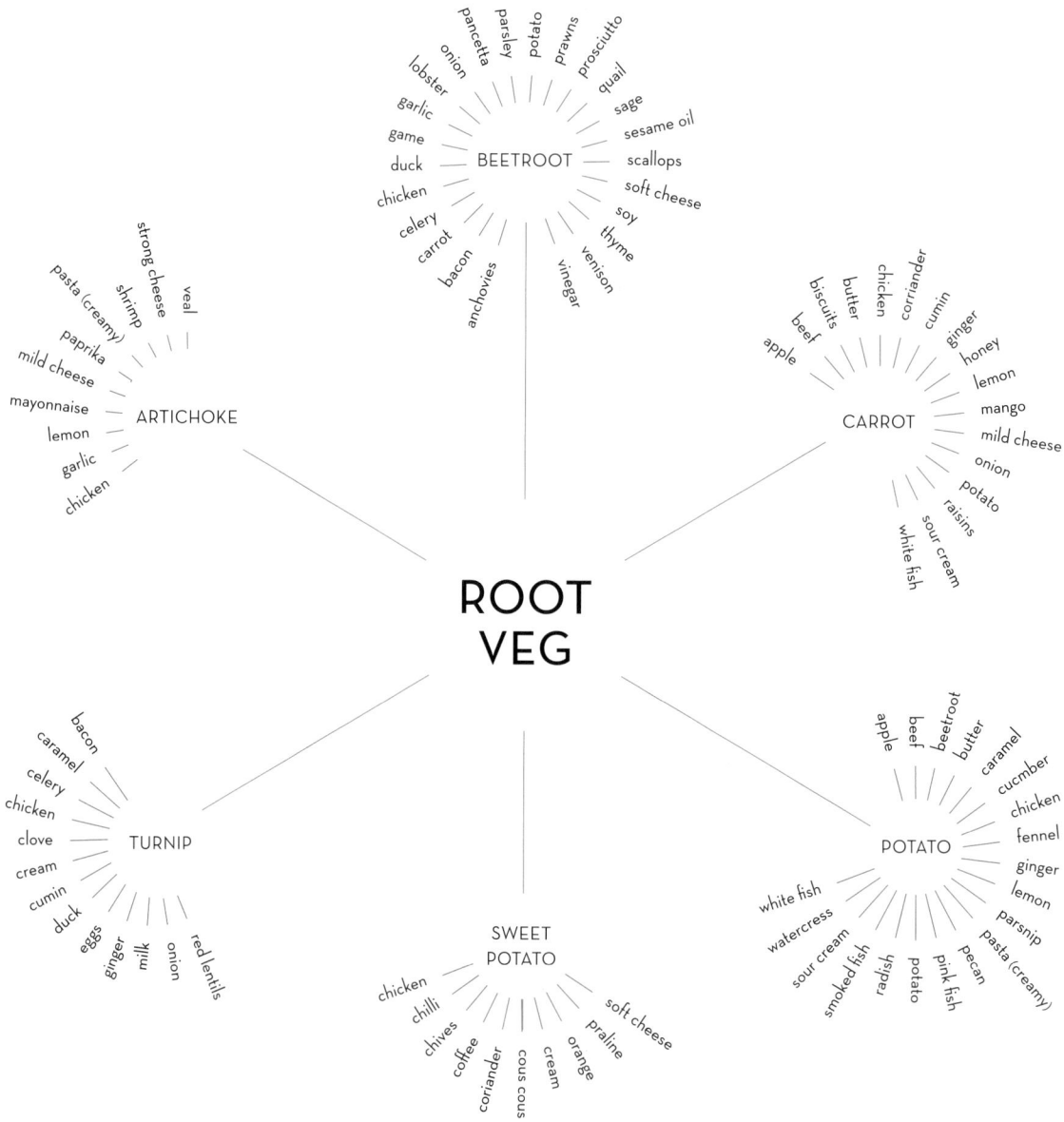
ROOT VEG
BEETROOT
pancetta
parsley
potato
prawns
prosciutto
quail
sage
sesame oil
scallops
soft cheese
soy
thyme
venison
vinegar
anchovies
bacon
carrot
celery
chicken
duck
game
garlic
lobster
onion
ARTICHOKE
strong cheese
veal
pasta (creamy)
shrimp
paprika
mild cheese
mayonnaise
lemon
garlic
chicken
CARROT
chicken
corriander
cumin
butter
biscuits
beef
apple
ginger
honey
lemon
mango
mild cheese
onion
potato
raisins
sour cream
white fish
TURNIP
bacon
caramel
celery
chicken
clove
cream
cumin
duck
eggs
ginger
milk
onion
red lentils
SWEET POTATO
chicken
chilli
chives
coffee
coriander
cous cous
cream
orange
praline
soft cheese
POTATO
apple
beef
beetroot
butter
caramel
cucmber
chicken
fennel
ginger
lemon
parsnip
pasta (creamy)
pecan
pink fish
potato
radish
smoked fish
sour cream
watercress
white fish

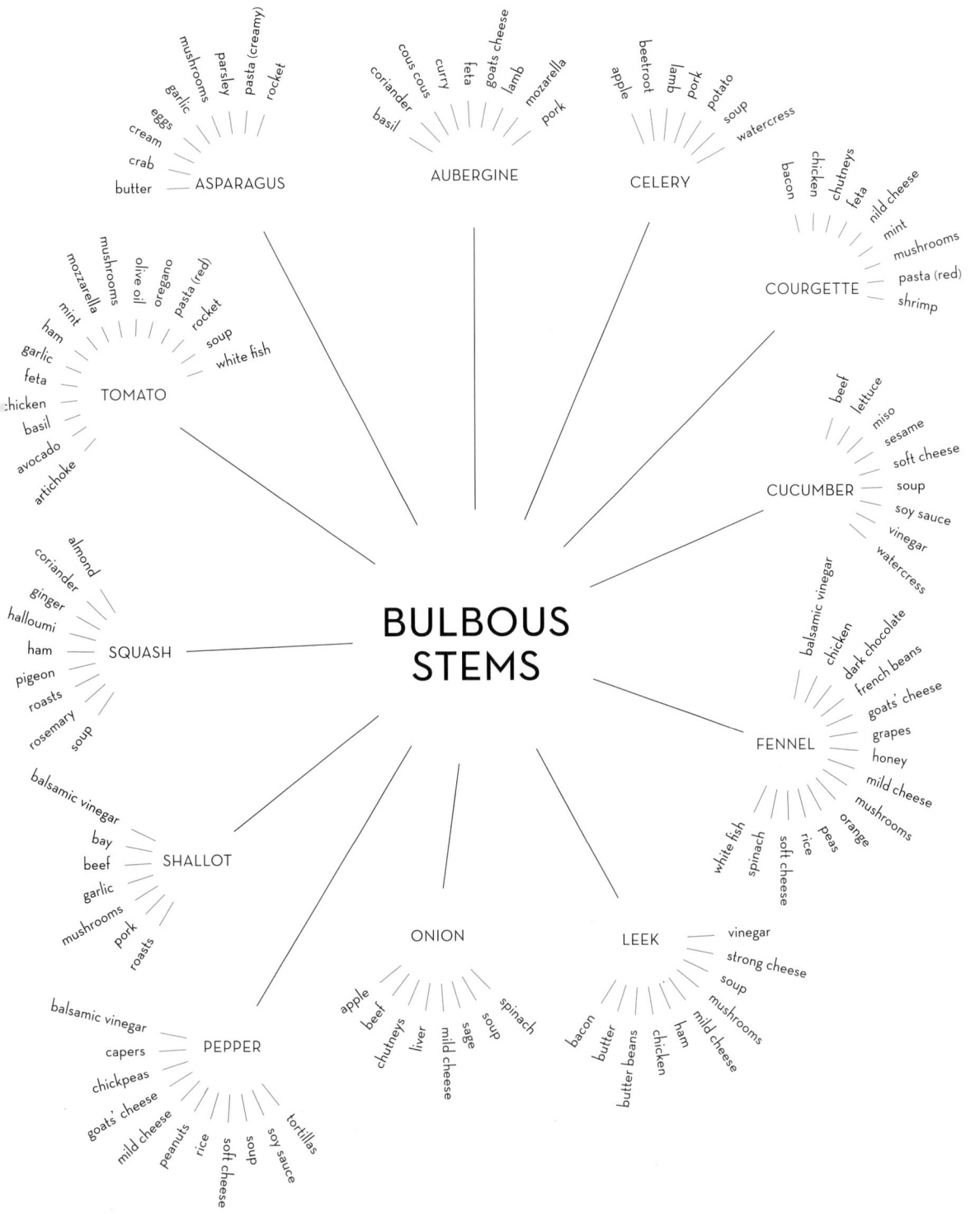

source: general internet and bbc.co.uk/food

Sunlight

TWO MAIN TYPES OF ULTRAVIOLET

UVA	UVB	UVC
Ages your skin	Burns your skin	UVC blocked by atmosphere

% REACHING GROUND

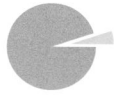

RELATED SKIN CANCER

Carcinoma (nasty)

Melanoma (deadly)

SUNSCREEN PROTECTION

STAR SYSTEM

SUN FACTOR (SPF)

How much sunscreen?

1 Divide your body into eleven zones

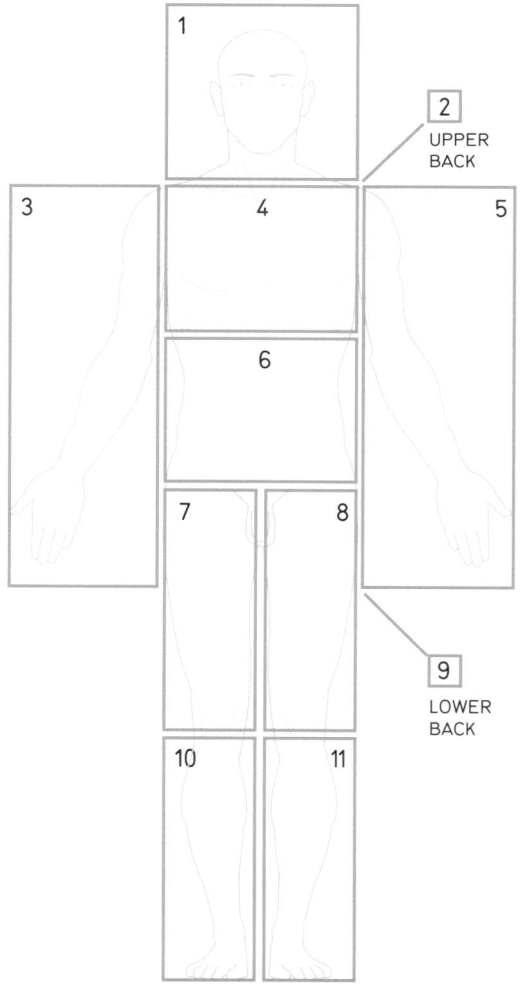

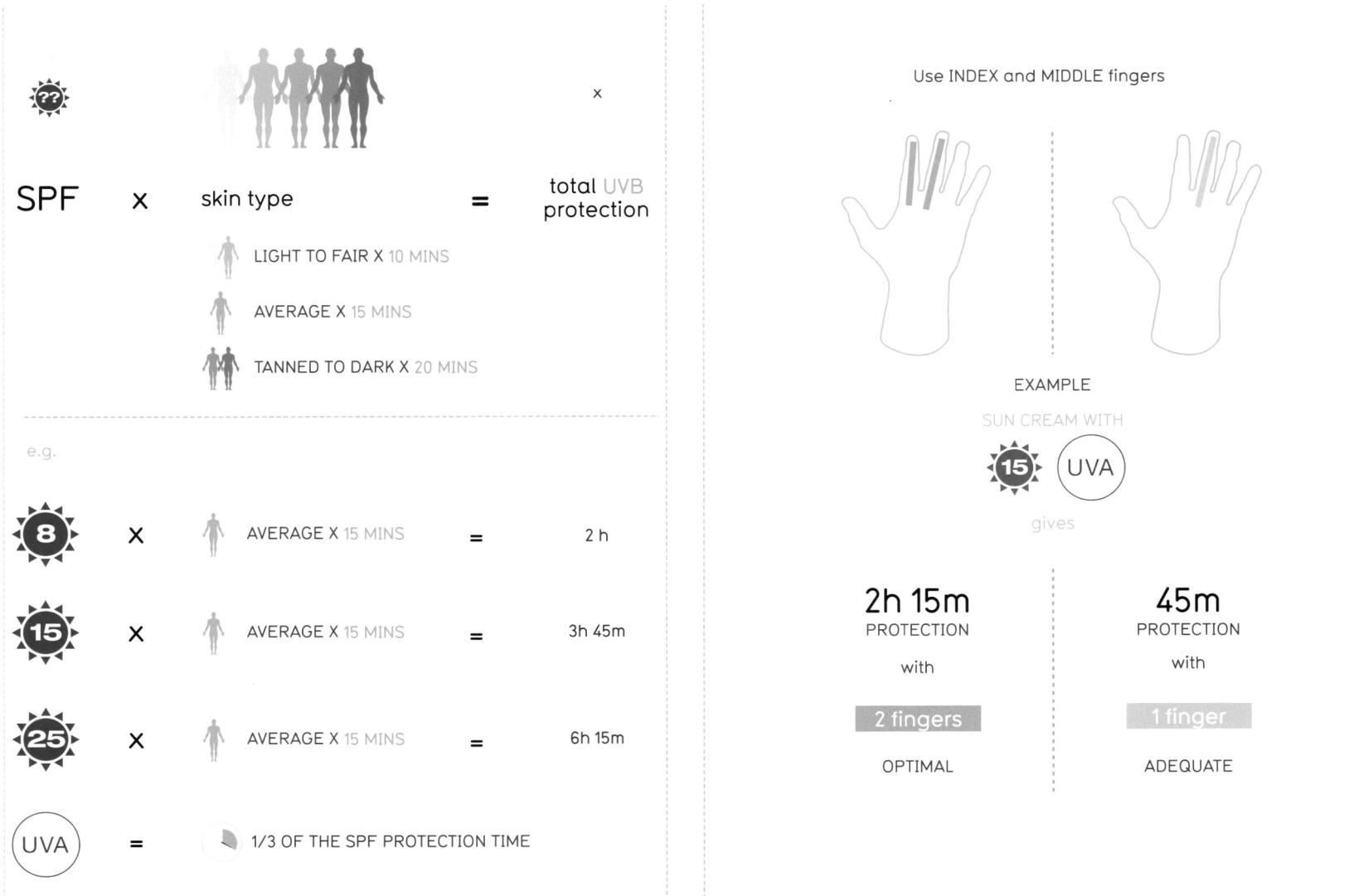

The Sunscreen Smokescreen

How often?

Previous wisdom

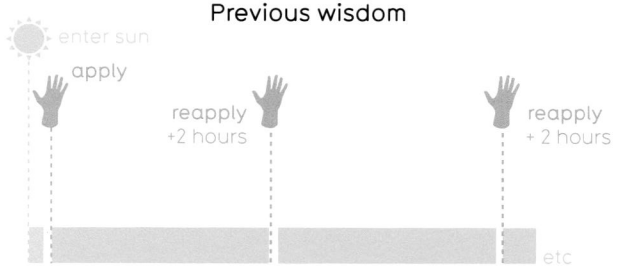

Current wisdom

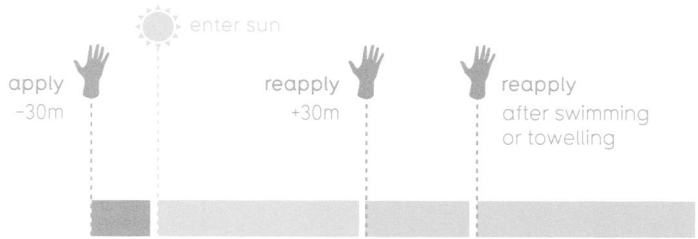

Intuitive wisdom

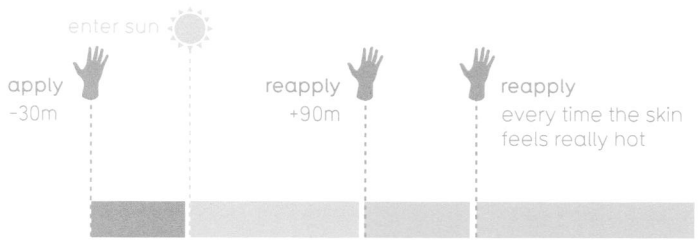

Sunlight & skin cancers

SKIN CANCER	Squamous Cell Carcinoma	Basal Cell Carcinoma	Melanoma
WHAT DOES IT AFFECT?	Lining of the skin (epithelium)	Deepest skin tissue layer (basal layer)	Cells that tan skin (melanocytes)
% OF SKIN CANCERS	20%	75%	5%
% OF CASES CAUSED BY SUNLIGHT	90% UVA	90% UVB	65% UVB
% OF SUFFERERS WHO DIE	0.4% (nasty)	0.07% (normally curable)	13% (deadly)

IN COMPARISON

brain 68%
breast 10%
colon 35%

CLOUD COVER

Thick clouds

reduce UV radiation by 80-99%

REFLECTIONS

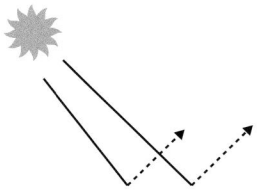

UV reflections

fresh snow	80%
dry sand	20
grass	10
water	10

ALTITUDE

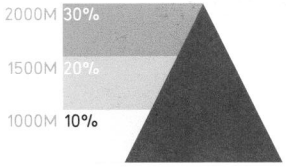

Snow burn

At 2,000 m above sea level UV radiation can be 30% more intense

Cases of the cancer per 100,000 people

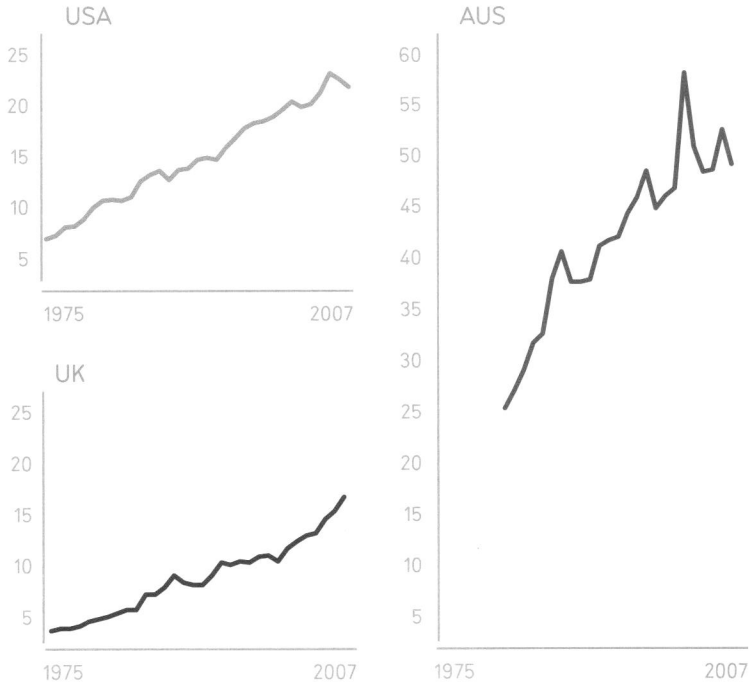

Don't forget - the sun is good!

20 mins of daily sunlight (without sunscreen) gives you a healthy dose of Vitamin D essential for health

Substantially more heart attack victims survive if struck during summer

Significantly more elderly people die in winter January, February and March

source: per capita data from Newscientist.com, Unstats.un.org, NationMaster.com

The Poison

Margarita

Martini

Manhattan

Mai Tai

Cosmopolitan

White Russian

Long Island Iced Tea

Mojito

Harvey Wallbanger

Whiskey Sour

Daiquiri

Bloody Mary

The Remedy

Hangover cures from around the world

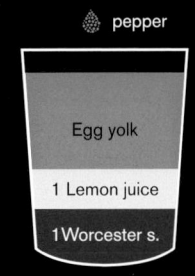

Traditional

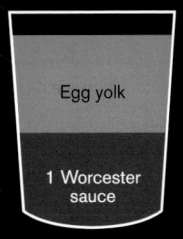

American

Dutch

Polish

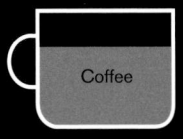

Italian

French

Isotonic

Icelandic

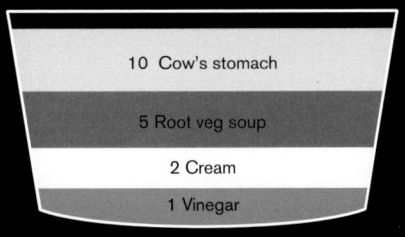

Romanian

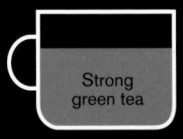

Chinese

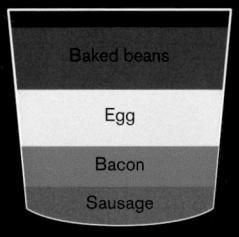

British

Medical

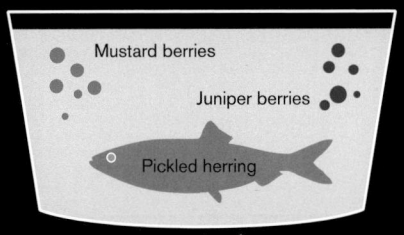

Germanic

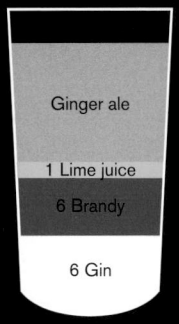

Hedonistic

source: Google

Salad Dressings

All in proportion

Vinaigrette

Ranch

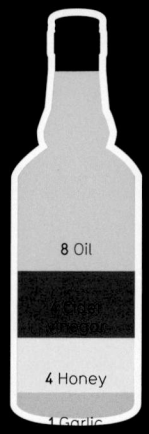

Honey

Creamy Herb

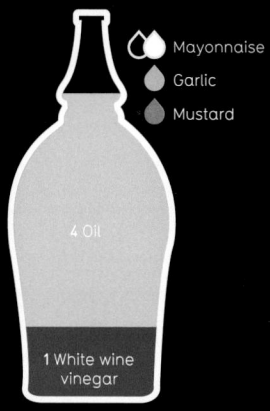

Creamy Garlic

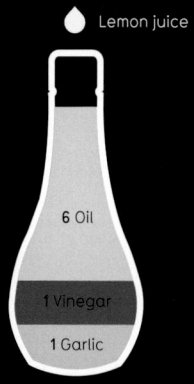

Oil, Lemon & Garlic

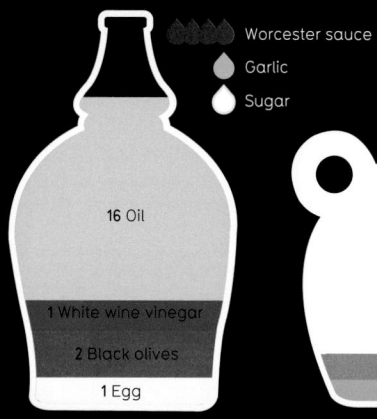

Thousand Island

Lemon, Herb & Yoghurt

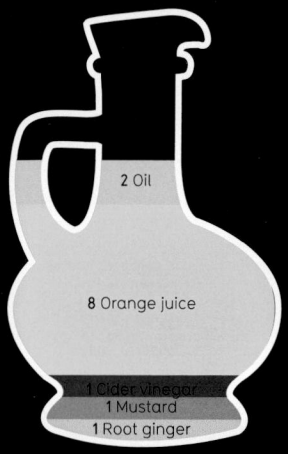

Orange

Oil & Lemon

Caesar

Curry

source: Googl

Not Nice

Food colourings linked to unpleasant health effects

source: Centre for Science in the Public Interest, Cspinet.org

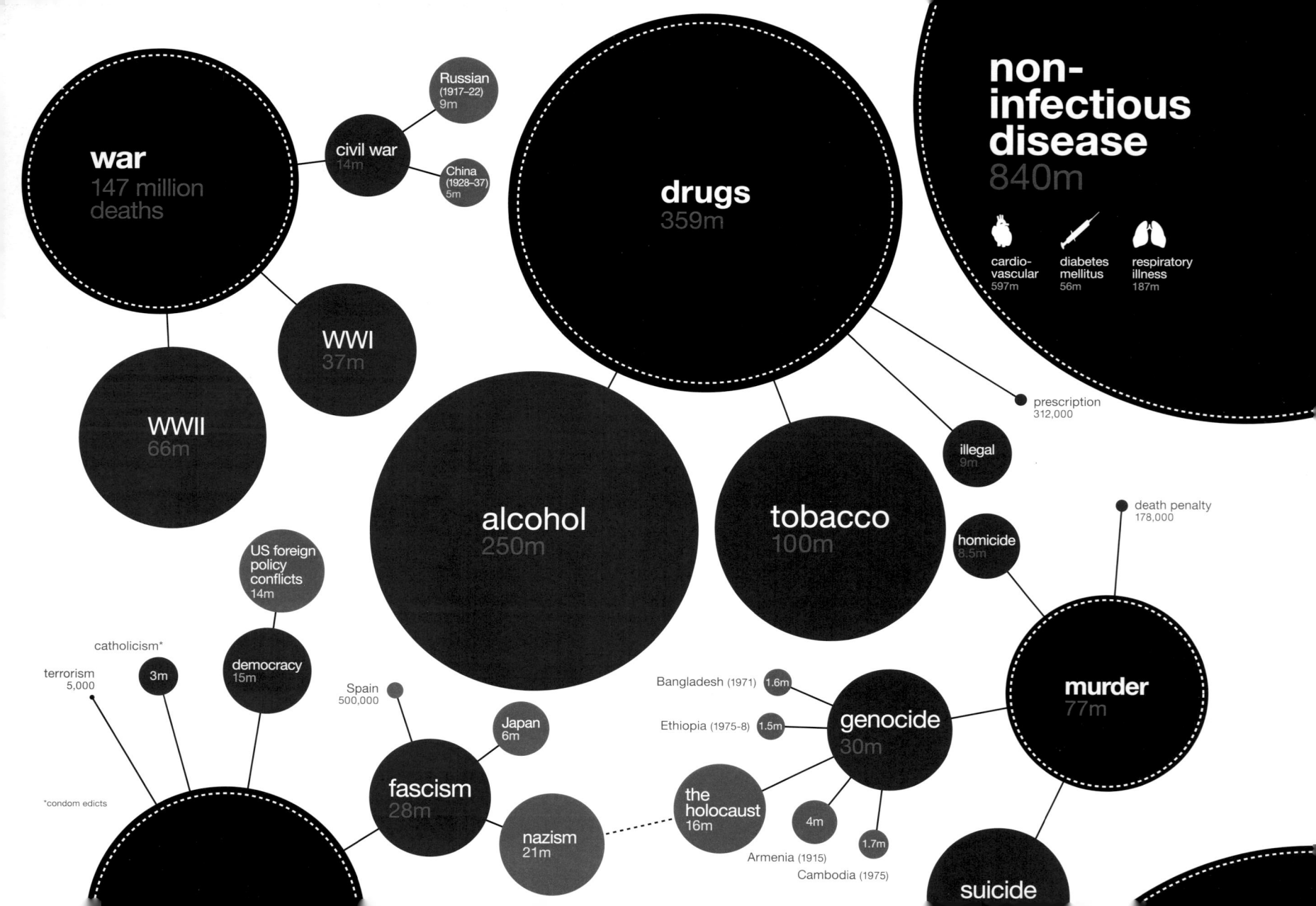
war
147 million deaths
civil war
14m
Russian (1917–22) 9m
China (1928–37) 5m
WWI
37m
WWII
66m
drugs
359m
non-infectious disease
840m
cardio-vascular
597m
diabetes mellitus
56m
respiratory illness
187m
prescription
312,000
illegal
9m
alcohol
250m
tobacco
100m
homicide
8.5m
death penalty
178,000
US foreign policy conflicts
14m
catholicism*
3m
terrorism
5,000
democracy
15m
Spain
500,000
Japan
6m
fascism
28m
nazism
21m
Bangladesh (1971)
1.6m
Ethiopia (1975-8)
1.5m
genocide
30m
murder
77m
the holocaust
16m
4m
1.7m
Armenia (1915)
Cambodia (1975)
*condom edicts
suicide

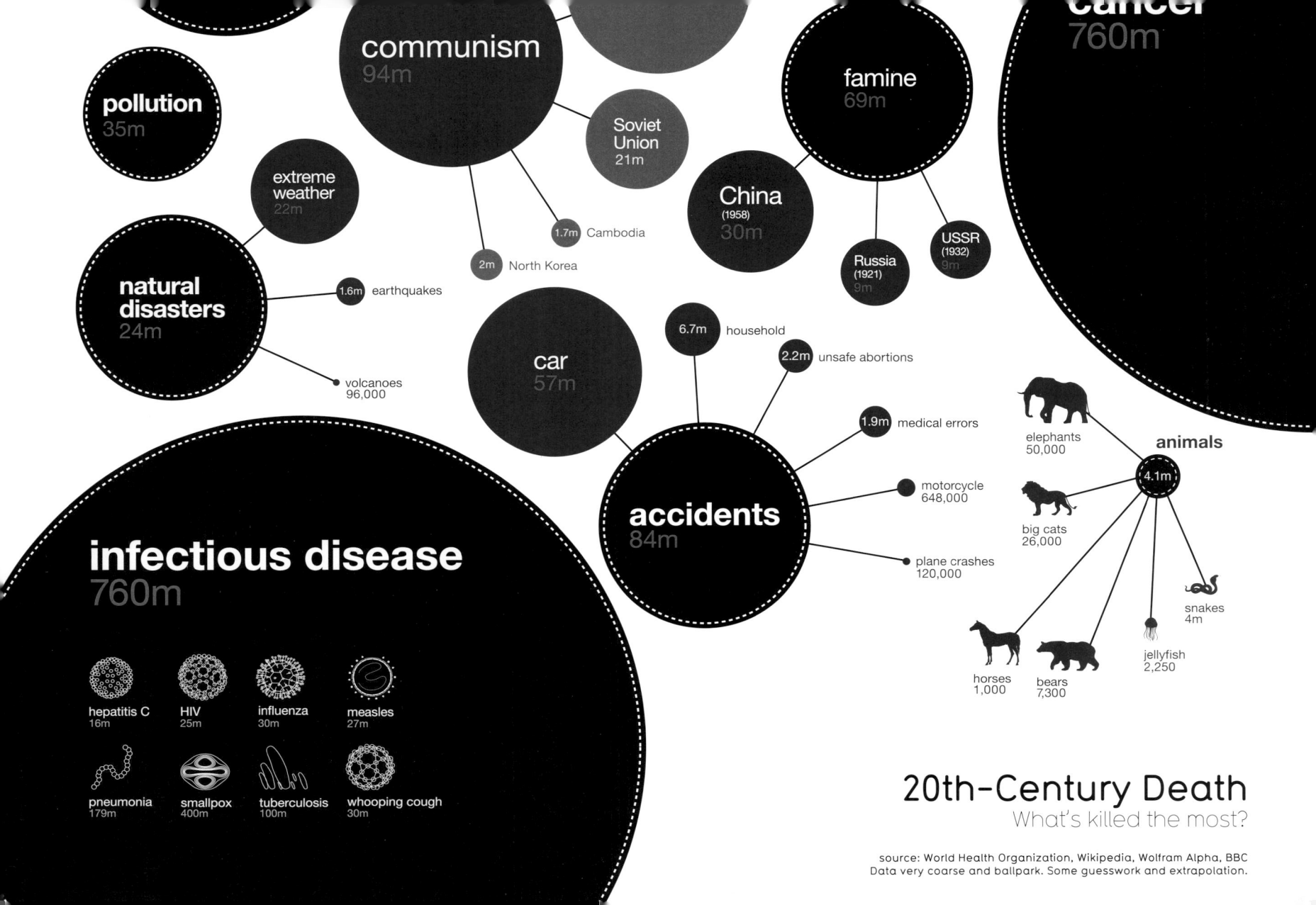

20th-Century Death

What's killed the most?

source: World Health Organization, Wikipedia, Wolfram Alpha, BBC
Data very coarse and ballpark. Some guesswork and extrapolation.

THE GLOBAL WARMING SCEPTICS

We don't believe there is any credible evidence that mankind's activities are the cause of global warming if that's even happening at all. There's only circumstantial evidence of a link between carbon dioxide levels and rising global temperatures.

THE SCIENTIFIC CONSENSUS

The earth's climate is rapidly warming. The cause is a thickening layer of carbon dioxide pollution, caused by humanity's activities. It traps heat in the atmosphere, creating a "greenhouse effect" that heats the earth. A rise in global temperatures of 3 to 9 degrees will cause devastation.

Rising CO_2 levels are not always linked with rising temperatures

Because of extreme weather, Arctic temperature is often a dramatic barometer of global climate. But the temperatures there match poorly with human CO_2 emissions.

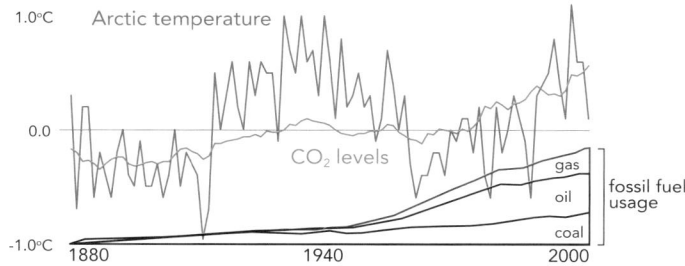

source: Polvakov et al 2002. NASA

A single graph for a single small area is not enough evidence

You can't draw conclusions about the warming of the whole planet just by looking at a small area. It's like comparing apples and pears. It's impossible to tell what caused the warming of the Arctic in the 1930. Or whether it's the same mechanism that's causing global warming today.

In the past, CO_2 rises have occured after temperature rises

Recognize this from *An Inconvenient Truth*? Al Gore famously showed that temperature and CO_2 are clearly linked back over 400,000 years. But if you zoom in....

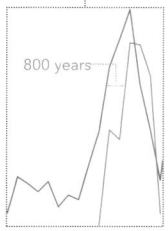

...you see that CO_2 levels rise 800 years after the temperature does. This massive lag proves that CO_2 can't cause global warming!

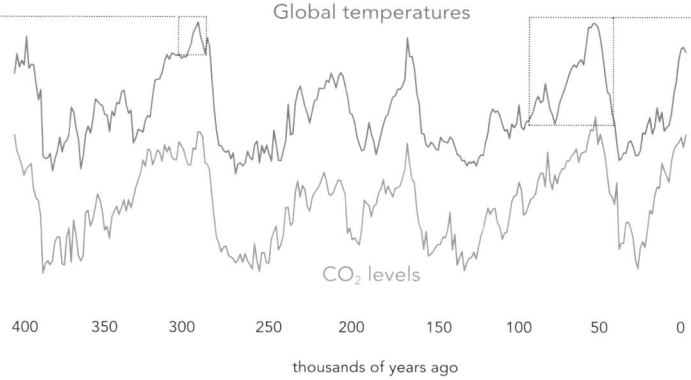

source: Vostok ice core, Petit et al 2002

We don't claim CO_2 caused temperature rises in the past

We say, because of its greenhouse effect, CO_2 makes natural temperature rises worse. Much worse in fact.

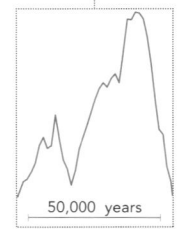

Historically, global warming cycles last 5000 years. The 800-year lag only shows that CO_2 did not cause the first 16% of warming. The other 4200 years were likely to have been caused by a CO_2

We don't even have accurate temperature records

90% of temperature recording stations are on land. 70% of the world's surface is ocean. Cities and towns heat the atmosphere around land-based weather stations enough to distort the record of historical temperatures. It's called the urban heat island effect. And it's why we can't trust temperature records.

Global weather recording stations

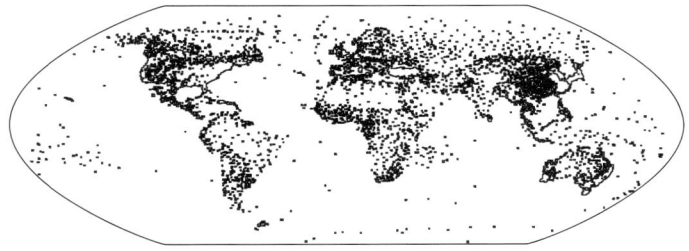

source: National Environmental Satellite Data and Information Service

We do have accurate temperature records

Distortion of temperature records is a very real phenomenon. But it's one climate scientists are well aware of. Detailed filters are used to remove the effect from the records.

It was actually hotter in medieval times than today

Between AD 800 and 1300 was a Medieval Warm Period where temperatures were very high. Grapes were grown in England. The Vikings colonized Greenland. This occurred centuries before we began pumping CO_2 into the atmosphere. More proof that CO_2 and temperature are not linked. Because of this – and to make 20th-century warming look unique – UN scientists constantly play down this medieval period in their data.

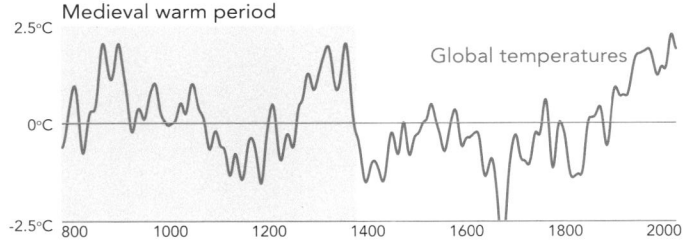

source: NESDIS (smoothed data)

It was hotter in some areas of the world and not in others

This was likely a local warming, rather than a global warming, equivalent to warming today. Ice cores show us that there were periods of both cold and warmth at the time. And there's no evidence it affected the southern hemisphere at all.

The records also show that the earth may have been slightly cooler (by 0.03 degrees Celsius) during the 'medieval warm period' than today.

The famous "hockey stick" temperature graph has been discredited

Made famous by Al Gore, the "hockey stick" graph shows that 20th-century temperatures are showing an alarming rise. But the hockey stick appears or disappears depending on the statistical methods employed. So unreliable has it become that the UN's International Panel On Climate Change dropped it from their 2007 report.

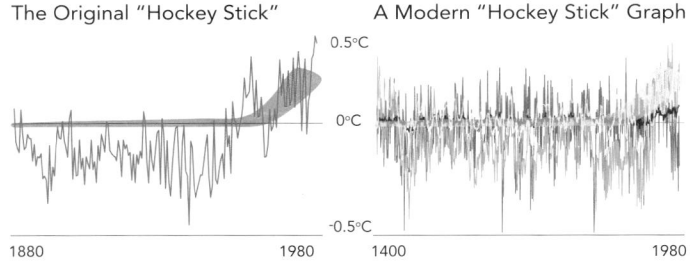

source: Author's composite Briffa Ammann & Wahl Mann 2003 Mann 1998

Reworked, enhanced versions still show the "hockey stick" shape

The hockey stick is 8 years old. There are dozens of other newer, more detailed temperature reconstructions. Each one is different due to different methods and data. But they all show similar striking patterns: the 20th century is the warmest of the entire record. And that warming is most dramatic after 1920 (when industrial activity started releasing CO_2 into the atmosphere).

THE GLOBAL WARMING SCEPTICS

THE SCIENTIFIC CONSENSUS

Ice core data is unreliable

A lot of our temperature records come from measuring the gases trapped in ice cores. These are segments of deep ice unmelted for hundreds of thousands of years. The trapped air inside acts as "photographs" of the contents of the atmosphere going back millennia. But ice-cores are not "closed systems" that preserve ancient air perfectly. Air can get in and out. Water can also absorb the gases, changing the result. And deep ice is under huge amounts of pressure. Enough to squeeze gas out. All in all this adds up to make ice cores unreliable.

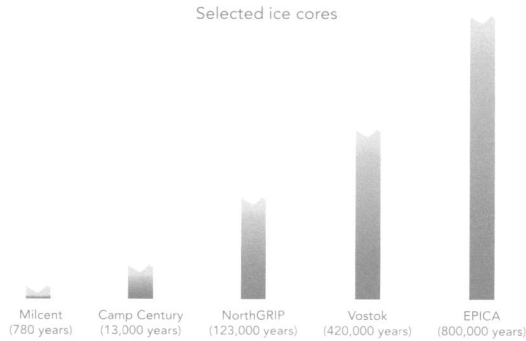

Ice records are reliable

Ice core data is taken from many different samples to reduce errors. Also, other evidence (temperature records, tree rings, etc) back these readings up. All these results combined make the records very reliable.

The predictions of future global warming don't depend on ice cores. But ice cores do show that the climate is sensitive to changes in cycles and that CO_2 has a strong influence.

Overall, CO_2 levels from different ice cores are remarkably similar.

When the evidence doesn't fit, the scientists edit the evidence

Ice core data from Siple in the Arctic shows the concentrations of CO_2 in the atmosphere in 1890 to be 328 parts per million. However, according to the consensus, that level was not reached until 1973. So the rise in CO_2 levels happens 83 years too early.

To fix it, scientists moved the graph 83 years to the right to make the data exactly fit.

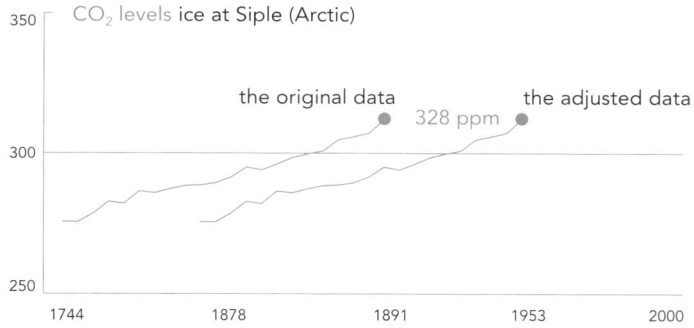

Scientists correct their results when new evidence comes to light

No other ice core data in the world shows CO_2 levels rising above 290 parts per million in the last 650,000 years. It's possible it might have happened for a year or a day. But consistently, no.

Some areas of ice are more porous than others. At Siple, the more recent shallow ice was quite porous. So new air was able to circulate quite far down. That affected the record.

We detected and compensated for this. That's why the data has been shifted.

CO_2 stays in the atmosphere for only 5 to 10 years, not the 50–200 years stated by UN scientists

The ocean absorbs the CO_2 so it can't accumulate to dangerous levels in the atmosphere. In fact, the oceans are so vast they can absorb 50 times as much CO_2 as there is in the atmosphere – more than all the fossil fuels on the planet!

Conclusion: humans can't have been emitting CO_2 fast enough to account for all the extra CO_2 in the atmosphere.

CO_2 absorption by the oceans

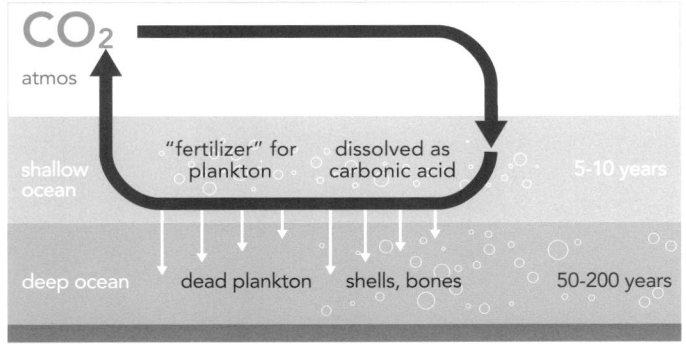

When you take the entire complex ocean-climate system into account 50–200 years is more accurate

CO_2 is absorbed in 5 to 10 years by the *shallow* ocean. Not the deep ocean. It takes 50–200 years for CO_2 to be mixed into the deep ocean where it stays. CO_2 in the shallow ocean, however, is prone to escaping back into the atmosphere. So CO_2 absorbed by the ocean often comes straight back out again.

Also the more carbon the ocean absorbs, the less it's able to absorb. It becomes saturated. It's a very complex process. But if you take the entire ocean-climate system, full absorption of atmospheric CO_2 takes around 50,000 years.

SCEPTICAL CONCLUSION

Man-made CO_2 cannot be driving climate change

Whatever affects global temperatures and causes global warming is not CO_2. Whatever the cause, it works like this: the cause affects the climate balance, then the temperature changes accordingly. The oceans then adjust over a period of decades and centuries. Then the balance of CO_2 in the atmosphere increases.

So the global panic about CO_2 causing global warming is baseless and fear-mongering. The UN's reports on the matter are biased, unscientific and alarmist.

CONSENSUS CONCLUSION

Man-made CO_2 is driving climate change this time

We don't claim that greenhouse gases are the major cause of the ice ages and warming cycles. What drives climate change has long been believed to be the variation in the earth's orbit around the sun over thousands of years.

In a normal warming cycle, the sun heats the earth, the earth gets hotter. The oceans warm up, releasing huge amounts of CO_2. This creates a greenhouse effect that makes warming much, much more intense.

That's why humanity's release of CO_2 is so perilous. We're out of step with the natural cycle. And we haven't even got to the stage where the oceans warm up.

source: Solomon, Lawrence, The Deniers (Richard Vigilante Books, 2008), RealClimate.org

Behind Every Great Man...

Dictators' wives

Wife	Nadezhda Alliluyeva	Eva Braun	Yang Kaihui	Imelda Marcos	Mirjana (Mira) Markovic
Husband	Stalin	Hitler	Mao	Marcos	Milosevic
Pre-marital occupation	clerk	assistant and model	communist!	beauty queen	professor of sociology
How they met	her father sheltered Stalin in 1911 after he escaped from Siberian exile	she was assistant to his personal photographer	her father was Mao's teacher	whirlwind courtship during "holy week"	at school, she borrowed his card to rent *Antigone* from the library. Oh yeah
Years of marriage	13	about 40 minutes	8	35	32
Children					
Rumoured quality of marriage	strained and violent	changeable	troubled	good	very good
Political power rating	none		none		
Key governmental roles	none	none	prominent female member of party	Governor of Manila, Ambassador plenipotentiary	puppet-master, leader o "Yugoslav United Left"
Style rating	none				
Nickname	none	The Rolleiflex Girl	none	The Steel Butterfly	The Red Witch
Notable talents	none – super dull	photography, athletics	very intelligent	none	politics
Trademark/idiosyncrasy	left-handed	nude sunbathing	feminist	very ostentatious and flamboyant	would berate her husba in front of state officials, wore only black Versace
Obsessions and pathologies	suicide	lots of make-up	good communists don't covet material things	shoes, clothes, paintings	media products, plastic surgeons, rich friends
Most salacious rumour	she was Stalin's daughter	she was pregnant when she died OR she didn't sleep in the same room as Hitler	said she would have killed herself when she and Mao divorced if she didn't have kids	sent a plane to pick up white sand from Australia for her beach resort	ordered the murder of Ivan Stambolic, a rival to her husband. Had at lea four officials killed after they disagreed with her. Disappeared a journalis who criticized her.
Reason for death	officially "appendicitis" – really, shot	suicide – bit into a cyanide capsule	publicly executed by the Nationalists	still alive	still alive

ace Marufu	Khieu Ponnary	Jiang Qing	Carmen Polo	Sajida Talfah	He Zizhen
ugabe	Pol Pot	Mao	Franco	Hussein	Mao
ecretary	teacher	actress	none	teacher	communist!
orked as his secretary en became his mistress	at university. She came from a privileged background. He did not	at the Chinese Communist HQ. She "joined the revolution"	family connections	arranged marriage (her father is his uncle)	introduced by a classmate of her elder brother
13	23	39	52	43	7
good	good at start, terrible when she flipped	bad	good	crazy – many family feuds	bad
one	President of the Democratic Kampuchea Women's Association	key member of the politburo & infamous "gang of four"	key advisor and censor of the press	none	none
s Grace	Old Virgin	Madame Mao	La Señora	none	none
opping nce spent £75,000 on a opping spree in Paris)	inspiring young communists	photography, seduction	being glamorous	paranoia	excellent markswoman
ending - called one of e £500,000 palaces she d built, "Gracelands"	paranoia	sexy and chic, in the gossip columns	always accompanied her husband EVERYWHERE	none	none
hates journalists	Communist ideologies, PARANOIA	hypochondriac, insomnia, hyper-sensitive, paranoid	completely isolated herself in her old age	paranoid	nervous breakdown/ insomnia
es the Reserve Bank Zimbabwe as her own nk account. Spent over 0m and transferred ge funds to build luxury operties in Malaysia	Pol Pot couldn't bear to look at her when she became ill and avoided her	entertained her prison jailors by being their dinner (and bed) companion	smuggled 300 million pesetas worth of gold, jewellery & medals	none	none
ll alive	natural causes	allegedly hanged herself	old age	no one knows where she is...	old age

source: Wikipedia

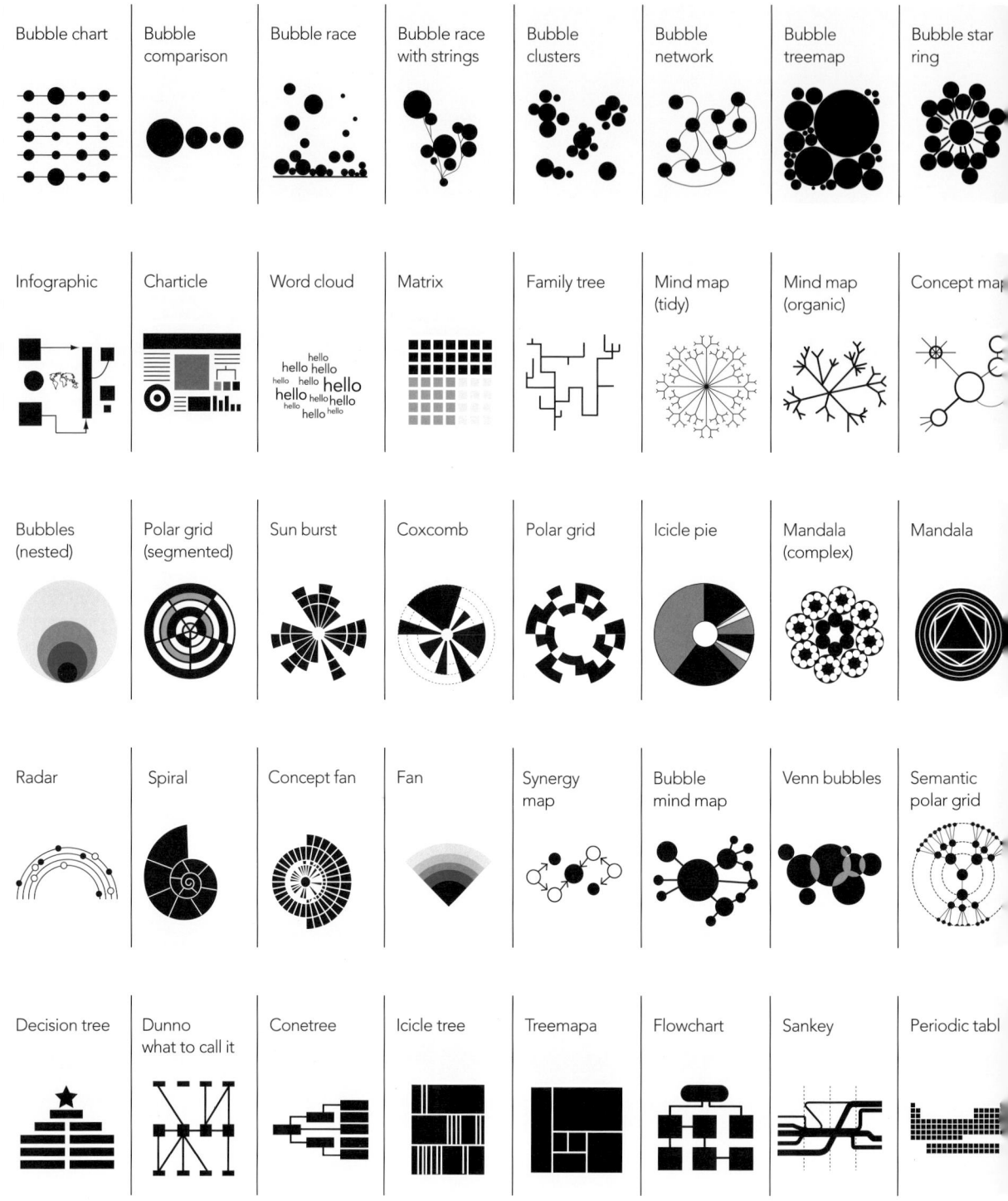

Types of Information Visualization

source: Edward Tufte, visual-literacy.o

Pass the...

A table of condiments that periodically go bad

Tz (1) Tzatziki — 2 days											Sa (2) Salsa — 2 days	Gu (3) Guacamole — 2 days
Ps (4) Peanut/ Satay sauce — 2 days										Be (5) Beef extract — 3 days	L (6) Lemon Juice — 3 days	Sc (7) Sour cream — 3 days
Ss (8) Sweet and sour sauce — 3 days	Ra (9) Raita — 5 days	Mg (10) Meat gravy — 5 days	Hu (11) Hummus — 5 days	Ma[1] (12) home-made mayonnaise — 1 week	Wc (13) Whipped cream — 1 week	Og (14) Onion gravy — 1 week	O (15) Oyster sauce — 2 weeks	Cu (16) Custard — 3 weeks	Lc (17) Lime chutney — 3 weeks	Pa (18) Parmesan cheese — 3 weeks	B (19) Butter — 3 weeks	M (20) Margarine — 3 weeks
Gs (21) Granulated sweetener — 3 weeks	J (22) Jam — 1 month	Tr (23) Treacle — 1 month	Mg (24) Mango chutney — 1 month	T (25) Tomato chutney — 1 month	Vg (26) Vegetable gravy — 1 month	Bq (27) BBQ sauce — 1 month	Ch (28) Chilli sauce — 1 month	Pl (29) Plum sauce — 1 month	Hs (30) Hoisin sauce — 1 month	Fd (31) French dressing — 1 month	Dm (32) Dijon mustard — 1 month	Lc (33) Lemon curd — 6 weeks
Bs (34) Brown sauce — 6 weeks	H (35) Horseradish — 6 weeks	K (36) Ketchup — 6 weeks	Mi (37) Mint sauce — 6 weeks	Ta (38) Tartar sauce — 6 weeks	Pk (39) Pickle — 6 weeks	Pi (40) Picalilli — 6 weeks	Sp (41) Sweet pickle — 6 weeks	Id (42) Italian dressing — 6 weeks	Td (43) Thousand island dressing — 6 weeks	Ma (44) Mayonnaise — 2 months	Sc (45) Salad cream — 2 months	Fs (46) Flaxseed oil — 2 months
Ca (47) Cayenne pepper — 3 months	Ch (48) Chilli powder — 3 months	Bm (49) Brown mustard — 3 months	Wa (50) Wasabi — 3 months	Ma (51) Marmalade — 6 months	Pb (52) Peanut butter — 6 months	Y (53) Yeast extract — 6 months	Ta (54) Tahini — 6 months	Ms (55) Maple syrup — 1 year	Pa (56) Palm oil — 1 year	P (57) Peanut oil — 1 year	So (58) Soybean oil — 1 year	Sf (59) Sunflower oil — 1 year
C (60) Cocoa — 1 year	Bb (61) Black pepper — 1 year	Ym (62) Yellow mustard — 18 months	Wv (63) White wine vinegar — 2 years	Cv (64) Cider vinegar — 2 years	W (65) Worcester sauce — 2 years	Sy (66) Soy sauce — 3 years	Ol (67) Olive oil — 4 years	Bv (68) Balsamic vinegar — 5 years	Mv (69) Malt vinegar — indefinite	H (70) Honey — indefinite	Sa (71) Salt — indefinite	Su (72) Sugar — indefinite

idea: Internet Apocryphal / source: Google

NATURE vs NURTURE

Your genes control everything. Hair colour. Behaviour. Intelligence. Personality. Sure, environment has a role, but it's your genes that rule you.

You learn pretty much everything you do. From standing and walking to talking and socializing. Your environment and your choices make you who you are...

Most behaviour is genetic. Genes for speech, empathy and even altruism all evolved when we lived as hunter-gatherers on the ancient grasslands of Africa.

The evidence for that ancient lifestyle is complete guesswork.

The proof is in the brain. It has evolved "modules" for all human abilities, even for religious experience!

Nah. Those "structures" could simply be projections of human interpretation on the brain. Behaviour isn't genetically evolved. We learn it.

Oh yeah? Animal breeders know it takes only a few generations of controlled mating to influence behaviours like fierceness or tameness in dogs.

Dogs, maybe. But complex human behaviour like musical ability or humour? C'mon. These are learnt. In fact, learning, we now know, changes the physical structure of the brain! So much for genes.

Genes change the brain too. And at a more fundamental level, before your so-called "choices" come in. Try "deciding" to override a genetic expression. You can't! Hah!

Most genetic expression, from traits to behaviours, are triggered by your environment. Nurture comes first!

Okay then, what about behavioural problems such as depression, mental illness and autism? They're all highly inheritable.

Yeah, it's fashionable to say that, yes. But, even after

Ahhhhh but behavioural disorders like autism are highly inheritable. In identical twins, if one twin is autistic, the other has a 60% chance of being autistic. In non-identical twins the chance is only 5%. That goes for intelligence too.

In autism, maybe. But you can't then stretch it to all behaviour and certainly not intelligence. Intelligent parents *teach* their kids to be intelligent.

But don't intelligent parents also provide the genes for high IQ? Twins separated at birth are often remarkably similar in IQ and personality, even when they haven't met. This proves there are genetic influences for everything. Even taste in music!

Yeah, but if it was all genes, you'd expect identical twins to be 100% the same. Figures for IQ may be high. But it's way less, to non-existent, for other traits like personality.

But identical twins reared apart become more alike, even when they haven't met. That means that genes must shape our personalities.

Hmmmmmm. Many studies of twins are flawed and biased. Often they just compare identical twins reared apart after birth. They don't use "controls" of unrelated people with the same background as the twins to check that age, gender, ethnicity and cultural environment are not also influencing personality. The whole field is biased.

Pffff.

Grrrrr!

CONCLUSION

50-50

Both nature and nurture each contribute
(in arguable proportions) to who we are.
They also "speak the same language".
That is, they both change the structure of the brain.
In summary, humans are dynamic creative organisms.
Learning and experience amplify the effect of genes on behaviour.

source: Skeptic.com

Postmodernism

Postmodernism is pretty much a buzz word now. Anything – and everything – can be described as postmodern now. The design of a building. The samples used in a record. The layout of a page. The collective mood of a generation. Cultural or political fragmentation. The rise of blogging and crowd-wisdom. Anything that starts with the word "meta". But what does it mean?

In art, where it all began, it's a style of sorts. Ironic and parodying. Very playful and very knowing. Knowing of history, culture, and often knowing of itself. Postmodern art and entertainment is often self-conscious. It calls attention to itself as a piece of art, or a production, or something constructed. A character who knows they are a character in a novel, for example. Or even the appearance of an author in their own book. (Like me, David, writing this. Hello.)

Overall, postmodern art says there's no difference between refined and popular culture, "high" or "low" brow. It rejects genres and hierarchies. Instead, it embraces complexity, contradiction, ambiguity, diversity, interconnectedness, and criss-crossing referentiality.

The idea is: let's not pretend that art can make meaning or is even meaningful. Let's just play with nonsense.

All of this springs from the discovery of a new relationship to truth. In a postmodern perspective, truth is a not single thing "out there" to be discovered. Instead truth must be assembled or constructed. Sometimes, it's constructed visibly, from many different components (i.e. scientists gathering results of multiple studies). Other times, it happens invisibly by society, or by cultural mechanisms and other processes that can't be easily seen by the individual.

So when someone "speaks the truth", what they are saying is actually an assemblage of their schooling, their cultural background, and the thoughts and opinion they've absorbed from their environment. In a way, you could say that their culture is speaking through them.

For that reason, it becomes more accurate and safer in postmodern times, to assemble truth with the help of other people, rather than just decide it independently.

A clear example of this is the scientific method. Any scientist can do an experiment and declare a discovery about the world. But teams of other scientists must verify or "peer-review" that truth before it's safe to accept it. The truth here has been assembled by many people.

All the time, though, there is an understanding that even this final "truth" may well just be temporary or convenient, a place-holder to be changed or binned later on. (Well, that *should* be the case. Even scientific discoveries have a tendency to harden into dogma.)

If you accept this key postmodern insight, then immediately it becomes impossible for any individual to have a superior belief. There's no such thing as "absolute truth". No one "knows" the truth. Or can have a better truth than someone else. If an individual – or a group, organization or government – does claims to have truth and declares that truth to you, they are likely to be attempting to overpower and control you.

Confusingly, these kinds of entities are known as "Modernist". Modernity is all about order and rationality. The more ordered a society is, Modernists believe, the better it functions. If "order" is superior, then anything that promotes "disorder" has to be wrong. Taken to an extreme, that means anything different from the norm – ideas, beliefs, people – must be excluded. Or even destroyed. In the history of Western culture this has usually meant anyone non-white, non-male, non-heterosexual and non-rational.

This is one reason why tension still erupts between holders of "absolute truth" (say the Church) and postmodern secular societies. Or between an entity like an undemocratic government which seeks to control its populace and the internet, a truly postmodern piece of technology. This is because postmodernity has a powerful weapon that can very easily and very quickly corrode Modernist structures built on "old-fashioned" absolute truth: *deconstruction*.

If all truth is constructed, then deconstruction becomes useful. Really useful. If you deconstruct something, its meanings, intentions and agendas separate and rise to the surface very quickly – and everything quickly unravels.

Take a novel, for example. You can deconstruct the structure of the text, and the personality of the characters. Then you can deconstruct the author's life story, their psychological background, and their culture and see how that influenced the text. If you keep going, you can start on the structure of human language and thought. Beyond that, a vast layer of human symbols. Beyond that ... well, you can just keep going...

Belief systems and modernist structures protect themselves from threats like deconstruction with "grand narratives". These are compelling stories to explain and justify why a certain belief system exists. They work to gloss over and mask the contradictions, instabilities and general "scariness" inherent in nature and human life.

Liberate the entire working class. Peace on Earth. There is one true God. Hollywood is one big happy family. History is progress. One day we will know everything. These are all grand narratives.

All modern societies – even those based on science – depend on these myths. Postmodernism rejects them on principle. Instead it goes for "mini-narratives", stories that explain small local events – all with an awareness that any situation, no matter how small, reflects in some way the global pattern of things. Think global, act local, basically.

So a postmodern society, unglossed-over by a grand narrative, must embrace the values of postmodernity as its key values. That means that complexity, diversity, contradiction, ambiguity, and interconnectedness all become central. In social terms that means a lack of obvious hierarchies (equal rights for all), embracing diversity (multi-culturalism), and that all voices should be heard (consensus). Interconnectedness is reflected in our technology and communications. In the 21st century anything that cannot be stored by a computer ceases to be knowledge.

That's the goal, anyway. There are pitfalls. Runaway postmodernism creates a grey goo of no-meaning. Infinite consensus creates paralysis. Over-connection leads to saturation. Too much diversity leads to disconnection. Complexity to confusion.

So in the midst of all this confusion and noise and diversity, without a grand narrative, who are you? Postmodern personal values are not moral but instead values of participation, self-expression, creativity. The focus of spirituality shifts from security in absolute given truth to a search for significance in a chaotic world. The idea that there is anything stable or permanent disappears. The floor drops away. And you are left there, playing with nonsense.

source: constructed from Wikipedia, an essay by Mary Klages, University of Colorado, Wisegeek.com

Death Spiral

You're going to go one way. Which way?

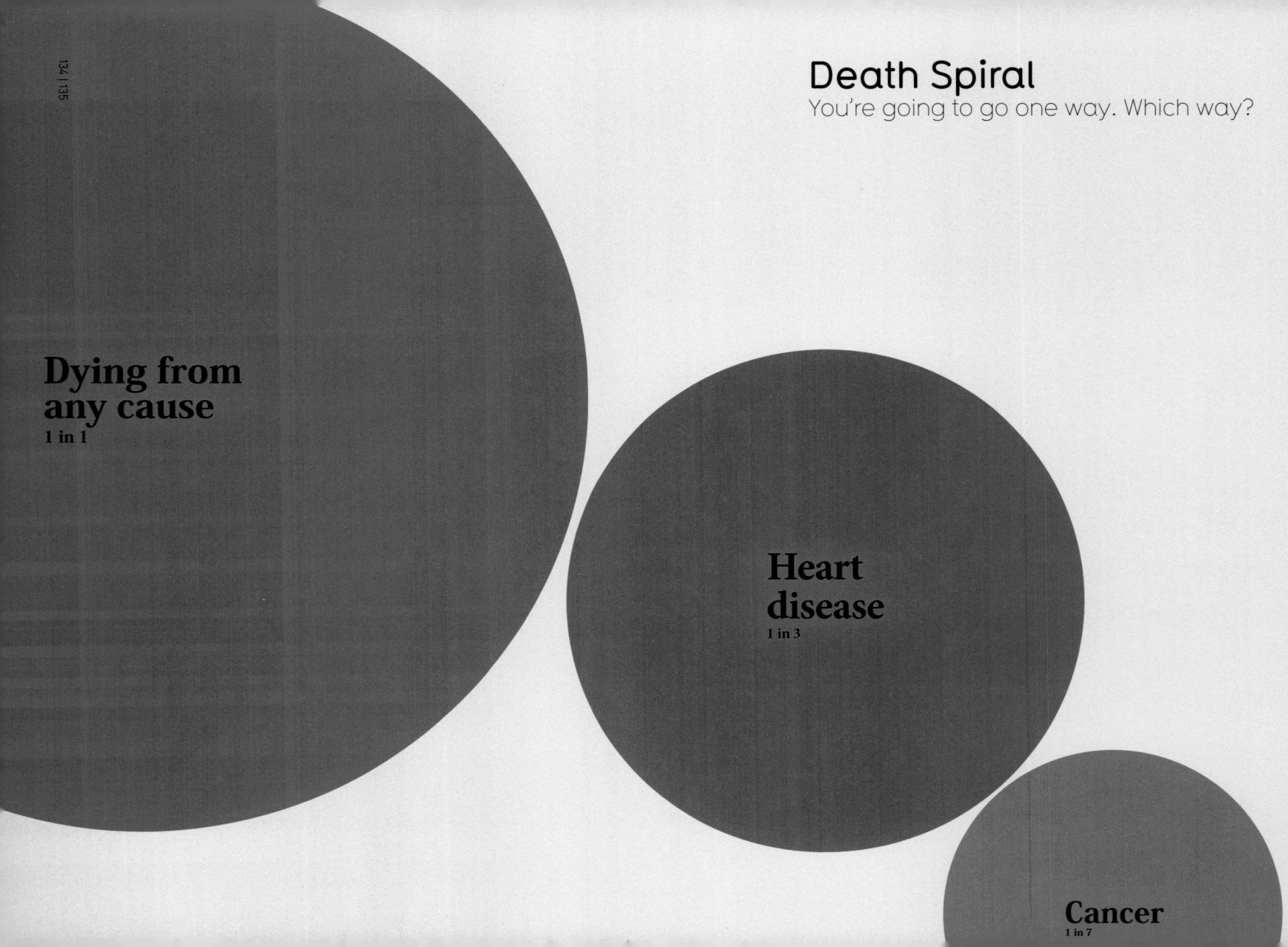

Stroke
1 in 23
Bus /train accident
1 in 77
Ageing sun engulfs Earth
Medical error (hospital)
1 in 300
Assault by firearm
1 in 323
House fire
1 in 1431
Diabetes
1 in 4096
Freak lawnmower accident
1 in 5300
Passive smoking
1 in 7895
Electrocution (home)
1 in 9308
Suicide
1 in 9380
Assault
1 in 16,421
Hernia
1 in 16,742
Murder
1 in 18,000
Drug overdose
1 in 18,125
Car accident
1 in 18,585
Flu
1 in 19,415
Falling down
1 in 20,666
Skin cancer
1 in 29,500
Power-line accident
1 in 40,103
Super volcano
Destroys climate
Tsunami (coastal dweller)
1 in 50,000
Walking down the street
1 in 52,000
Food poisoning
1 in 55,600
Avalanche
1 in 78,535
Accidental drowning
1 in 79,065
Fire
1 in 81,524
Choking
1 in 97,000
Explosion
1 in 107,787
Magnetic Field Reversal
Earth fried by cosmic radiation
personal threats – planetary threats
source: Guardian.co.uk, Time, Google
Dog attack
1 in 147,717
Act of nature
1 in 225,107
Runaway climate change
Earth cooked
Falling off a boat
1 in 400,900
Freezing
1 in 469,000
Asteroid impact
1 in 500,000
Bicycle accident
1 in 578,000
Terrorist attack (overseas)
1 in 658,000
Drowning in the bath
1 in 685,000
Choking on your own vomit
1 in 740,000
Heat stroke
1 in 930,000
Fireworks accident
1 in 1,000,000
Asteroid collision
Seismic shock wave de
Falling out of bed
1 in 72,000,000
Falling off a ladde
1 in 2,300,000
Lightning
1 in 2,320,000
Flood
We all drown
Legal execution
1 in 3,441,325
Ozone layer des
UV radiation kill
Nuclear accident
1 in 10,000,000
Global nuclear war
That was our planet, yo
Plane crash
1 in 11,000,000
Bee sting
1 in 15,000,000
Bubonic plague
1 in 30,000,000
Super Virus
Typhoon of nightmear
1 in 30,589,556
Crushing the planet
Galactic magnetic cloud collapses
Wormhole black hole
Tears planet apart
1 in 32,000,000
Mountain lion attack
1 in 35,000,000
Freak solar flare
Flies us all
Grey goo
Runaway avocado eats us
Blogging
1 in 35,000,000
Mad Cow Disease
1 in 40,000,000
Amusement park accident
1 in 72,300,000
SARS
1 in 100,000,000
Gamma ray burst
Nearby dying star irradiates us
Copernicic revolution
All hail our new robotic overlords
Hadron Collider accident
Oops! Scientists create a black hole
Alien invasion
All hail our new extraterrestrial overlords
Falling coconut
1 in 250,000,000
Omega Point
Storage capacity of universe hit
New Ice Age
Planet freezes
Shark attack
1 in 578,000,000
Meteor landing on your house
1 in 182, 139,00,000
Biblical apocalypse
Jesus returns for Judgement Day

Google Insights

The intensity of certain search terms compared

Beer vs Wine

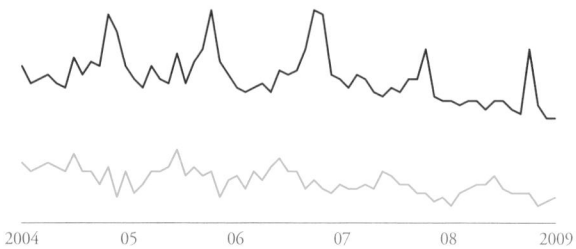

Tea vs Coffee

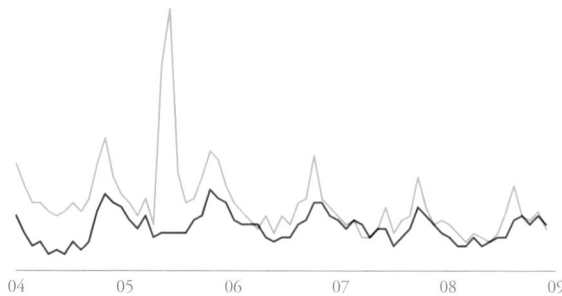

Lipstick vs Recession

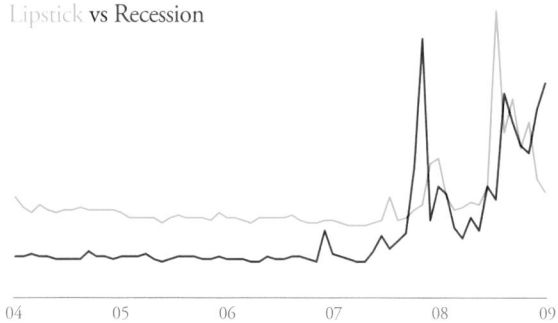

Marriage vs Divorce

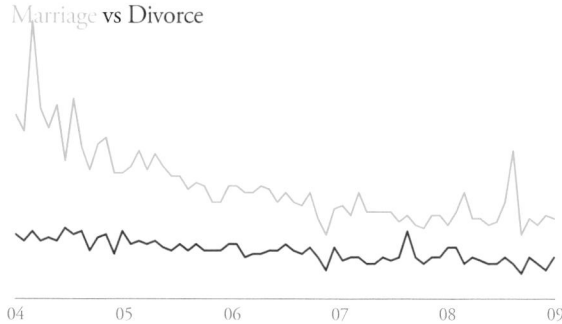

Microsoft vs Apple

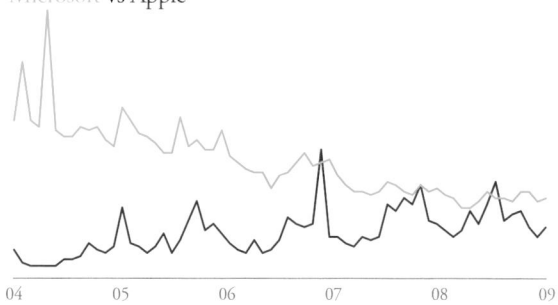

MySpace vs Facebook

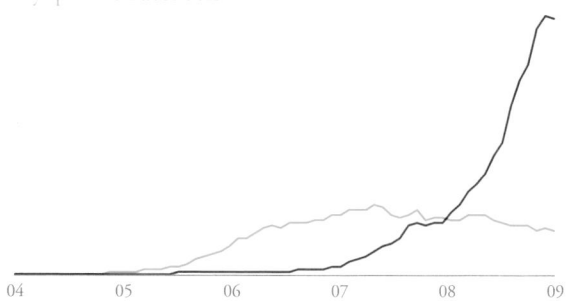

Cornflakes vs Muesli vs Porridge

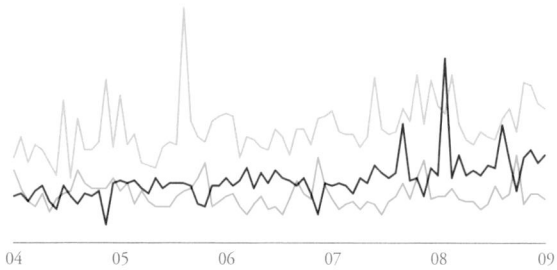

Cornflakes vs Muesli vs Porridge vs Toast

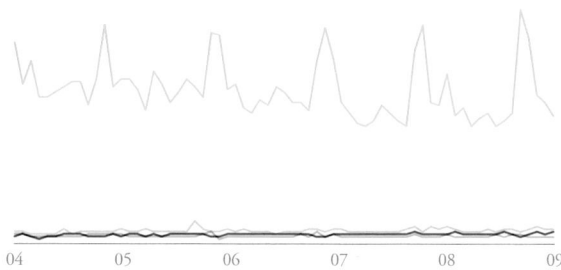

What's Better than Sex?

PTO for the answer

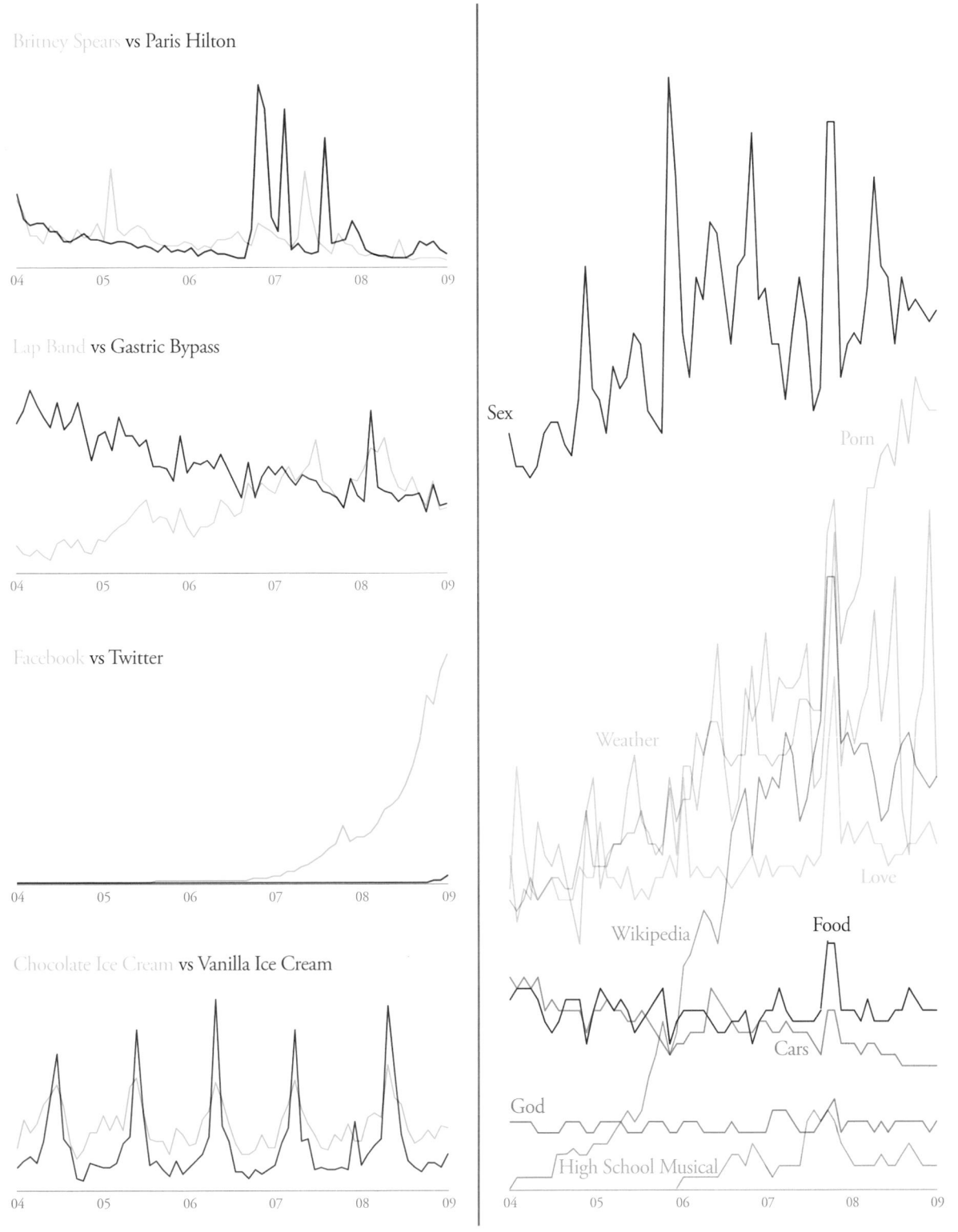

source: Google Insights

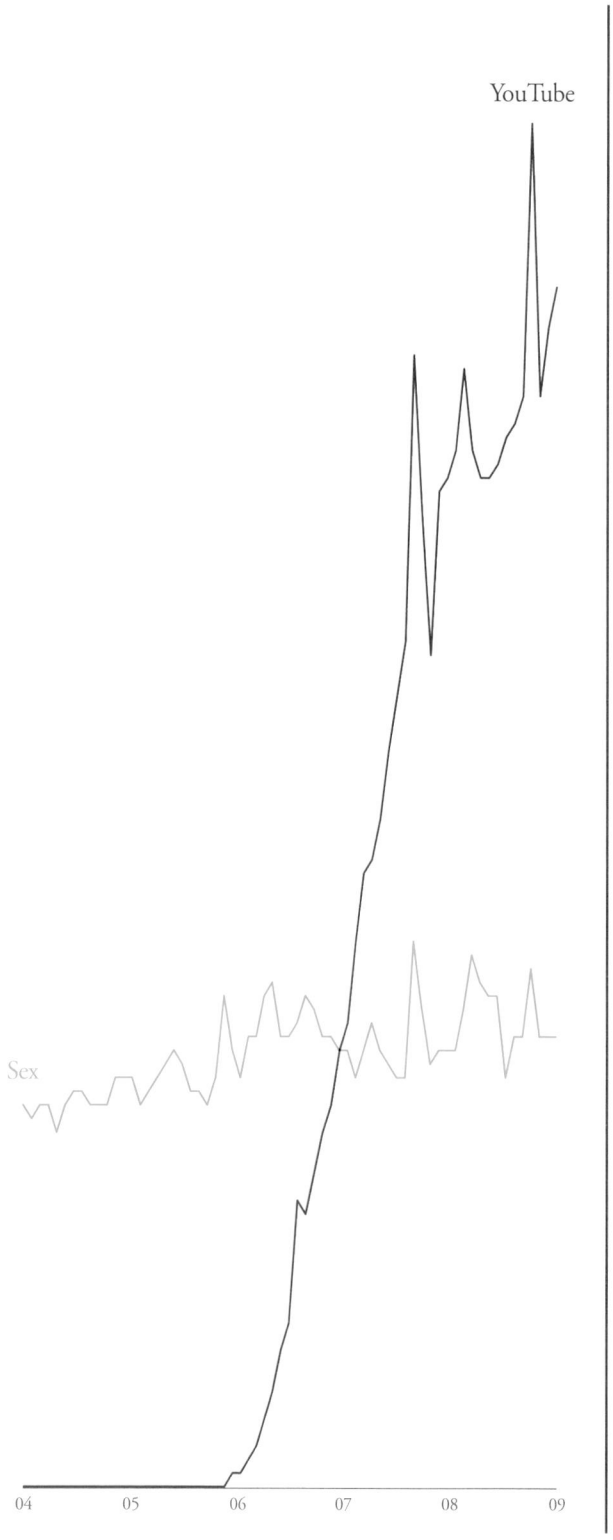
YouTube
Sex
04
05
06
07
08
09

Kyoto Targets

target

% on target

% off target

% on target (with "extras")

extras if a country can't meet its carbon reduction targets, it can invest overseas in carbon trading and infrastructure schemes to offset its debt. Cheat!

ullseye!

Greece

Germany

Sweden

England

n target

these countries look like they're doing very well due of a lack of pre-1997 records to compare against

Bulgaria

Czech Republic

Hungary

Poland

Romania

Slovak Republic

ependent on "extras"

Belgium

Croatia

Portugal

Slovenia

France

Netherlands

ff target

Austria

Finland

Ireland

Luxembourg

Japan

Norway

ail

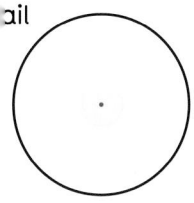

Canada

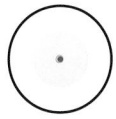

Denmark

Italy

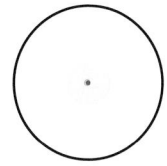

Scotland

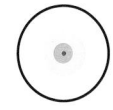

Spain

Switzerland

Despite Kyoto, the EU's carbon emmissions has increased by 1% by 2012

source: European Environment Agency

The Varieties of Romantic Relationship

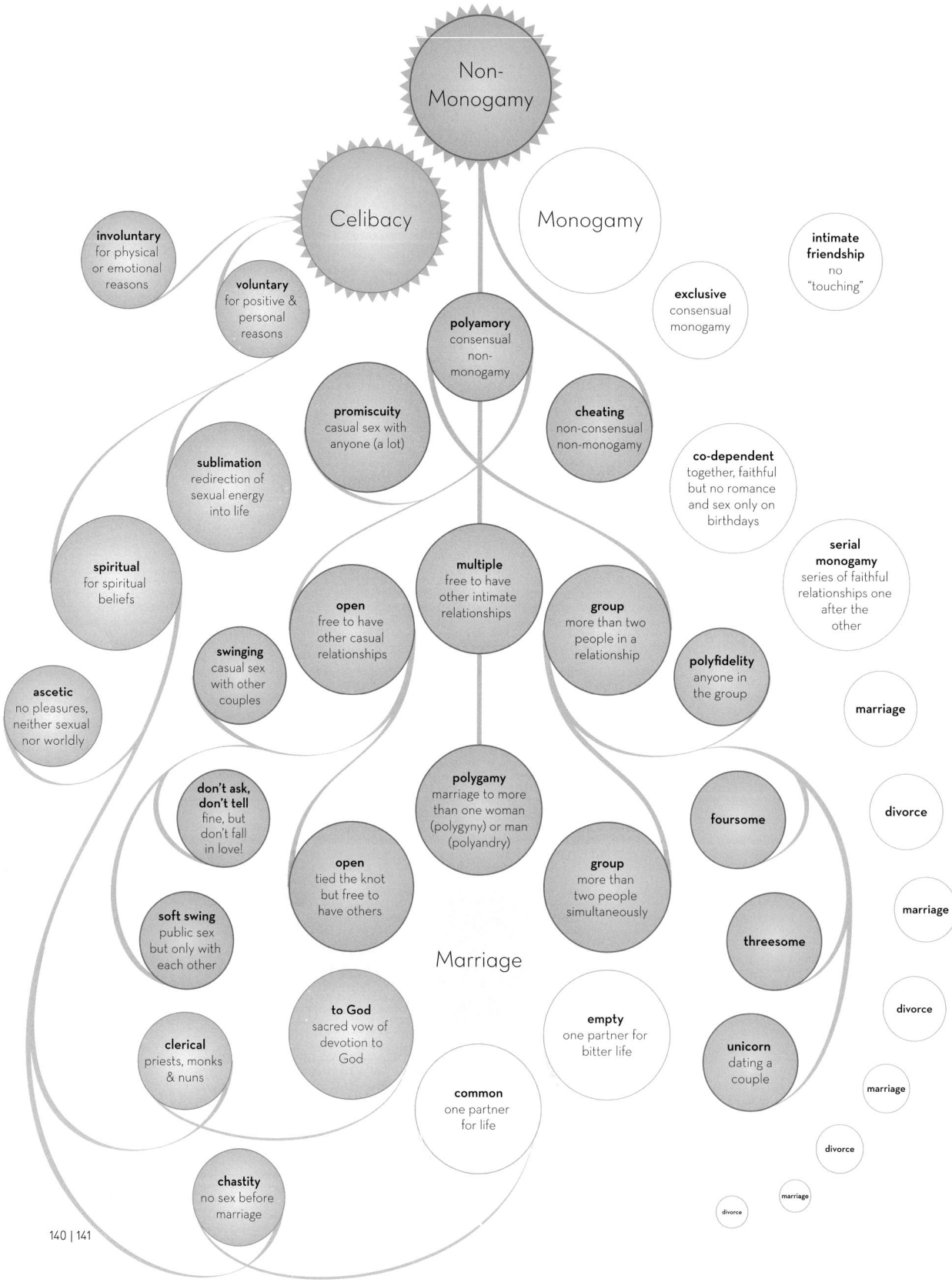

The Evolution of Marriage in the West

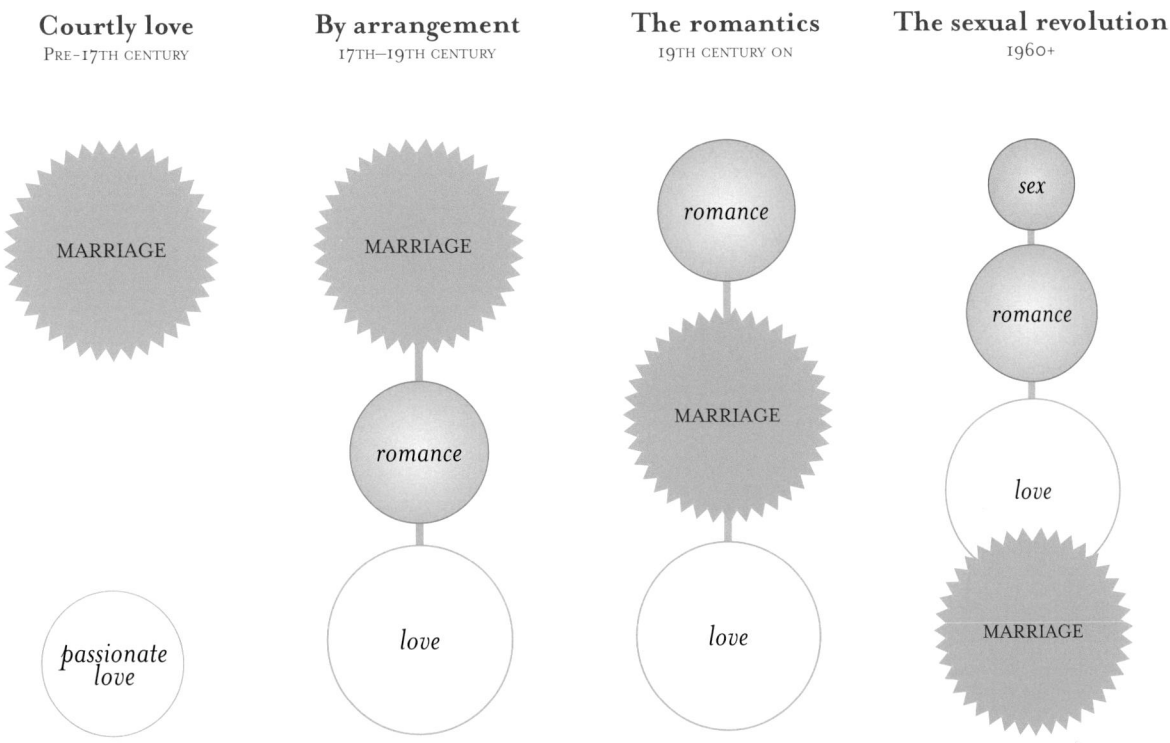

Marriage an economic and political contract negotiated by amilies. Love, a divine madness, ways found outside of marriage.

Marriages arranged but expected to lead to romance and, ultimately, love.

Romance, the essential spark that leads first to marriage and then to enduring love.

Sexual gratification and pleasure necessary for romance. That may, in turn, lead to love and *only* then to marriage.

source: Wikipedia

30 Years Makes a Difference

LAKE CHAD

THE ARAL SEA

OZONE HOLE

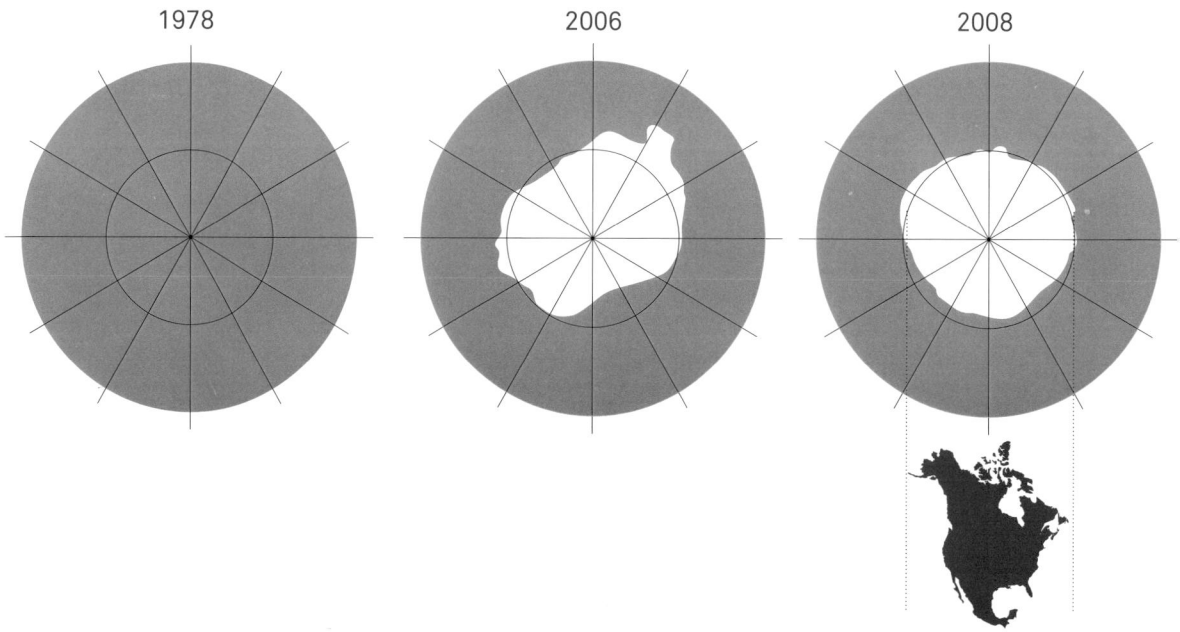

NORTH POLAR ICE CAP

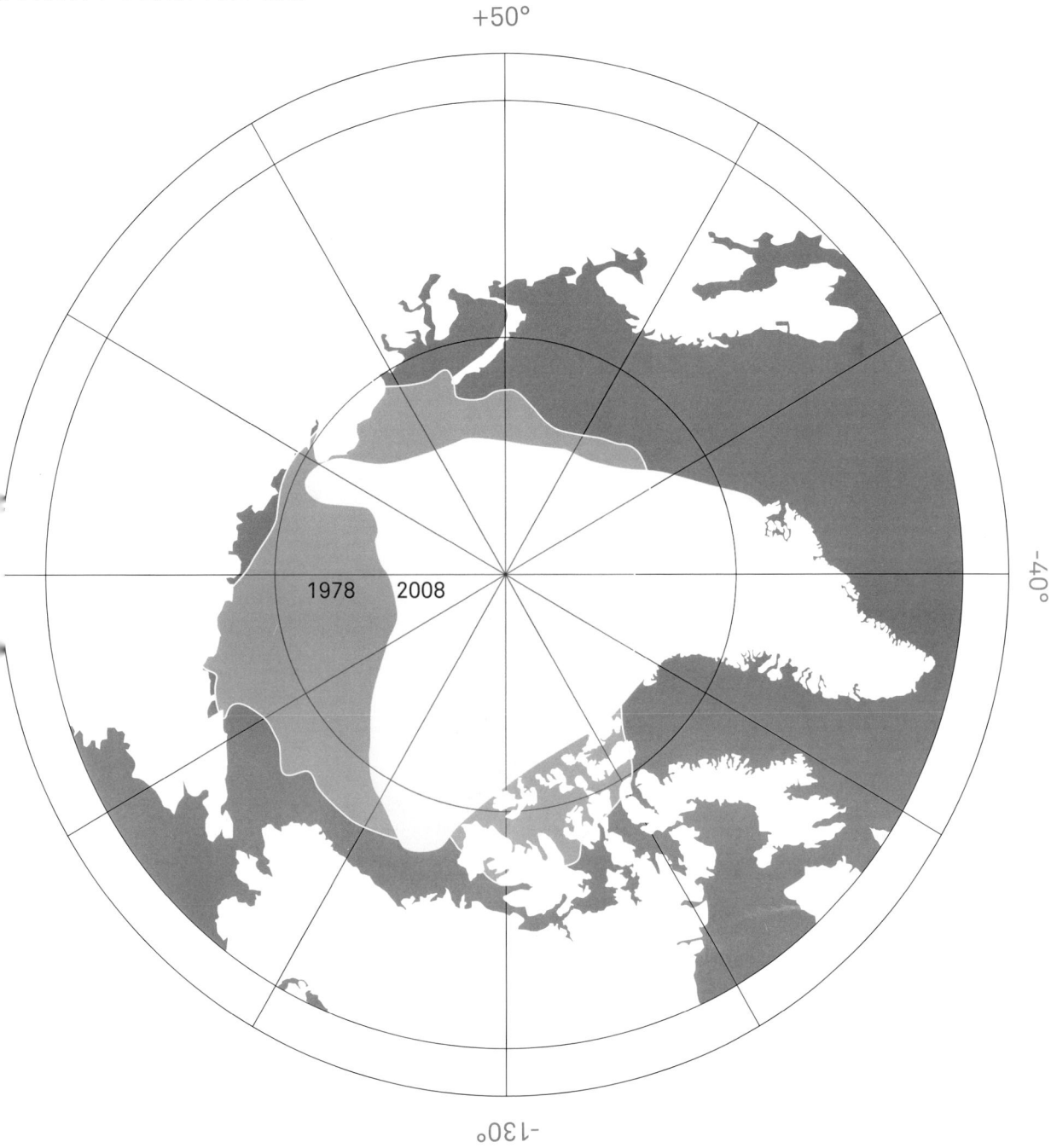

source: NASA

Horoscoped

Most common words

red words unique to each star sign
source: 60,000 scraped star sign predictions

Better than Bacon

The real centre of the Hollywood universe

A study of over 1 million films and actors at the website oracleofbacon.org has revealed a series of actors who are way better connectors for the game Six Degrees of Kevin Bacon than Mr Bacon himself.

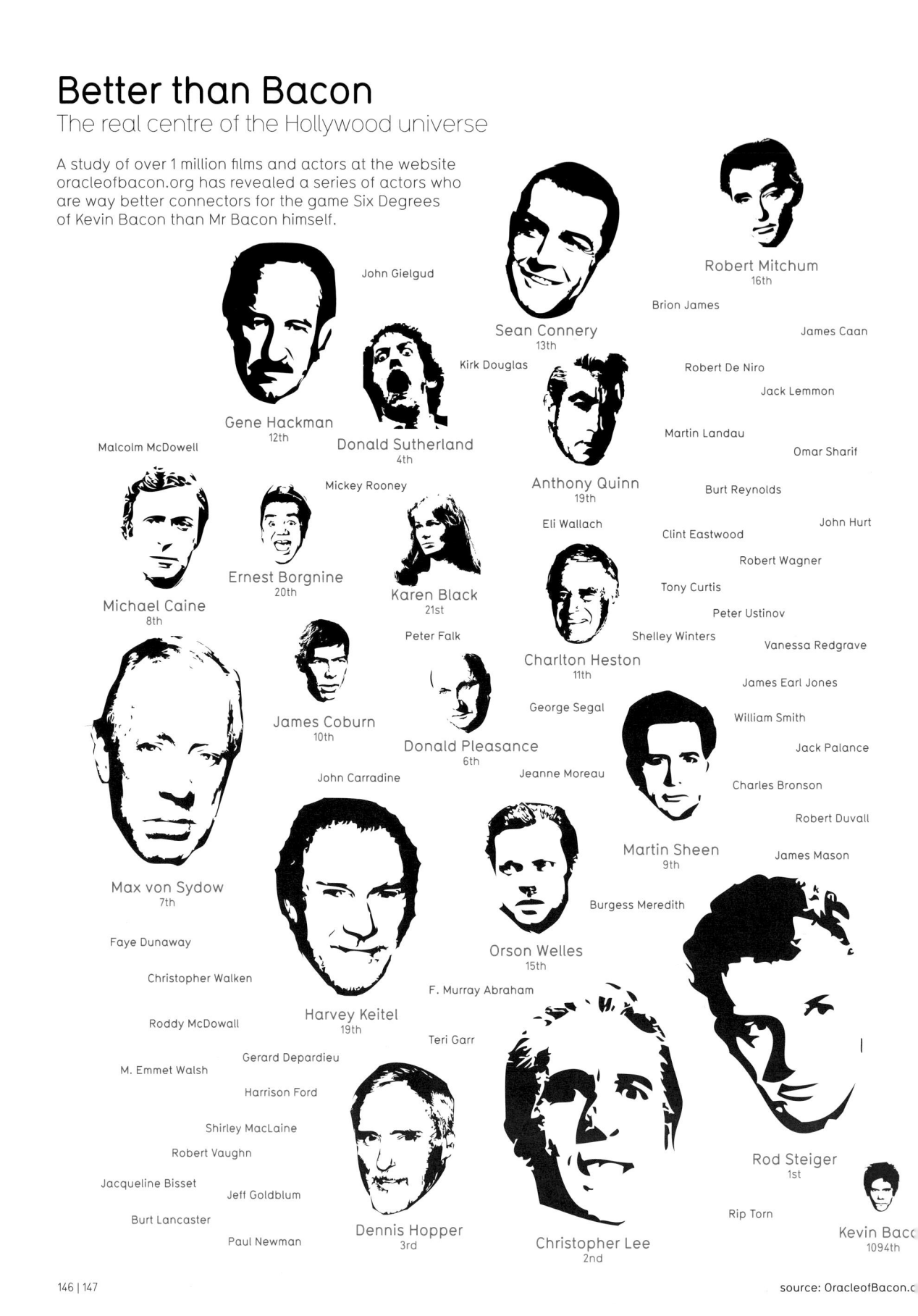

source: OracleofBacon.c

Calculating the Chances

Five-year cancer survival rates

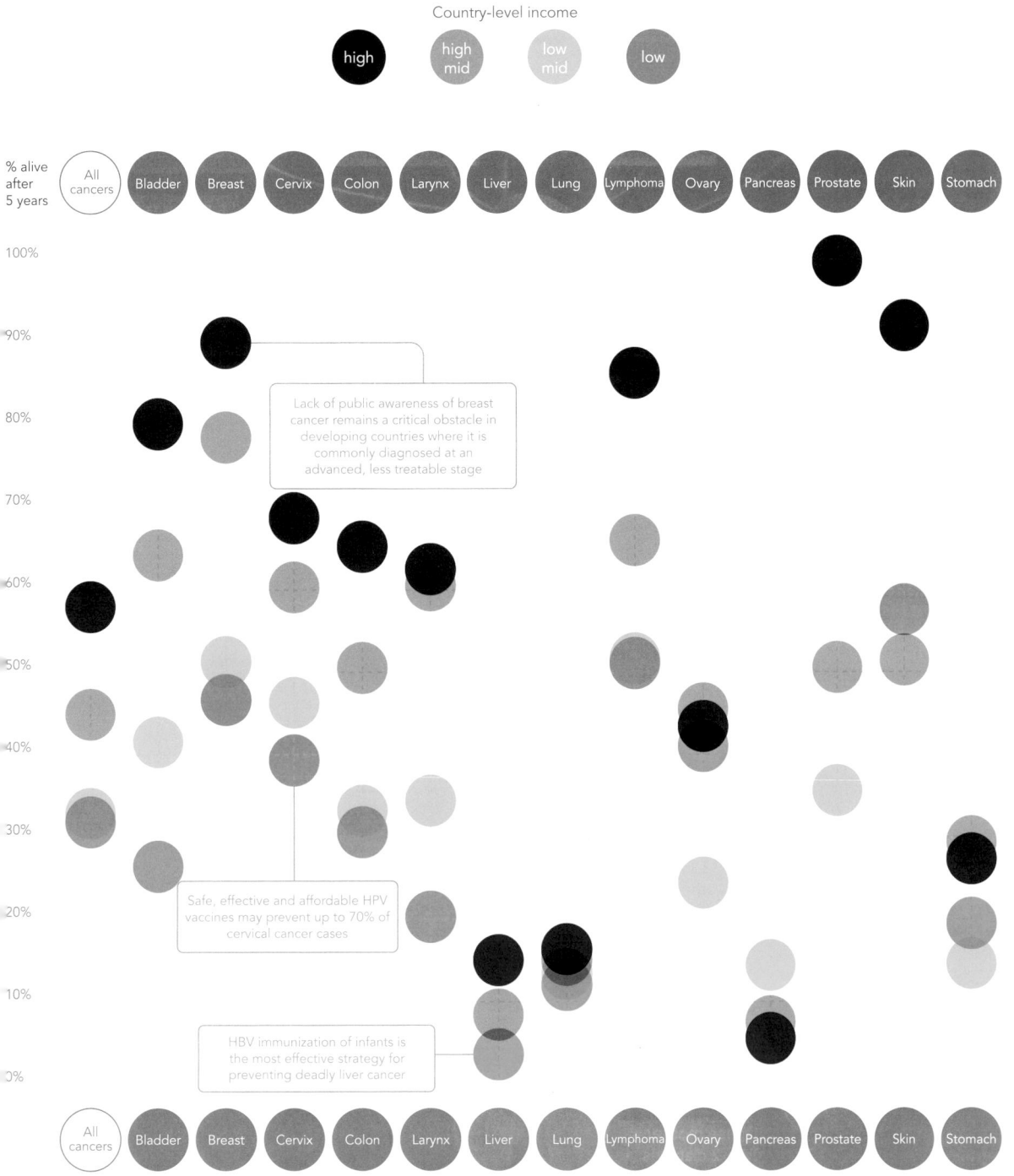

note: lack of colour spot means missing data // data: bit.ly/cancerburden
source: International Agency for Research on Cancer, UK Office for National Statistics, National Cancer Institute

Some Things You Can't Avoid

Characteristics and behaviours that increase the likelihood of certain ailments

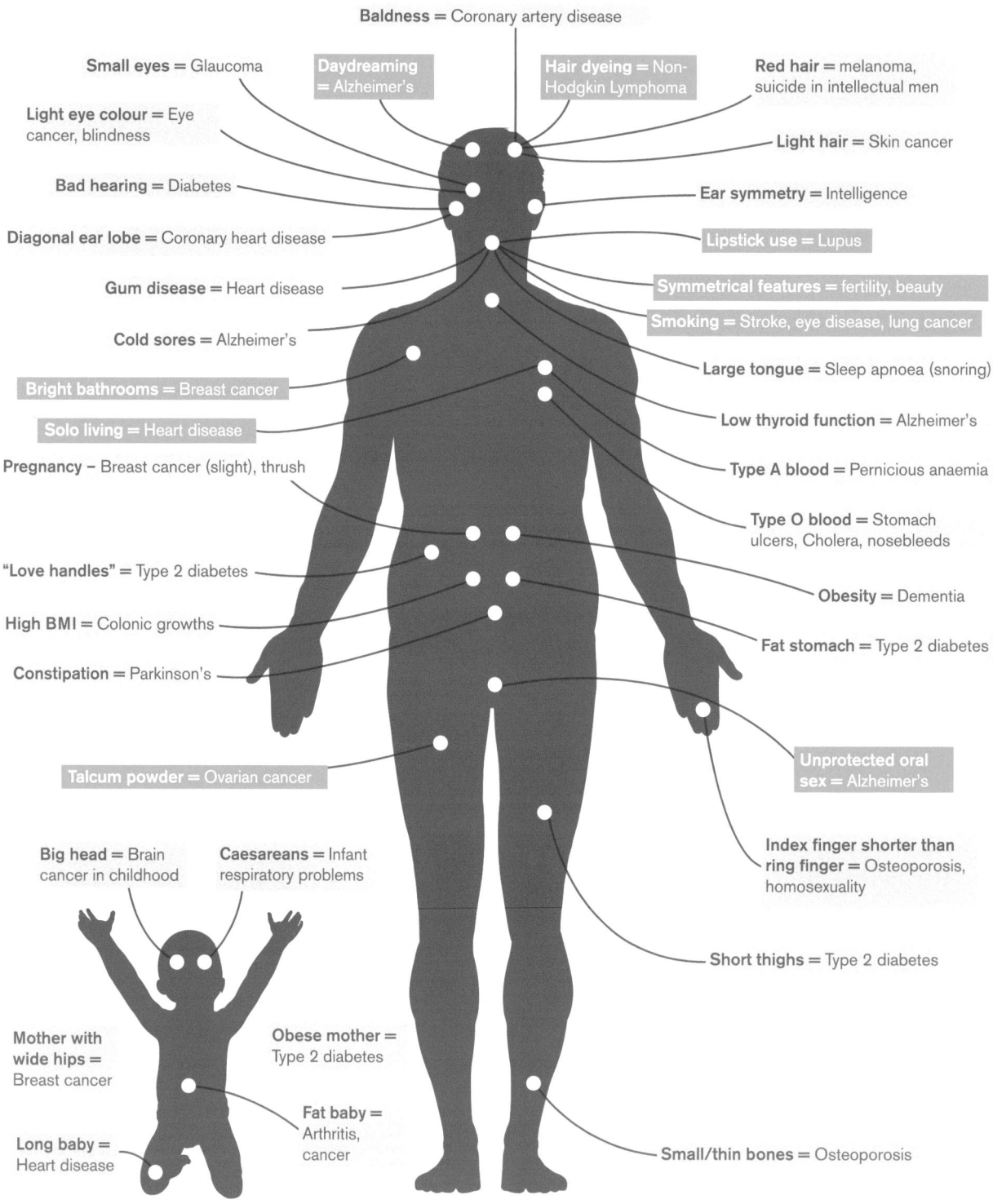

Or decrease the likelihood

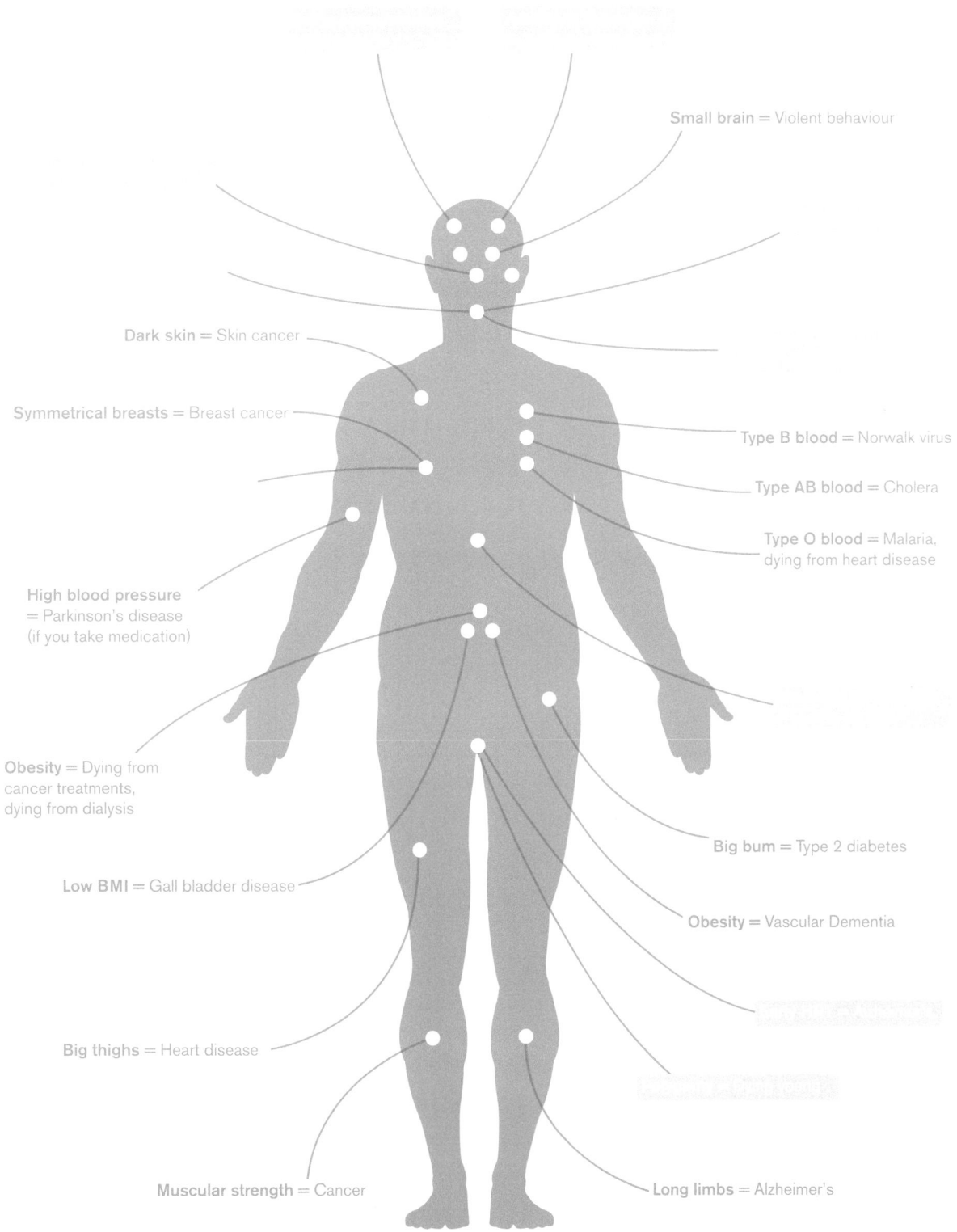

source: PubMed, Medscape.com, HealthDay, biomedicine.org, eupedia.com, Reuters, yale.edu, NHSdirect.nhs.uk

By Descent

Decreased risk – increased risk

African-American

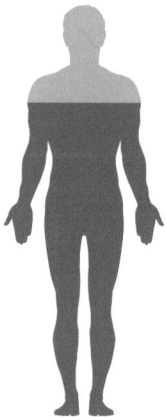

Skin cancer

Coeliac disease (wheat intolerance)

Head, neck and lung cancer

Obesity

Diabetes

Glaucoma

Hypertension

Alzheimer's

Sickle cell anaemia

European

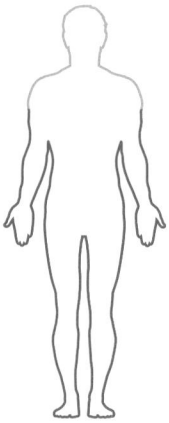

Premature birth

Osteoporosis

Lactose intolerance

Deep vein thrombosis

Heart disease

Type 2 diabetes

Dupuytren's disease

Skin cancer

MS

Asian

Skin cancer

Osteoporosis

Nosebleeds

TB

Type 2 diabetes

Heart disease

Jaundice

Wheat intolerance

Bone marrow cancer

By Gender

Decreased risk – increased risk

Female

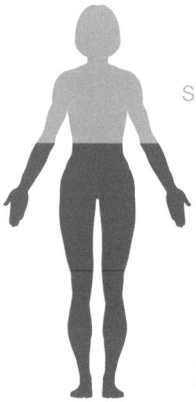

Lung cancer

Diabetes

Sickle cell anaemia

Stroke

Skin cancer

Rheumatoid arthritis

Obesity

Depression

Glaucoma

Coeliac disease

Alzheimer's

Male

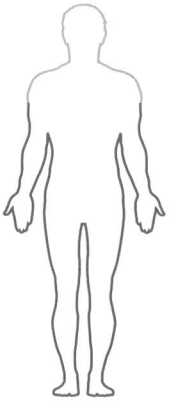

Multiple Sclerosis

Osteoporosis

Lactose intolerance

Dupuytren's disease — thickening of the tissues of the palm causing the fingers to bend inwards

Skin cancer

Deep vein thrombosis

Gout

Heart disease

Type 2 diabetes

source: PubMed, Medscape.com, HealthDay, biomedicine.org, eupedia.com, Reuters, yale.edu, NHSdirect.nhs.u

Body By

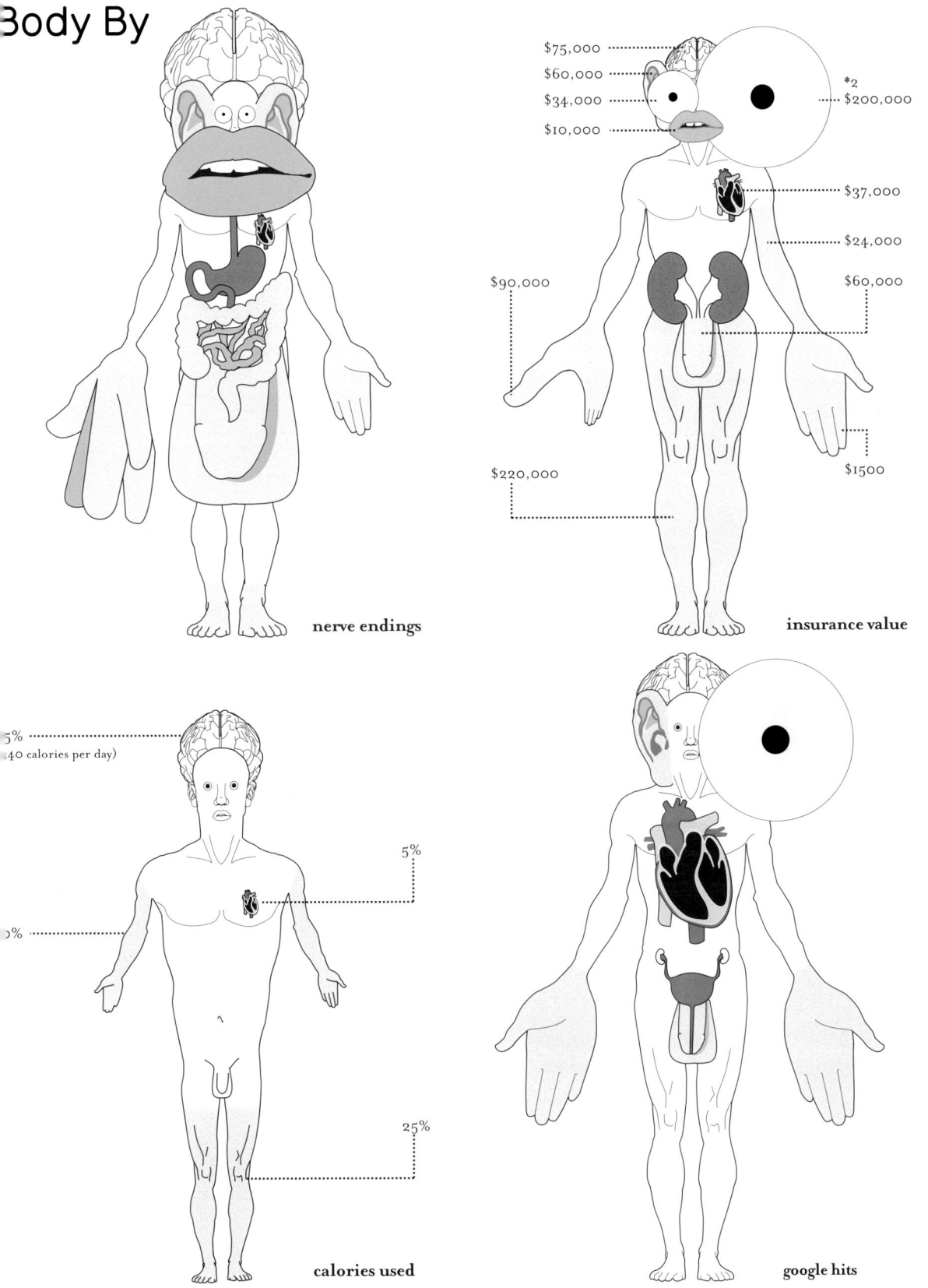

source: Google, Wikipedia

Microbes Most Dangerous

By survival time outside the body

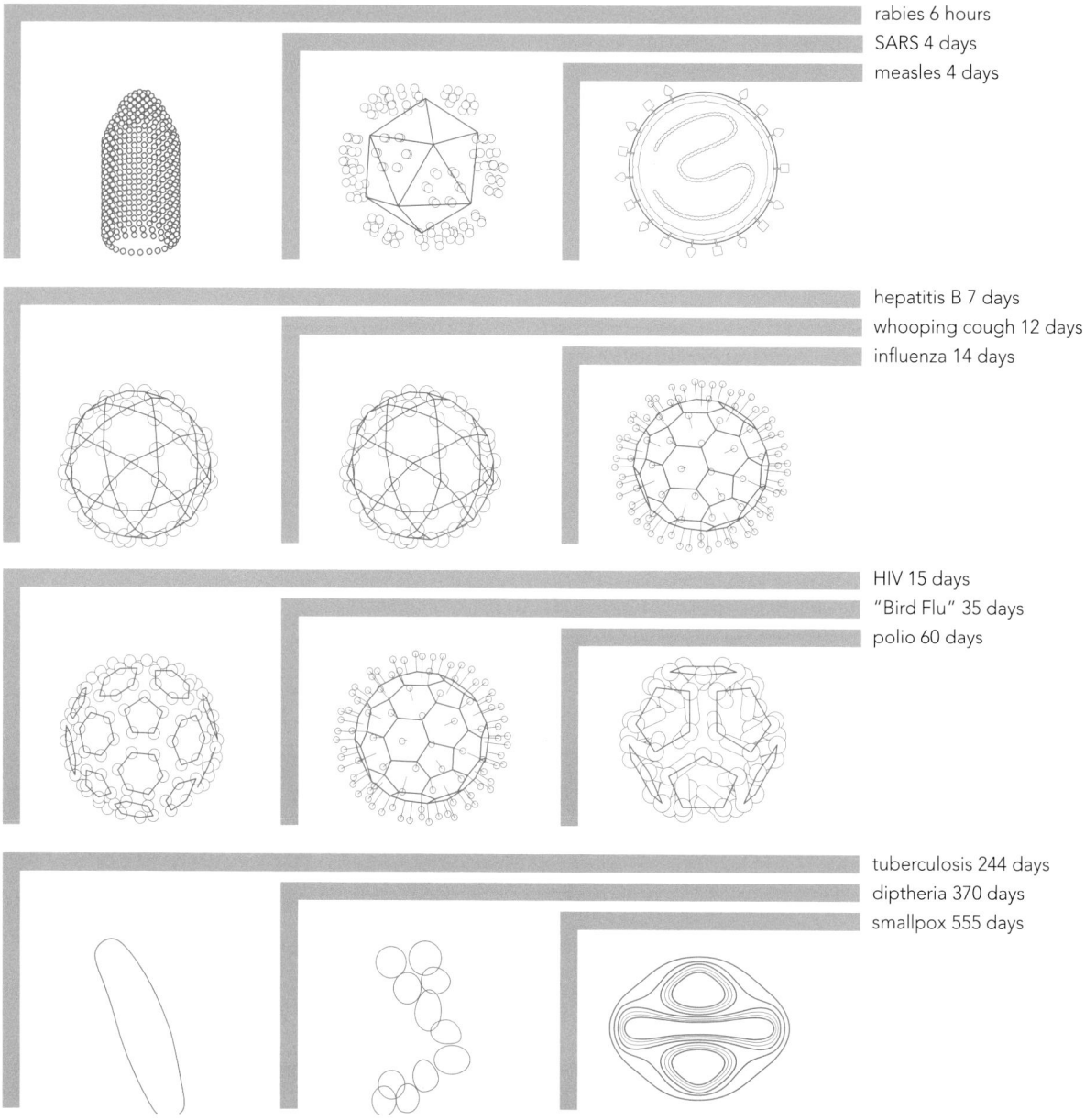

source: Centre For Disease Control & Prevention, NewScientist.com. Design inspired by Geig

Cosmetic Ingredients

Shampoo. Suntan lotion. Soap. Cleanser. Lipstick.

CHLORHEXIDINE DIGLUCONATE, 1,4-DIOXANE, ACETATE, ACETONE, ACETYLATED LANOLIN ALCOHOL, ACRYLATES COPOLYMER, ACRYLATES / OCTYLPROPENAMIDE COPOLYMER, ALCOHOL DENAT, ALCOHOL SD-40, ALGAE/SEAWEED EXTRACT, ALLANTOIN, ALPHA HYDROXY ACID, ALPHA LIPOIC ACID, ALPHA-ISOMETHYL IONONE, AMMONIUM LAURETH SULFATE, AMMONIUM LAURYL SULPHATE, ANGELICA ANTHOS FLAVOUR, JAPGOLDWORD, ARACHIDYL PROPIONATE, ASCORBIC ACID, ASCORBYL PALMITATE, BEESWAX, BENZALKONIUM CHLORIDE, BENZOIC ACID, BENZOYL PEROXIDE, BENZYL SALICYLATE, BETA HYDROXY ACID (SALICYLIC ACID), BORIC ACID, BUTYL METHOXYDIBENZOYLMETHANE, BUTYLATED HYDROXYANISOLE, BUTYLENE GLYCOL DICAPRYLATE/DICAPRATE, BUTYLPARABEN, BUTYLPHENYL METHYLPROPIONAL, C12-15 ALKYL BENZOATE, CAFFEINE, CAMPHOR, CARBOMERS (ESP. 940, 941, 934, 980, 981), CARICA PAPAYA (PAPAYA) EXTRACT, CARNAUBA WAX, CAVIAR (FISH EXTRACT), CELLULOSE, CERAMIDES, CETALKONIUM CHLORIDE, CETEARETH, CETEARYL ALCOHOL, CHAMOMILLA RECUTITA (CHAMOMILE), CL 14700 (E125), CL 191140 (YELLOW 5 ALUMINIUM LAKE), CITRONELLOL, COCAMIDE MEA, COCAMIDOPROPYL BETAINE, COLLAGEN, COUMARIN, CYCLIC HYDROXY ACID, CYCLOMETHICONE, D&C RED NO. 6 BARIUM LAKE, DIETHANOLAMINE (DEA), DIETHYLHEXYL BUTAMIDO TRIAZONE, DIEMETHICONE, DIOCTYL SODIUM SULFOSUCCINATE, DISODIUM COCOAMPHODIACETATE, DISODIUM LAURYL PHENYL ETHER DISULFONATE, DMDM HYDANTOIN, EDTA, ELASTIN, ELLAGIC ACID, ETHYL ALCOHOL (ETHANOL), ETHYLPARABEN, EUGENOL, FD&C YELLOW NO. 5 ALUMINUM LAKE, GLYCERIN, GLYCERYL STEARATE, GLYCIN, GLYCOGEN, GLYCOL STEARATE, GLYCOLIC ACID, GRAPE SEED EXTRACT, GREEN TEA EXTRACT (CAMELLIA SINENSIS), HEXYL CINNAMAL, HYALURONIC ACID, HYDROGEN PEROXIDE, HYDROLYZED COLLAGEN, HYDROQUINONE, HYDROXYLSOHEXYL 3-CYCLOHEXENE CARBOXALDEHYDE, ISOPROPYL ALCOHOL, ISOPROPYL ISOSTEARATE, ISOPROPYL IANOLATE, ISOPROPYL MYRISTATE, ISOPROPYL PALMITATE, ISOSTEARAMIDOPROPYL ETHYLDIMONIUM ETHOSULFATE, ISOSTEARIC ACID, KAOLINE (CHINA CLAY), KOJIC ACID, L-ERGOTHIONEINE, LACTIC ACID, LAMINARIA DIGITATA (HORSEHAIR KELP), LANOLIN, LECITHIN, LICORICE EXTRACT (BHT), LIGHT MINERAL OIL, LIMONENE, LINALOOL, LINOLEAMIDOPROPYL, LINOLEIC ACID, LYSINE, METHYLISOTHIAZOLINONE, METHYLPARABEN, MINERAL OIL, MYRISTYL MYRISTATE, MYRTRIMONIUM BROMIDE, OCTOCRYLENE, OCTYL METHOXYCINNAMATE, OCTYL PALMITATE, OCTYLDODECANOL, OLEYL ALCOHOL, OXYBENZONE (BENZOPHENONE-3), PABA (PARA-AMINOBENZOIC ACID), PADIMATE 0, PANTHENOL, PARABEN, PARAFFIN, PARFUM, PC-DIMONIUM CHLORIDE PHOSPHATE, PEG-40 CASTOR OIL, PETROLATUM, PHENOXYETHANOL, PHENYL TRIMETHICONE, PHENYLBENZIMIDAZOLE SULFONIC ACID, PHTHALATES, POLY HYDROXY ACID, POLYBUTENE, PROLINE, PROPYLENE GLYCOL, PROPYLPARABEN, QUATERNIUM-15, RESVERATROL, RETINOL (ALSO VITAMIN A), RETINYL PALMITATE, RETINAL PALMITATE POLYPEPTIDE, ROSE HIPS, SALYCYLIC ACID, SILICONE (DIMETHYL SILICONE), SILICA, SILK POWDER, SILK PROTEINS, SODIUM ACRYLATES/C10-30 ALKYL ACRYLATE CROSSPOLYMER, SODIUM BICARBONATE, SODIUM BORATE, SODIUM CETEARYL SULFATE, SODIUM CHLORIDE, SODIUM FLUORIDE, SODIUM HYALURONATE, SODIUM LAUREL SULFATE, SODIUM LAURETH SULFATE, SODIUM LAURYL SULFATE, SODIUM METHACRYLATE, SORBIC ACID, SORBITOL (MINERAL OIL), STEARIC ACID, SULFUR, TALC, TAPIOCA STARCH, TARTARIC ACID, TITANIUM DIOXIDE, TOCOPHERYL ACETATE, TRICLOSAN, TRIDECETH-12, TRIMETHOXYCAPRYLYLSILANE, TRISODIUM EDTA, TYROSINE, VITAMIN A (RETINOL), VITAMIN B, VITAMIN C (CITRIC ACID), VITAMIN D, VITAMIN E (TOCOPHEROL), WATER, WHITE PETROLATUM, WHITE WAX, XANTHAN GUM

GOOD FINE OKAY NASTY TOXIC DEADLY

source: CosmeticDatabase.com, Environmental Working Group

Things That'll Give You Cancer

Source: the media

abortio
acrylamid
agent orang
Nut mould. Nasty. — alcohol aldrin alfatoxir
asphalt fumes atrazin
meat benzene benzadin
High doses in smokers linked to lung cancer — betacarotene betel nuts birth
bread breasts bus stations cadmiun
Fungicide — captan carbon tetrachloride career
Vinyl acetate in gum — foods chewing gum Chinese food Chinese herb
chlordane chlorinated camphen
chloroform cholesterol chromium coalta
curry cyclamates dairy products DDT deodorants deple
diesel exhaust diet soda dimethylsulphat
Safe — epichlorhydrin ethilenedibromide ethnic belie
Lack of real contact alters our biology apparently — facebook fat fibre fluoridation flying formaldehyc
gingerbread global warming gluteraldehyde granite grille
supplements heliobacter pylori hepatitis B
In poorly ventilated spaces — bone mass HRT hydrazine hydrogen peroxide incens
Higher risk of breast cancer — laxatives lead left-handedness Lindane Listerine lov
Minimal risk — mammograms manganese menopause methylbromid
No link. Now proven. — mixed spices mobile phones moisturizers mould MTB
breast feeding not having a twin nuclear power
Contains carcinogens — juice oxygenated gasoline oyster sauce ozo
When mouldy — PCBs peanuts pesticides pet birds plast
Itís the creosote. Donít lick. — PVC radio masts radon railway sleeper
sausage dye selenium semi conductor plant
soy sauce statins stress strontium styren
sunscreen talc testosterone tetrachloroethyle
Probably okay — tooth fillings toothpaste tooth whitenin
underarm-shaving unvented stove
vegetables vinyl bromid
vitamins vitreous fibres wallpap
well water wifi win
x-rays

no risk maybe a risk **definite risk**

crylonitril

r pollution alar — Pesticide & fruit spray

rsenic **asbestos**

ZT babyfood **barbecued**

enzopyrene **beryllium**

ontrol pills bottled water bracken — Only if contaminated

alcium channel blockers cannabis — Linked to testicular cancer but also has anti-tumour effects

r women car fumes casual sex celery **charred**

oplements chinese medicine chips chloramphenicol — Antibiotic

hlorinated water **chlorodiphenyl**

fee **coke ovens** cooked foods crackers creosote — May help combat cancer

nium depression **dichloryacetylene dieldrin**

nitrotouluene **dioxane** **dioxin** dogs — unproven links to breast cancer

hyleacrilate ethylene **ethylenedichloride** Ex-Lax

ee radicals french fries fruit frying **gasoline** genes

eat **Gulf war** **hair dye** hamburgers health — Linked to many cancers

rus hexachlorbutadiene hexachlorethane high

fertility jewellery **Kepone** **kissing** lack of exercise — Kissing disease (infectious mononucleosis)

holesterol low fibre diet magnetic fields **malonaldehyde**

ethylenechloride microwave ovens milk hormones

ckel night lighting **nightshifts** **nitrates not** — Probable cause of cancer

ants Nutrasweet **oestrogen** olestra olive oil orange

zone depletion papaya **passive smoking**

bags polio vaccine power lines proteins Prozac

dmeat Roundup saccharin salmon salt sausage — Most red meat linked to bowel cancer

having shellfish sick buildings smoked fish — Air quality

lphuric acid **sunbeds** **sunlight**

ght bras toast toasters **tobacco**

n stations **trichloroethylene** tritium

anium **UV radiation**

nyl chloride vinyl toys

ight gain welding fumes

ter **wood dust** work

source: UK and US media reports [via numberwatch.co.uk], Wikipedia

Types of Coffee

Espresso
[ess-press-oh]

Espresso Macchiato
[ess-press-oh mah-ke-ah-toe]

Espresso con Par
[ess-press-oh kon pawn-

Caffé Latte
[caf-ay lah-tey]

Flat White
[Fla-te-why-te]

Caffé Breve
[caf-ay brev-ay]

Cappuccino
[kap-oo-chee-noh]

Caffé Mocha
[caf-ay moh-kuh]

Americano
[uh-mer-i-kan-oh]

Caffeine content

Freddo
[fred-oh]

Marocchino
[mar-oh-cheen-oh]

Stretto
[stret-toh]

Ristretto
[wrist-tret-oh]

Irish
[eye-rish]

Granita con Panna
[gran-ee-ta-kon-pan-na]

Corretto
[kor-ret-oh]

Con Leche
[kon-letch-eh]

Crappa
[krap-aaahhh!]

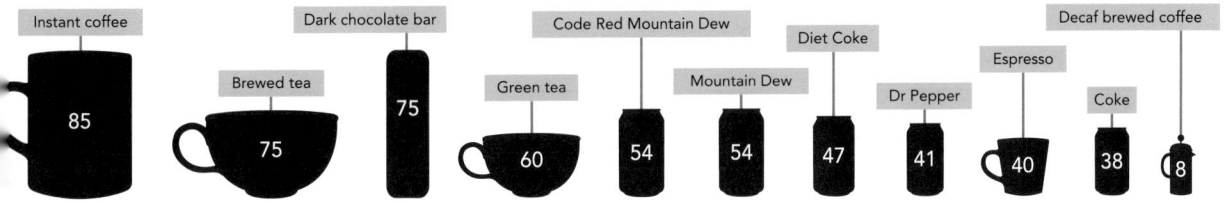

idea: Lokesh Dhakar @ lokeshdhakar.com

Tons of Carbon

Emissions per year

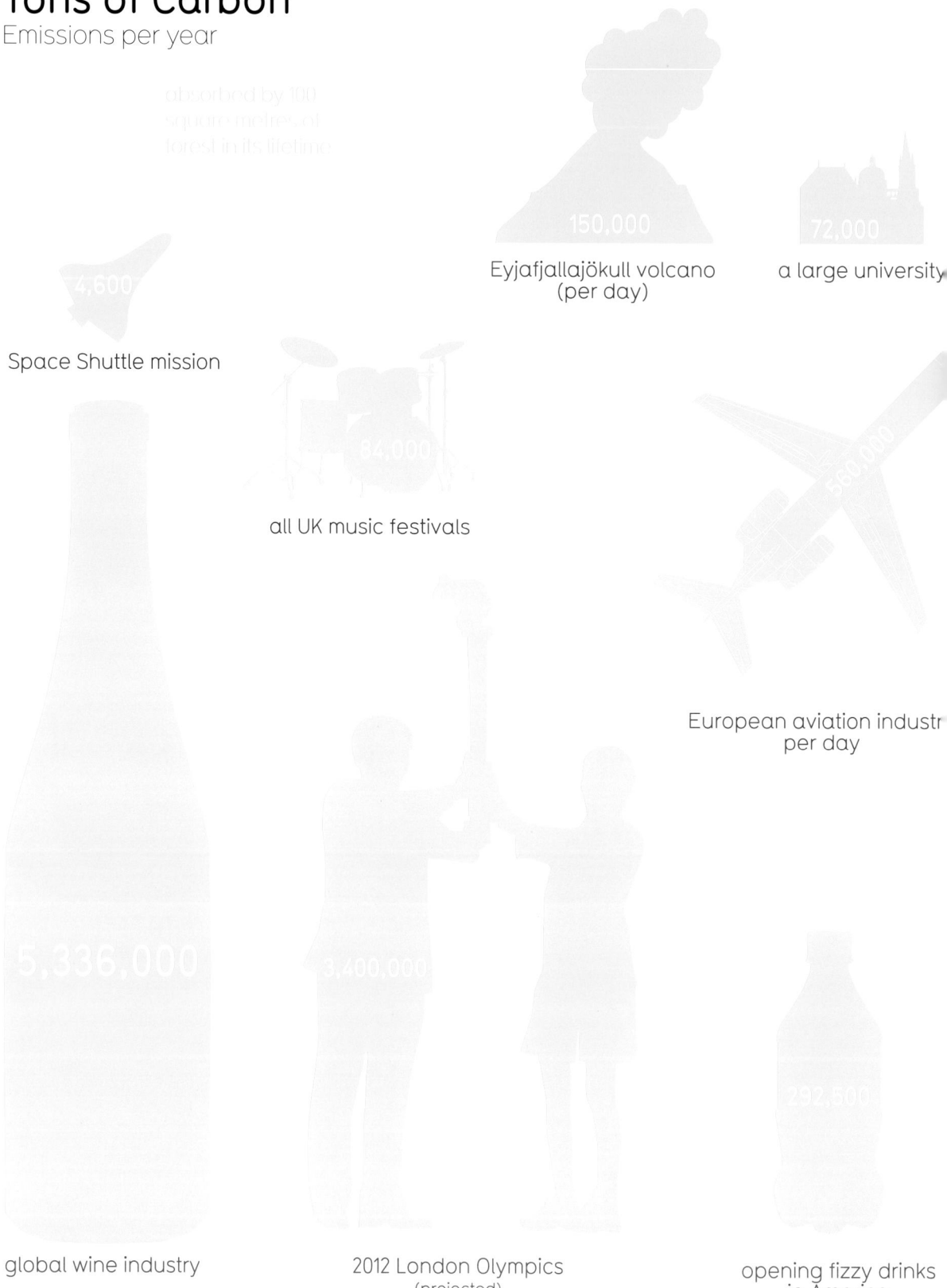

Megatons of Carbon

Emissions per year

all measurements in tons

Articles of War

Most edited Wikipedia pages

Technicality · Political · Ethics · Ethnic Feuds · American Cultural Superiority · Religion · Culture War · Animal Rights · Star Wars

Page
Key battle or dispute
Total no. of page edits

page creation date
2001

The Beatles

Should they be listed in "traditional" order or alphabetically? And is it "The Beatles" or "the Beatles"?

17,608 edits

Cat

"Owner", "caregiver", or "human companion"? Which words describe the correct relationship between man and beast:

10,996

Jesus

A very long dispute over whether to use B.C. or A.D. Jesus!

21,864

Alumin(i)um

MASSIVE fight

5,462

Sulfur or Sulphur?

3,950

Death Star

120km or 160km in diameter?

1,856

Brazil or Brasil?

11,751

Cow Tipping

Appropriate to include a picture of a cow with the caption "An unsuspecting potential victim"?

2,155

Fossil fuel for reciprocating piston engines equipped with spark plugs

Should this substance be called "gasoline" or "petrol"? *2,927*

André the Giant

How tall was he? 7'4"? 6'10"? Was his height even consistent?

3,766

J. K. Rowling

Pronounced "rolling" or does it rhyme with "howling"?

5,950

Wikipedia

Is Jimmy Wales the founder or a co-founder with Larry Sanger?

29,041

Christianity

An argument about syntax in a sentence regarding the Church's historical definition of orthodoxy and heresy.

15,647

Nikola Tesla

Born of Serbian parents in Austrian Empire, which became a part of the Hungarian half of Austria-Hungary and is now in Croatia. Category nightmare!

7,449

Anus

Should article use an image of a human anus? If so, male or female? Hairless or "moderately hairy"?

2000

As there was no year zero, the millennium we are currently in

Feces

Should this page include a picture of a

Tiger

The "most powerful living cat"?

5,303

Potato chip

Flavored or

Arachnophobia

Appropriate to include a huge picture of a tarantula on a page about fear of spiders?

640

Freddie Mercury

Of Iranian, Indian, Parsi or Azeri ancestry?

11,439

Iron Maiden

Which is more famous – the band or the torture device?

9,388

Kiev, capital of Ukraine

Kiev (Russian) or Kyiv (Ukranian)? Edit war involved both Russian and Ukrainian governments.

3,026

User: Jimbo Wales

A war over the background colour of various parts of the user page.

8,721

Hummus

Should hummus be in the "Israeli cuisine" category, or is it a purely Arab food the Zionists have illegally occupied?

2,076

Limp Bizkit

Are the band "nu metal/rapcore" or "rapcore/nu metal"?

6,372

Star Wars

Are Anakin Skywalker and Darth Vader the same character? What order should the films appear in? Should actors from the Special Editions be credited?

12,869

U2

Are Bono's harmonica skills relevant in an encyclopedia entry?

10,367

Jennifer Aniston

American or American-born? Greek American? English-American?

6,536

John Logie Baird

Can you be both Scottish and British?

1,122

Mayonnaise

Does traditional Mayonnaise contain lemon juice or not?

1,984

source: Wikipedia

Articles of War

Most edited Wikipedia pages

Technicality · Political · Ethics · Ethnic Feuds · American Cultural Superiority · Religion · Culture War · Animal Rights · Star Wars

Page
Key battle or dispute
Total no. of page edits

page creation date
2003

Futurama
Was protagonist Fry cryonically frozen or crygenically frozen (or even cryogenically frozen)?
8,731

Grey/Gray Squirrel
Slow and remorseless edit war over this spelling.
1,124

Palin
Is the politician more famous than the Monty Python member?
289

John Kerry
Was his Purple Heart awarded for a "wound" or a "minor wound"? Was it "bandaged" or just "wrapped with gauze"?
12,629

Silent Hill 3
What is the last name of the video game's protagonist?
3,095

Ann Coulter
Was the right-wing US commentator born in 1961 or 1963?
10,790

Preteen
Are they 8–12 years old? 9–12? 10–12? 8–13? Even 17 years old?
544

Jimmy Wales
The Wikipedia founder edited his own birthdate
8,628

Yoghurt or Yogurt?
One of the biggest and longest-running Wikipedia edit wars. Seriously.
3,135

Grace Kelly and Cher

Gay icons?

2,282

Money (Pink Floyd song)

What exactly is this song's time signature? 7/8, 7/4 or even 21/8?

573

character articles

Drawn-out edit wars over the correct heights and weights of fictional characters

2,147

2006 Atlantic Hurricane Season

Tropical Storm Zeta formed on 30 December, 2005 and lasted until 6 January, 2006. Which hurricane season does this count as?

3,254

Cute

Is it NPOV (Neutral Point of View) to say an animal is "cute"?

21

House MD

Should we mention the show's lack of Asian diversity?

8,423

Pwned

What does this piece of geek slang actually mean? Who invented it? How do you pronounce it?

26

Wii

"Wii", "Nintendo Wii" or "the Wii"? Should "wee" link here or to the article on urine?

20,077

US Election 2008

Is Stephen Colbert considered a serious candidate? If so, was it Stephen Colbert (comedian) or Stephen Colbert (character)?

14,957

Angels & Airwaves is/are a band

British English requires "are" as the band comprises multiple people. American English requires "is", as the band is a singular entity. FIGHT!

8,055

Clover (Creature)

Cloverfield, Clover, The Cloverfield creature, or Clover (creature)?

1,654

Compact Disc

Is a tradename and so should be capitalized. HOWEVER the logo says "Compact disc".

3,888

Sega Genesis & Sega Mega Drive

What's the proper name for the article when both names are used? Surely something can't be two things at the same time? An eight-month debate.

3,670

Pregnancy

The picture of a nude pregnant women in this article provoked an enormous debate – and even the intervention of Wikipedia founder, Jimmy Wales.

5,671

source: Wikipedia

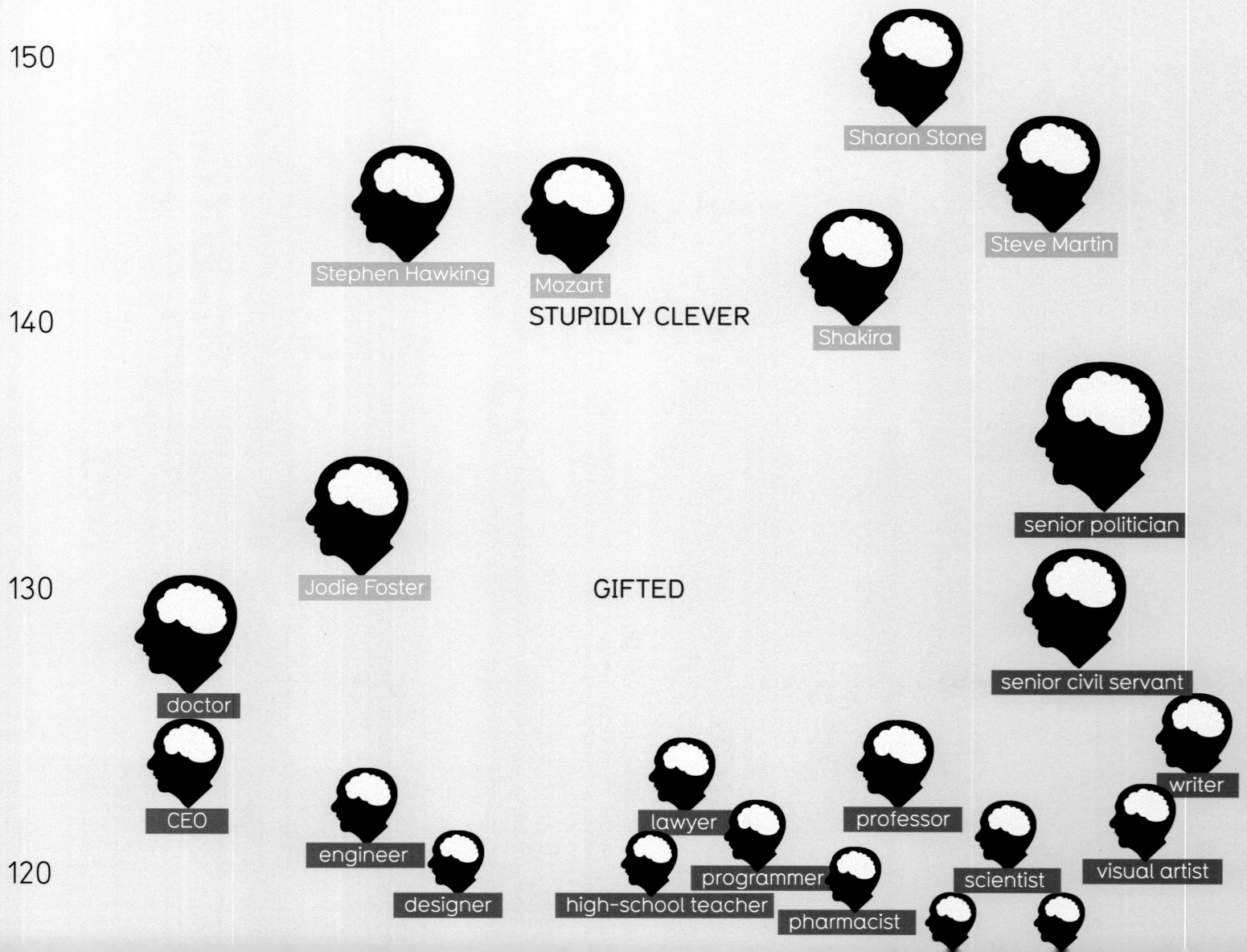
150
140
130
120
Sharon Stone
Steve Martin
Stephen Hawking
Mozart
STUPIDLY CLEVER
Shakira
senior politician
Jodie Foster
GIFTED
senior civil servant
doctor
writer
CEO
lawyer
professor
engineer
programmer
scientist
visual artist
designer
high-school teacher
pharmacist

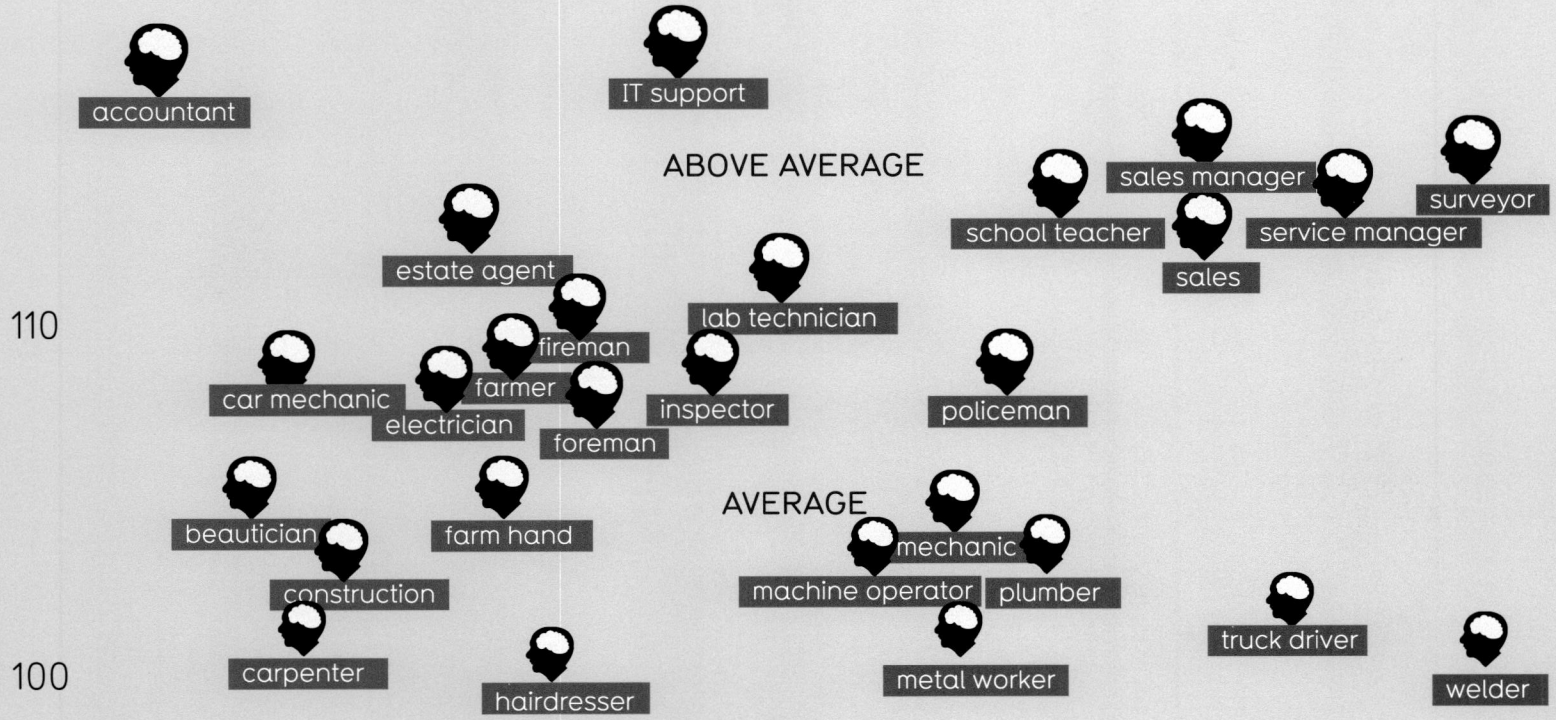

Who Clever are You?

Average IQs of different callings

source: University of Wisconsin Henmon–Nelson IQ Distributions 1992–94 via Hauser, Robert M (2002)

The Buzz vs The Bulge

Caffeine vs Calories

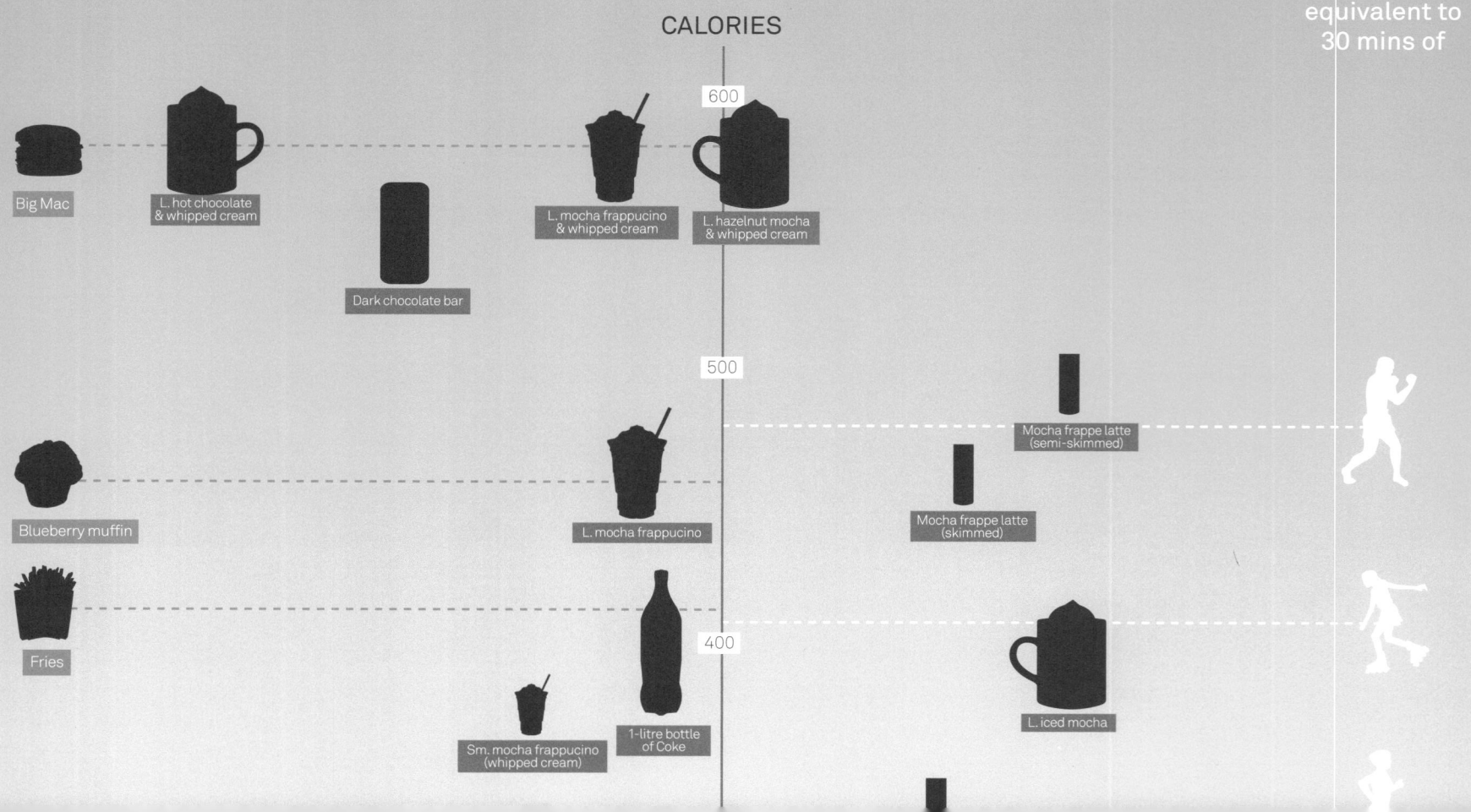

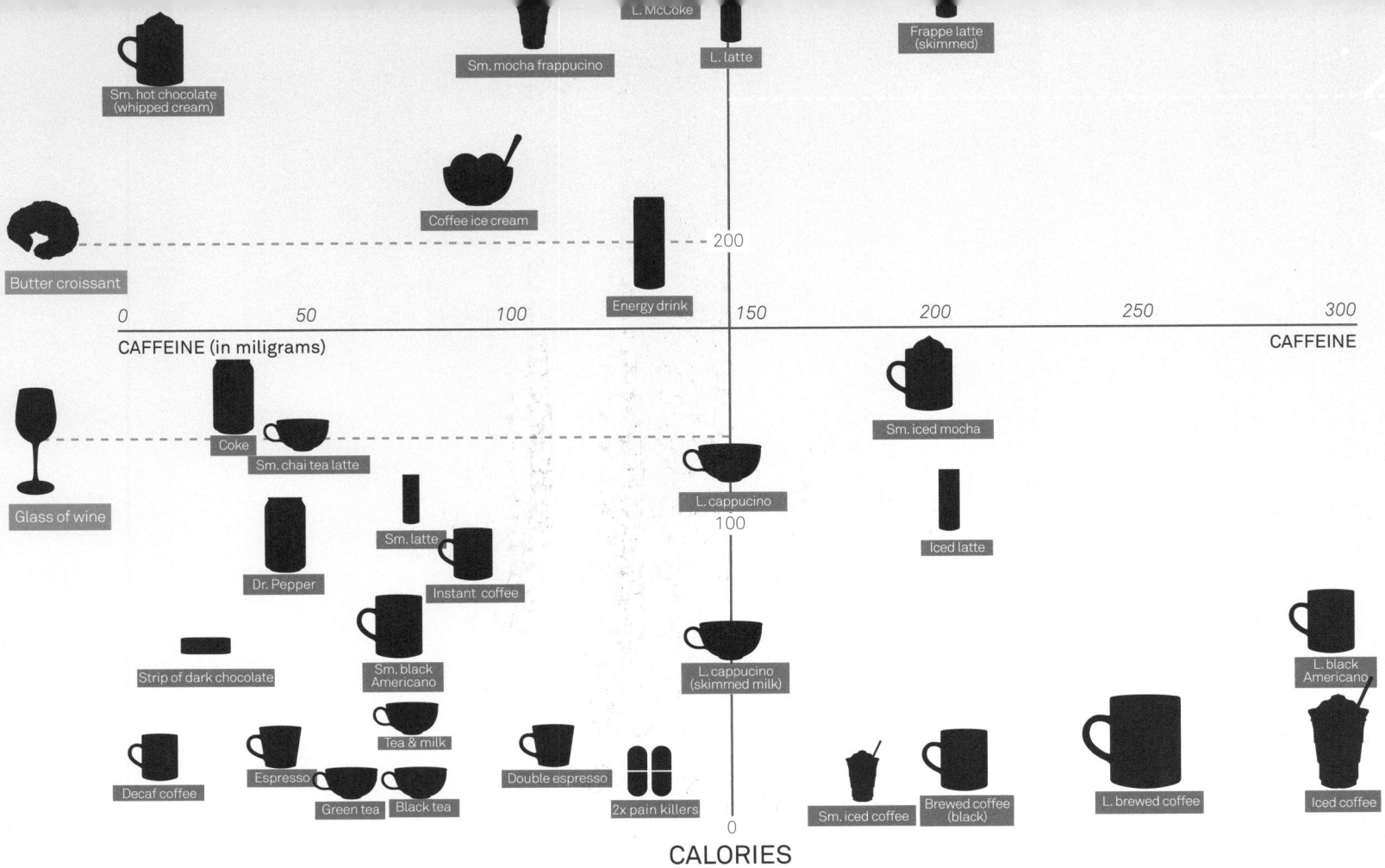

Source: Guardian Data Store, Starbucks.co.uk, Calorie-Counter.com

Daily Diets

How do they stack up?

	MORNING	AFTERNOON
ATKINS	omelette, tomato	salmon, salad
LOW G.I.	porridge, skim milk, oj	carrot & barley soup
WEIGHT WATCHERS	porridge & raisins, brown sugar	small burger, salad, apple
ZONE	grapes, rye toast, fruit, peanut butter	
CABBAGE SOUP	fruit	cabbage soup
DETOX	oats, yoghurt, fruit	tzatziki, veg crudités
JUICE DIET	carrot & apple	carrot & veg juice
CALORIE COUNTING	4 tbsp branflakes, skim milk, apple	mozzarella, tomato & avocado salad, french bread
MEDITERRANEAN	toast, yoghurt, blueberries, almonds	chickpea salad
WEIGHT GAIN	6 x cream cheese bagels, yoghurt, oj	pitta bread, tuna, lentil soup, apple juice
SUNLIGHT	sunlight	sunlight
SCARSDALE	grapefruit, toast, black coffee	assorted cold cuts, stewed tomatoes

EVENING				SNACKAGE		WATER
grilled chicken			veg	chocolate shake	granola bar	x 8
wholewheat pasta bake				yoghurt	raspberries	x 8
tuna steak	olive sauce	assorted veg	french bread	fat-free yoghurt		x 8
grapes	rye bread	olive oil	peanut butter			x 8
cabbage soup				fruit		x 8
potato & bean casserole				yoghurt	fruit	x 8
veg juice						x 8
roast pork				hummus	cruditès	x 8
spinach frittata				hummus	crisp bread	x 8
spaghetti	salami	bread	milk	bread & jam	ice cream	x 8
vitamin D				oxygen		x 8
shellfish	salad		veg	hummus		x 8

Calories In
Average load

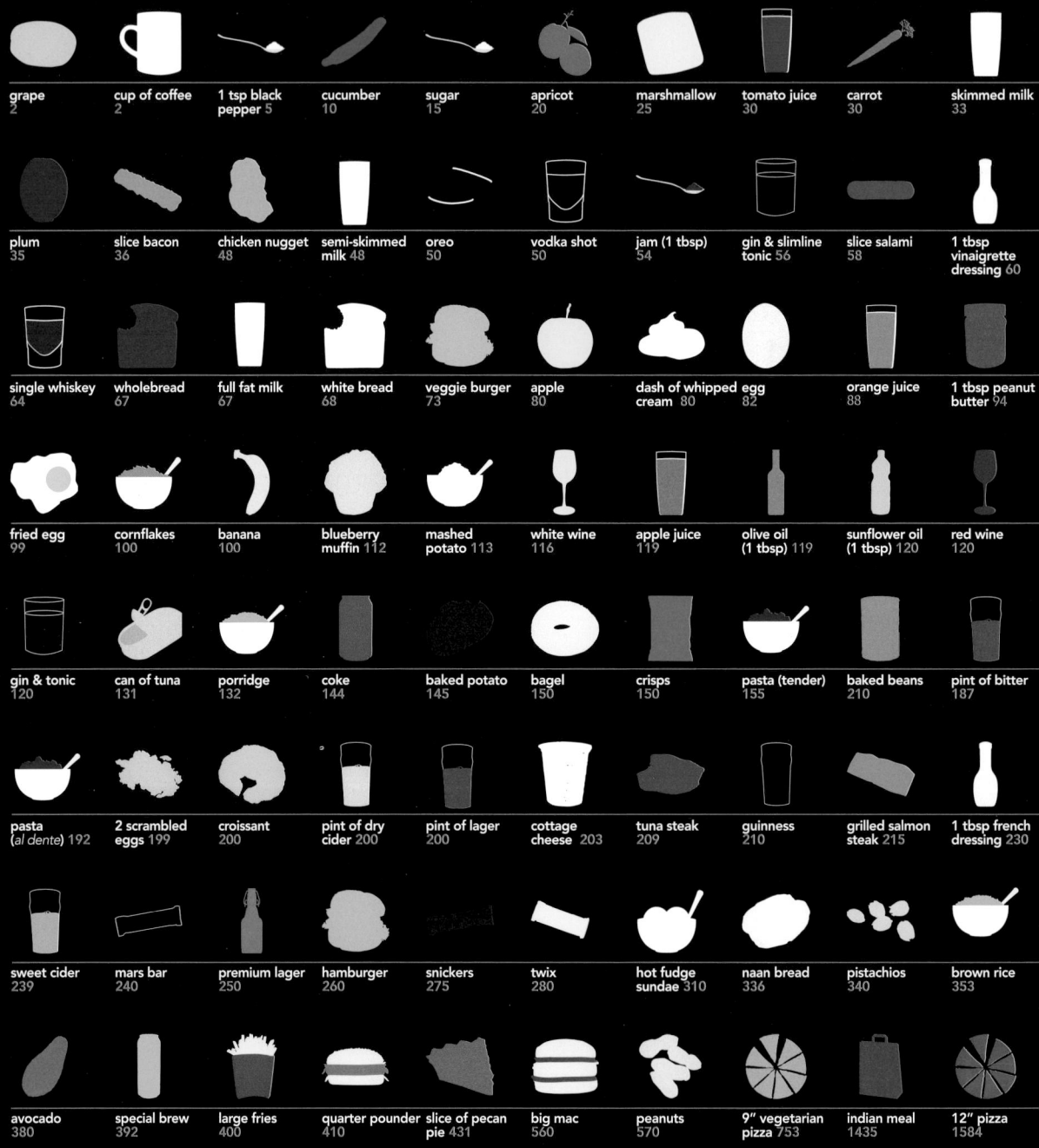

Calories Out

Average burn for 30 minutes of...

source: cross-referenced from various dieting websites

Types of Facial Hair

A little hair says a lot about a man

Major
Al-Assad, Hafez
Syria (ruled 1971-2000)
Killed: 25,000

Traditional
Al-Bashir, Omar
Sudan (1989-)
Killed: 400,000

Painter's Brush
Kai-Shek, Chiang
China (1928-31)
Killed: 30,000

Pyramid
Franco, Francisco
Spain (1939-75)
Killed: 30,000

Freestyle
King Abdullah
Saudi Arabia (2005-)
Killed: -

Chevron
Lenin, Vladimir Ilyich
Russia (1917-24)
Killed: 30,000

Handlebar
Stalin, Joseph
Soviet Union (1924-53)
Killed: 23,000,000

Natural Full
Castro, Fidel
Cuba (1976-2008)
Killed: 30,000

Horseshoe
Habre, Hissene
Chad (1982-90)
Killed: 40,000

Toothbrush
Hitler, Adolf
Germany (1933-45)
Killed: 58,000,000

Walrus
Hussein, Saddam
Iraq (1979-2003)
Killed: 6,000,000

Zappa
Mengitsu, Haile Maiam
Ethiopa (1987-91)
Killed: 150,000

Fu Manchu
Temujin, Genghis Khan
Mongolia (1205-27)
Killed: millions

Nu Geek
McCandless
UK (1971)
Killed: 0

source: Wikipedia and general web

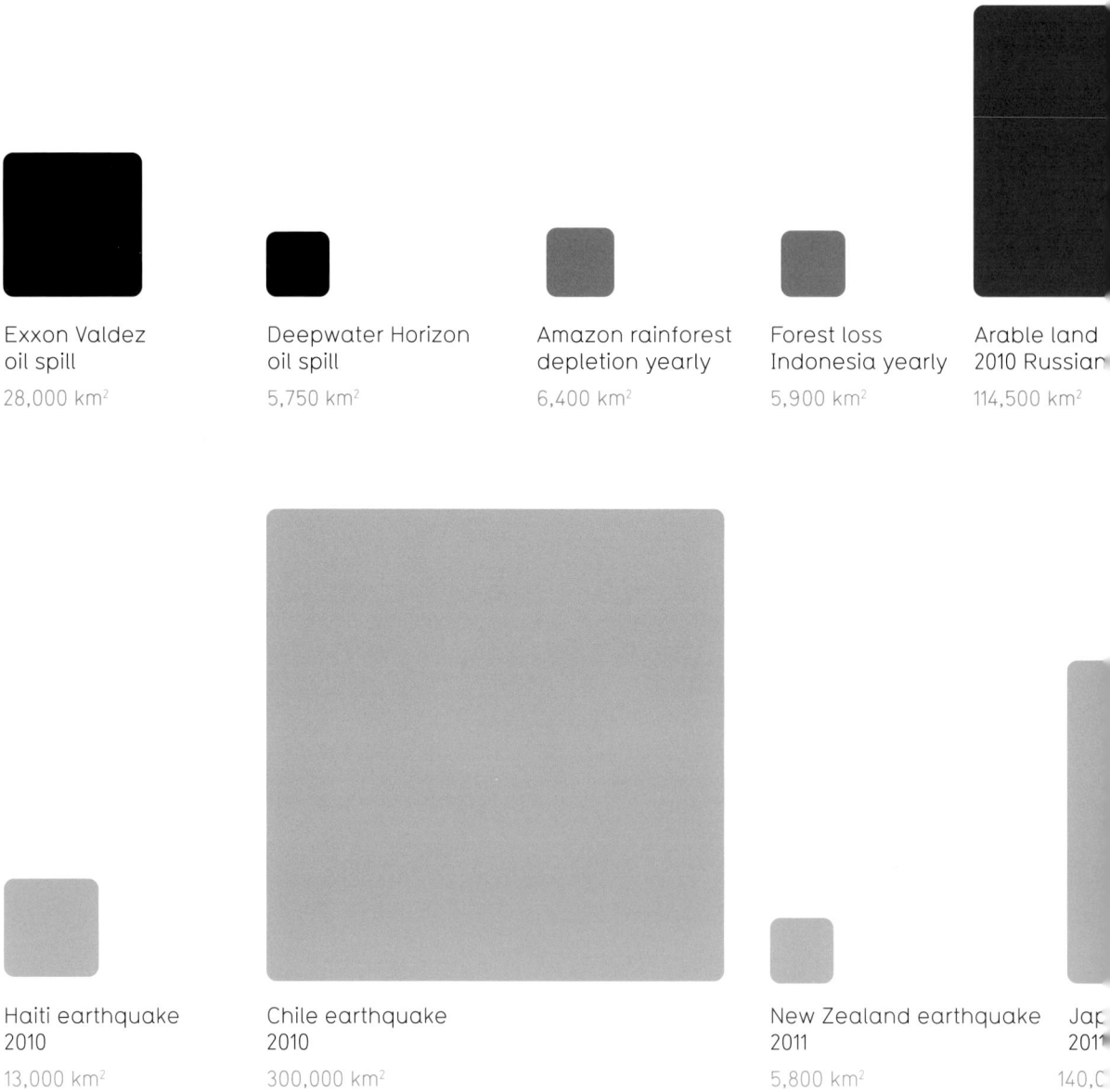

Scale of Devastation

Square kilometres

Wildfires during 2010
Russian heat wave

8,800 km²

Chernobyl
exclusion zone

1,300 km²

United Kingdom surface area

242,000 km²

kistan floods 2010

500 km²

Australia floods 2010

850,000 km²

Sources: USGS, ScienceDirect, Wikipedia

Amphibian Extinction Rates

Canaries in a coal mine?

Normal rate

1x

1990

200x

Chrytid fungus

Habitat Loss

UV-Radiation

Insecticides

In the 1930s, the African clawed frog was popular as a pregnancy test. Doctors would inject a female frog with a woman's urine. If the frog laid any eggs, the woman was pregnant. Alas the frog was also an immune carrier of the deadly chytrid fungus. Escaped frogs gradually spread the fungus around the world.

Even a tiny amount of malathion, the most common insecticide in the US, can lead to a devastating chain reaction that destroys bottom-dwelling algae, the primary food of tadpoles. Malathion, together with the pesticide Atrazine, are considered key factors in the loss of entire populations of amphibians.

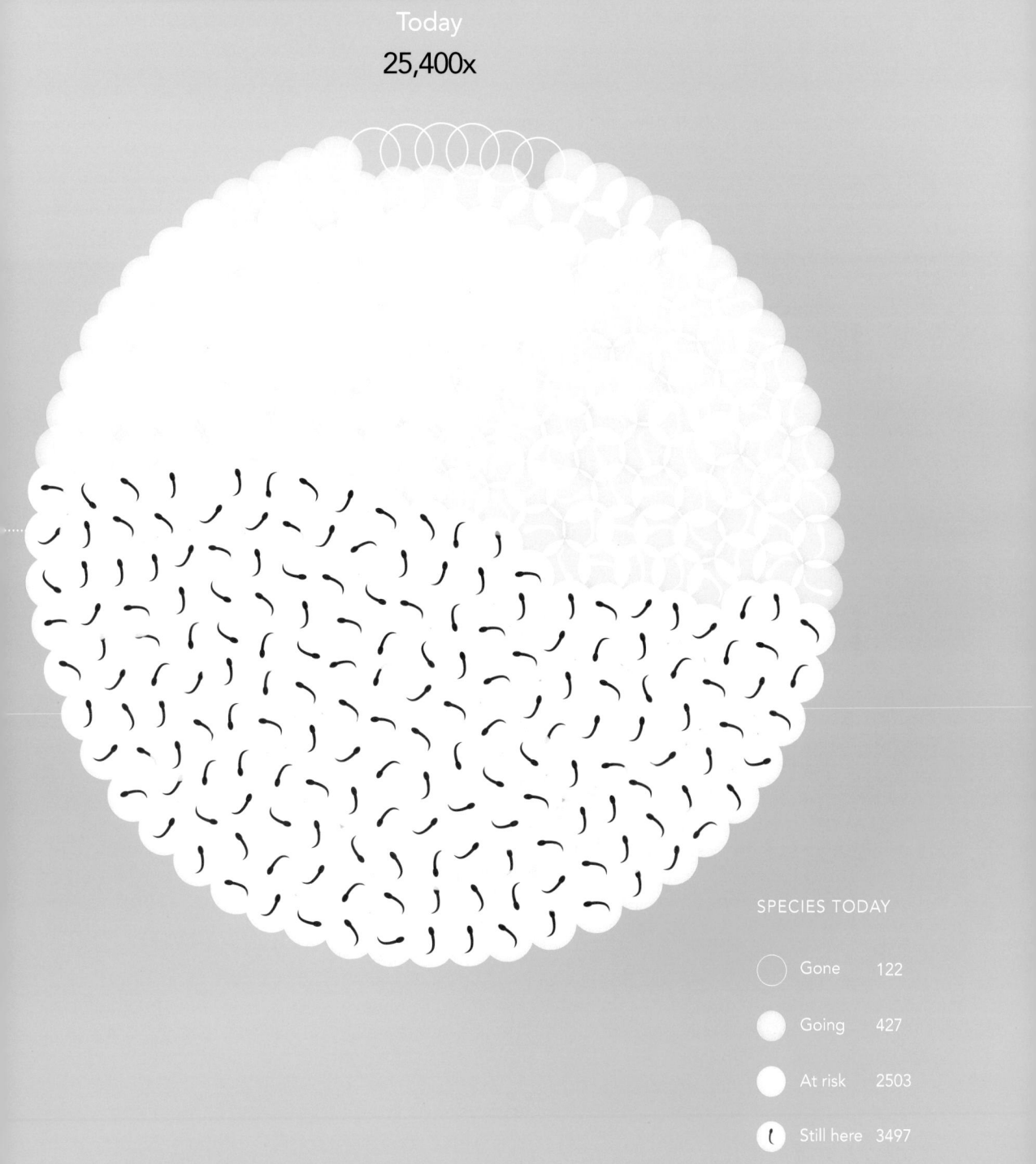

source: National Academy of Sciences, Discovery.com

Motive

Searches for the phrase "we broke up because..."

he couldn't keep his hands to himself "we're at different stages in our lives" she was cheating wit
women he wanted to experience the whole college thing he said he needed space he's a complet
idiot with **I don't clip my toenails enough** I was cheating on him so he made-ou
the guy I was cheating on him with c
Drugs of Def Jam of her partying ways his parents don't like me his girlfriend got suspicious he
husband needs oral sex I didn't love her i too much control him of all of the time he spent on his attempt
to break into film-making we had different life goals of religious reasons – he refused to worship me c
my drinking – I binge drink he has a small pee-pee and wouldn't buy me any jewellery I smothered he
we didn't have anything in common and everything was completely physical of parental disapproval
he pressured me into having sex **she just realized I'm a better friend**
I have a high-pitched voice!
I wasn't comfortable telling her who I really am we fell out of love he couldn't keep his hands to himse
he is traumatized by his former relationship and can't reach his feelings for anything or anyone. We
well, my family has money i moved. i want him back more than i can say I basically caught him in bed
with one of his co-workers he liked another guy. Yes, a guy he was short and kind of looked like a gian
mole that stood upright of one of those arguments she was way too hurt by my lack of effort to ca
her I "bug" him I was overprotective? he lied too much & went crazy & punched a hole in the wall h
made out with my friend i realized me being insecure due to the hurtful past experiences, was not goin
to enable us to take our **he doesn't have "love" for me** relationship to the nex
level he said i wasnt treating him right. an
i wasnt of time and dist. I was a complete arsehole to her of this election i asked "are we ok?
caused she seemed a little weird lately and she said next time you ask that again we are thru we fough
a lot and several red flags kept showing up I felt that he deserved better than me. I needed help. I hav
abandonment, insecurity, and anxiety issues she wants to find herself as an individual she likes to dea
with her problems alone and not to really share them he thinks his career won't match up to mine
realized that I had been gradually developing strong feelings for one of her close friends He belonge
to a different religion and wanted me to convert not because I got somebody pregnant she hurt m
on Valentines night we love each other? we had never been with anyone else and we felt it was to
serious for our age **of artistic differences** We Were On A Break And I Starte
To Treat Him Bad i lied about my age I can't make hir
stay with me He's in love with his mother I'm "immature" & like to party too much..... ummm hello I'r
twenty-one!!!! I couldn't have a tree she didn't want to change her FB status of the stock market I'r
passive I wouldn't submit to his views on what a wife should be we couldn't agree on a sex positio
together he only saw me as a weekend fling he has a fatal flaw, as caring, romantic, and intuitive as h
is, he has a horrid temper... I felt that he wasn't present in the relationship. I felt alone while seeing hir
he was gay I feel that I hurt her too much and I feel she deserves better i told simple lie
(small lies that i didnt have to tell) im too **he told people I was crazy**
"clingy" he cheated on me twice and
it was a year ago I was jealous that he swiped her ass with her credit card, and not mine sh
was too flirty she just realized I'm a better friend. he always ignored me and got mad over an
little thing. He was extremely jealous he messed around with my worse enemy the sex wa
bad his fear of commitment?!? he is not financially stable I am dangerous no reaso

source: searches for "we broke up because..." on Facebook, Twitter & Google. Apologies for heterosexual bi

Timing

Most common break-up times, according to Facebook status updates

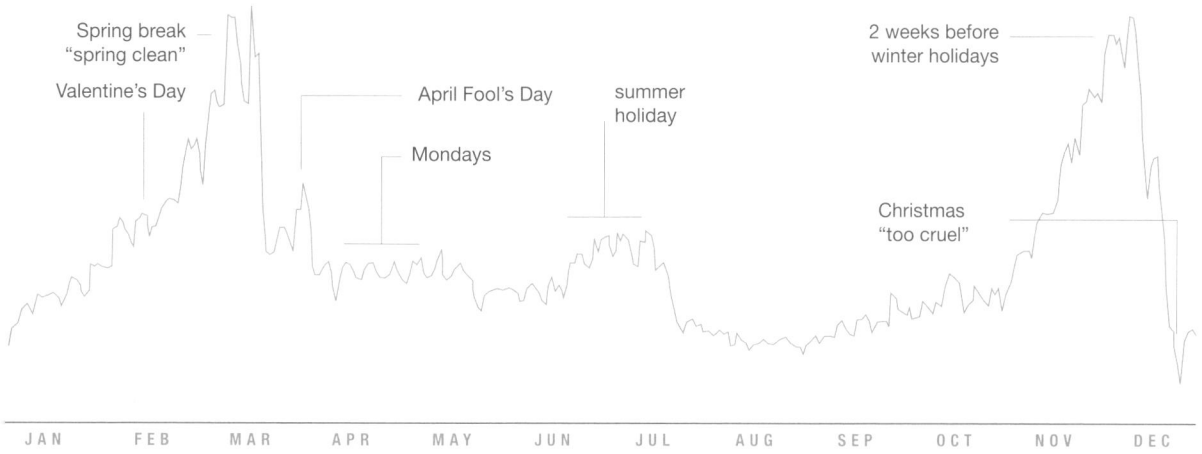

source: Facebook lexicon

Delivery

Most common methods of break-up

Those born before 1975

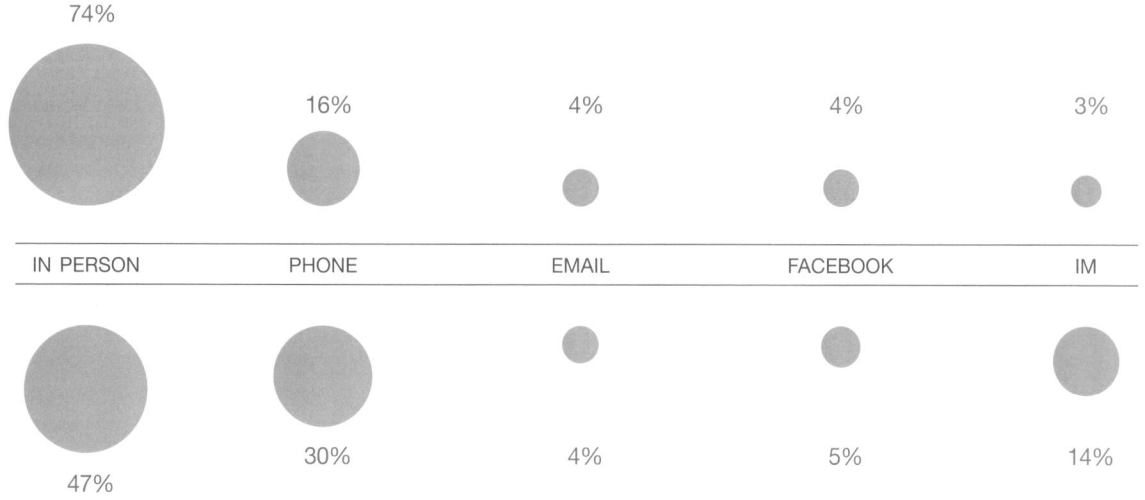

Those born after 1984

source: survey of 10,000 Twitter users

Good News

It's all we could find. Sorry.

Booming trees & plants

Thanks to climate change. source: NASA 2006

National smoking bans

source: Wikipedia

Smokers quitting

source: Cancer Council Victoria, 2008

Russian health spending

source: WHO 2006

The Good of Bush

Stuff that improved under Dubya

Artificial limb research funds

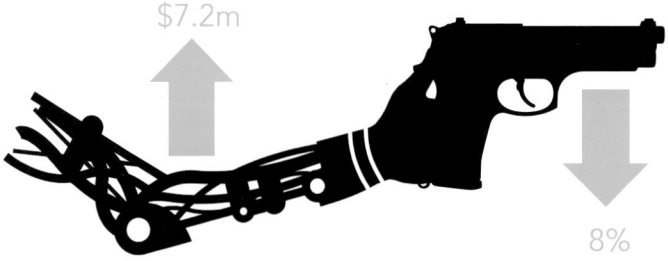

source: Christian Science Monitor

Violent crime

8%

source: US Dept. of Justice

Painkiller sales

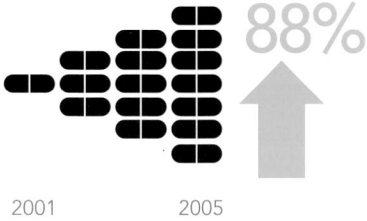

source: Pharmatimes

Roads in Afghanistan

Mobile phones & cancer

source: 20-year 420,000-person Danish study

CFC usage

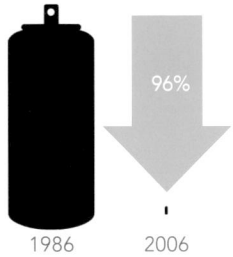

source: NASA

Gender pay gap

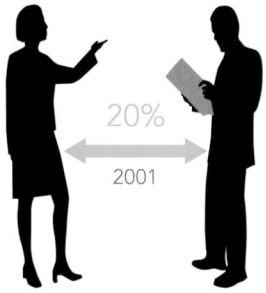

Shark attacks

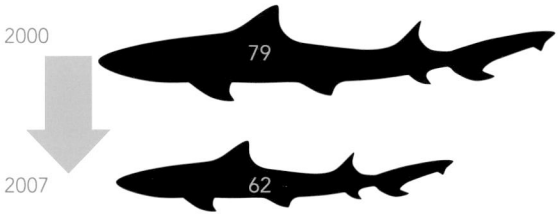

source: University of Florida

Leaded fuel

source: UN

source: OECD

Patients getting free anti-viral drugs in Africa

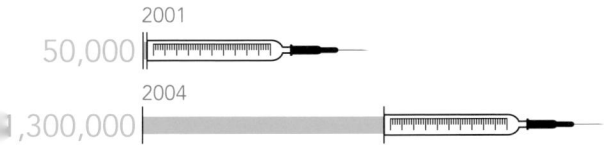

source: Independent newspaper

Education budget

Racial gaps in results

source: US Dept. of Education

12350 km
2008

source: USAID

Immortality

Biographies of the famously long-lived examined for clues to longevity

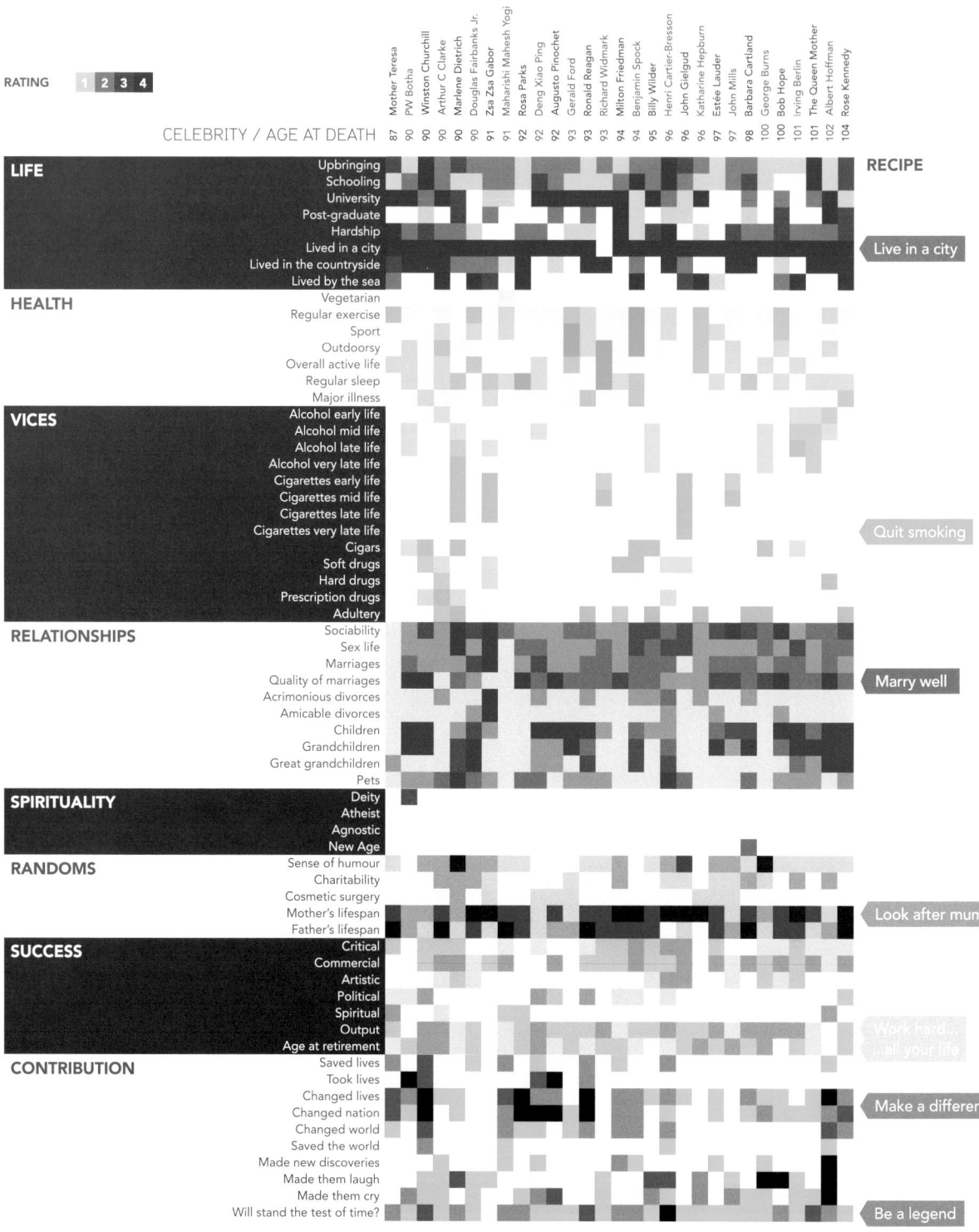

source: Wikipedi

War Chests

Who has the biggest military budget per year?

USA
$711bn

China
$142 bn

Russia
$71 bn

UK
$63 bn

France
$62 bn

Japan
$59 bn

India
$48 bn

Saudi Arabia
$48 bn

Germany
$46 bn

Brazil
$35 bn

War Chests II

Who has the biggest military budget as a % of GDP?

Saudi Arabia
7.1%

Israel
7%

Oman
5.3%

USA
4.7%

Iraq
4.6%

Kuwait
3.8%

Jordan
3.7%

Azerbaijan
3.3%

Algeria
3.2%

Angola
3.1%

UK 2.8%
(21st)

source: Stockholm International Peace Research Institute, sipri.org

2012: The End of the World?

Sceptics vs Believers

2012 BELIEVERS

We believe cataclysmic or transformative events will occur in the year 2012

Mayan archaeological, mythological, and numerological sources all point to December 21st 2012 as a momentous date in the history of humanity.

The planet and its inhabitants may undergo a positive physical or spiritual transformation. Or the date may mark the beginning of an apocalypse...

2012 SCEPTICS

We do not believe anything significant, transformative or apocalyptic will happen in the year 2012

The idea of a global event occurring in 2012 based on any interpretation of the Mayan calendar is rejected as pseudoscience by the scientific community.

It is also considered a misrepresentation of Mayan history by Mayanist scholars.

2012 MAYAN PROPHECY? 2012

BELIEVERS

The ancient Mayans predicted the end of the world in 2012

The Mayan's longest calendar, The Long Count, lasts approximately 5,125 years (13 baktuns) and ends around December 21st 2012.

The end of the calendar signifies the end of a great cycle and the end of the world.

SCEPTICS

The Mayans did not predict the end of the world in 2012

Scholars disagree about the end date. Also different Mayan city states had different Long Counts. Some lasted 7,886 years (20 baktuns).

The end of the calendar did not mean the end of creation. Mayans celebrated the ends of cycles. Predictions were also made for events after the calendar ended.

BELIEVERS

The Mayan's "Hunab Ku" symbol signifies their understanding of cosmic forces on humanity

This Hunab Ku, the name of Mayan diety, is a leading symbol of the 2012 movement. The Hunab Ku bears a resemblance to both a ying-yang symbol and a spiral galaxy. Just an amazing coincidence?

SCEPTICS

This isn't a Mayan symbol. It's Aztec and has no known assocation to "Hunab Ku" or the Mayans

This symbol was originally rectangular and used by the Aztecs, not the Mayans, as a ritual cloak design known as "The Mantle of Lip Plugs". It was turned into a circular symbol and associated with the Milky way by the New Age author Jose Arguelles in 1987.

THE MAYANS COUNTED IN BASE 20 (fingers & toes) ⬭ = 0 ● = 1 ▬ = 5

3,200,000's						▬▬▬▬ *
160,000's					▬▬	⬭
8000's				▬▬	⬭	⬭
400's			▬▬	⬭	⬭	⬭
20's		●	⬭	⬭	⬭	⬭
1's	●	⬭	⬭	⬭	⬭	⬭
mayan	kin	winal	tun	katun	baktun	13 x baktuns
solar time	**1** day	**20** days	**360** days	**19.7** years	**394.3** years	**5125.36** years

*N.B. this final Mayan number may be incorrect

Image: S. Gronemeyer

START DATE: **AUG 11th or 13th 3113 BCE** END DATE: **DEC 21st or 23rd 2012 AD**

TORTUGUERO MONUMENT 6

SOME OF THE INSCRIPTION IS ILLEGIBLE

BELIEVERS

Mayan texts are full of references to 2012 (date 13.0.0.0.0 in Mayan).

Present-day Mayan elders believe that 2012 is the year of the transformational "shift".

SCEPTICS

The only reference to 2012 is carved in one single monument found in Tortuguero, Mexico. (And the long count calendar used in Tortuguero was a 7,886 year, 20 baktun, version.)

Very few modern day Mayans use the Long Count calendar. It was only recently discovered by archaeologists. "Apocalypse" is a Western concept that has little to do with Mayan belief.

PRECESSION OF THE EQUINOXES

A wobble in the Earth's axis slowly traces out a cone over approximately 25,685 years. This means the constellations shift by 1 degree every 72 years. A full rotation is called a Precession.

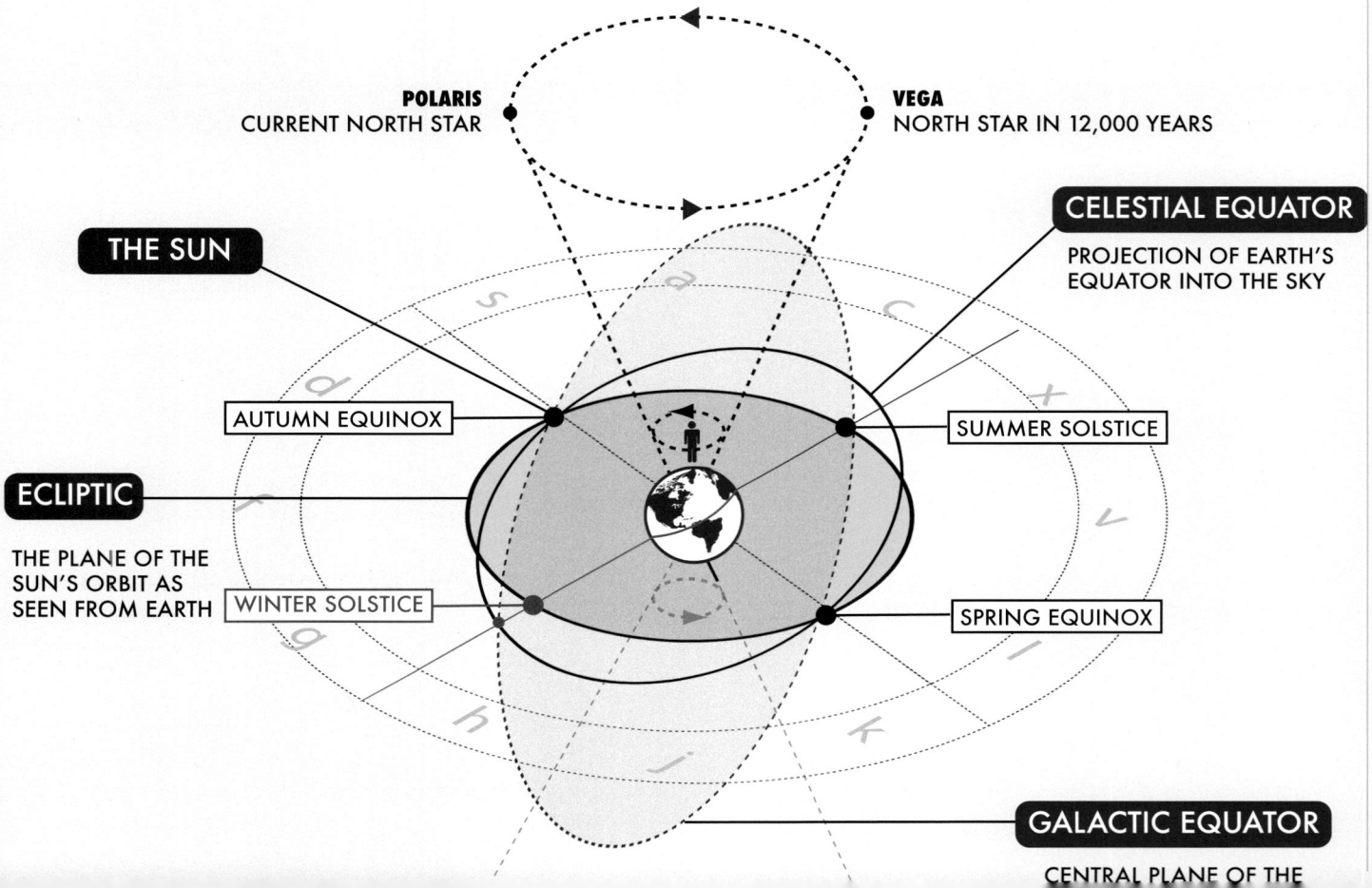

December 21st 2012 is a significant celestial date

That date marks the completion of a 26,000 year celestial cycle: "The Precession of the Equinoxes"

December 21st 2012 is not massively significant

True. But such are the vast timespans involved, the "completion" actually occurs over 36 years, not a single day.

BELIEVERS

Galactic Alignment

The Winter solstice December 21st 2012 is a unique moment when the equators of the Earth, the Sun and the Milky Way all fall miraculously into alignment.

SCEPTICS

Galactic Non-Alignment

The most precise alignment already happened – in 1998

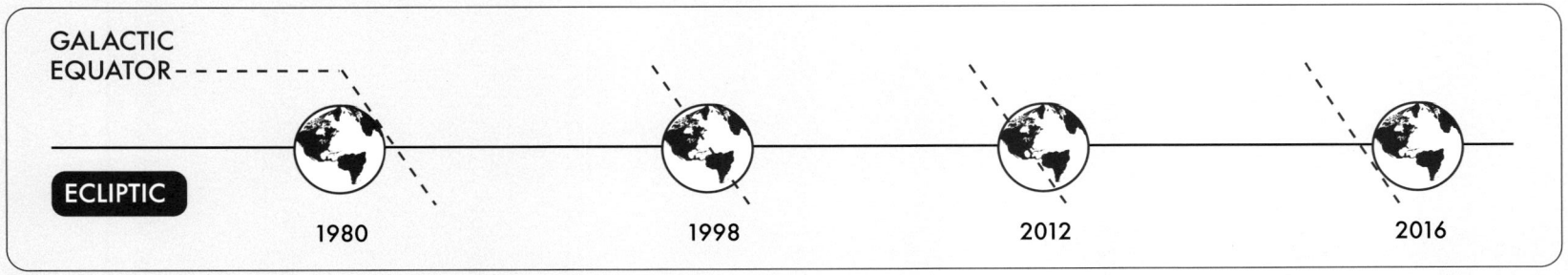

BELIEVERS

The Earth will pass through the Galactic plane

In 2012, the planet will physically move through the disk at the centre of the Milky Way and pass through to the other side.

SCEPTICS

The Earth is nowhere near the galactic plane

We are currently around 24 light years north of the plane. We won't cross it for around 27 million years.

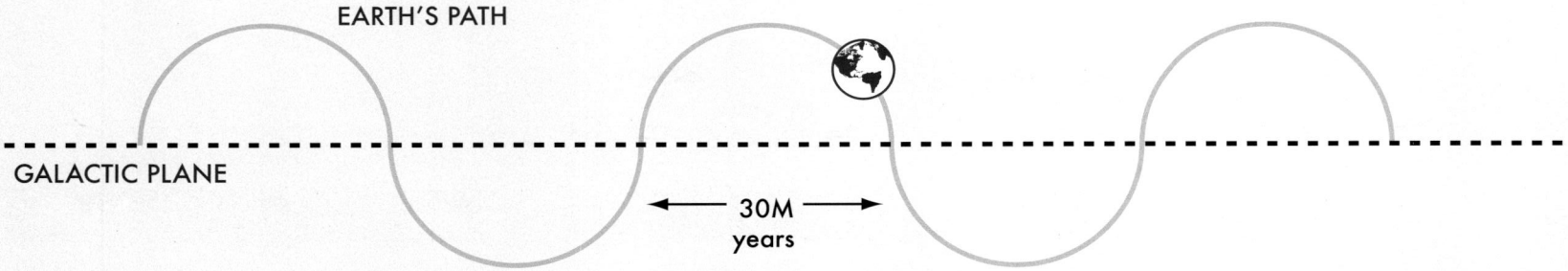

source: diagnosis2012.co.uk, realitysandwich.com, Associated Press, Astronomy Answers, Skeptical Inquirer, NASA

Red vs Blue

Scientists have discovered that when two evenly matched teams compete, the team wearing red wins most often

American Football		American Football		Football		Football	
San Francisco 49ers	Denver Broncos	Kansas City Chiefs	Tennessee Titans/ Houston Oilers	Arsenal	Chelsea	Bayern Munich	Schal
Handball		Baseball		Ice Hockey		Rugby League	
Norway	France	LA Anaheim Angels	Toronto Blue Jays	Detroit Red Wings	Columbus Blue Jackets	Wigan Warriors	Leeds Rhin
Rugby Union		Ten Pin Bowling		Politics		Politics	
Gloucester	Bristol	USA	Europe	Republican	Democrats	Labour	Conservati

Red win 8

Blue win 2

source: Hill & Barton, University of Durham, Journal of Sports Sciences [via Nature], Wikipedia

Man's Humanity to Man

Ah, that's better

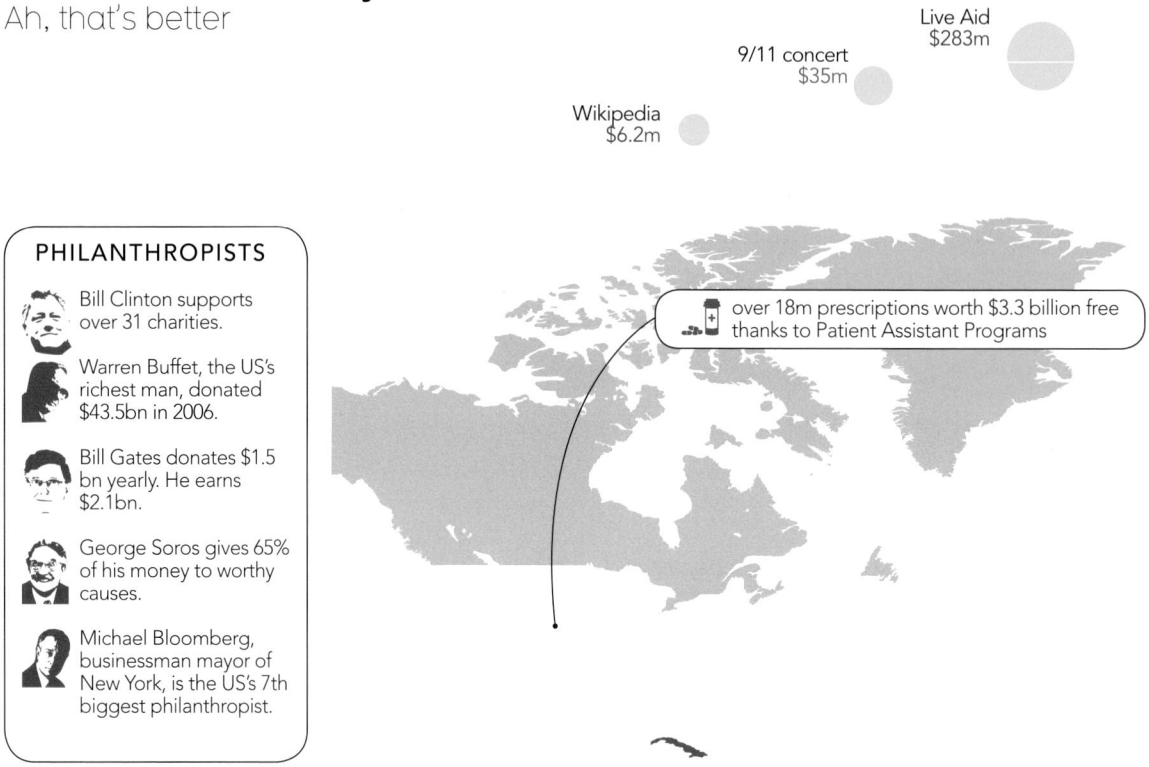

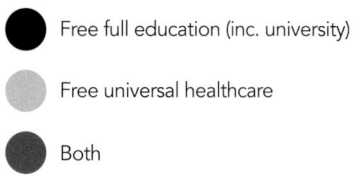

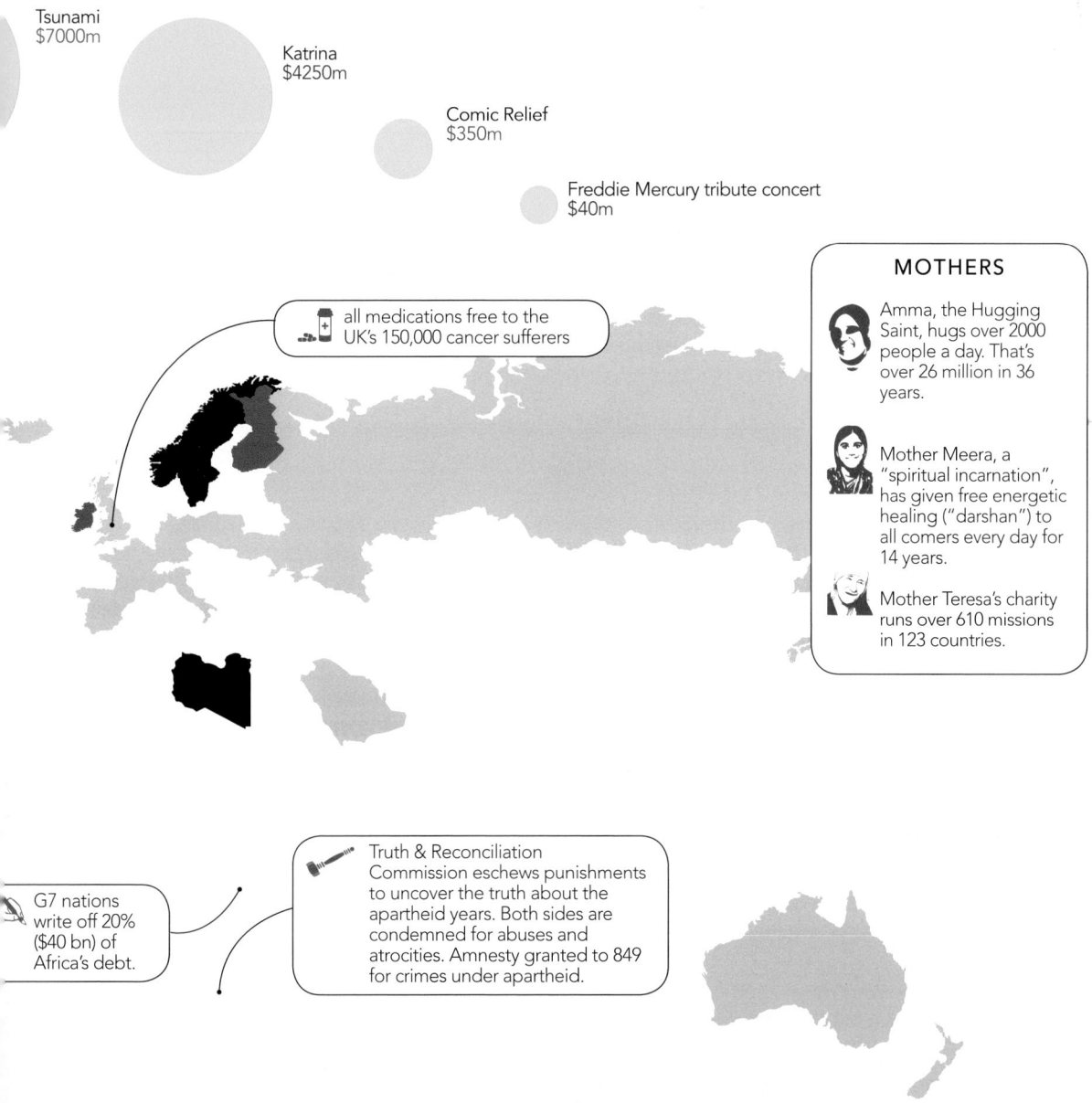

PEOPLE POWER non-violent revolutions

- **Berlin Wall, Germany 1989** After weeks of civil unrest, the East German government allowed its citizens to cross into West Germany. The wall was quickly dismantled.
- **Velvet Revolution, Czech Republic 1989** 500,000 took to the streets to overthrow the communist government without a shot being fired.
- **Bulldozer Revolution, Serbia 2000** Slobodan Milosevic usurped. Named after a bulldozer operator who charged the HQ of Serbian State Television.
- **Rose Revolution, Georgia 2003** A disputed election led to the peaceful overthrow of president-elect Eduard Shevardnadze.
- **Orange Revolution, Ukraine 2004** Thousands protested against a presidential election marred by fraud and corruption. Election annulled.
- **Blue Revolution, Kuwait 2005** Kuwaitis protested in support of giving women the vote. The government gave in and women voted for the first time in 2007.

source: Wikipedia, Unicef.org, Forbes.com, Un.org

Fast Internet

Most popular search terms 2006

Most popular search terms 2008

idea: Christian Lange coccu.de source: Google Zeitgeist.
Years after 2009 not plotted due to dominance of Facebook.

Most popular search terms 2009

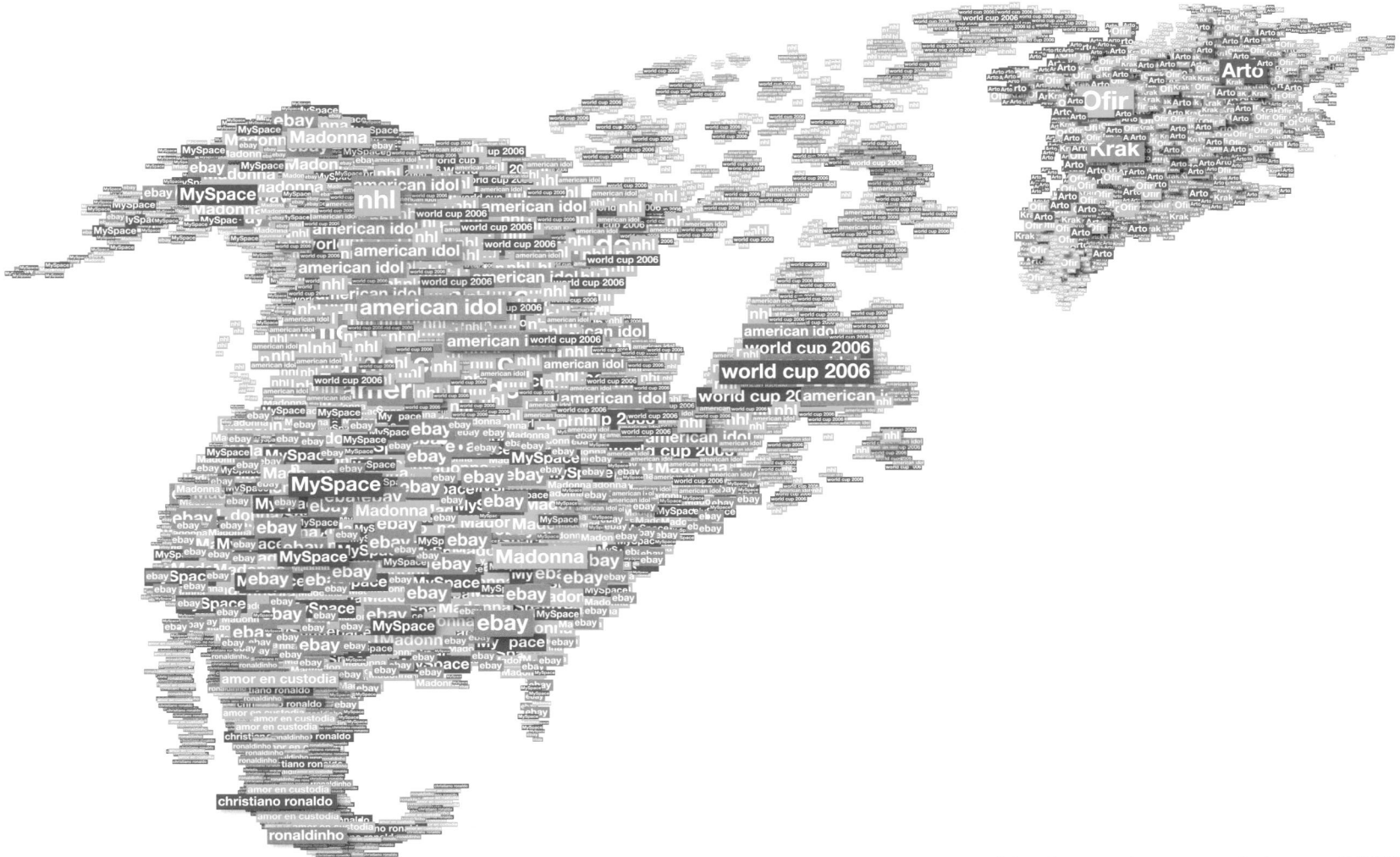

Most popular search terms 2006

Most popular search terms 2008

Most popular search terms 2009

idea: Christian Lange coccu.de source: Google Zeitgeist.
Years after 2009 not plotted due to dominance of Facebook.

Time to Get Away

Legally required paid annual leave in days per year

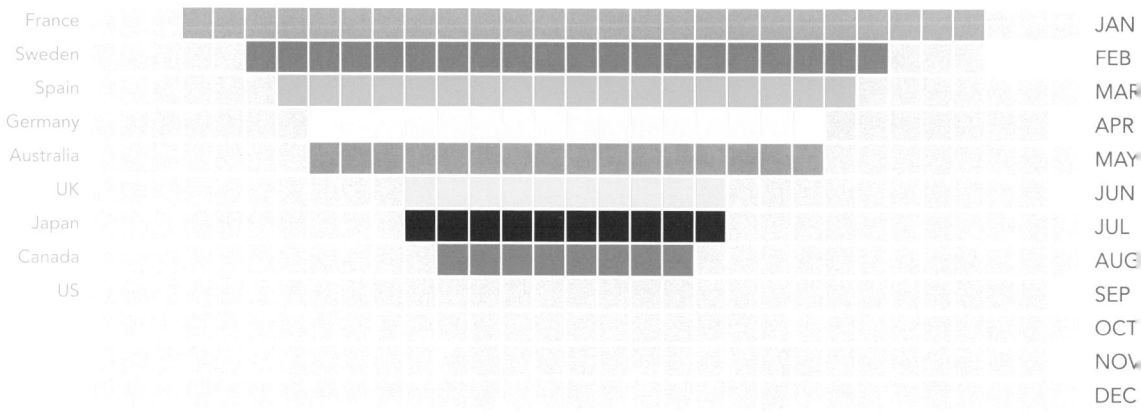

source: Centre for Economic & Policy Research, 2007

Lack of Conviction

Rape in England and Wales

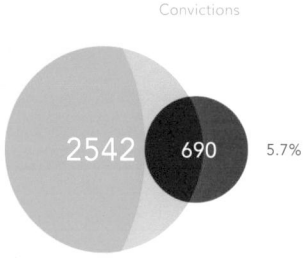

source: UK Home Office

Trafficking

World internet bandwidth usage

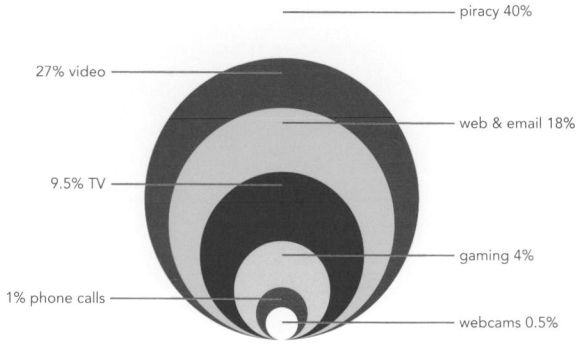

source: Cisco visual networking index

Fat Chance

Who has the most influence on your weight?

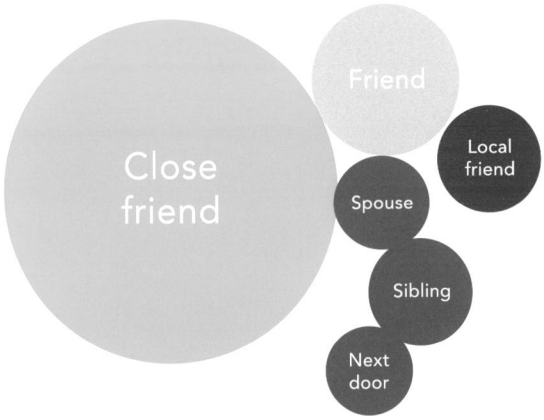

Source: N.Fowler, J.Christakis, N. England Journal of Medicine [via New Scientist]

Shooting Stars

Worldwide yearly arms sales

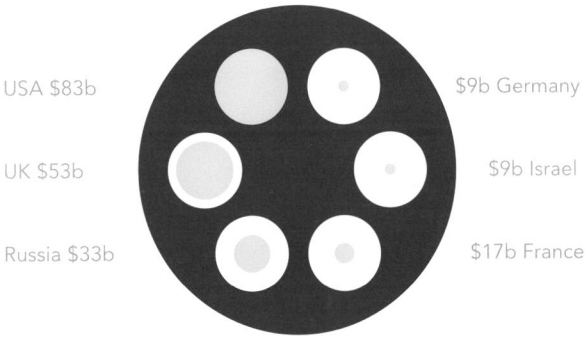

source: Guardian.co.uk

Caused by Global Warming

According to media reports

CLIMATE CHANGE Alaska reshaping, oak deaths, ozone repair slowing, El Niño intensification, Gulf Stream failure, new islands, sinking lands, melting alps, mud slides, volcanic eruptions, subsidence, wildfires, earthquakes, tsunamis RANDOMS witchcraft executions, violin decline, killer cornflakes, tabasco tragedy, truffle shortage, tomato rot, fashion disasters, gingerbread house collapse, mammoth dung melt, UFO sightings, mango harvest failure ANIMALS cannibal polar bears, brain-eating amoebas, aggressive elephants, cougar attacks, stronger salmon, rampant robins, shark attacks, confused birds THE EARTH! light dimming, slowing down, spins faster, wobbling, exploding SOCIAL PROBLEMS floods of migrants, suicides, drop in brothel profits, civil unrest, increased taxes, teenage drinking, early marriages, crumbling roads, deformed railways, traffic jams FOOD soaring prices, sour grapes, shop closures, haggis threat, maple syrup shortage, rice shortage, beer shortage! THE TREES! growth increase, growth decline, more colourful, less colourful HEALTH PROBLEMS dog disease, cholera, bubonic plague, airport malaria, asthma, cataracts, smaller brains, HIV, heart disease, depression LESS moose, geese, ducks, puffins, koalas EVEN LESS krill, fish, glaciers, antarctic ice, ice sheets, avalanches, coral reef MOUNTAINS shrinking, taller, flowering, breaking up INVASIONS rat, crabgrass, wasp, beatle, midge, cockroach, stingrays, walrus, giant pythons, giant oysters, giant squid MORE HEALTH PROBLEMS salmonella, kidney stones, anxiety, childhood insomnia, frostbite, fainting, dermatitis, fever, encephalitis, declining circumcision, diarrhoea, fever, dengue, yellow, west nile, hay DISASTER! boredom, next ice age, cannibalism, societal collapse, release of ancient frozen viruses, rioting and nuclear war, computer models, terrorism, accelerated evolution, conflict with Russia, billions of deaths, the end of the world as we know it

Source: UK and US media reports [via numberswatch.co.uk]

Life Times

How will you spend your 77.8 years?

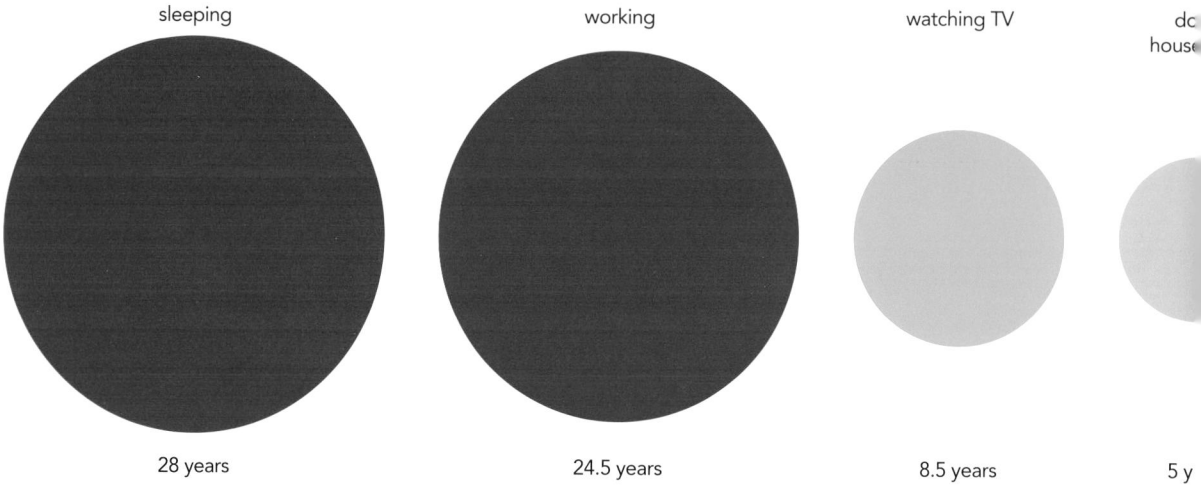

Visible Spectrum

Current best guess for the composition of the universe Dark energy // Dark matter // Intergalactic gas // Normo

Invisible

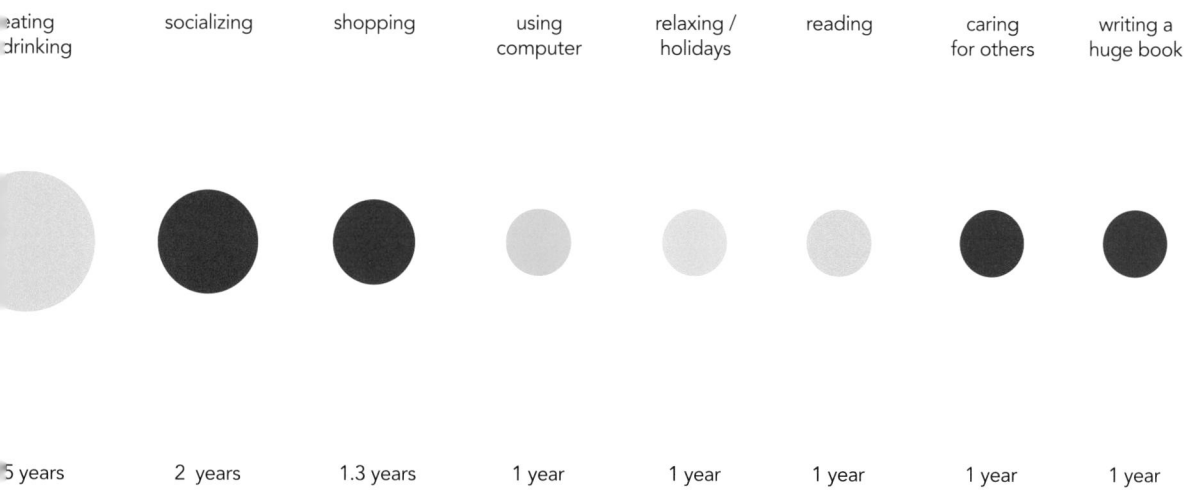

source: American Bureau of Labor Statistics 2007

source: Wikipedia

Peters Projection

The true size of the continents

The standard "Mercator" world map inflates the size of nations depending on their distance from the equator. This means that many developing countries end up much smaller than they are in reality (i.e. most of Africa). The Peters Projection corrects this.

source: Wikipedia

Alternative Medicine

Scientific evidence for complementary therapies

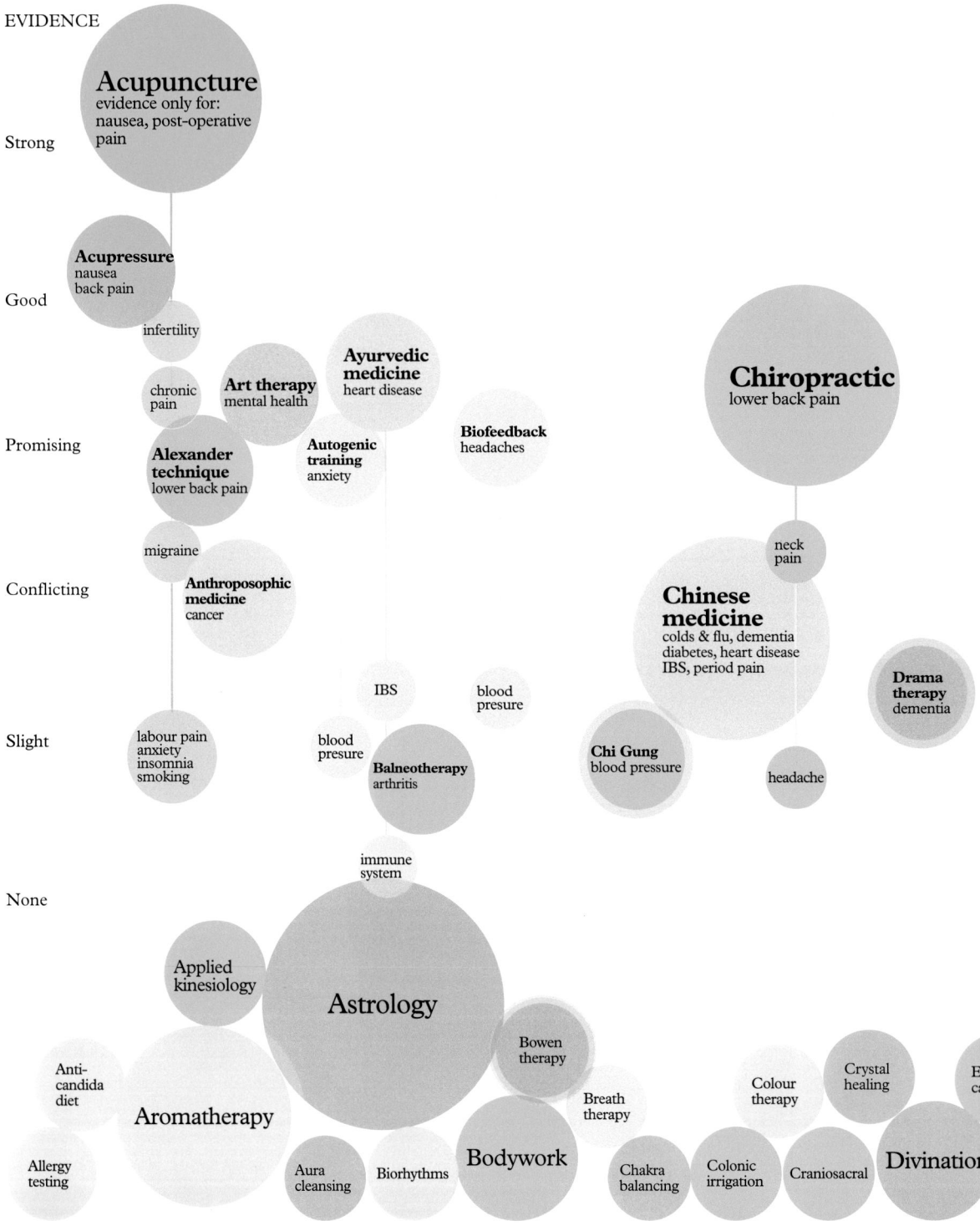

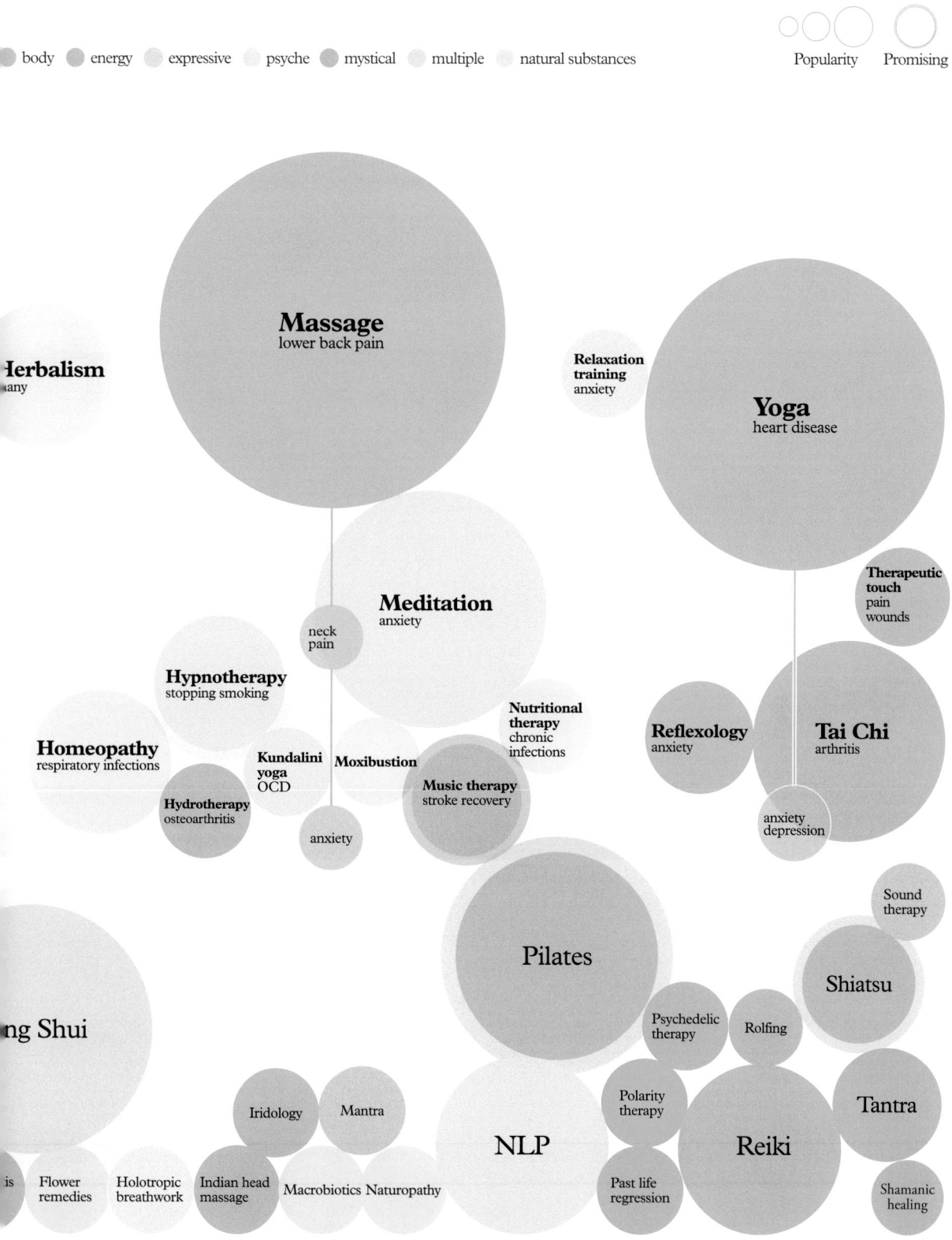

source: Cochrane.org and other English-language meta-studies (via Pubmed.org)

Radiation Dosage

Risk of harm is dependent on both the **dose** and the **dose rate** (the time the body is exposed to that dose).

So a dose of 1,000 mSv over an hour is considerably more damaging than a dose of 1,000 mSv over a year.

Exposure Time

Instant | **Hours** | **One Day** | **One Year**

microsieverts (μSv)

0.1 μSv

0.1 — Airport security scan (backscatter X-ray)
Eating a banana

0.25 — Airport security scan maximum permitted

1.0 μSv

1.0 — Using a cathode-ray computer monitor for a year

5.0 — Dental X-ray

7.5 — Per day in Tokyo, 250km SW of Fukushima plant (+107 days after the disaster, 28 June 2011)

10 μSv

10 — Background dose received by an average person on an average day (varies wildly)

40 — Flight from New York to LA

70 — Living in a stone, brick or concrete building for a year

80 — Average total dose per person within 10 miles of the Three Mile Island Accident (1979)

100 μSv

100 — Chest X-ray; One hour dose 3km SW of Fukushima plant (+83 days after the disaster, 3 June 2011)

250 — Release limit for a nuclear power plant for a year

400 — Yearly dose per person from food

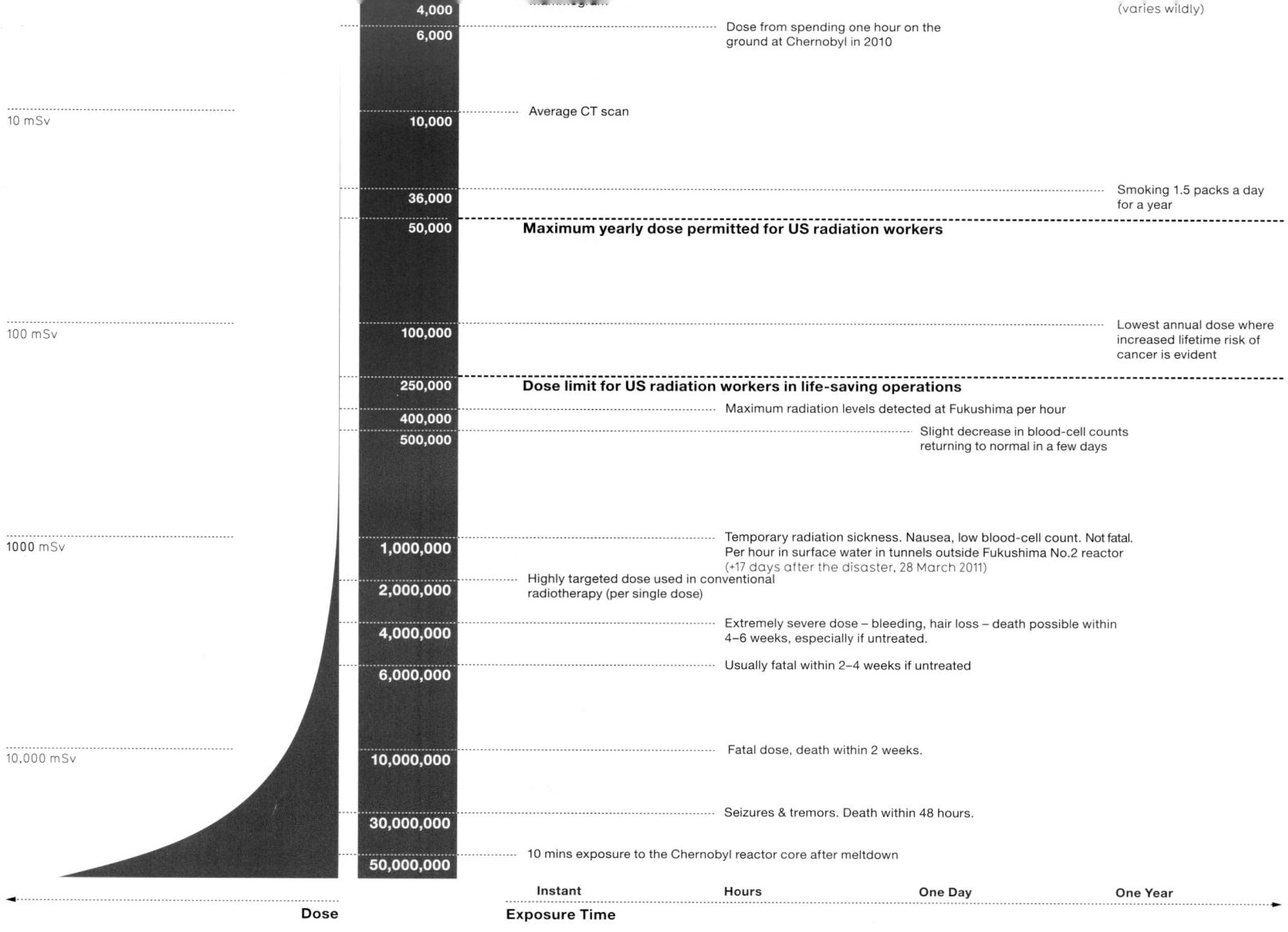

source: EPA, BBC, Guardian Datablog

Being Defensive

How psychotherapy sees you

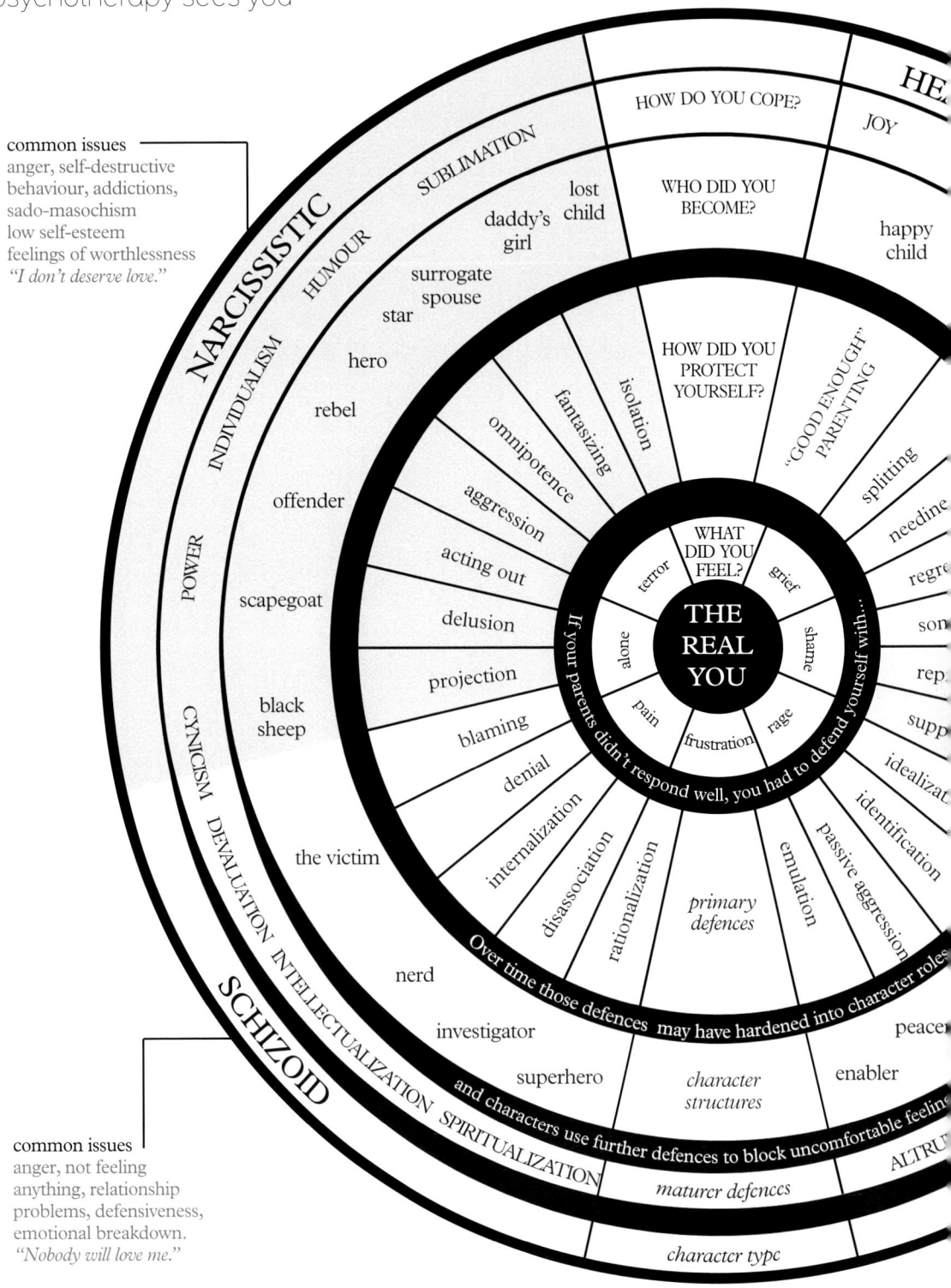

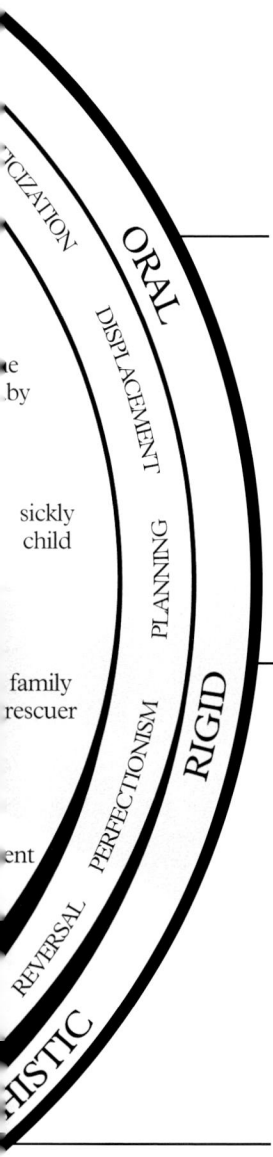

common issues
addictions, manic depression, lethargy, rage, suicidal impulses, chaotic lifestyle
"I can't get love for myself."

common issues
sex-love-intimacy problems, stress, inflexibility, failed relationships, compulsions, coldness, nervous breakdown
"I don't know what love is."

common issues
obsessive compulsions, abusive relationships, fear, anxiety, phobias, self-harm, obesity, depression, nervous breakdown.
"I'll be loved if I'm good."

PRIMARY DEFENCES

acting out
turn it into behaviour

aggression
attacking

blaming
someone else's fault

delusion
lie to yourself & believe it

denial
it's not happening

disassociation
go numb

distortion
changing the story to fit

emulation
copy what you know

fantasizing
go into other worlds

idealization
over-regard for others

identification
forge an alliance

internalization
holding it all in

isolation
separate off feelings

neediness
over-dependence on another

omnipotence
all powerful, no weakness

passive aggression
indirect & concealed attacks

projection
put your feelings on someone

regression
revert back to immaturity

rationalization
a false but plausible excuse

repression
unconsciously burying it

somatization
turn it into a physical illness

splitting
good/bad, love/hatred

suppression
consciously burying it

MATURER DEFENCES

altruism
efface it with good deeds

cynicism
everything is false

devaluation
it doesn't matter

displacement
find a teddy bear

eroticization
safety in sex

humour
deflect with jokes

individualism
celebrate it

intellectualization
turn it into safe concepts

perfectionism
never slip up again

planning
safety in organization

power
control everyone

reversal
do the opposite of how you feel

spiritualization
it's all a divine purpose

sublimation
make art out of it

undoing
constant acts of compensation

source: the work of Freud, Heinz Kohut, John Bradshaw and A.H. Almaas

Being Defensive

How psychotherapy works

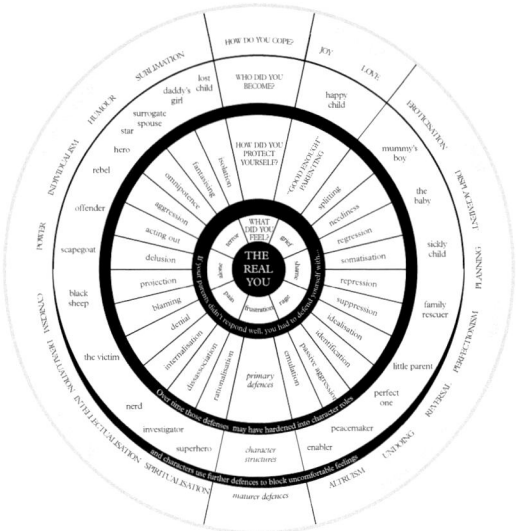

You slowly build a relationship of trust and intimacy with the therapist. That allows you to investigate, explore and ultimately learn to drop your outer defences without feeling threatened.

Exploring your life history, you re-experience situations and relationships from childhood in slow motion with the therapist. This way you can bring adult awareness and understanding to those experiences.

Some types of therapy and their target areas

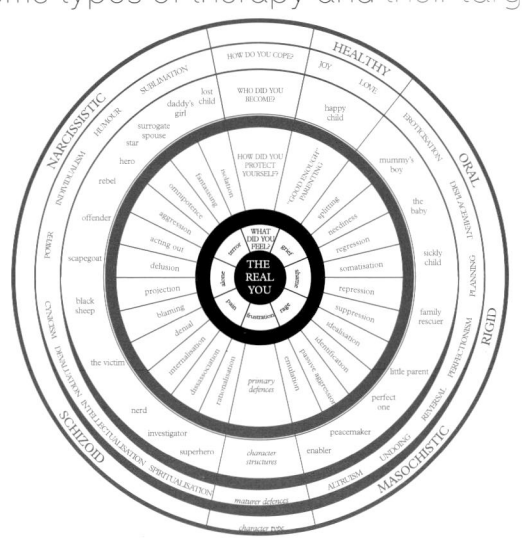

PSYCHOANALYSIS Explores the connection between (possibly "forgotten") events in early life and current disturbances and stress. Talking freely allows fantasies, feelings, dreams and memories to emerge more easily.

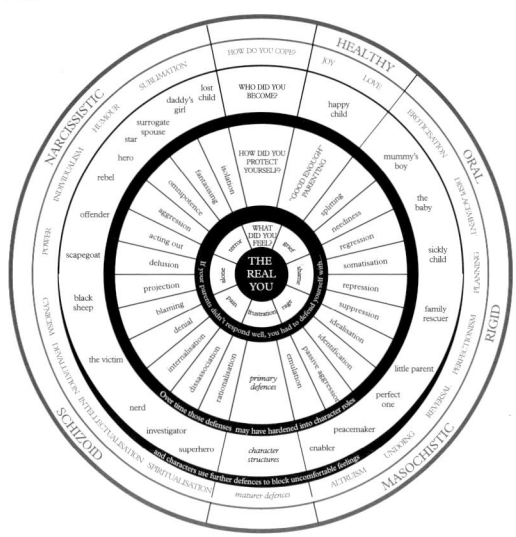

COGNITIVE-BEHAVIOURAL THERAPY Uncovering and understanding how inaccurate thoughts, beliefs and assumptions can lead to inaccurate interpretations of events and so to negative emotions and behaviours.

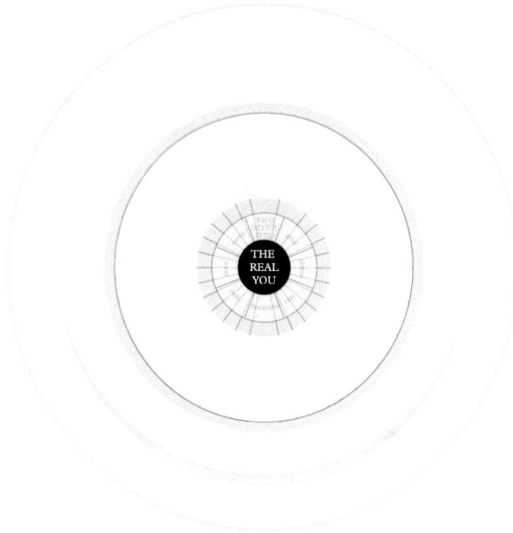

As those experiences are re-felt, digested, understood and perhaps resolved, the difficult and unbearable feelings you weren't able to feel at the time can also be felt. Deeper blocks and resistances may be revealed.

As those feelings are repeatedly felt, you learn to understand, tolerate and deal with them. The "real you", underneath all the defences, can be felt. Nothing really changes. All your defences are still there. You just feel less blocked and become more "transparent".

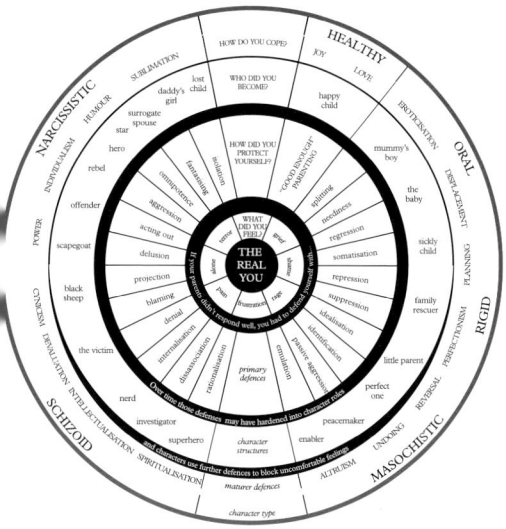

ANTI-DEPRESSANTS Reducing the intensity of symptoms of depression and anxiety and other symptoms of psychological disturbance and distress through regular use of psychiatric medicine.

source: Wikipedia, psychotherapy.org.uk

Most Popular US Girls' Names

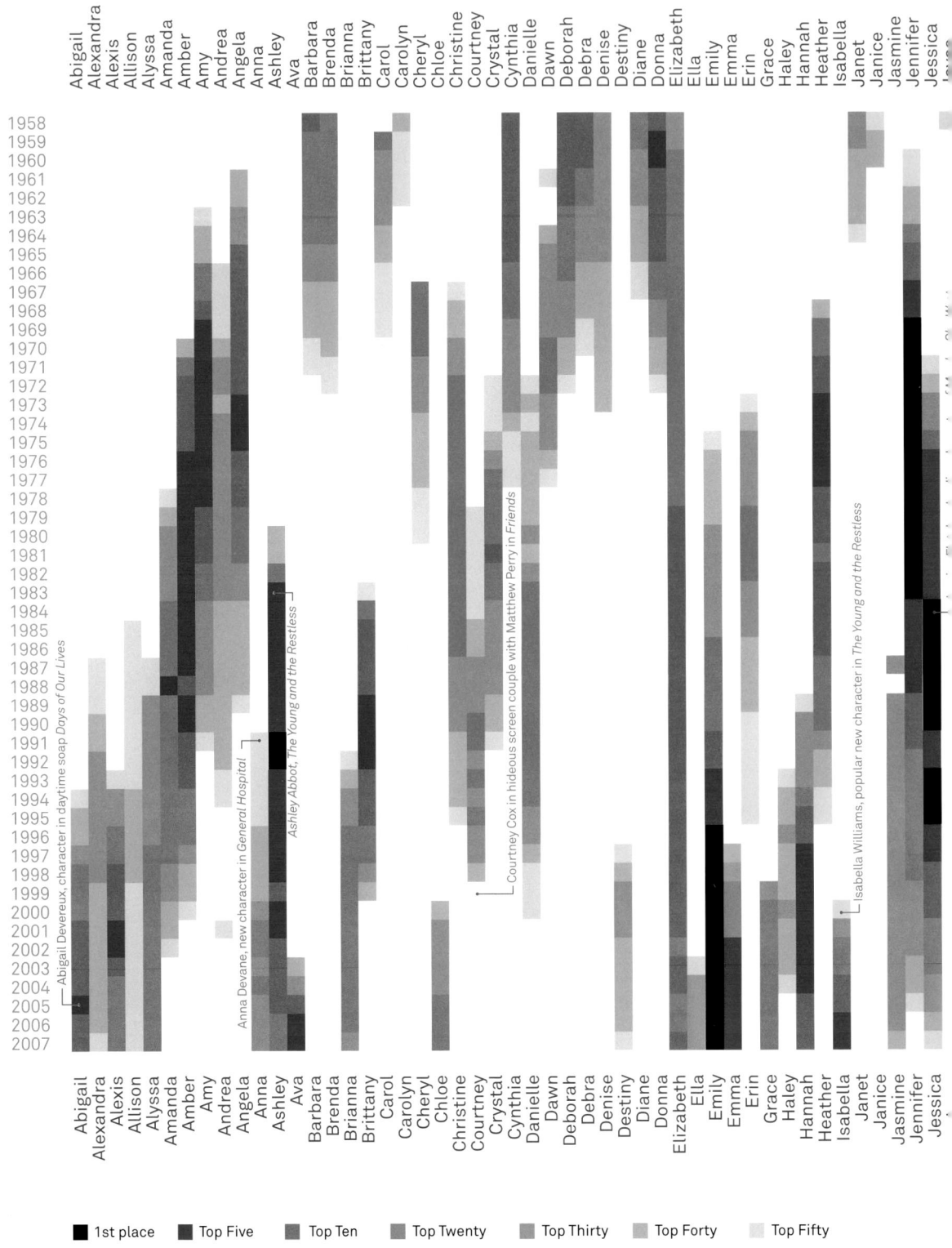

source: US Social Security Administration @ ssa.gov

Most Popular US Boys' Names

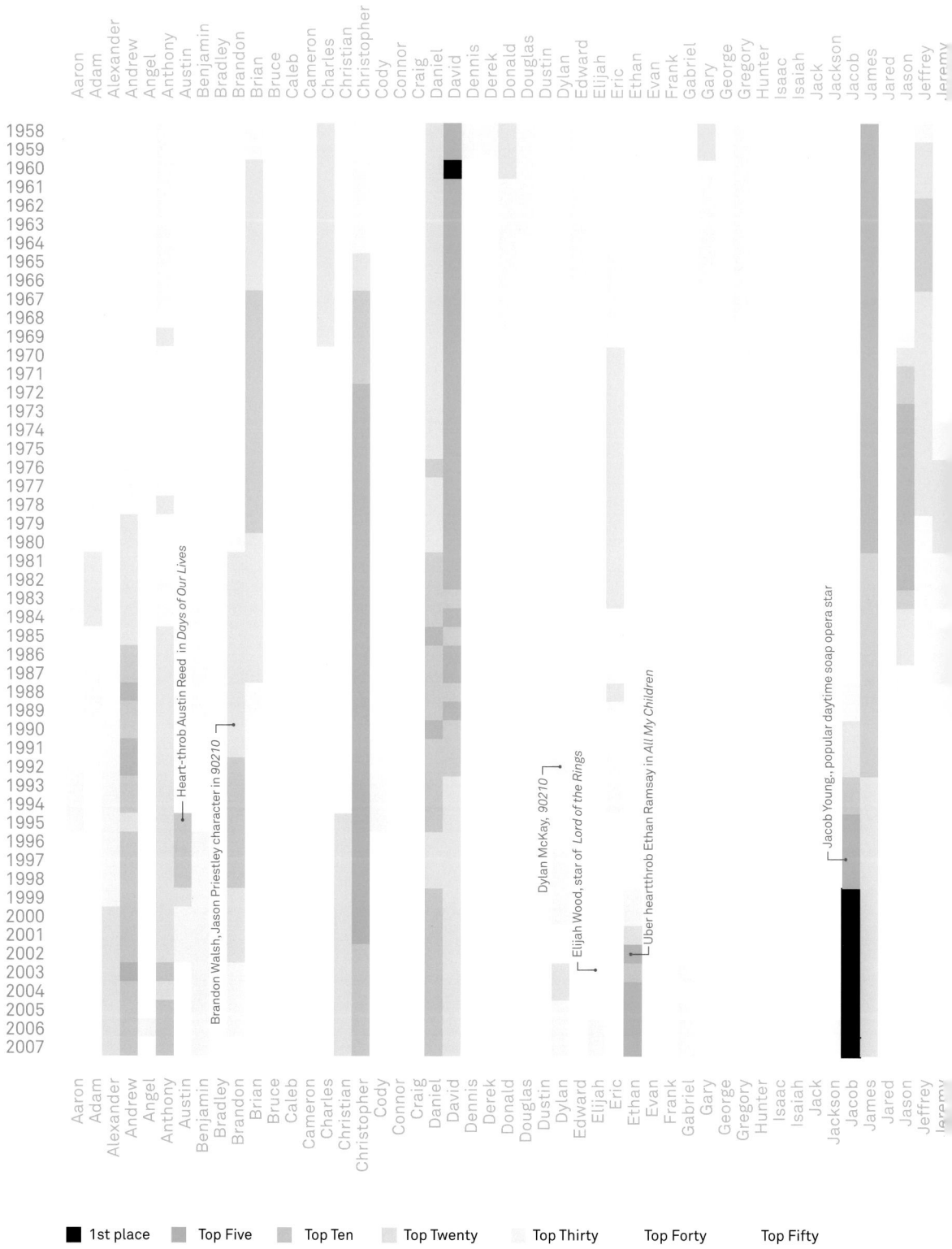

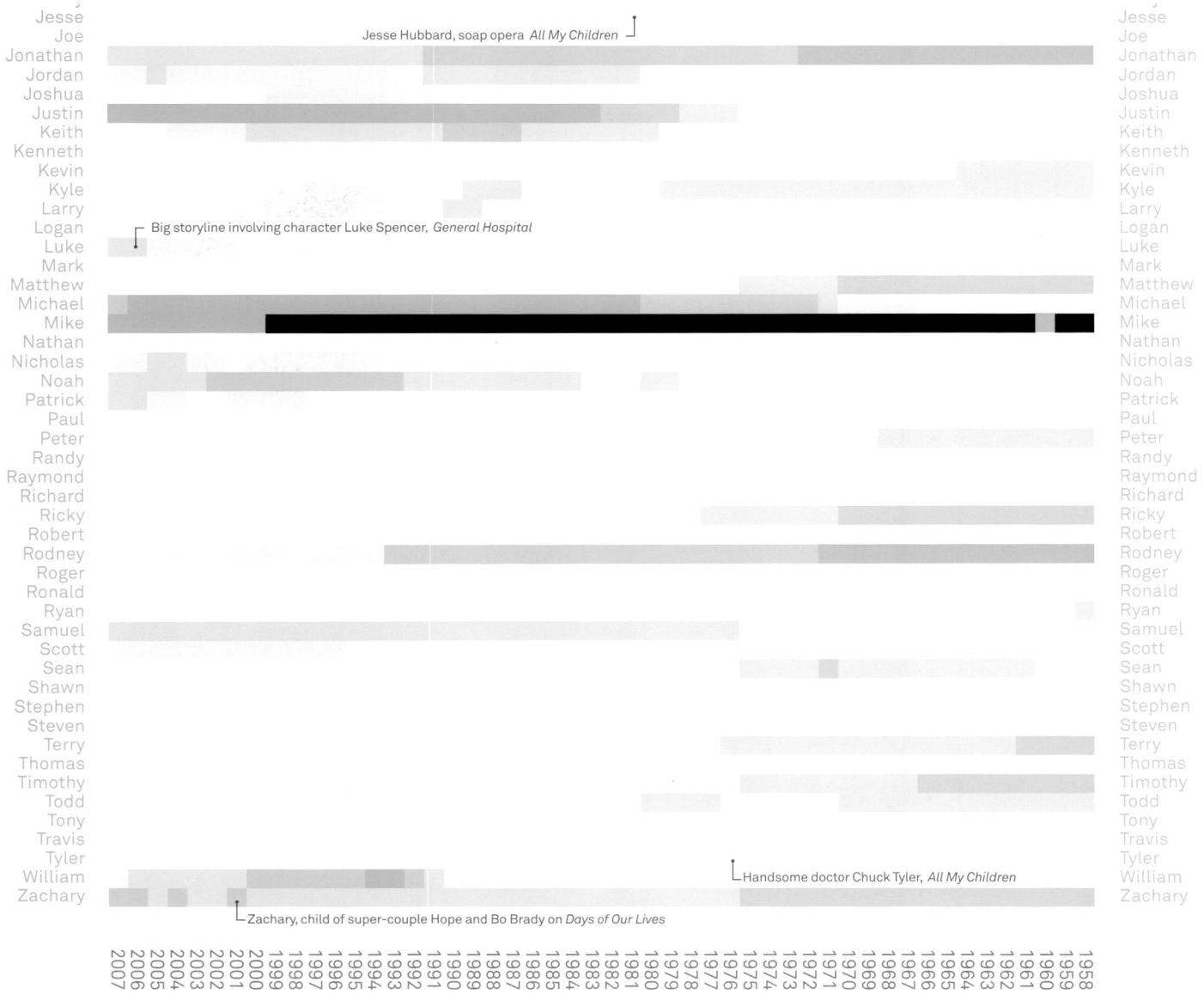

source: US Social Security Administration @ ssa.gov

The Middle East

A relationship map

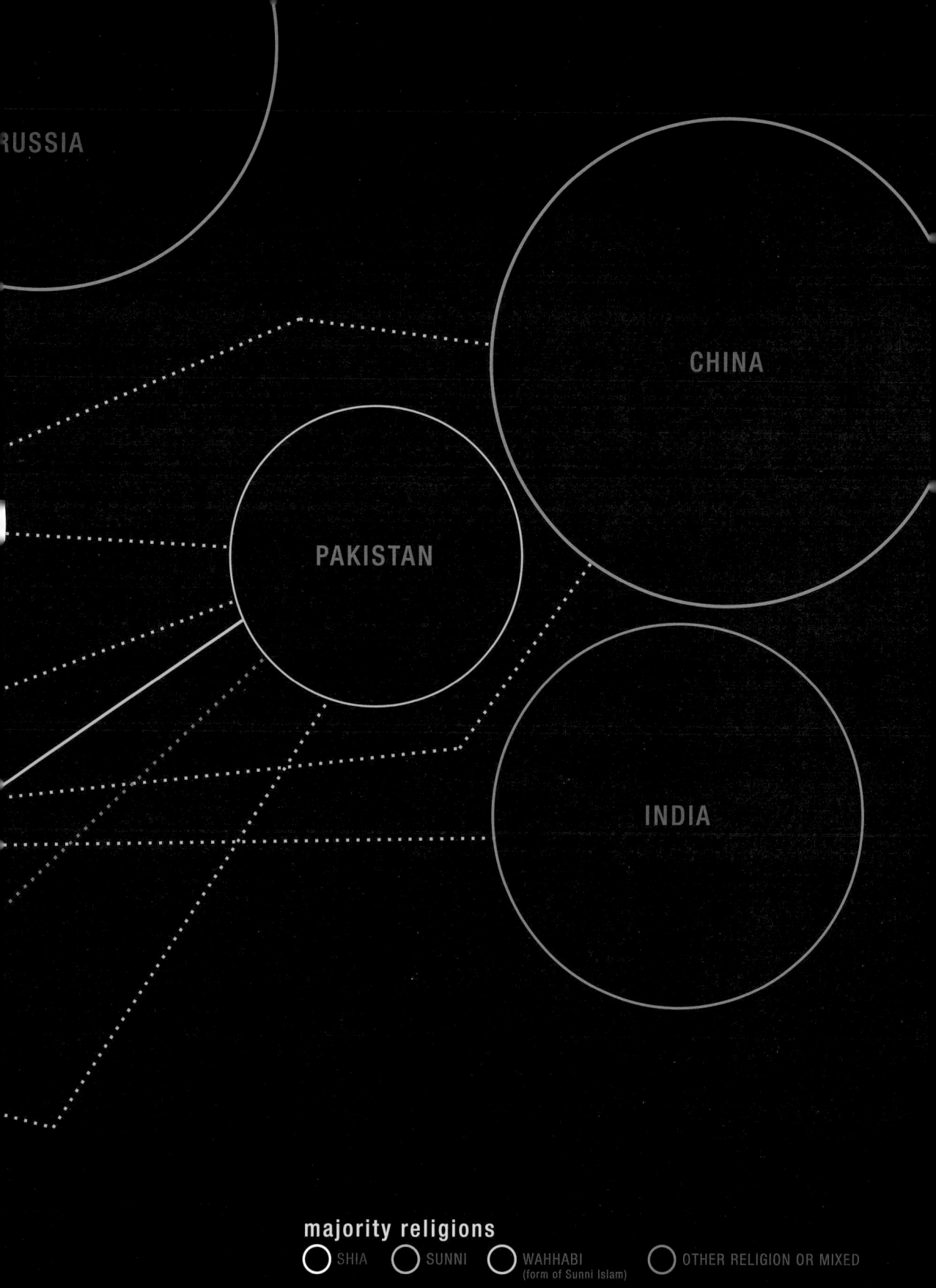
RUSSIA
CHINA
PAKISTAN
INDIA
majority religions
SHIA
SUNNI
WAHHABI
(form of Sunni Islam)
OTHER RELIGION OR MIXED
source: Orgnet.com, New York Times

The Middle East: Some Context

Palestinian territories

Oil States

Who has the world's oil?

Oil States

Who'll have the world's oil?

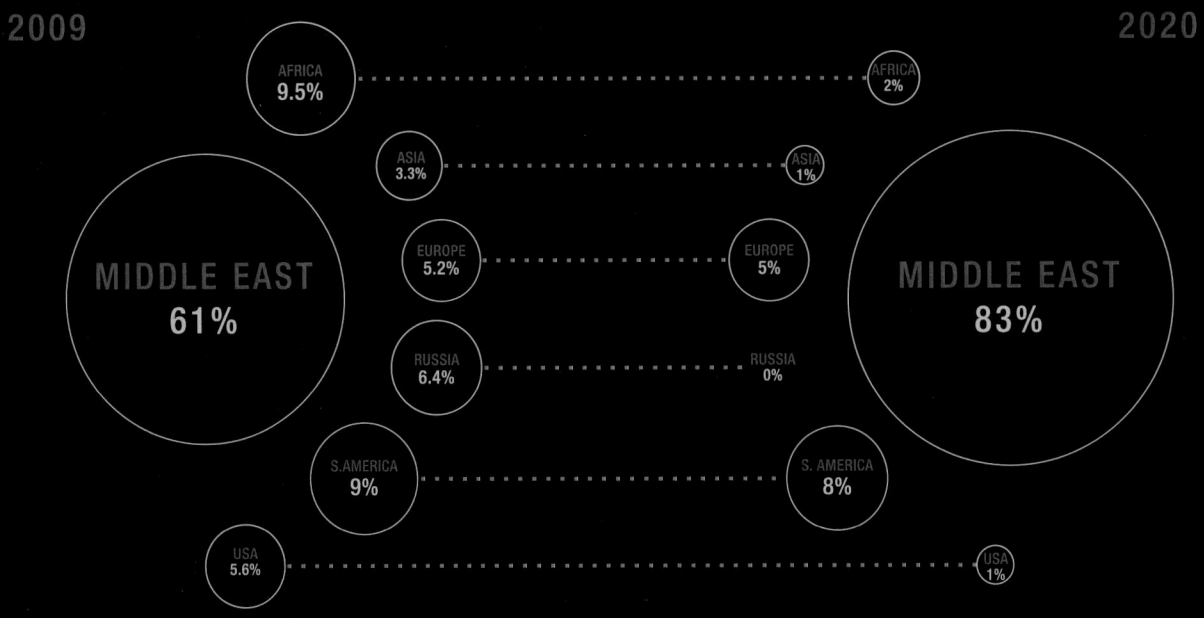

source: BP Statistical Review of the Year 2008, Wikiped

'he Future of Energy

lace your bets

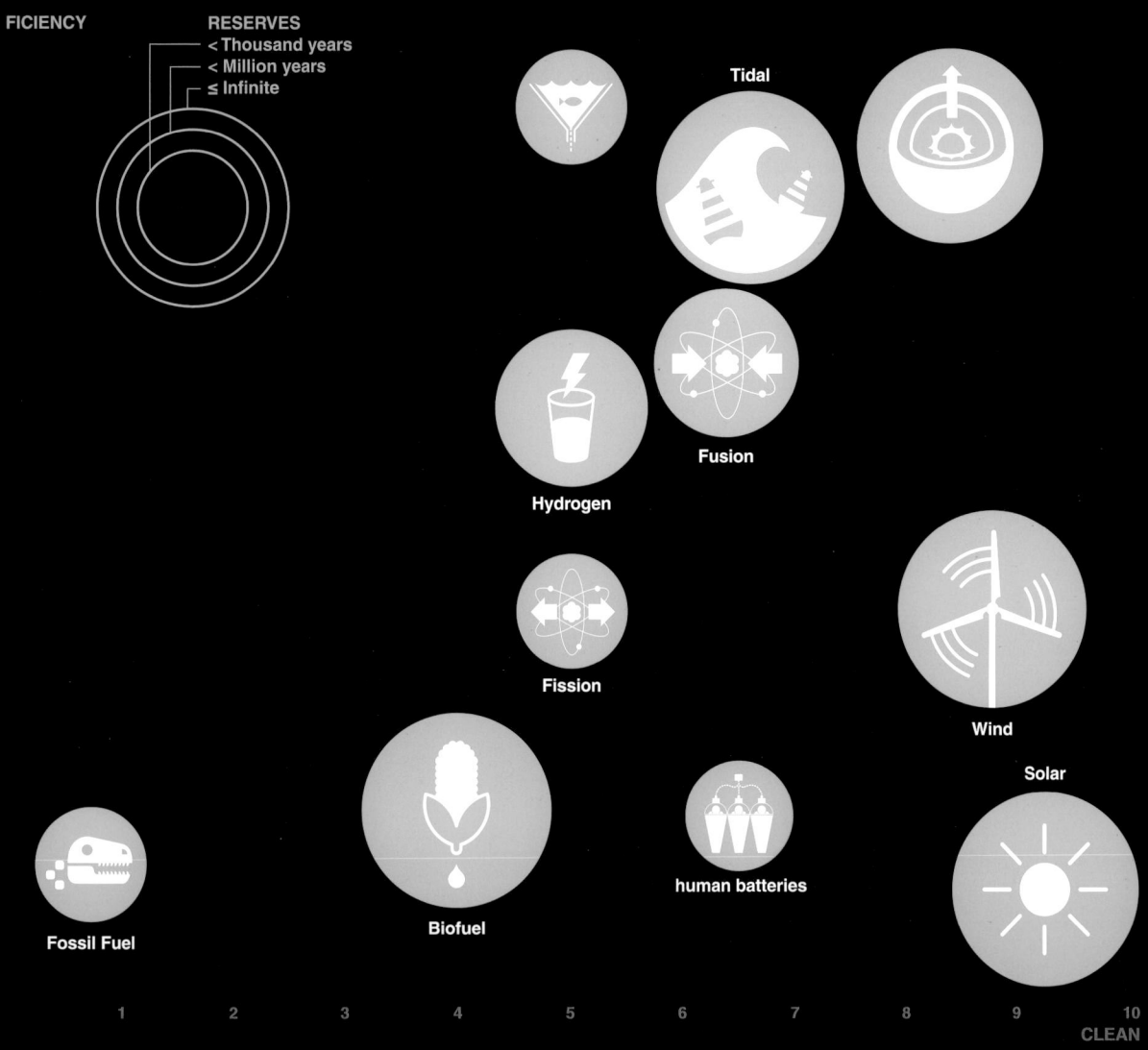

ofuel – To replace all of America's petrol nsumption with bio-fuel from plants would ke three-quarters of all the cultivated land the face of the Earth.

ssil Fuel – By products: sulphur dioxide, bon monoxide, methane, poisonous tals like lead, uranium and, of course, CO_2.

othermal – Drilling for free heat under earth's surface has lots of advantages d is pollution-free. Iceland gets 20% its energy this way. But watch out for thquakes!

man Batteries – The energy in the food eded to feed human power sources is eater than the energy generated. D'oh!

Hydroelectric – There's an unavoidable built-in limit to dams. There are only so many places you can put them. And space is running out...

Hydrogen – Currently 96% of hydrogen is made using fossil fuels.

Nuclear Fission – To meet the world's electricity needs from nuclear power would require 2230 more nuclear power stations. There are currently 439 in operation. They can take 5–10 years to build.

Nuclear Fusion – Recreates the temperatures at the heart of the sun. Generates much less nuclear waste than fission. But no one can work out how to do it. "At least 50 years away".

Solar – To replace all current electricity production in the US with solar power would take an area of approximately 3500 square miles (3% of Arizona's land area) covered in solar panels. In most areas of the world, solar panels would cover 85% of household water heating needs.

Tidal – Several question marks remain. Mostly related to its impact on environment and biodiversity.

Wind – Turbines covering about 0.5% of all US land would power the entire country. Around 73,000 to 144,000 5-megawatt wind turbines could power electric cars for every single American.

source: Wikipedia, USGS

Most Successful Rock Bands

True rock success got nothin' to do with selling records

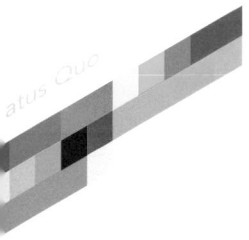

- Sex/drugs in album titles
- Longest time to finish album
- Offshoot groups
- Solo albums
- Disbanded and reformed
- Severe musical differences
- Largest single audience
- Onstage breakdowns
- Likelihood of cancelling gigs

- Visits to rehab
- Alcoholic members
- Heavy drug-using members
- Hotel room trashings
- Own-vomit chokings
- Religious/occult dabblings
- God complex rating
- Groupies
- Divorces

- Sexual tension in band
- Supermodel relationships
- Record company disputes
- Court cases
- Hits critically panned
- Flops critically acclaimed
- Sheer ardency of fans
- Number of mansions
- Number of islands

- Number of estates
- Glib political statements
- Disastrous TV appearances
- Feature films made
- Tribute bands
- Riffs heard in guitar shops
- '"Greatest Hits" albums

source: Wikipedia

22 Stories

P=The Protagonist

Fish out of Water P tries to co
in a completely different place
time/world.
Mr Bean, Trading Places

Discovery Through a major upheaval, P discovers a truth about themselves and a better understanding of life.
Close Encounters, Ben-Hur

Escape P trapped by antagonistic forces and must escape. Pronto.
Poseidon Adventure, Saw

Journey & Return P goes on a
physical journey and returns changed.
Wizard of Oz, Star Wars

Temptation P has to make a moral choice between right and wrong.
The Godfather, The Sting

Rags to Riches P is poor, then rich.
Trading Places, La Vie en rose

The Riddle P has to solve a puzzle or a crime.
The Da Vinci Code, Chinatown

Metamorphosis P literally changes into something else (i.e. a werewolf, hulk, giant cockroach).
Spiderman, Pinocchio

Rescue P must save someone who is trapped physically or emotionally.
The Golden Compass, Die Hard

Tragedy P is brought down by a fatal flaw in their character or by forces out of their control.
One Flew Over the Cuckoo's Nest, Atonement

ove A couple meet and ercome obstacles to discover ue love. Or – tragically – don't.
tanic, Grease

Monster Force A monster / alien / something scary and supernatural must be fought and overcome.
Jaws, The Exorcist

Revenge P retaliates against another for a real or imagined injury.
Batman, Kill Bill

Transformation P lives through a series of events that change them as a person.
Pretty Woman, Muriel's Wedding

aturation P has an experience at matures them or starts new stage of life, often dulthood.
e Graduate, Juno

Pursuit P has to chase somebody or something, usually in a hide-and-seek fashion.
Goldfinger, Bourne Ultimatum

Rivalry P must triumph over an adversary to attain an object or goal.
Rocky, The Outsiders

Underdog Total loser faces overwhelming odds but wins in the end.
Slumdog Millionaire, Forrest Gump

omedy A series of mplications leads P into diculous situations.
hostbusters, Airplane

Quest P searches for a person, place or thing, overcoming a number of challenges.
Raiders of the Lost Ark, Lord of the Rings

Sacrifice P must make a difficult choice between pleasing themselves or a higher purpose (e.g. love, honour).
300, 3:10 to Yuma

Wretched Excess P pushes the limits of acceptable behaviour, destroying themselves in the process.
There Will Be Blood, Citizen Kane

source: Tennesse Screenwriting Association, Robert McKee's *Story*

Most Profitable Hollywood Stories 2007

Average profitability: 301% Average quality: 51% Most common stories: Love Pursuit

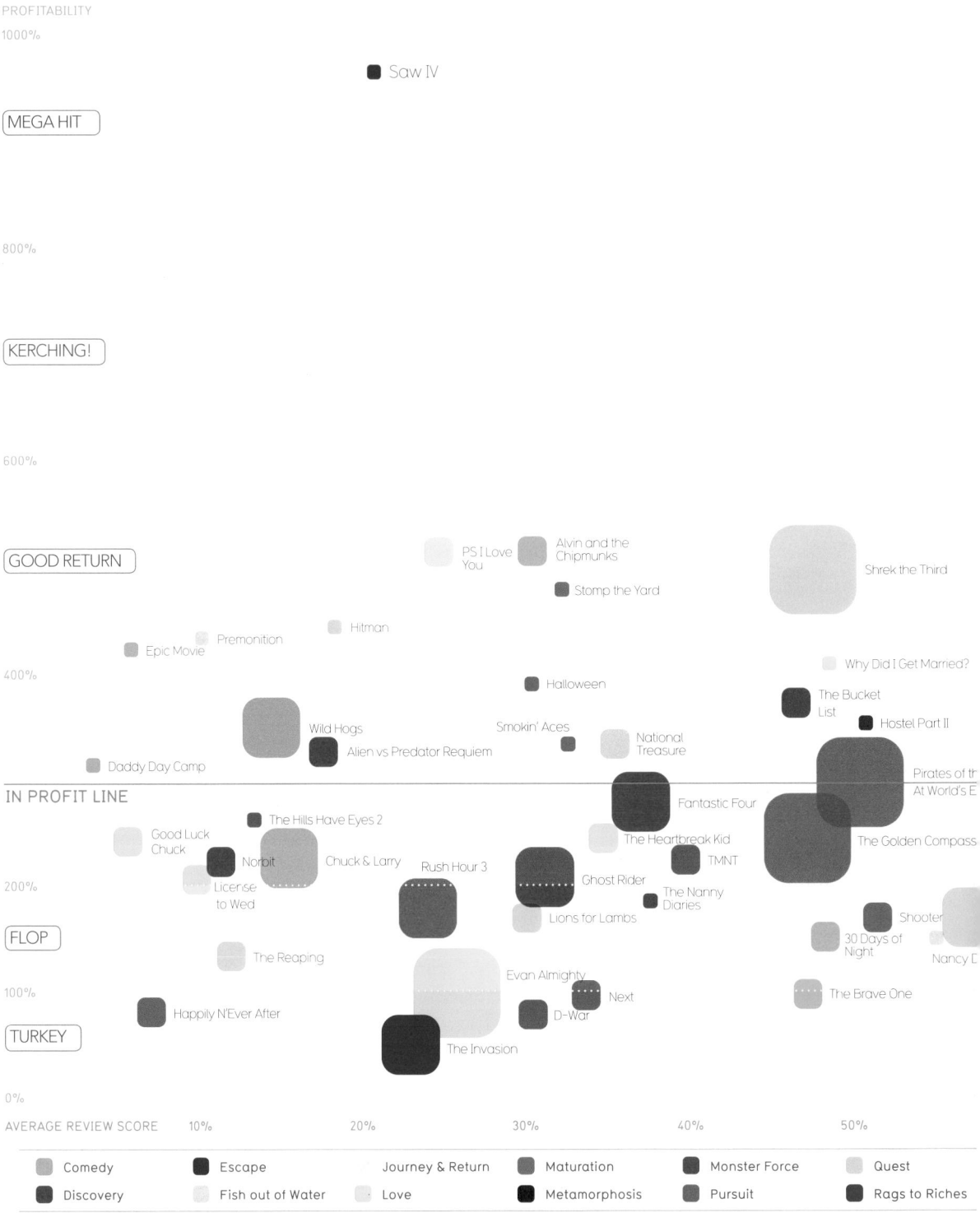

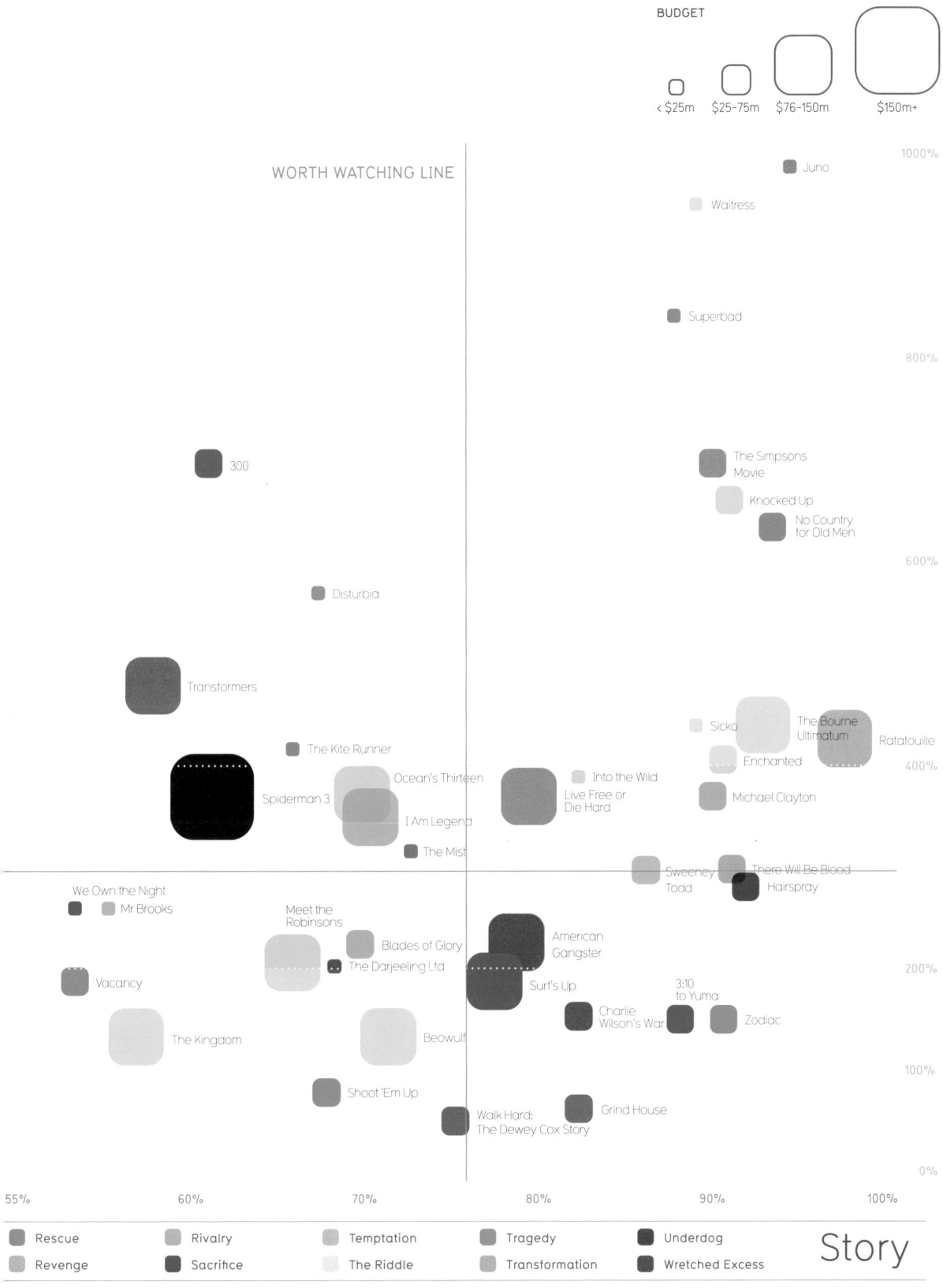

source: BoxOfficeMojo.com, The-Numbers.com, Wikipedia, IMDB.com & RottenTomatoes.com. Note: reported film budgets are notoriously unreliable (especially for flops)

Most Profitable Hollywood Stories 2008

Average profitability: 278% Average quality: 46% Most common stories: Love Discovery

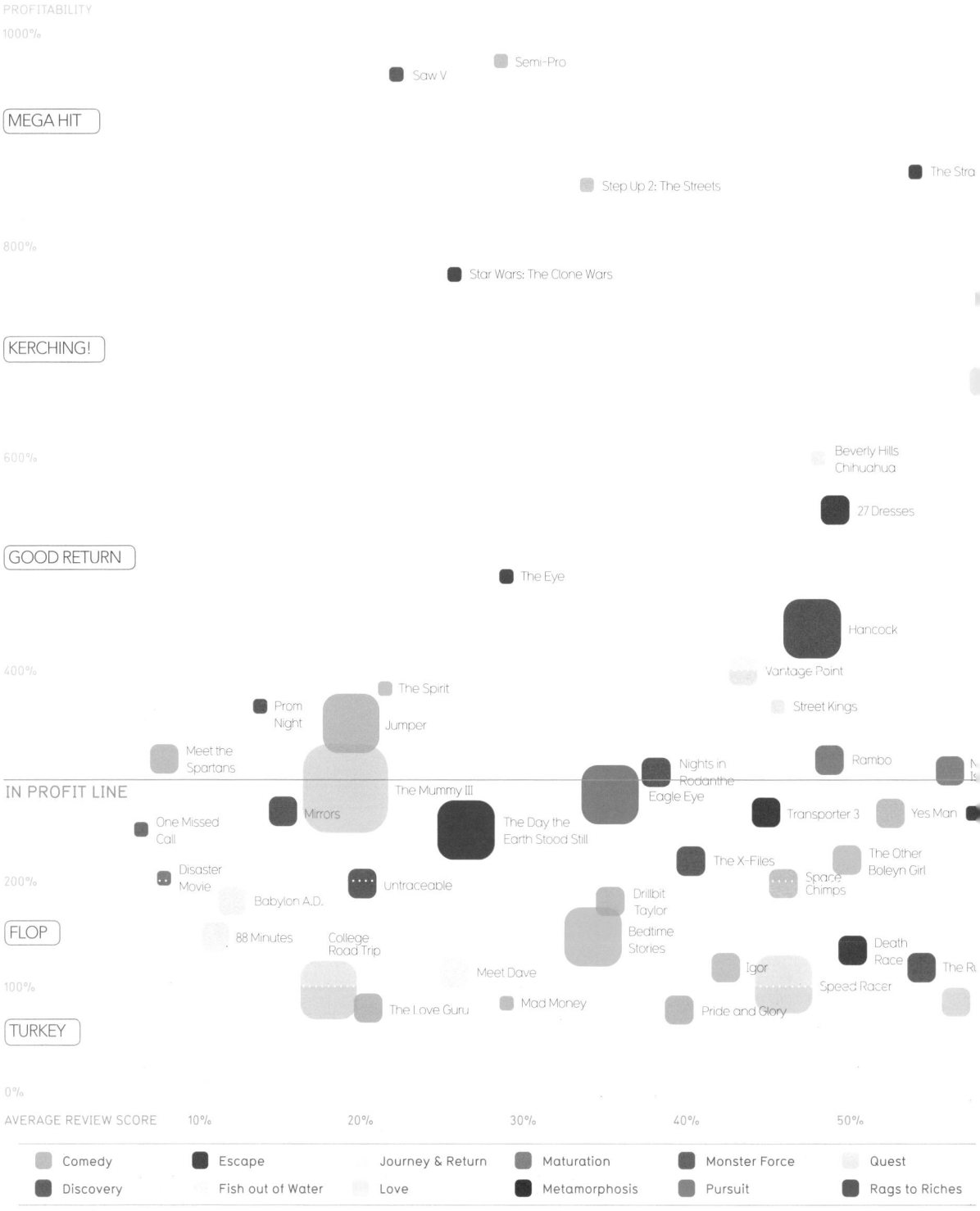

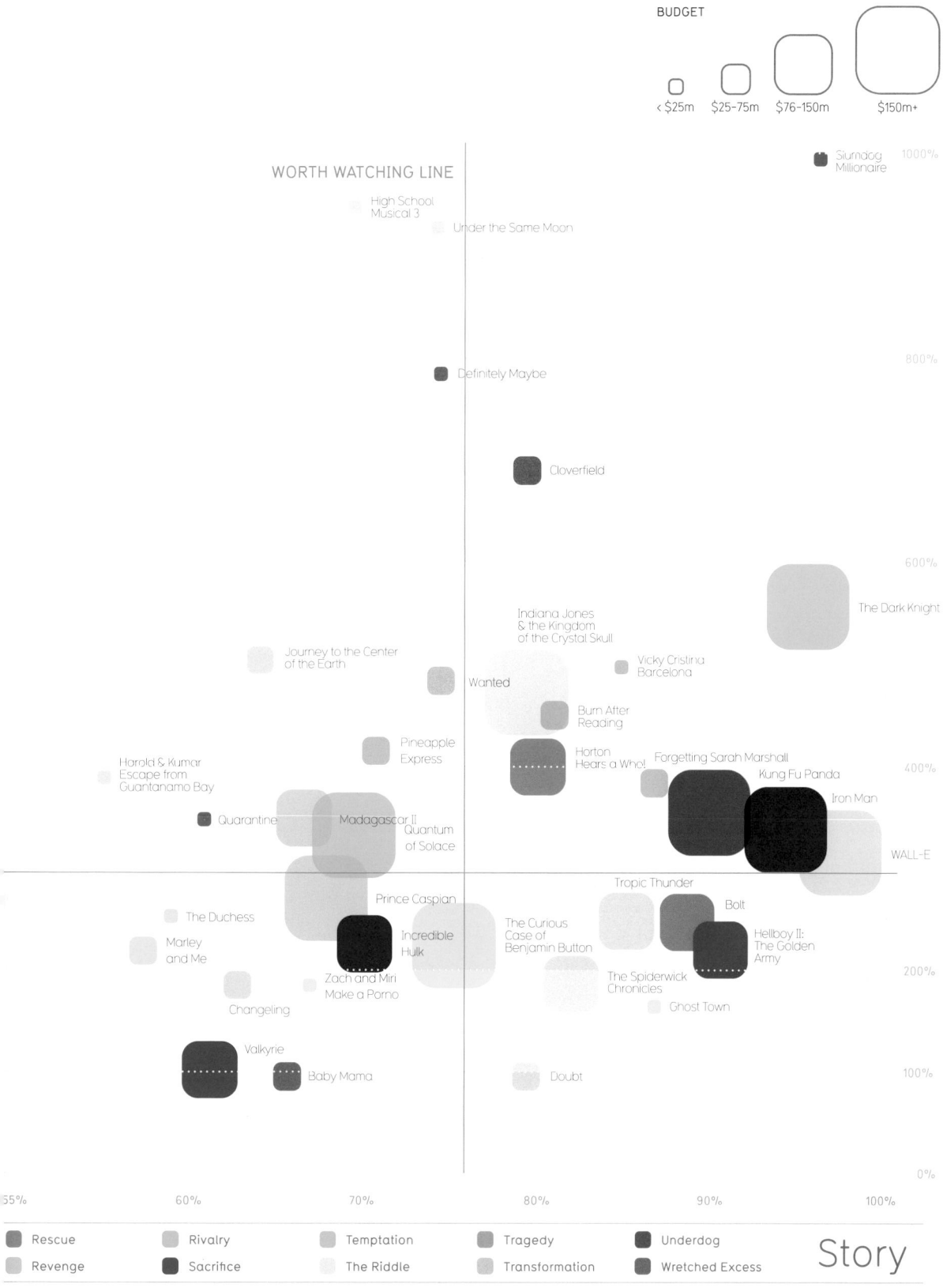

source: BoxOfficeMojo.com, The-Numbers.com, Wikipedia, IMDB.com & RottenTomatoes.com. Note: reported film budgets are notoriously unreliable (especially for flops)

Most Profitable Hollywood Stories 2009

Average profitability: 308% Average quality: 47% Most common stories: Quest Comedy

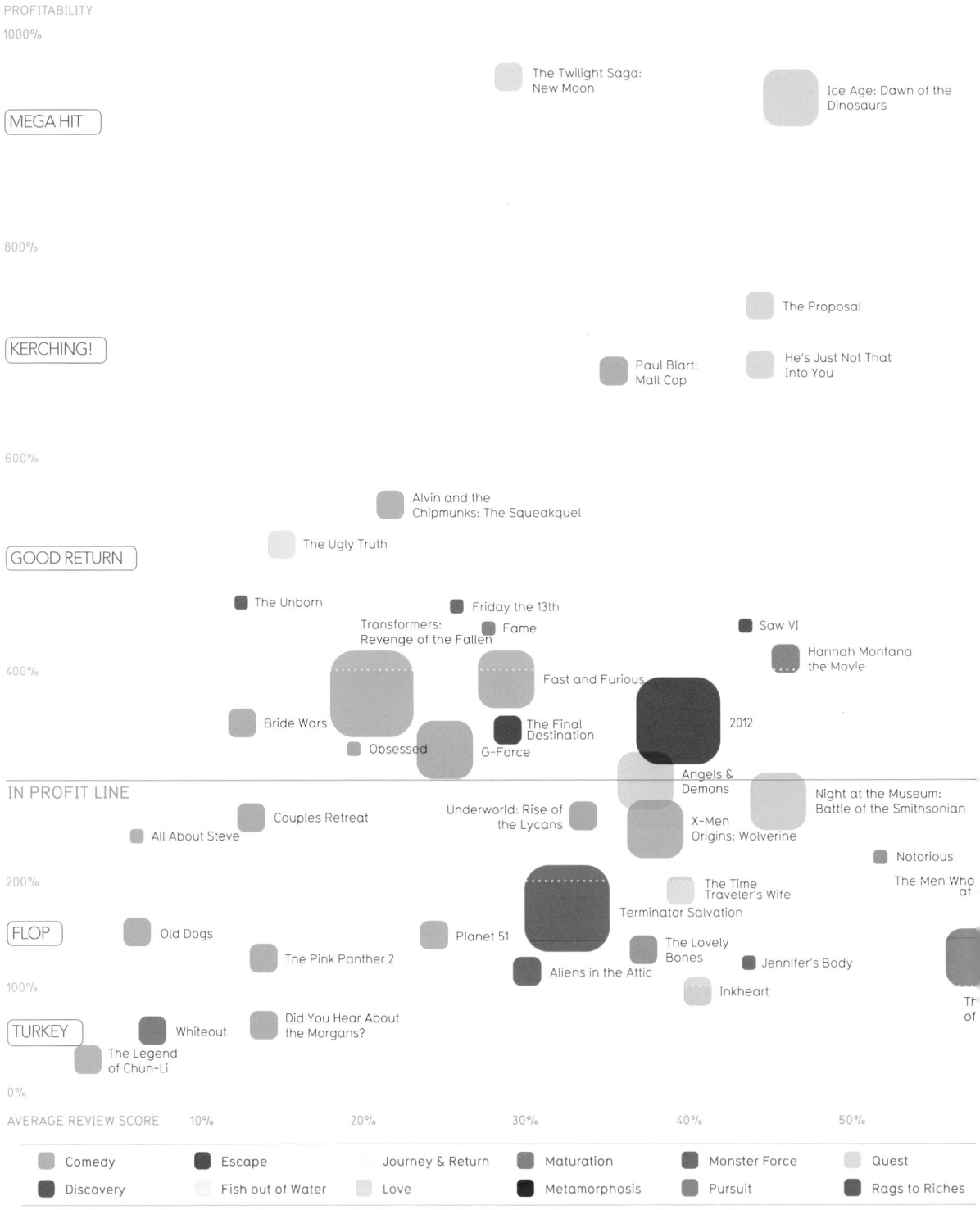

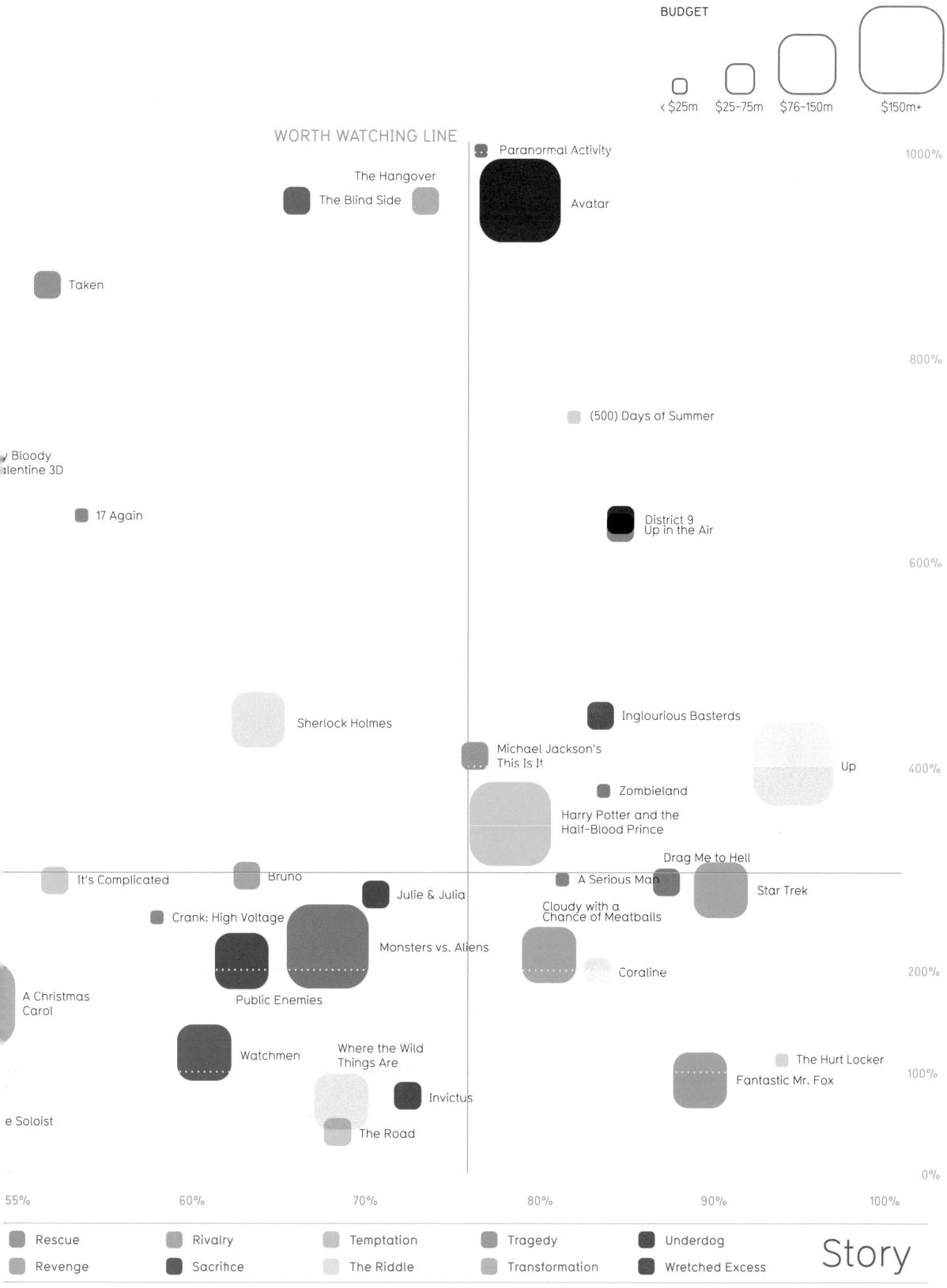

source: BoxOfficeMojo.com, The-Numbers.com, Wikipedia, IMDB.com & RottenTomatoes.com. Note: reported film budgets are notoriously unreliable (especially for flops)

Most Profitable Hollywood Stories 2010

Average profitability: 277% Average quality: 49% Most common stories: Love Comedy

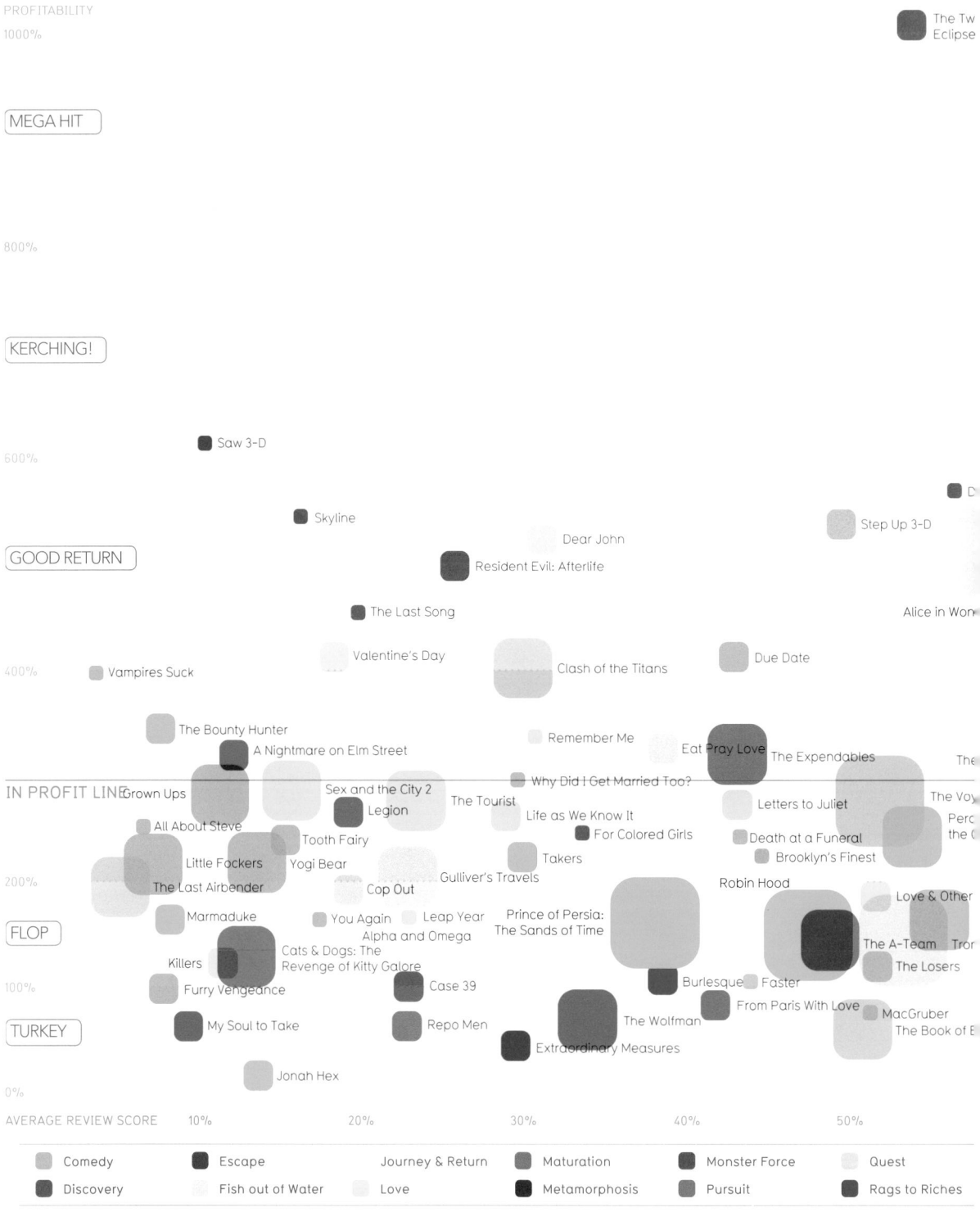

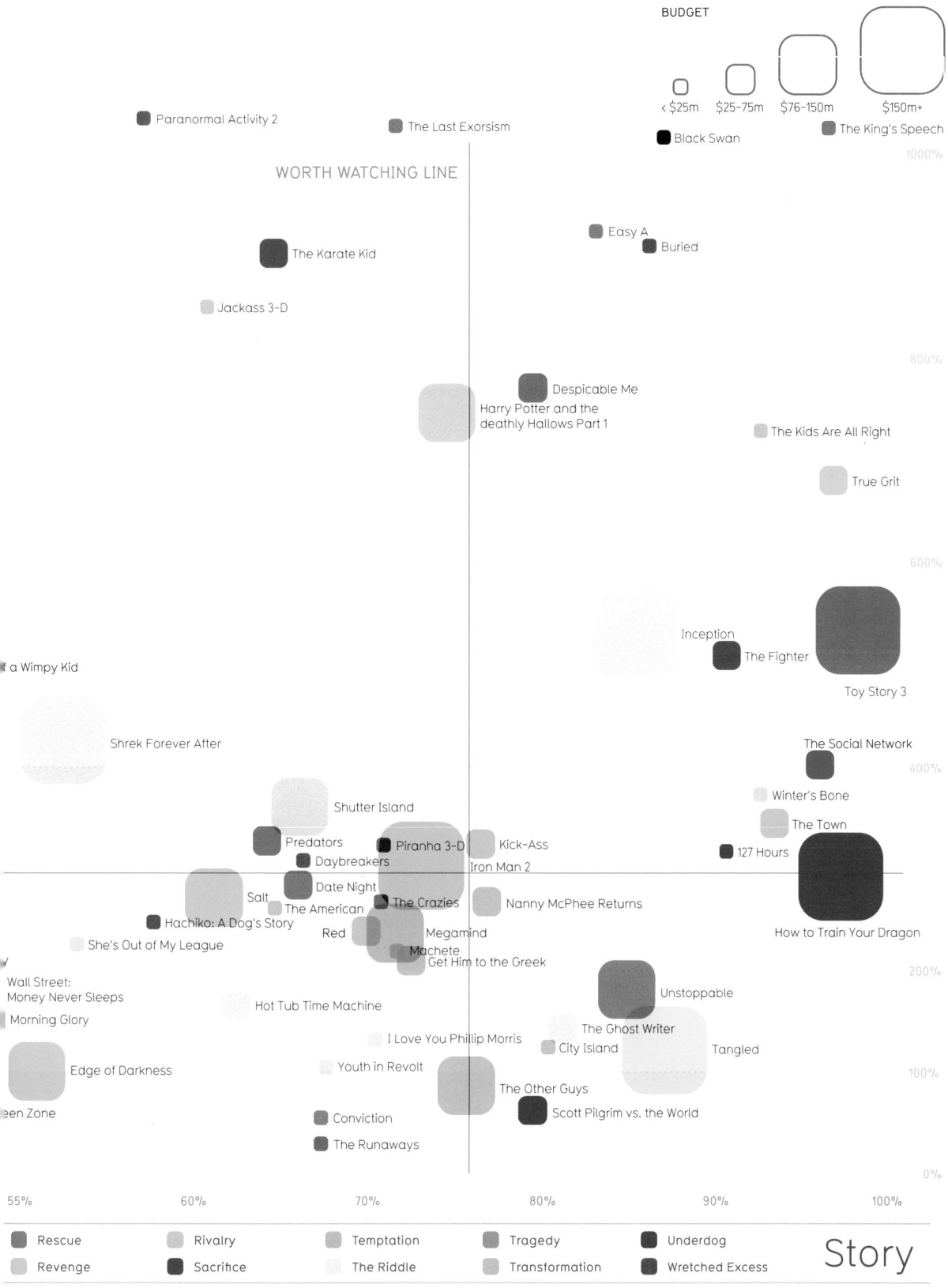

source: BoxOfficeMojo.com, The-Numbers.com, Wikipedia, IMDB.com & RottenTomatoes.com. Note: reported film budgets are notoriously unreliable (especially for flops)

Most Profitable Hollywood Stories 2011

Average profitability: 289% Average quality: 54% Most common stories: Quest Monster

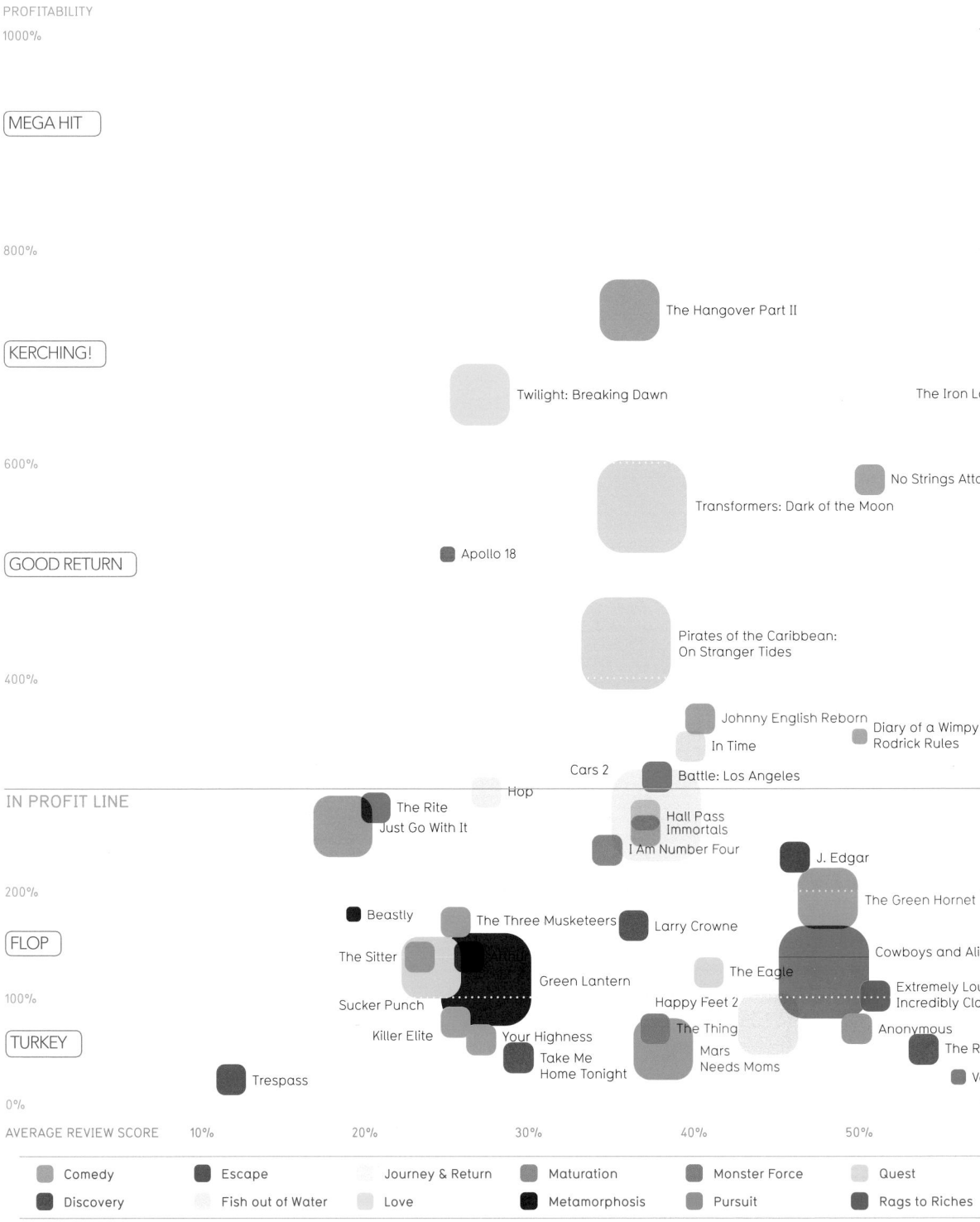

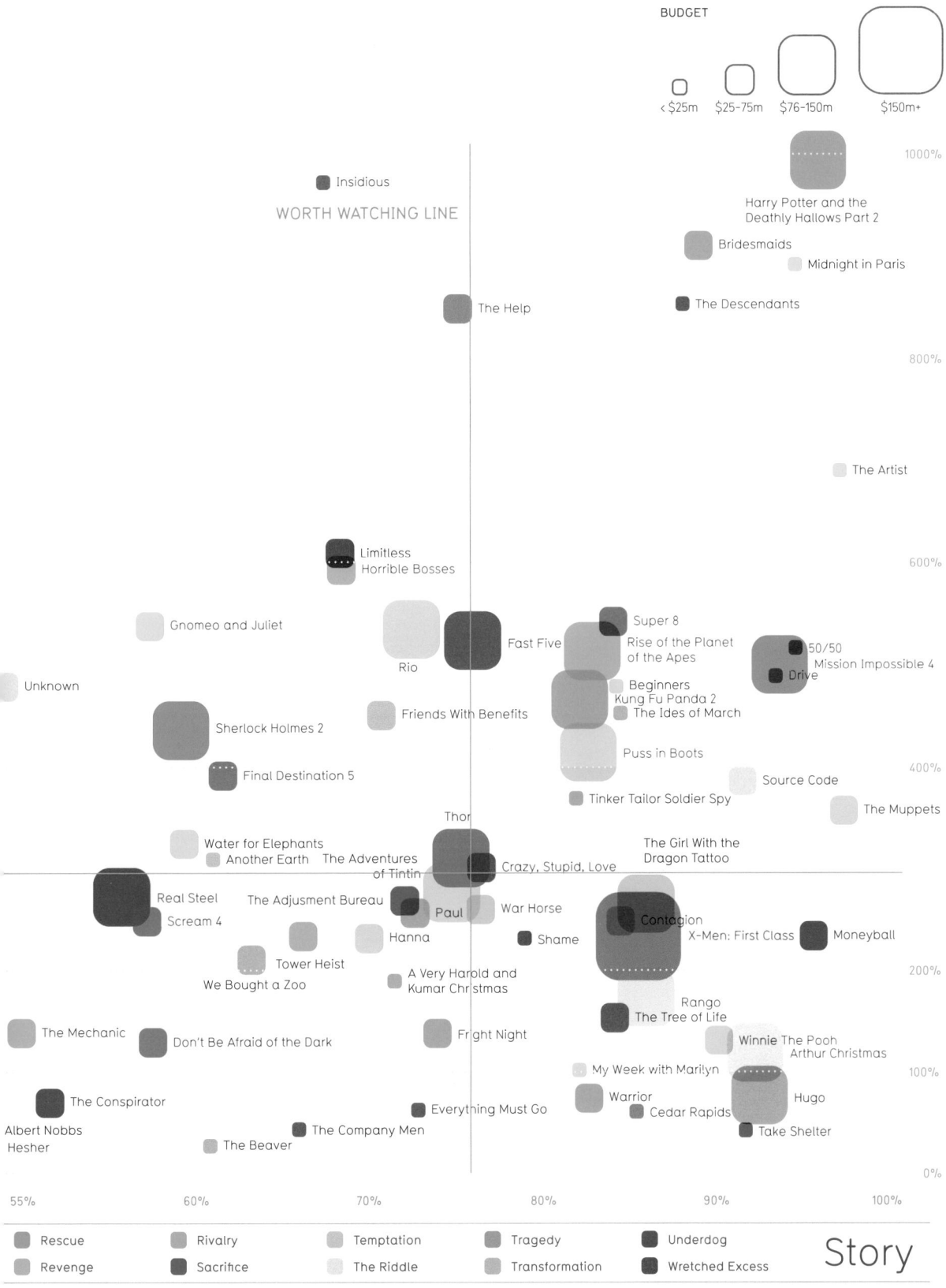

source: BoxOfficeMojo.com, The-Numbers.com, Wikipedia, IMDB.com & RottenTomatoes.com. Note: reported film budgets are notoriously unreliable (especially for flops)

Most Profitable Stories of All Time

Average budget: 43m Average quality: 83% Most common stories: Quest Monster Force

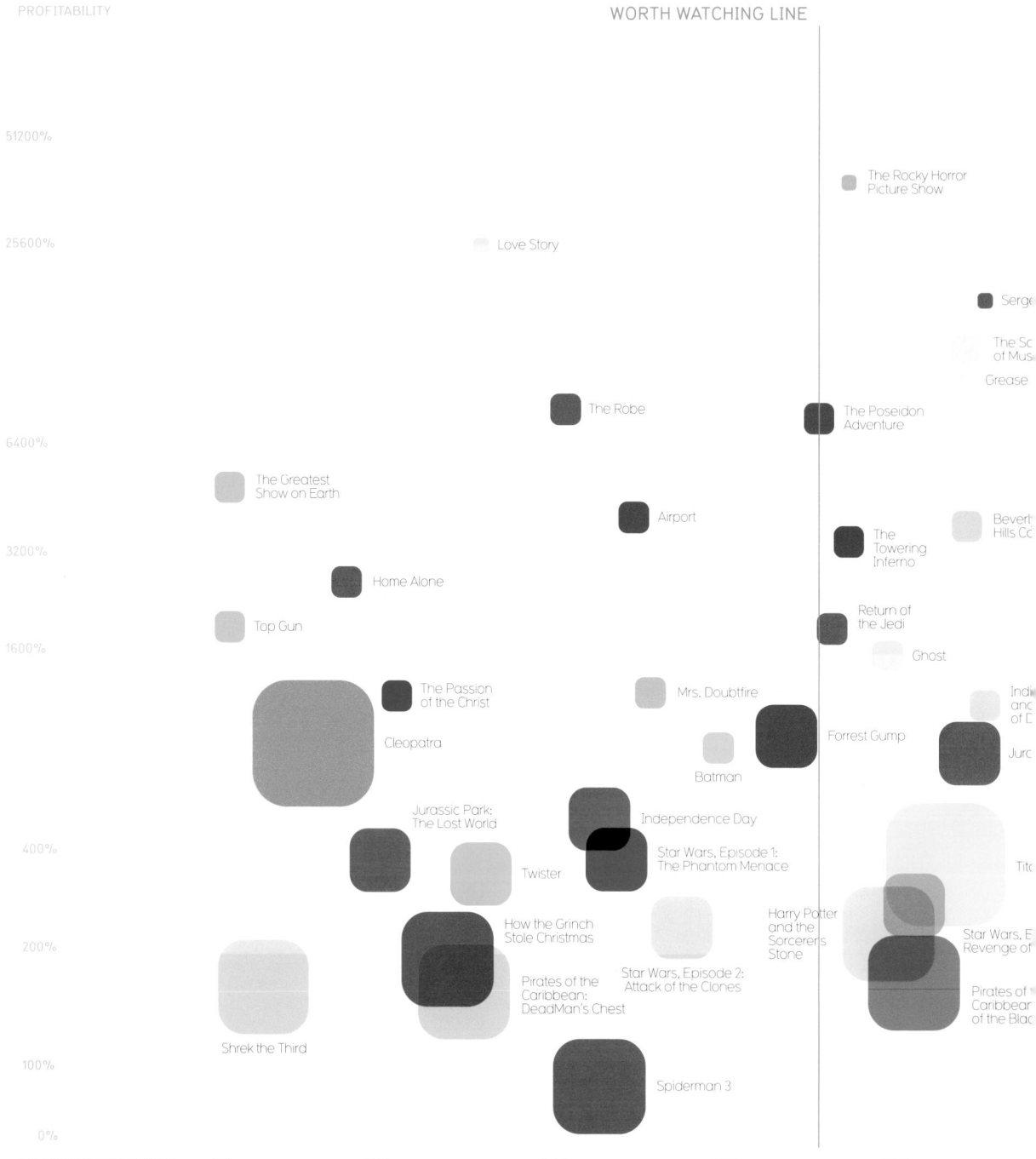

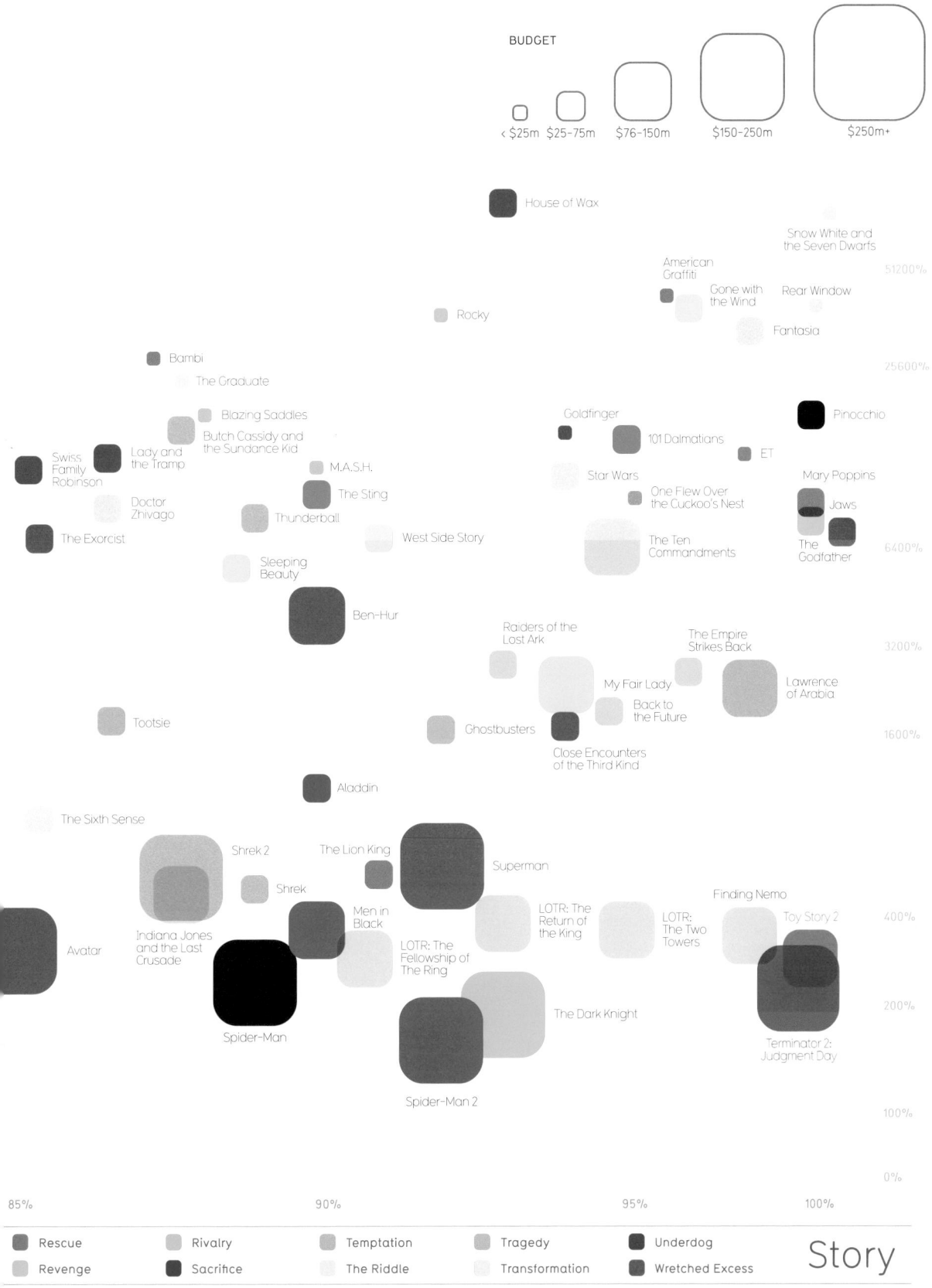

source: BoxOfficeMojo.com, Wikipedia. Budgets inflation adjusted to 2010 dollars

Enneagram

A personality-type system based around an ancient symbol of perpetual motion. Each type is formed from a key defence against the world. Which one are you?

		I am...	I want to...	Virtue
1	**Reformer**	Reasonable and objective	Be good and have integrity	Serenity
2	**Helper**	Caring and loving	Feel love	Humility
3	**Achiever**	Outstanding and effective	Feel valuable	Honesty
4	**Individualist**	Intuitive and sensitive	Be myself	Balance
5	**Investigator**	Intelligent, perceptive	Be capable and competent	Detachment
6	**Loyalist**	Committed, dependable	Have support and guidance	Courage
7	**Enthusiast**	Reasonable and objective	Be satisfied and content	Sobriety
8	**Challenger**	Strong, assertive	Protect myself	Innocence
9	**Peacemaker**	Peaceful, easygoing	Have peace of mind	Action

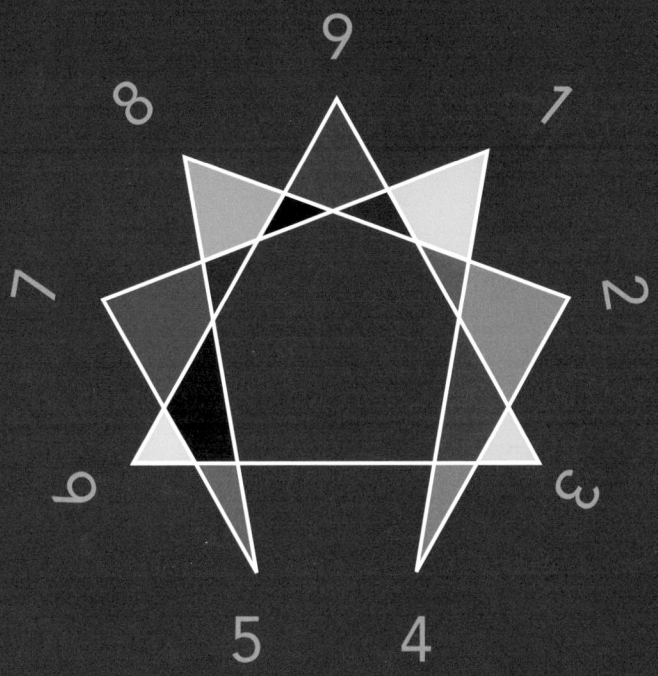

Hidden complaint	I fear being...	Flaw	Saving grace
am usually right. Others should listen to me.	Bad, wrong	Resentment	Sensible
m always loving. Others take me for granted.	Unloved	Flattery	Empathic
am a superior person. Others are jealous	Worthless	Vanity	Eagerness
don't really fit in. I am different from others.	Insignificant	Melancholy	Self-aware
m so smart. Others can't understand me.	Helpless or incompetent	Stinginess	No bullshit
do what I'm told . Others don't	Without support	Worrying	Friendly
m happy. But others don't give me enough.	In pain	Over-Planning	Enthusiasm
m fighting to survive. Others take advantage.	Harmed or controlled	Vengeance	Strength
am content. Others pressure me to change.	Lost and separated	Laziness	Fluidity

source: Wikipedia, EnneagramInstitute.com

Selling Your Soul

Workers on Amazon.com's Mechanical Turk asked to draw their souls

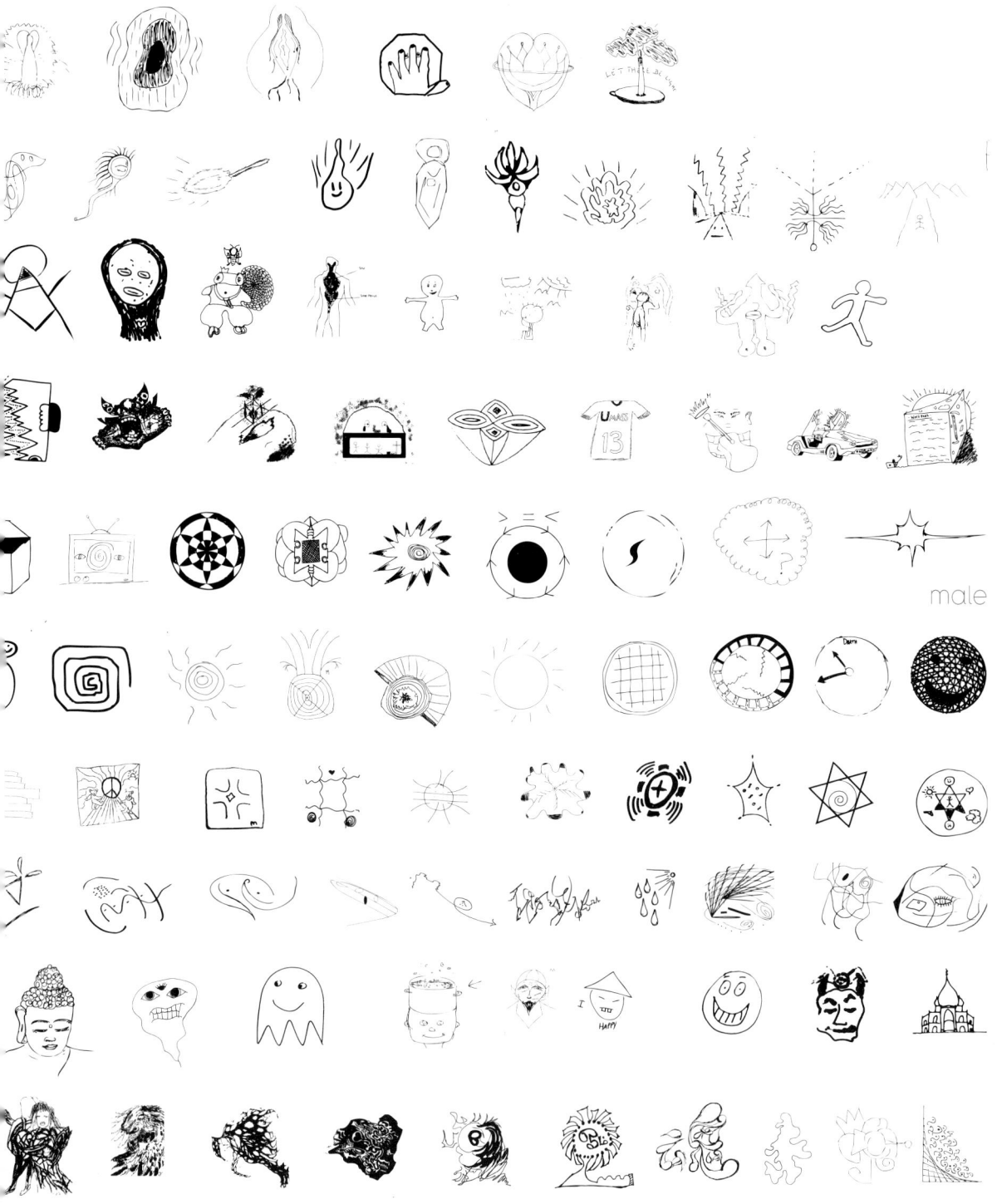

Amazon's Mechanical Turk is a "cloud workforce" of people happy to do microjobs for micropayments ($0.25 and up). 200 people were asked to draw a picture of their soul for the author's ongoing collection. Muhahahahahahahaha...

source: Mturk.com. Thanks to all Turkers who took part!

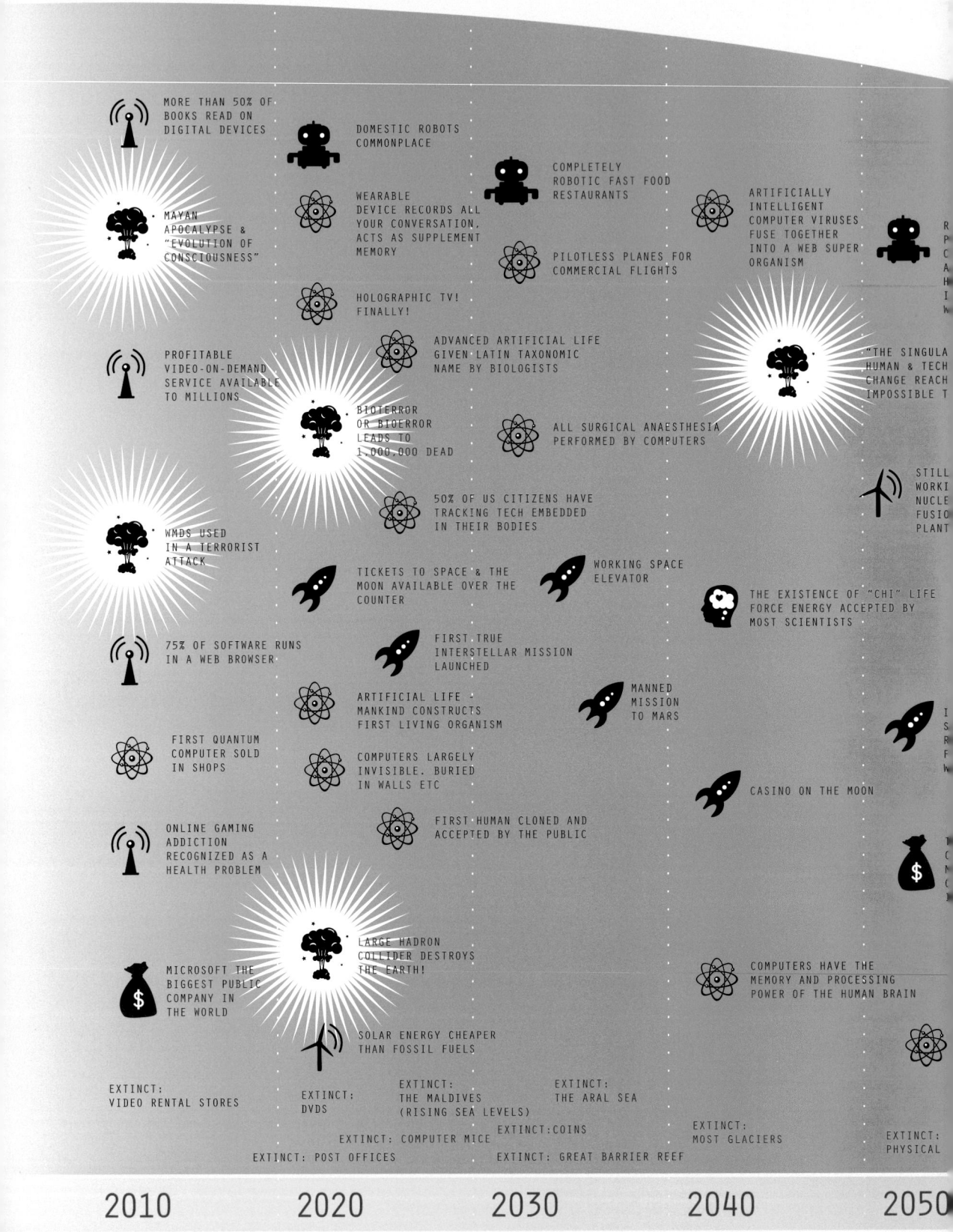
MORE THAN 50% OF BOOKS READ ON DIGITAL DEVICES
DOMESTIC ROBOTS COMMONPLACE
COMPLETELY ROBOTIC FAST FOOD RESTAURANTS
MAYAN APOCALYPSE & "EVOLUTION OF CONSCIOUSNESS"
WEARABLE DEVICE RECORDS ALL YOUR CONVERSATION, ACTS AS SUPPLEMENT MEMORY
ARTIFICIALLY INTELLIGENT COMPUTER VIRUSES FUSE TOGETHER INTO A WEB SUPER ORGANISM
PILOTLESS PLANES FOR COMMERCIAL FLIGHTS
HOLOGRAPHIC TV! FINALLY!
PROFITABLE VIDEO-ON-DEMAND SERVICE AVAILABLE TO MILLIONS
ADVANCED ARTIFICIAL LIFE GIVEN LATIN TAXONOMIC NAME BY BIOLOGISTS
BIOTERROR OR BIOERROR LEADS TO 1,000,000 DEAD
ALL SURGICAL ANAESTHESIA PERFORMED BY COMPUTERS
50% OF US CITIZENS HAVE TRACKING TECH EMBEDDED IN THEIR BODIES
WMDS USED IN A TERRORIST ATTACK
TICKETS TO SPACE & THE MOON AVAILABLE OVER THE COUNTER
WORKING SPACE ELEVATOR
THE EXISTENCE OF "CHI" LIFE FORCE ENERGY ACCEPTED BY MOST SCIENTISTS
75% OF SOFTWARE RUNS IN A WEB BROWSER
FIRST TRUE INTERSTELLAR MISSION LAUNCHED
ARTIFICIAL LIFE - MANKIND CONSTRUCTS FIRST LIVING ORGANISM
MANNED MISSION TO MARS
FIRST QUANTUM COMPUTER SOLD IN SHOPS
COMPUTERS LARGELY INVISIBLE. BURIED IN WALLS ETC
CASINO ON THE MOON
FIRST HUMAN CLONED AND ACCEPTED BY THE PUBLIC
ONLINE GAMING ADDICTION RECOGNIZED AS A HEALTH PROBLEM
LARGE HADRON COLLIDER DESTROYS THE EARTH!
MICROSOFT THE BIGGEST PUBLIC COMPANY IN THE WORLD
COMPUTERS HAVE THE MEMORY AND PROCESSING POWER OF THE HUMAN BRAIN
SOLAR ENERGY CHEAPER THAN FOSSIL FUELS
EXTINCT: VIDEO RENTAL STORES
EXTINCT: DVDS
EXTINCT: THE MALDIVES (RISING SEA LEVELS)
EXTINCT: THE ARAL SEA
EXTINCT: COINS
EXTINCT: COMPUTER MICE
EXTINCT: MOST GLACIERS
EXTINCT: POST OFFICES
EXTINCT: GREAT BARRIER REEF
EXTINCT: PHYSICAL
2010
2020
2030
2040
2050

The Future of the Future

At longbets.org leading thinkers gather to place bets on future predictions

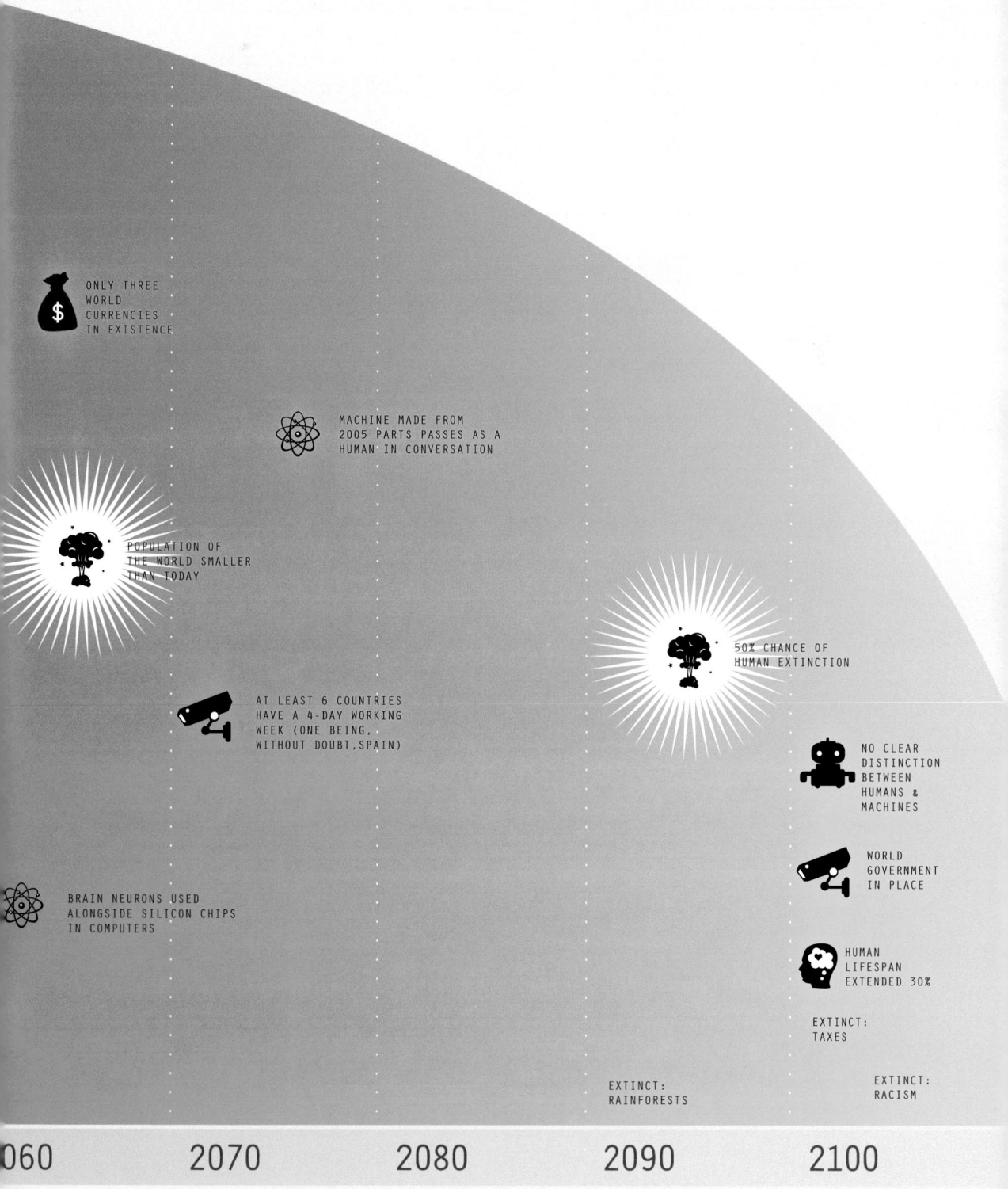

source: longbets.org

Making the Book

The first six months

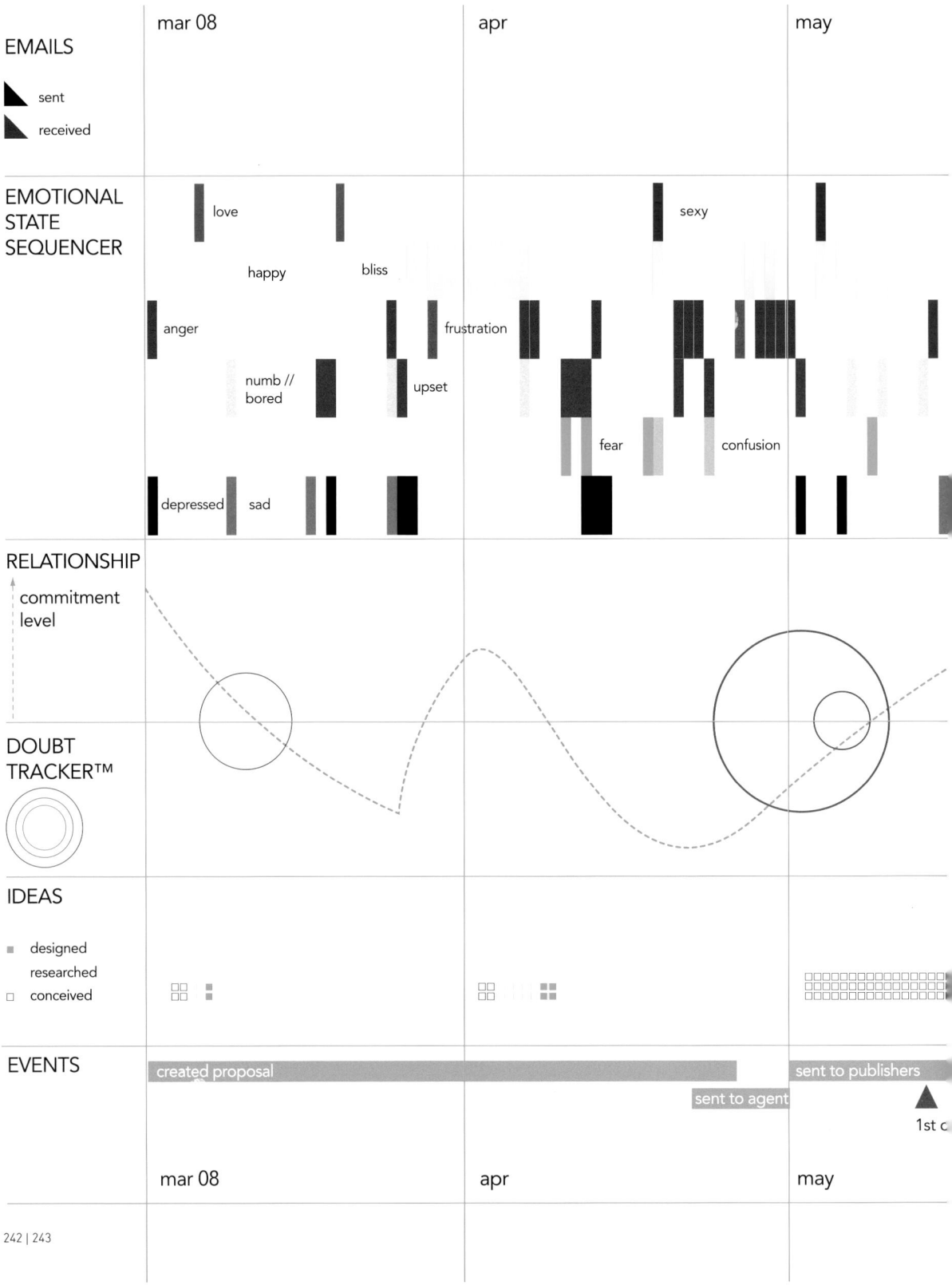

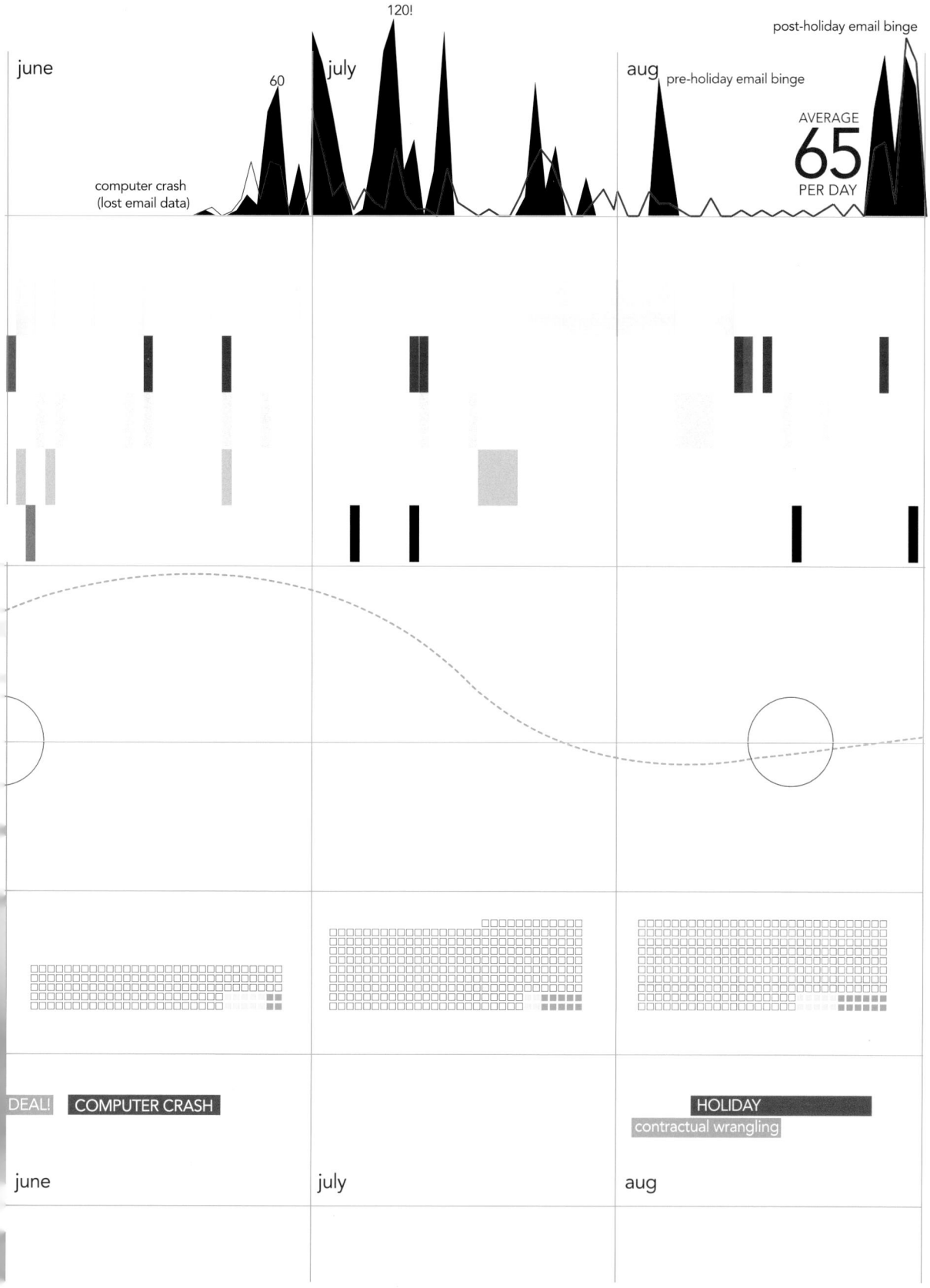
120!
post-holiday email binge
june
60
july
aug
pre-holiday email binge
AVERAGE
65
PER DAY
computer crash
(lost email data)
DEAL!
COMPUTER CRASH
HOLIDAY
contractual wrangling
june
july
aug

Making the Book

The last six months

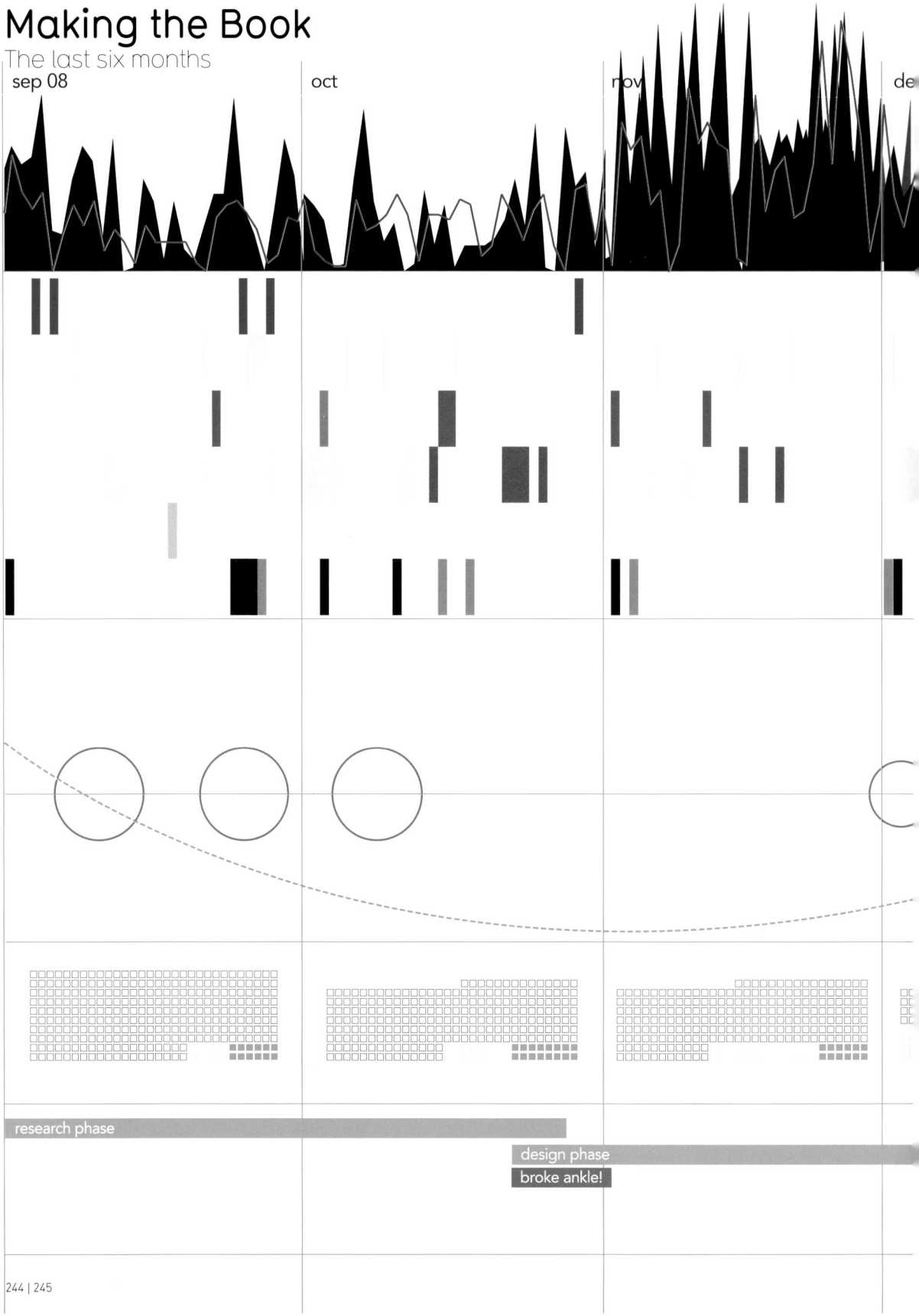

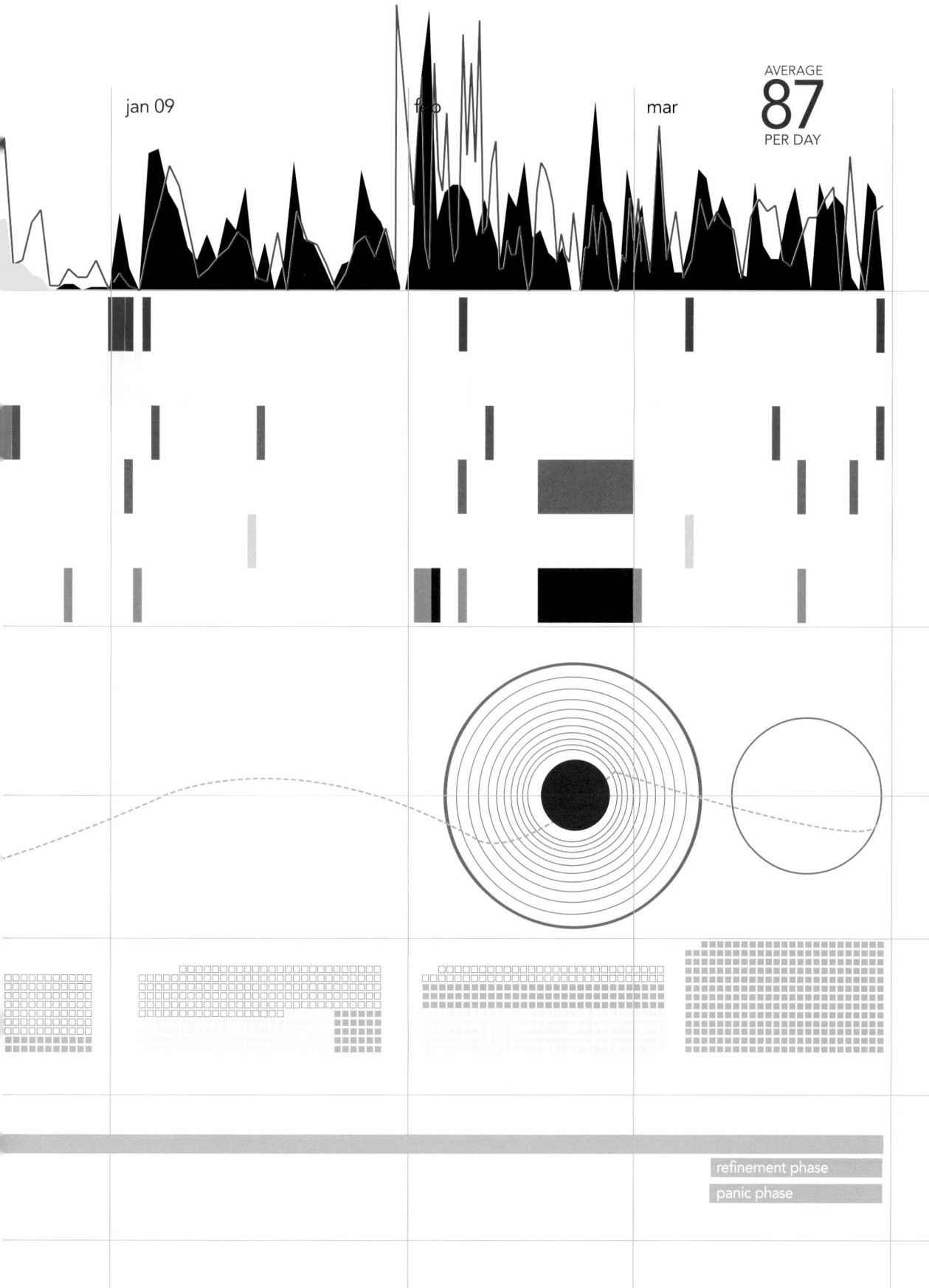
jan 09
feb
mar
AVERAGE
87
PER DAY
refinement phase
panic phase

Acknowledge Map

Thanks to all who helped and supported

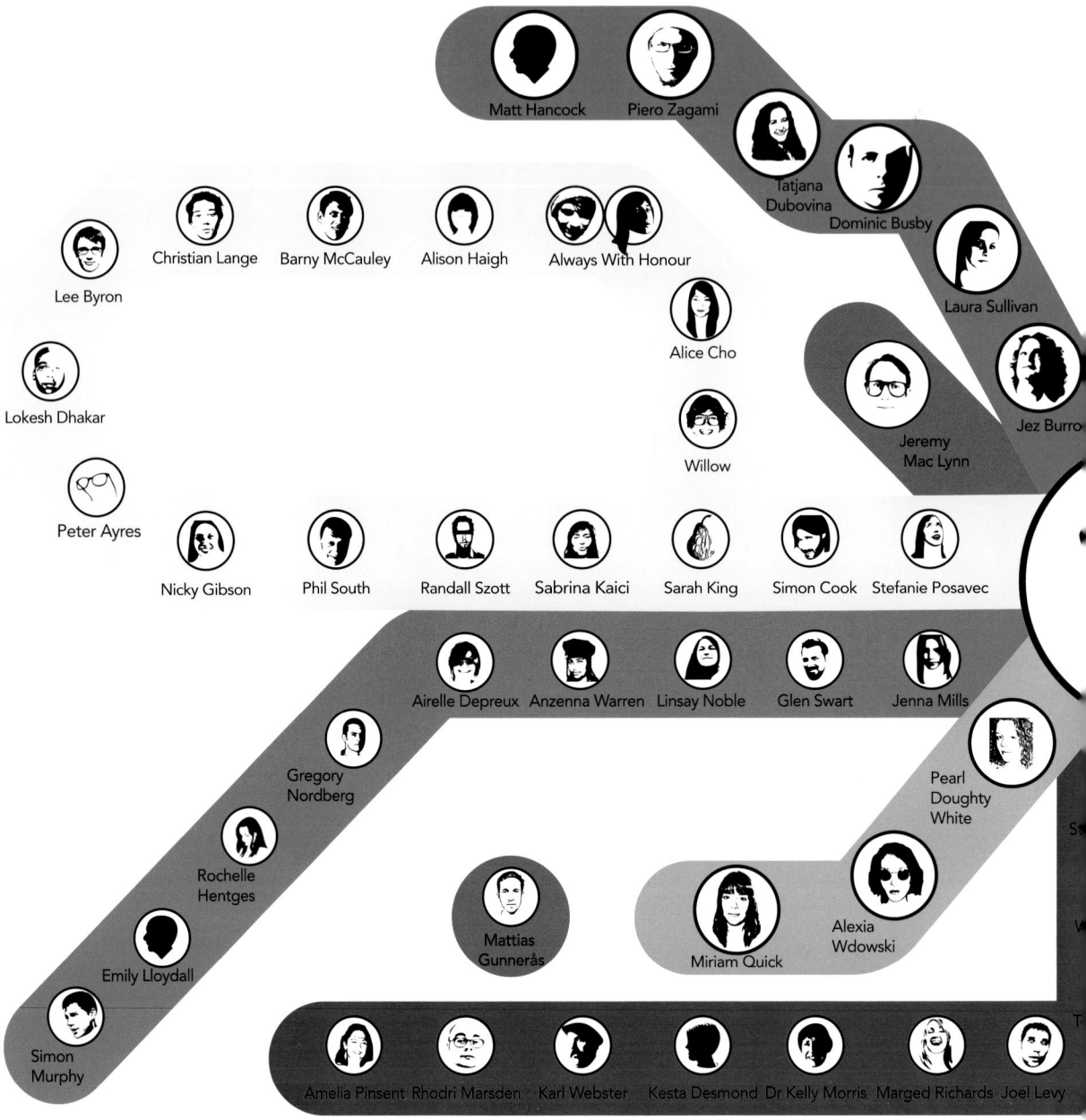

MANY THANKS TO: Vincent Ahrend, Kathryn Ariel, Dr David Archer, Steve Beckett, Delfina Bottesini, Laura Brudenell, Candy Chang, Susanne Cook Greuter, Dave Cooper, Kesta Desmond, Robert Downes, Danielle Engelman, Edward Farmer, Richard Henry, Dr Phil Howard, Claudia Hofmeister, Aegir Hallmundur, Becky Jones, Dongwoo Kim, Jenny McIvor, Priscila Moura, Mar O'Connor, Kate O'Driscoll, Dr. Lori Plutchik, Laura Price, Richar Rogers, Miriam Quick Twitter Army, Mechanical Turkers.

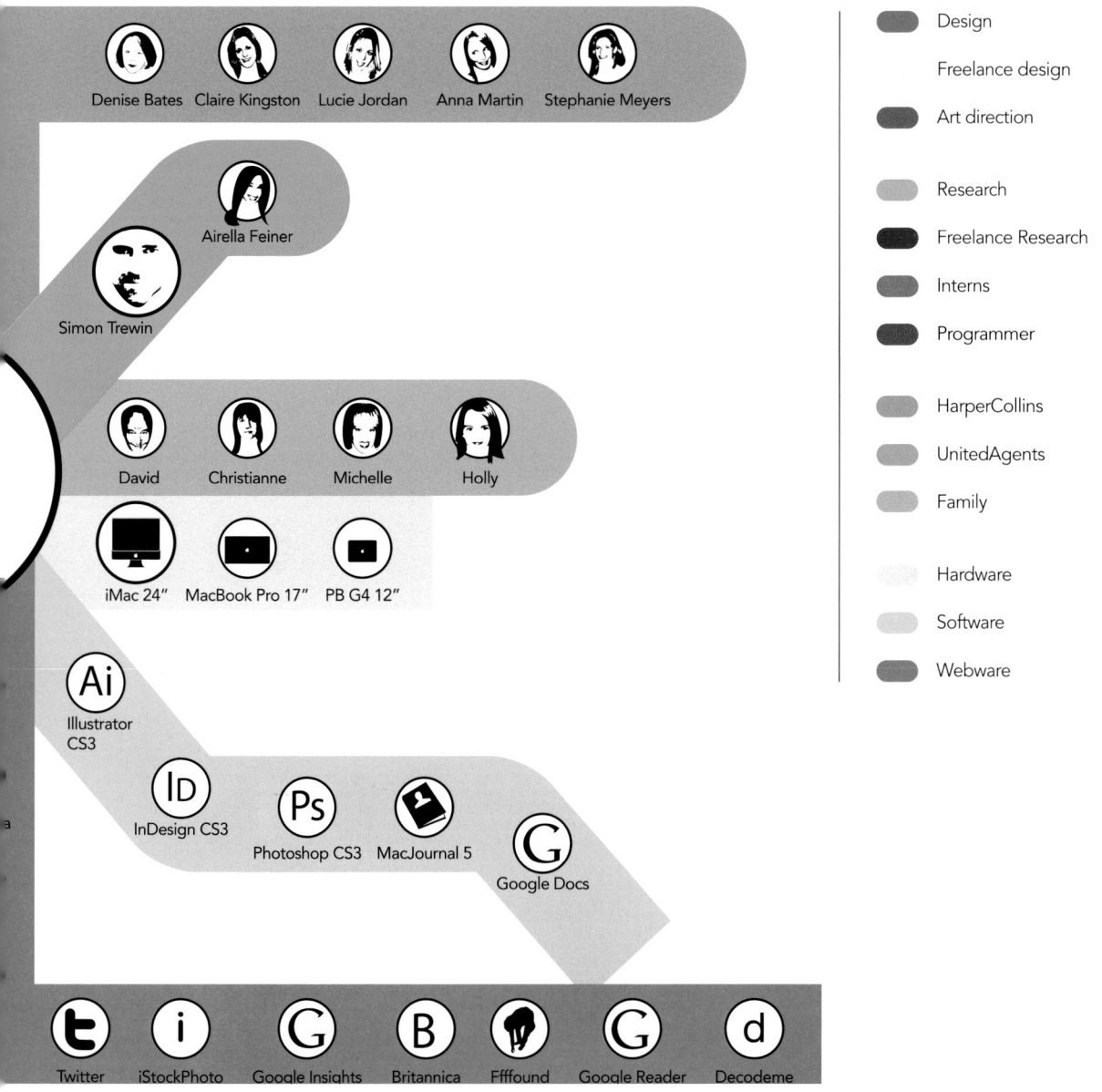
Denise Bates
Claire Kingston
Lucie Jordan
Anna Martin
Stephanie Meyers
Airella Feiner
Simon Trewin
David
Christianne
Michelle
Holly
iMac 24"
MacBook Pro 17"
PB G4 12"
Ai
Illustrator CS3
ID
InDesign CS3
Ps
Photoshop CS3
MacJournal 5
G
Google Docs
Twitter
iStockPhoto
Google Insights
Britannica
Ffffound
Google Reader
Decodeme
Design
Freelance design
Art direction
Research
Freelance Research
Interns
Programmer
HarperCollins
UnitedAgents
Family
Hardware
Software
Webware

Bibliograph

Inspiration and source material

Schott, Ben, *Schott's Almanac* 2007 (London: Bloomsbury Publishing Plc., 2007)

Tufte, Edward R., *Envisioning Information* (Cheshire, Connecticut: Graphics Press LLC, 2005)

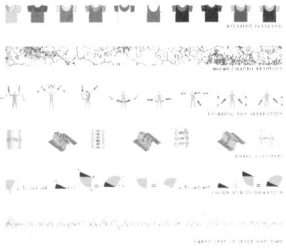

Fry, Ben, *Visualizing Data* (Sebastopol, CA: O'Reilly Media, Inc., 2008)

Abrams, Janet and Peter Hall, *Else/Where: Mapping* (Minneapolis: University of Minneapolis Design Institute, 2006)

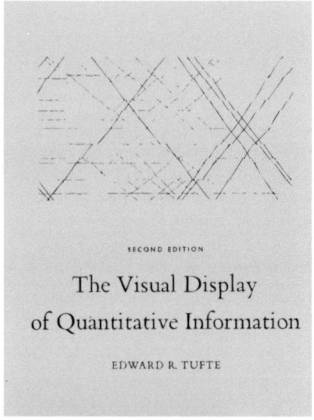

Tufte, Edward R., *The Visual Display of Quantitative Information* (Cheshire, Connecticut: Graphics Press LLC, 2006)

Bakhtiar, Laleh, *Sufi* (New York: Thames and Hudson Inc., 2004)

Levitt, Steven D. and Stephen J. Dubner, *Freakonomics* (London: Penguin Books, 2006)

Ayers, Ian, *Super Crunchers* (London: Random House, Inc., 2008)

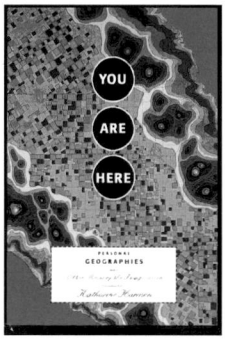

Harmon, Katharine, *You Are Here* (New York: Princeton Architectural Press, 2004)

Solomon, Lawrence, *The Deniers* (Richard Vigilante Books, 2008)

mage Credits

TOCK IMAGES neubauwelt.com

TOCK IMAGES istockphoto.com

734147 - appleuzr 4213783 - hypergon 1639568 - FreeTransform 2886642 - lacreme 7214514 -red_frog 7772263 -red_frog 4417544 - redmal

INGS dafont.com

YeoSport

VC Fonts Sold Out B

VC Fonts Sold Out C

ONTS lineto.com

ype 1451 - ABCDEFGHIJKLMNOPQRSTUVWXYZabcdefghijklmnopqrstuvwxyz1234567890

kkurat - ABCDEFGHIJKLMNOPQRSTUVWXYZabcdefghijklmnopqrstuvwxyz1234567890

ONTS linotype.com

venir - ABCDEFGHIJKLMNOPQRSTUVWXYZabcdefghijklmnopqrstuvwxyz1234567890

InformationIsBeautiful.net

Visit the website for the book

discover more
our blog covers visual journalism, unusual infographics, far-out data visualizations

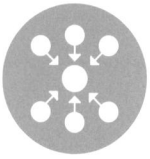

be involved
crowdsource and help us investigate, research and unearth facts and information for new designs

get animated
play with interactive visuals and animations

have a play
access the data and research used in this book and find editable versions of some images

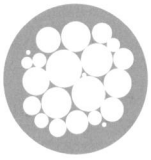

find extra stuff
tons of new diagrams, idea maps, bubble charts, factoramas, knowledgescapes and infomaps...

twitter: @infobeautiful // facebook.com/pages/Information-Is-Beautiful

Can Drugs Make You Happy?

RUGGIEST Largest % of population using illegal drugs (7% or more)

gentina, Australia, Belize, Canada, Chile, Czech Rep, Denmark, England & Wales, onia, France, Ghana, Ireland, Israel, Italy, Jamaica, Kyrgyzstan, Latvia, Lebanon, xembourg, Madagascar, New Zealand, Nigeria, Spain, Switzerland, Uruguay, A, Venezuela, Zambia, Zimbabwe

rce: Guardian Data blog, UN

HAPPIEST by Happiness Index Rating (above 6.8/10)

gentina, Australia, Austria, Belgium, Belize, Brazil, Canada, Chile, Colombia, sta Rica, Cyprus, Denmark, El Salvador, England & Wales, Finland, Guatemala, land, Ireland, Italy, Luxembourg, Malta, Mexico, Netherlands, New Zealand, rway, Saudi Arabia, Singapore, Spain, Sweden, Switzerland, Thailand, Trinidad & bago, UAE, USA, Venezuela

irce: Erasmus University Rotterdam, Worlddatabaseofhappiness.eur.nl

LISSED OUT! where happiness strongly correlates with drug use

gentina, Australia, Belize, Canada, Chile, Denmark, England & Wales, Ireland, ly, Luxembourg, New Zealand, Spain, Switzerland, USA, Venezuela

42%

for fun. correlation is not cause

in't Nothing Going On But The Rent

oney and divorce in a co-dependent relationship?

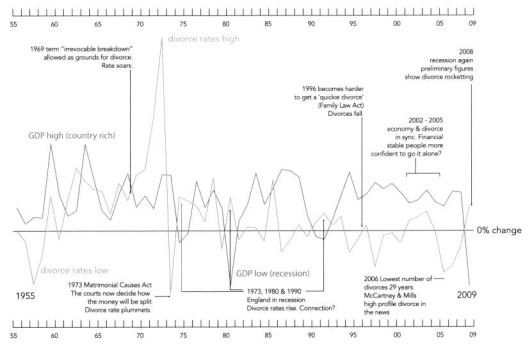

Selling Out

How much do music artists earn online?

For solo artist to earn US monthly min. wage $1,160

format		$	they must sell	label REVENUE	artist
	Self-pressed CD	$9.99	143	$0.0	$0
cdbaby	CD album	$9.99	155	$0.0	$7.50
	retail album CD (high end royalty deal)	$9.99	1,161	$2.00	$1.00
NAPSTER iTunes	album download	$9.99	1,229	$6.29	$0.94
cdbaby	MP3 download	$0.99	1,562	$0.0	$0.74
cdbaby	MP3 download via iTunes	$0.99	2,044	$0.0	$0.57
	retail album CD (low end royalty deal)	$9.99	3,871	$2.00	$0.30
amazon iTunes	Track download	$0.99	12,399	$0.63	$0.09
Rhapsody	Stream	$fixed	849,817 plays per month	$0.0091	$0.0022

format			to earn minimum wage	label REVENUE	artist
last.fm	Free on demand stream	$fixed	1,546,667 plays per month	$0.00015	$0.005

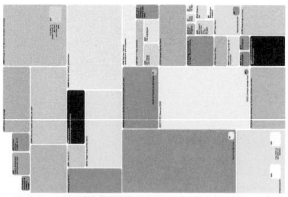
The Billion-Dollar-O-Gram
010

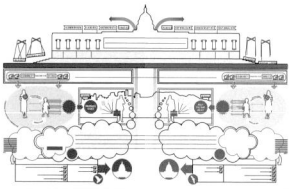
Left vs Right
014

Time Lines
016

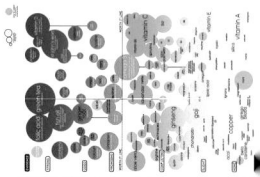
Snake Oil?
018

International Number Ones
020

Mountains out of Molehills
022

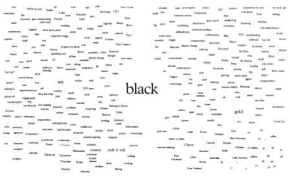

X "is the new" Black
024

Small Carbon
026

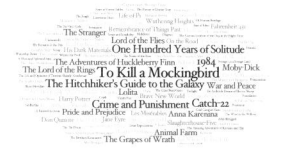

Books Everyone Should Read
028

Which Fish are Okay to Eat?
030

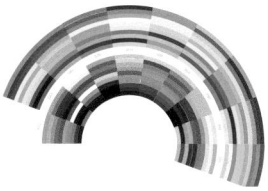
The 'In' Colours
032

Three's a Magic Number
036

Who Runs the World?
038

Who *Really* Runs the World?
040

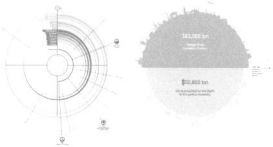
Stock Check
042

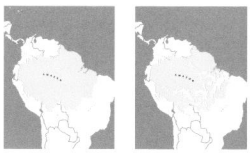
Amazon
044

Creation Myths
046

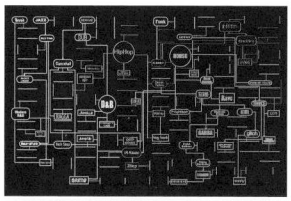
Dance Genre-ology
048

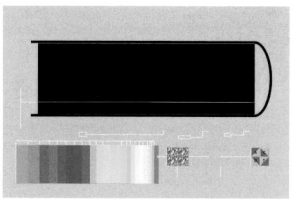
The Book of You
050

The Book of Me
052

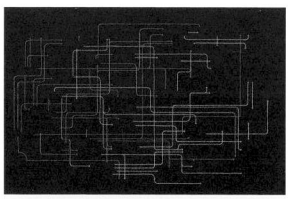
Rock Genre-ology
058

Simple Part I
060

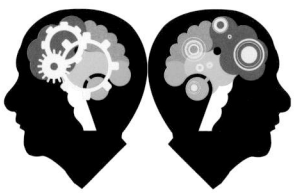
What is Consciousness?
066

Carbon Conscious
068

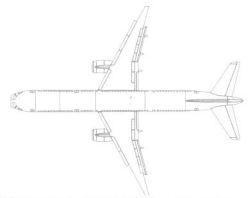
educe Your Chance of Dying
a Plane Crash 072

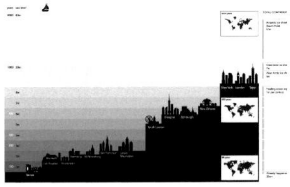
Rising Sea Levels
074

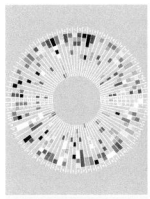
Colours &
Culture 076

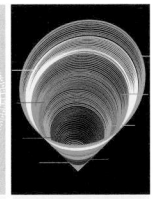
Stages of You
077

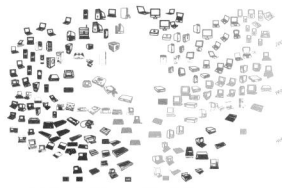
Personal Computer Evolution
084

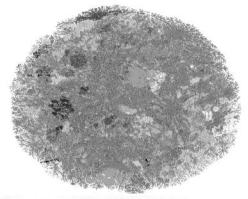
ne One Machine
86

What Does China Censor
Online? 092

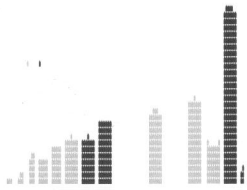
Water Towers
094

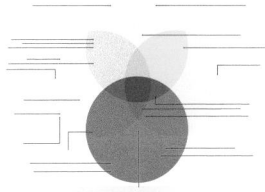
Drugs World
096

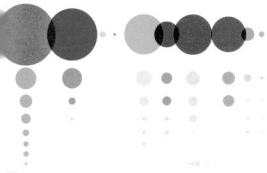
orld Religions
98

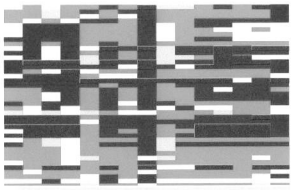
Moral Matrix
100

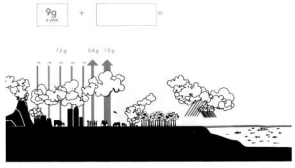
The Carbon Dioxide Cycle
102

Low Resolution
104

aste Buds
06

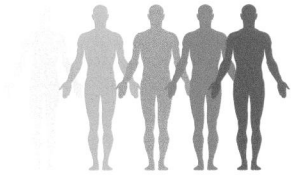
The Sunscreen Smokescreen
Part 1 112

The Sunscreen Smokescreens
Part 2 114

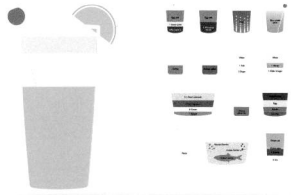
The Poison / The Remedy
116

alad
ressings 118

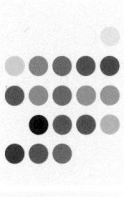
Not Nice

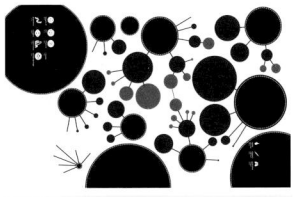
20th-Century Death
120

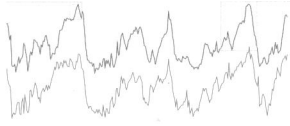
Climate Sceptics vs The
Consensus 122

Behind Every Great Man...
126

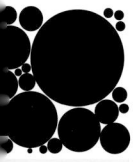
ypes of Info
iz 128

Pass the...
129

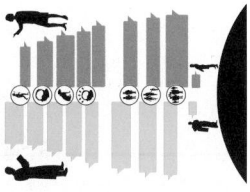
Nature vs Nuture
130

Postmodernism
132

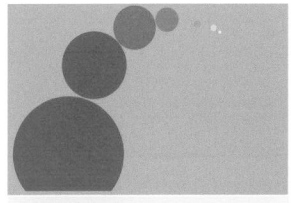
Death Spiral
134

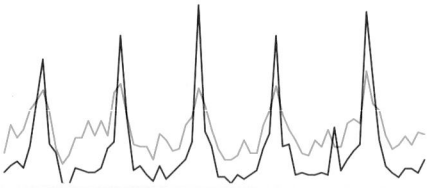
Google Insights
136

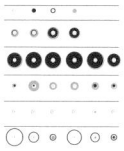
On Target?

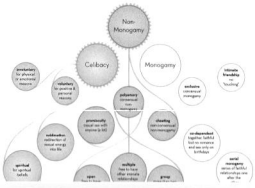

The Varieties of Romantic Relationship 140

30 Years Makes a Difference
142

Horoscoped
144

Better than Bacon 146

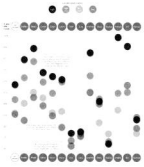
What are the Chances? 147

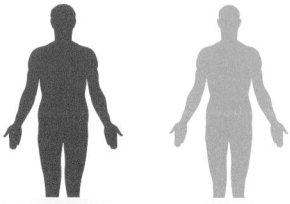
Some Things You Can't Avoid
148

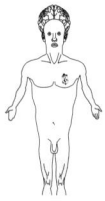
Body By
151

Microbes Mos
Dangerous 15

Cosmetic Ingredients 153

Things That'll Give You Cancer
154

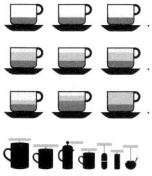
Types of Coffee
156

Big Carbon
158

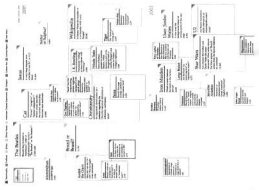
Articles of War I
160

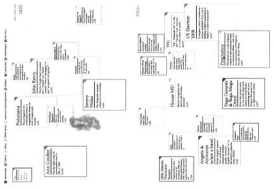
Articles of War II
162

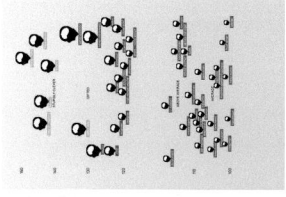
Who Clever are You?
164

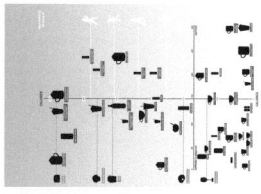
The Buzz vs The Bulge
166

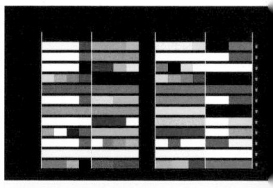
Daily Diets
168

Calories In, Calories Out
170

Types of Facial Hair
172

Scale of Devastation
174

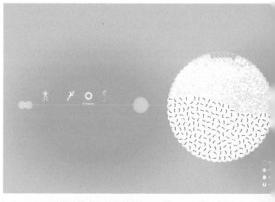
Amphibian Extinction Rates
176

Motive, Timing & Delivery
178

Good News
180

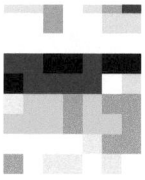
Immortality
182

War Chests
183

2012: The End of the World?
Part 1 184

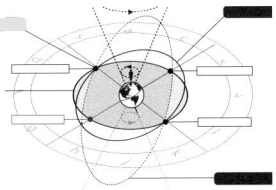
012: The End of the World?
art 2 186

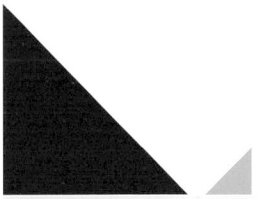
Red vs Blue
188

Man's Humanity To Man
190

Fast Internet
192

mple Part II
98

Peters Projection
202

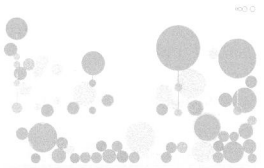
Alternative Medicine
204

Radiation Dosage
206

eing Defensive
08

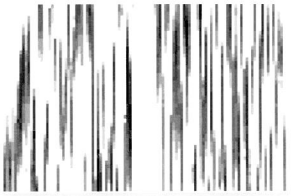
Most Popular US Girls' Names
212

Most Popular US Boys' Names
214

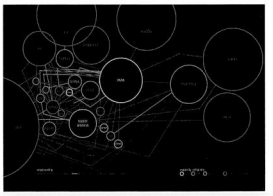
The Middle East
216

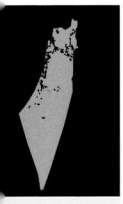
he Middle
ast 218

The Future of
Energy 219

Most Successful Rock Bands
220

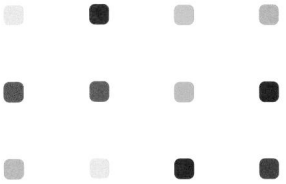
Stories
222

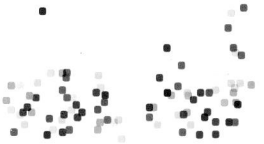
Most Profitable Stories 2007–2011
224

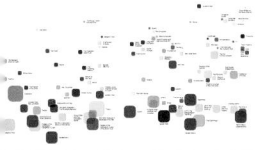
lost Profitable Stories of All
ime 234

The Enneagram
236

Selling Your Soul
238

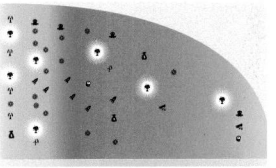
The Future of the Future
240

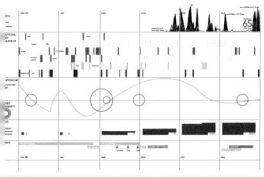
Making the Book
42

Acknowledge Map
246

DISCARD